GETTING CULTURE

GETTING CULTURE

Incorporating Diversity Across
the Curriculum

Edited by
Regan A. R. Gurung and
Loreto R. Prieto

STERLING, VIRGINIA

COPYRIGHT © 2009 BY
STYLUS PUBLISHING, LLC.

Published by Stylus Publishing, LLC
22883 Quicksilver Drive
Sterling, Virginia 20166-2102

Library of Congress Cataloging-in-Publication-Data
Getting culture : incorporating diversity across the
curriculum / edited by Regan A.R. Gurung and Loreto R.
Prieto. — 1st ed.
    p. cm.
    Includes bibliographical references and index.
    ISBN 978-1-57922-279-6 (hardcover : alk. paper) —
ISBN 978-1-57922-280-2 (pbk. : alk. paper)
1. Multicultural education—United States.
2. Interdisciplinary approach in education—United States.
I. Gurung, Regan A. R. II. Prieto, Loreto R.
    LC1099.3.G48 2009
    370.1170973—dc22

                                                    2008051359

13-digit ISBN: 978-1-57922-279-6 (cloth)
13-digit ISBN: 978-1-57922-280-2 (paper)

Printed in the United States of America

All first editions printed on acid-free paper
that meets the American National Standards Institute
Z39-48 Standard.

Bulk Purchases

Quantity discounts are available for use in workshops
and for staff development.
Call 1-800-232-0223

First Edition, 2009

10 9 8 7 6 5 4 3 2 1

To all those who work quietly and tirelessly, even in the face of hardship and occasional discouragement, to better educate students about diversity

CONTENTS

SECTION TWO—FEMINISM AND DIVERSITY EDUCATION

SECTION THREE—THE INCLUSIVE CLASSROOM

SECTION FOUR—DIVERSITY AND ONLINE ENVIRONMENTS

ACKNOWLEDGMENTS

We extend our deepest gratitude to Dr. Bill Hill (Kennesaw State University, Georgia). His vision and leadership, which gave rise to the annual "Best Practices" conference series, made this text possible. We also thank our panel of expert reviewers, Drs. Tresmaine Grimes (Iona College, New York), Linh Littleford (Ball State University, Indiana), Richard Vellayo (Pace University, New York), and Kristin Vespia (University of Wisconsin-Green Bay), who assisted in editorial duties. Finally, we thank the scholars who contributed their works to this text. Without their experience as educators, their passion for the topics, and their perseverance through the editorial and publishing process, we would not have this wonderful product to offer teachers and students across the disciplines. Special thanks go to John von Knorring, president and publisher of Stylus, and his staff for making this project a reality.

What does it mean to be culturally diverse? People vary in attitudes, beliefs, and behaviors, many of which are strongly tied to their culture. "Culture" is reflected in many physical and socially constructed forms: race and ethnicity, sex, gender, religion, geographical location, physical ability, and sexual orientation, among many others. People also have many different ancestral immigration histories. These human differences only scratch the surface of cultural diversity. The United States boasts a variety of cultural groups, and cultural variance increases dramatically as we look more broadly around the world.

No longer are nation-states, including the United States, isolated beings and actors in the world. No longer are ocean or land boundaries meaningful in this global twenty-first century. No longer can we remain ignorant of others in the world. No longer can we deny that our actions and human interactions have global consequences. We are now citizens of the world, teachers and students alike, learning about the cultural differences that abound within and outside of our own personal lives and experiences.

In this book, we provide a set of "best practices" for teaching about the cultural diversity present in our world. This book features current scholarship, conceptual discussion, and practical techniques on effectively teaching about diversity. The authors provide the most up-to-date thinking and the concrete practices of experienced educators to optimally teach about diversity, broadly defined.

Higher education has paid an increasing amount of attention to cultural differences, and there is clear consensus that educating our students about cultural diversity is critical (e.g., Branche, Mullennix, & Cohen, 2007). We live in a culturally diverse world, and educating about cultural differences can help alleviate many of the societal problems resulting from cultural ignorance, stereotyping, and prejudice. How can we best do this? What are the conceptual issues involved in reaching this goal? In this book, we aim to provide a valuable resource to answer these questions.

The perennial problem for teachers is that there is never a single, up-to-date resource on teaching students about diversity, especially one that includes a focus on international issues. Some pedagogical journals publish collections of previous work, but these have become dated. Teachers, regardless of their own cultural backgrounds and experiences, need a current resource to teach effectively about diversity. Manuals or media that accompany many diversity texts sometimes provide techniques to incorporate diversity in the classroom, but these are rarely detailed or developed enough to be of real utility. They provide little help in improving overall teaching effectiveness in diversity courses and often do not deal with critical and difficult issues surrounding teaching about diversity. For example, no current text addresses issues such as instructor burnout related to the pressures and challenges in teaching about diversity; provides pragmatic and tested ways of overcoming student misconceptions; or satisfactorily deals with student resistance and the emotions that can result during discussions concerning diversity.

Our book not only addresses the technical aspects of teaching about diversity but also tackles the enduring, broad-based challenges of the course. We go beyond teaching tips to introduce a more scholarly approach to teaching about diversity. As stated by Dennis Bok, president emeritus of Harvard, in his recent book *Our Underachieving Colleges* (2005), one of the major problems in higher education is not just *what* we are teaching (e.g., distribution requirements), but *how* we are teaching it. We believe that the broad conceptual issues we raise will stimulate readers' thinking and that the techniques we present will generate fresh ideas for instructors. The term *best practice* implies that, where feasible, there is empirical support for the effectiveness of a teaching technique. This book is among the few on this subject that uses this framework.

Our book is a response to the growing need in the broad academic community for guidance on how to integrate culture into the curriculum and to teach courses on diversity. *Getting Culture* is a scholarly but pedagogically practical attempt to provide a showcase for best practices in teaching about diversity across the academic disciplines. Instructors from high school through graduate school and from the liberal arts and sciences to the applied and professional schools will find useful resources in our text. The book is intended to serve as a core reference for faculty members who are creating courses on diversity as well as for those who are integrating diversity into their existing courses. Many of its ideas and suggestions can be incorporated into any class that includes a discussion of diversity issues or has a diverse student enrollment. In addition, this book can inform and guide department chairs and other administrators in the design and implementation of diversity initiatives.

Most of the chapters in this book are based on presentations delivered at the recent 2006 conference, *Reaching Out: Best Practices in Teaching About Diversity and International Issues*, held in Atlanta, Georgia, which focused on innovative and effective strategies and techniques for teaching diversity across the curriculum.

The book is organized into six major sections: *General Issues in Teaching About Diversity, Feminism and Diversity Education, The Inclusive Classroom, Diversity and Online Environments, Methods and Techniques for Faculty and Diversity Trainers,* and finally, *Diversity Across Educational Settings.*

Chapters in the opening section focus on key factors such as distinguishing teaching to a diverse audience from teaching about diversity, and contrasting incorporating culture across the curriculum with the practice of instituting diversity distribution requirements. The *Feminism and Diversity Education* section provides resources and information to help ensure an affirming and equitable experience in the classroom for women. Exposing students to international issues is the focus of *The Inclusive Classroom* section, which provides ideas on incorporating diverse national worldviews into the U.S.-based curriculum. Chapters in this section help instructors identify key pedagogical processes that can optimize students' learning about diversity issues, especially those from culturally diverse backgrounds. *Diversity and Online Environments* addresses the booming area of technology-based pedagogy and how a focus on diversity is a key element to effective instruction within this realm. Chapters in *Methods and Techniques for Faculty and Diversity Trainers* provide hands-on practical demonstrations for immediate use in class. The authors of these chapters include brief literature reviews of research on their specific topic, with emphasis on intracultural variations (and similarities), explicit descriptions of procedures to ensure that any reader can replicate the demonstration (including materials needed, time taken, and space needed), discussions of possible variations on the demonstration, a summary of the range of responses students may have to the demonstration, and the potential ethical hazards of the demonstration. Finally, the *Diversity Across Educational Settings* section highlights the special considerations of teaching and learning at the high school, community college, and college levels, and the closing chapter, *Beyond the Classroom: An Experiential Model for Developing Multicultural Competence*, presents a model for going beyond university walls and influencing the state.

References

Bok, D. (2005). *Our underachieving colleges: A candid look at how much students learn and why they should be learning more.* Princeton, NJ: Princeton University Press.

Branche, J., Mullennix, J., & Cohn, E. R. (Eds.). (2007). *Diversity across the curriculum: A guide for faculty in higher education.* Boston: Anker.

SECTION ONE

GENERAL ISSUES IN TEACHING ABOUT DIVERSITY

1

TEACHING ABOUT CULTURE

David Matsumoto

The importance of culture is one of the most fascinating topics to emerge in recent years in psychology and one of the biggest challenges teachers and researchers face. The field has made amazing strides in improving our understanding of culture and its influence on human behavior in the past two decades. In this chapter, I discuss three primary topics relevant to teaching about culture: a definition of culture, the complexity of understanding individual behavior, and teaching goals. I hope to stimulate thinking about culture and its relationship to mental processes and behaviors to help improve teaching efforts in psychology concerning culture.

What Is Culture?

One of the major conceptual issues facing a researcher or teacher dealing with culture is a definition of culture. Scholars in the social sciences have proffered different definitions of culture over the past 150 years, and there will probably never be "the" definition with which all scholars agree. Nevertheless, I do believe that it is important to have a working definition, and to make that explicit in my work. I encourage all teachers of culture to do so as well.

Over the years, *culture* has been defined as all capabilities and habits learned as members of a society (Tylor, 1865); as social heredity (Linton, 1936); as patterns of and for behavior acquired and transmitted by symbols, constituting the distinct achievements of human groups, including their embodiments in artifacts (Kroeber & Kluckhohn, 1952/1963); and as the totality of equivalent and complementary learned meanings maintained by a human population, or by identifiable segments of a population, and transmitted from one generation to the next (Rohner, 1984). Some have defined culture as shared symbol systems transcending individuals (Geertz, 1975), whereas others define culture simply as the shared way of life of a group of people (Berry, Poortinga, Segall, & Dasen, 1992).

A limitation of many of these definitions, however, is that they may be applicable to many social animals. After all, fish swim in schools, wolves hunt in packs, lions roam in prides, bees communicate sources of food to each other, and even birds build nests and have nest eggs! Many social animals build relationships between themselves and the community; differentiate between ingroups and outgroups; negotiate issues concerning status, power, dominance, and hierarchy within groups; and distribute tasks.

Thus, culture as typically defined is not a uniquely human product. But certainly there are some things unique about human culture, and these are rooted in the fact that human social life is much more complex than that of nonhuman animals. Humans are members of multiple groups, each having its own purpose, hierarchy, and networking system, and humans move in and out of these multiple social groups and ecologies constantly. Human social life is also complex because of the incredible diversity in thoughts, feelings, and actions that humans are capable of having or engaging in. Conflicts can arise easily because of this diversity, and group survival is not possible without social coordination to reduce diversity in behavior in any situational context.

The considerable degree of social complexity in human social life brings with it enormous potential for social chaos, which can easily ensue if individuals are not coordinated well and relationships not organized systematically. Social chaos would set in if the behaviors of society's members were not regulated to a large degree. For example, driving without laws dictating which side of the road to drive on, how to make turns, and who has the right of way would lead to chaos on the roads.

One of the most important functions of human culture is to provide this necessary coordination and organization to prevent social chaos and to maintain social order. This aids individuals and groups in negotiating the social complexity of human social life, allowing humans to move seamlessly in and out of multiple social groups, adapting and adjusting behavior to these groups. Culture is what provides a system of rules for driving, preventing chaos on the roads.

Culture does this by providing a meaning and information system to its members. Thus, I define human culture as "a unique meaning and information system, shared by a group and transmitted across generations, that allows the group to meet basic needs of survival, by coordinating social behavior to achieve a viable existence, to transmit successful social behaviors, to pursue happiness and well-being, and to derive meaning from life" (Matsumoto, 2007; Matsumoto & Juang, 2007). Culture as a meaning system helps human groups deal with enormous social complexity by allowing for greater differentiations among social groups, by institutionalizing cultural practices and customs, and by prescribing social norms and expectations. Culture provides rules for all important aspects of human social life, such as mating, aggression, and cooperation. Moreover, cultures are constantly changing their rules, adapting them to local, ecological, environmental, and intellectual conditions. Culture as a meaning system is rooted in uniquely human cognitive behaviors, including language (Premack, 2004), belief that other people are intentional agents, self-other knowledge (Goffman, 1959; Tomasello, 1999), and continual building upon improvements and discoveries (ratcheting) (Tomasello, Kruger, & Ratner, 1993). And because groups communicate their solutions across generations, each generation need not create entirely new solutions, ensuring efficiency for survival.

Human cultures enable groups to meet basic needs of survival, such as meeting others to procreate and produce offspring, putting food on the table, providing shelter from the elements, and caring for daily biological essentials. Human culture also allows for complex social networks and relationships, the enhancement of the meaning of normal, daily activities, and the pursuit of happiness. It allows us to be creative in music, art, drama, and work. It allows us to seek recreation, to engage in sports, and to organize competitions, whether in the local community, a little league, or the Olympic Games. It allows us to search the sea and space, to develop an education system, and to create mathematics, an achievement no other species can claim. It allows us to go to the moon, to create a research laboratory on Antarctica, and to send probes to Mars and Jupiter. Unfortunately, it also allows us to have wars, create and improve on weapons of mass destruction, and recruit and train terrorists. Human culture does all this by creating and maintaining complex social systems, institutionalizing and improving cultural practices, creating beliefs about the world, and communicating this belief system or meaning system to other humans and subsequent generations, all in order to prevent social chaos and maintain social order.

Given this definition, culture is not race, ethnicity, or nationality. But culture gives these social constructs and other social constructs (e.g., sexual orientation, disabilities) meaning. Moreover, cultures around the world can be very similar in some respects and very different in others. Thus, when talking about culture, it's a good idea to think about the meaning systems involved, where they come from, and what similarities and differences they exhibit when compared with other cultures around the world.

The Complexity of Explaining Behavior of Individuals from Different Cultures

One of the problems teachers must face concerns how students deal with issues of diversity. Too often, presentations about culture emphasize differences more than similarities. Indeed, in psychology, "culture" is almost synonymous with "differences," and that definition keeps us from searching for common ground. Keep in mind that cultures as meaning and information systems help to produce both similarities and differences.

Typical work on culture also seems to imply, often not overtly, that Eurocentric or American perspectives are the norm and that other cultural perspectives are "unusual" or "outliers." Thus, it's a challenge to get students (and sometimes researchers!) to realize that they have unconscious cultural blinders that may lead them to make value judgments that are inappropriate. Here's what usually happens. We *observe* differences in what we would normally expect in people who *appear physically different* than ourselves. Then we interpret these differences as *cultural* differences.

Our interpretations *may* be correct; in fact, those differences may indeed be culture. But, our interpretations may be wrong. Incorrect interpretations occur because of biases we have when interpreting the behavior of others. For one, psychologists have a love of differences. In research, there is a bias in the political nature of publishing similarities versus differences in psychological research; it's easier to publish differences. When researchers attribute observed differences between people of different races, nationalities, ethnic groups, or any such participant variable to culture without empirical justification, I have called this attributional bias the *cultural attribution fallacy* (Matsumoto and Yoo, 2006).

Individuals, too, have such a bias when making such interpretations. When we are too quick to make inferences about cultural differences from the behavior of people who just happen to look different from ourselves, these biases actually help to reinforce our own sense of self-worth, oftentimes while denying such self-worth to others.

In reality, the sources of motivation for human behavior are complex. In a recent paper, I outlined three sources of such motivation: basic human nature, which includes dispositions, cognitive abilities, and universal psychological processes we are born with; culture, including unique situational meanings, social roles, and norms; and personality and individual differences, including role identities, narratives, values, and aggregate role experiences (Matsumoto, 2007). Undoubtedly there are other sources of behavior as well, and all of these contribute to producing the kinds of differences in individual and group behavior that we observe in our everyday lives and research.

We understand this level of complexity when explaining *our own* or *our group's* behaviors. But when we try to interpret the behavior of people with whom we are less familiar, our awareness of such complexity seems to go out the door. For instance, people of different cultures spontaneously categorize emotions into two groups (Demoulin et al., 2004; Rodriguez Torres et al., 2005). One involves those thought to be uniquely human emotions, such as contentment, delight, melancholia, or resignation; the other involves emotions thought to be shared by humans and animals (basic emotions). And, people of different cultures tend to attribute uniquely human emotions more to ingroups, and basic emotions more to outgroups, in an infrahumanization process (Cortes, Demoulin, Rodriguez, Rodrigues, & Leyens, 2005). That is, we don't consider people of other groups and cultures as human as we consider ourselves. Maybe this is because we have more intimate knowledge of the importance of all of these processes compared to people or groups we don't know. Or perhaps we have a bias in the way we want to interpret our own behaviors compared to those of others. Whatever the reason, we often forget this complexity when we interpret the behaviors of others and are often too quick in interpreting differences as culturally rooted.

One of the goals of understanding the relationship between culture and psychology is to understand the complexity of the sources of human motivation, and to learn how to apply that complexity when interpreting the behavior of others as well as ourselves. If students (and researchers) continue to simply interpret all group differences as cultural, that may serve only to promulgate stereotypes about people—which is ironic, because one of the goals of cultural psychology is to break down the power of stereotypes in describing people rigidly.

What Are We Teaching?

It's not easy to get students to delve into this complexity. The traditional approach in academia is to teach them about culture. When we do this, we should teach not solely cultural differences, but cultural similarities as well. If we understand culture from an environmental and adaptational framework, then it is easy to see how there can be both cultural similarities and differences. And I believe that understanding the basis of similarities among people and groups, along with differences, provides all of us with a common basis from which to understand each other.

That kind of traditional academic teaching involves knowledge-based outcomes, which are definitely important. But helping students gain skills that can aid them in navigating the difficulties of intercultural interactions or a multicultural life is also a valuable and worthy goal.

Research my colleagues and I have done over the years suggests that one very important outcome to consider for teachers interested in skill acquisition and development is emotion regulation (Matsumoto, Yoo, & LeRoux, in press). Emotion regulation is *the ability to manage and modify one's emotional reactions in order to achieve constructive, desirable outcomes.* It's clear from the research that, if individuals are to adapt and adjust well in dynamic, multicultural environments, they need a psychological engine that enables them to deal with the inevitable stresses that occur in that environment. Emotion regulation is a major part of that engine.

Traditional didactic courses that impart knowledge may not necessarily affect students' emotion regulation skills. Instead, emotion regulation and other psychological skills are probably best taught in experiential-based learning. This means that teachers who are interested in these kinds of student outcomes may need to create opportunities for students to have real-life intercultural experiences that produce real-life emotions. This could be achieved by incorporating role plays, simulations, and in- and out-of-class activities that expose students to differences that provoke emotional reactions. Informed and prepared faculty would then need to guide students in constructing and reconstructing their emotional experiences in order to get a better handle on them, which should then open the door to a greater range of cognitive knowledge stores. At the same time, those knowledge stores need to be introduced and incorporated so that student emotions become associated with a larger range of cognitive and behavioral repertoire than before the event. This means, of course, that faculty need to be comfortable in doing so, which may require the same kind of development on the part of the faculty.

In any case, I believe we need to give strong consideration to bolstering our typical knowledge-based approaches to teaching culture by (a) teaching similarities as well as differences, and (b) incorporating experiential-based learning that will have an effect on emotion regulation. The question, of course, is, what do we want our students to learn, and how can we deliver that knowledge? The answer may not lie in content, but in a hypothesis-testing type of critical thinking process that helps students engage with cultural differences. We can help students acquire this type of critical thinking if we model it ourselves in and out of our classrooms.

Conclusion

We have only scratched the surface in terms of understanding culture and its relationship to mental processes and behavior. In light of our world's increasingly pluralistic and multicultural tendencies, it's important for teachers to continue to be on the cutting edge of knowledge and teaching in this area so that students can emerge as more informed voyagers of the world who have some practical skills in engaging with the complexity of a diverse life. Our ability to understand, appreciate, respect, and interact with people of diverse cultures, lifestyles, and belief systems has implications not only for how we deal with friends, neighbors, colleagues, and strangers, but also for how we deal with other countries and cultures. Dealing with culture is a major challenge not only on a local scale, but also on a global scale, and it can mean the difference between war and peace. Hopefully, all of us, in our own ways, can help to make the world a better place through our teachings about culture and in our daily lives.

References

Berry, J. W., Poortinga, Y. H., Segall, M. H., & Dasen, P. R. (1992). *Cross-cultural psychology: Research and applications.* New York: Cambridge University Press.

Cortes, B. P., Demoulin, S., Rodriguez, R. T., Rodrigues, A. P., & Leyens, J.-P. (2005). Infrahumanization or familiarity? Attribution of uniquely human emotions to the self, the ingroup, and the outgroup. *Personality and Social Psychology Bulletin, 31*(2), 243–253.

Demoulin, S., Leyens, J.-P., Paladino, M. P., Rodriguez Torres, R., Rodriguez Perez, A., & Dovidio, J. F. (2004). Dimensions of "uniquely" and "nonuniquely" human emotions. *Cognition and Emotion, 18*, 71–96.

Geertz, C. (1975). From the natives' point of view: On the nature of anthropological understanding. *American Scientist, 63*, 47–53.

Goffman, E. (1959). *The presentation of self in everyday life.* Oxford, England: Doubleday.

Kroeber, A. L., & Kluckhohn, C. (1952/1963). *Culture: A critical review of concepts and definitions.* Cambridge, MA: Harvard University.

Linton, R. (1936). *The study of man: An introduction.* New York: Appleton.

Matsumoto, D. (2007). Culture, context, and behavior. *Journal of Personality, 75*(6), 1285–1320.

Matsumoto, D., & Juang, L. (2007). *Culture and Psychology* (4th ed.). Belmont, CA: Wadsworth.

Matsumoto, D., Yoo, S. H., & LeRoux, J. A. (2007). Emotion and intercultural communication. In H. Kotthoff & H. Spencer-Oatley (Eds.), *Handbook of applied linguistics* (Vol. 7: Intercultural Communication): Mouton de Gruyter Publishers.

Premack, D. (2004). Is language the key to human intelligence? *Science, 303*, 318–320.

Rodriguez Torres, R., Leyens, J.-P., Rodriguez Perez, A., Betancour Rodriguez, V., Quiles del Castillo, M. N., Demoulin, S., et al. (2005). The lay distinction between primary and secondary emotions: A spontaneous categorization? *International Journal of Psychology, 40*(2), 100–107.

Rohner, R. P. (1984). Toward a conception of culture for cross-cultural psychology. *Journal of Cross-Cultural Psychology, 15*, 111–138.

Tomasello, M. (1999). *The cultural origins of human cognition.* Cambridge, MA: Harvard University Press.

Tomasello, M., Kruger, A. C., & Ratner, H. H. (1993). Cultural learning. *Behavioural and Brain Sciences, 16*, 495–552.

Tylor, E. B. (1865). *Researches into the early history of mankind and development of civilisation.* London: John Murray.

2

GOT CULTURE?

Incorporating Culture into the Curriculum

Regan A. R. Gurung

To say that the world is getting increasingly diverse is to make a gross understatement and is now also trite and hackneyed. Whether from being "flattened" by technology or from increased rates of immigration and migration, the world is more diverse than it has ever been in the history of humankind. This is particularly the case in North America. Even the first U.S. Census in 1790 showed that the United States was a very diverse country (U.S. Bureau of the Census, 1976). Today, more than ever before, students in the United States and around the world must be well aware of cultural diversity and its consequences regardless of their own cultural backgrounds. Culture is part of the "web of significance" in which we live enmeshed (Geertz, 1973).

Learning about diversity and culture is a critical learning outcome for all students, not just those in the cultural majority. Universities around North America have instituted initiatives to diversify the curriculum by changing general education requirements, revising majors, creating new courses on culture, hiring more faculty of color, and trying to diversify the student body (Branche, Mullennix, & Cohn, 2007). Diversity, meaning all the ways in which people are different (Bucher, 2004; see also Matsumoto, this volume), has been defined in various ways, sometimes exclusively in relation to ethnicity and race, and sometimes also incorporating other differences such as disability and sexual orientation. Similarly, culture has been defined in many different ways (Gurung, 2010), and both terms can be used somewhat interchangeably. This chapter provides a broad overview of the major considerations needed to best incorporate culture into the curriculum. In many ways I set the stage for the chapters that follow in this book. I first provide a brief definition of culture, highlighting some of the major issues inherent in trying to define culture. I then discuss the different ways that faculty can bring more diversity to their classes.

Culture Defined

At first defining culture does not seem too difficult, but both trained academics and laypeople often mean different things when they discuss culture. (Matsumoto, in this volume, provides a more expansive discussion of this issue.) Many students use the words *culture, ethnicity,* and *race* as if they mean the same thing. People also think that culture represents a set of ideals, beliefs, or behaviors. Culture has many dimensions. If you ask someone what she thinks the dominant culture around her is, in most cases she will identify an ethnic category. Someone in Miami may respond with "Cuban." Someone in Minnesota may respond with "Scandinavian." When I ask that question in Green Bay, Wisconsin, people often respond with "Hispanic" or "Hmong" (people from Laos, near Vietnam). They sometimes say, "American Indian" because they think that I am asking for which ethnic group is most visible in town. In reality, culture can be a variety of things. The dominant culture in Green Bay is Catholic, but people rarely realize that religion also constitutes a form of culture.

Culture must be discussed and defined before one can determine how to incorporate it into the curriculum. There are many definitions of culture (Soudijn, Hutschemaekers, & Van de Vijver, 1990, analyzed 128 definitions). Culture can be broadly defined as a dynamic yet stable set of goals, beliefs, and attitudes shared by a group of people (Gurung, 2010). Culture can also include similar physical characteristics (e.g., skin color), similar psychological characteristics (e.g., levels of hostility), and common superficial features (e.g., hairstyle and clothing). Culture is dynamic because some of the beliefs held by members in a culture can change with time. However, a culture generally remains stable because its members change together. Their beliefs and attitudes can be implicit, learned by observation and passed on by word of mouth, or they can be explicit, written down as laws or rules for the group to follow. The most commonly described cultural groups are those defined by ethnicity, race, sex, and age.

Two of the most important aspects that define cultural groups are *socio-economic status (SES)* and *sex*. Although sex (including gender) has been in the curriculum for some time (e.g., gender studies, human sexuality classes, women's studies), socioeconomic status has only recently been incorporated into the curriculum. The poor make up a large percentage of Americans without health insurance. SES is related to a higher occurrence of most chronic and infectious disorders and to higher rates of nearly all major causes of mortality and morbidity (Gurung, 2010). SES is a critical aspect of culture because research shows it to be associated with a wide array of health, cognitive, and socioemotional outcomes, with effects beginning before birth and continuing into adulthood (Bradley & Corwyn, 2002).

Definitional Issues

Any discussion of culture has to be cognizant of a major trend in the literature. Whenever we talk about culture, we often tend to emphasize cultural differences. To some extent, this is a natural human tendency. Even if people who are relatively identical in age, ethnicity, and intelligence are randomly separated into two groups and forced to compete with each other, members of each group will tend to believe they are better than those of the other group. Even when not competing for resources, we still like to emphasize how we are different from other people. This behavior creates three major problems. First, this emphasis on differences often leads us to treat some groups better than others, favoring them for a range of activities and services. Second, by focusing on major group differences, we often forget that differences exist within a group as often as between groups. Some African Americans have the same values, attitudes, and beliefs as some Asian Americans, and the superficial ethnic difference should not be taken to automatically suggest that the two individuals are vastly different. Finally, and perhaps most importantly in the context of education, whenever we deal with an individual from an unfamiliar culture, we often use the key ways that he or she is different to define his or her entire culture. When students learn about how a culture is different, they automatically assume that every member of that culture is different.

When we consider incorporating culture and diversity into the curriculum, we have to consider the implications of how we define culture. My definition of culture is general and inclusive. It can be argued that by making such a broad definition I am downplaying the hardships faced by groups that have been historically discriminated against. Having ethnic and sex differences as major (or sole) parts of the university or department definition of culture may better facilitate the creation and requirements of courses on ethnicity and sex/gender. But having broader definitions may also make it easier for some instructors to avoid the more incendiary topics in diversity (e.g., racism and sexism) to focus on other forms of diversity that are somewhat less divisive (e.g., disability).

We should remember that cultural components interact. An individual has an ethnicity, a nationality, a sex, and many other components of culture. When we focus on only one of these (e.g., ethnicity) without noting how the one element interacts with others, we are missing out on the big picture. Human identity is complex, and focusing on only one element ignores that complexity. Sex and ethnicity provide a good example. As Lorde (1984) states, "By and large within the women's movement today, white women focus upon their oppression as women and ignore differences of race, sexual preference, class and age. There is a pretense to homogeneity of experience covered by the word sisterhood that does not exist" (p. 164). Figure 2.1 provides a useful graphic illustration of the importance of recognizing connectedness.

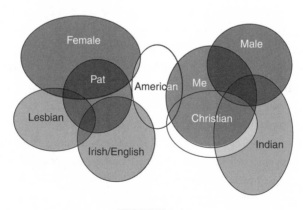

FIGURE 2.1

Cultural Components Interact

One final point in the context of definitions: There is a significant difference between teaching *about* diversity and teaching *to* a diverse student body; they require different skills and techniques. The chapters in this book primarily discuss the first type (teaching about diversity), although some also touch on the second (e.g., Hailstorks, this volume and the final section of this book).

Why Culture?

Some may wonder what the fuss is all about. Why should everyone incorporate culture into the curriculum? There are many different answers to this question, and perhaps one of them will suit you better than others. For many of us, there is no choice. Incorporating diversity is often a mandate handed down by our professional organizations, our university system or campus, or our department (Johns & Kelley Sipp, 2004). The American Psychological Association (APA), for example, urges that faculty "employ the constructs of multiculturalism and diversity in psychological education" (APA, 2003). In the field of psychology, one of the major competencies deemed critical by the Task Force on Undergraduate Psychology Major Competencies (Halonen et al., 2002) was that "students will recognize, understand and respect the complexity of sociocultural and international diversity."

Mandates aside, a sizable body of research suggests that being aware of cultural diversity can play a significant role in affect, behavior, and cognition (Gurin, 1999; Wlodkowski & Ginsberg, 1995). Gurin (1999) points out that students who had experienced the most diversity in classroom settings and in informal interactions with their classmates showed the greatest engagement in active thinking processes and the greatest growth in intellectual and academic skills. Experience with diversity is especially effective in moderating stereotyping and prejudice.

Although research helps to counteract skepticism, the importance of culture is relatively clear if we take a look at life and experience. Culture is part of who we are; our identity is based on interrelated cultural aspects—our ethnicity, our nationality, and our religious outlooks. This is particularly important for students and faculty of European ancestry, for whom being "White" is often associated with not having as much culture as others. As Prieto and

Robinson (both this volume) point out, even those of European descent have cultural richness and a cultural identity. Furthermore, because we live in a diverse world, it seems fitting that we have culturally diverse curricula. Such curricula will help ensure the full and equal participation of all groups in society, a goal of the social justice approach (see Goldstein, this volume). Finally, a diverse curriculum that supports diverse student bodies improves recruitment and retention, two of the critical variables in college (Wang & Folger, 2004).

When asked why they do not cover cultural issues in their classes, our colleagues in the field have many different reactions and reasons, some of them valid. More often than not, however, they are more valid to the believer than in reality. These reasons vary, and you may have heard many of them yourself.

A common perception is that cultural diversity is tangential or irrelevant to the course. "It does not fit my course" is the oft-repeated refrain. Although this may be true in some areas, if one believes that cultural diversity is important, one needs to make the effort to make culture relevant. Instructors of physics or chemistry, for example, may be able to focus on equations and reactions that are constant across cultures. Although an introduction to physics or chemistry course may seem an odd place for cultural diversity, there is a large ethnic variance among the foremost proponents of physics and chemistry; the fields are not pure White (though they may appear and mostly are predominantly male). An easy way to incorporate diversity in these classes is to highlight contributions made to the discipline by diverse investigators (see Daniels, 2007, for biochemistry; Gunasekera and Friedrich this volume, for the Science Technology, Engineering, and Mathematics (STEM) areas; and Guthrie, 2004, for psychology). Finding the time to discuss the varying ethnicities of investigators creates another issue and leads to another common excuse: "There's no time to cover diversity." We make time for what we think is important.

Sometimes it is easier to shift the responsibility to other sources. Some faculty members, especially those who do not believe they are competent to talk about diversity (another common excuse for not doing it), may also believe that students should get their diversity information from specific courses instead of from each instructor. One model of incorporating culture is having special courses on diversity, such as Race and Ethnicity or Introduction to Women Studies. A majority of colleges, 68%, require that students take one or more diversity courses (Humphreys, 2000). Although this approach exposes students to diversity issues, it may marginalize culture. Students "have" to take the course and "get it taken care of" or "out of the way." They may therefore become dissatisfied with the course and may even resent the instructor (see Haynes, this volume).

One of the most inaccurate assumptions is that "basic theories apply to all cultures" and that therefore one does not need to spend time and energy discussing cultural variation. Although this sentiment may have reflected the state of the research perhaps 100 years ago, it is clearly not the case today (Matsumoto, 2007). There are many ways that cultures differ, and learning about them is important.

Another Model of Cultural Education

Requiring students to take a specialty course or courses in culture is only one way of incorporating culture into the curriculum. Another way is to infuse culture across the curriculum. This method is commonly used for writing. Many universities choose to have classes in every department pay more attention to writing and not just have it be the responsibility of the English Department (see Sewanee University; Kuh, et al., 2005). This method works well for culture too.

There are different ways of successfully managing infusion. Sometimes culture is introduced as a separate subject within a course in the form of a designated lecture or lectures, a separate chapter, or supplemental readings. Another method is to have culture be the thread throughout the class. Relevant cultural issues are mentioned in each lecture or every week, or a textbook is adopted that has a culture section in every chapter. Both these methods run the risk of making the "other" cultures discussed exotic or unique. The best method is to have culture be the fabric of the course, its main foundation (Banks & Banks, 2004; Kitano, 1997). There are many resources to help with this approach (Adams, Bell, & Griffin, 1997; Branche, Mullennix, & Cohn, 2007; Bronstein & Quina, 2003; Bucher, 2004; Fowler, & Mumford, 1999; Johns & Kelley Sipp, 2004; Kowalski, 2000; Simoni, Sexton-Radek, Yescavage, Richard, & Lundquist, 1999; Singelis, 1998; Timpson, Canetto, Borrayo, & Yang, 2003; Trimble, Stevenson, & Worell, 2004; Whittlesey, 2001; Wlodkowski & Ginsburg, 1995).

Key Guidelines for Incorporating Culture into the Curriculum

There are many pragmatic ways to better include culture into the curriculum and many places and opportunities to do so. It does take time and effort, but if you have bought this book and read this far in this chapter, you clearly have an interest in this important task. There are seven key items to keep in mind:

1. *Make it explicit.* If you are serious about educating about cultural diversity, do not steer away from acknowledging it. Clearly list your goal in your syllabus (e.g., "To provide valuable information on cultural differences"). Students should know that learning about cultural diversity is going to be stressed and is not something tangential to the course. You can walk the walk by designing your assignments to make sure students learn about culture, and even by picking a textbook that incorporates culture throughout. For example, the subtitle of the textbook I use to teach health psychology is "A Cultural Approach" (Gurung, 2010). It is clear to students that cultural diversity is going to feature strongly in class.

2. *Make it safe.* It is not always easy to talk about diversity. Many students are uncomfortable. Many faculty members are uncomfortable. It is important to set ground rules for discussion and to provide alternative responses to raising one's hand for sharing differences (Kees, 2003; Wlodkowski & Ginsburg, 1995). Members of different cultural groups have different comfort levels for class participation, and sometimes it is helpful to explicitly acknowledge these differences. Chapters in this book will greatly expand your awareness of things to watch out for.

3. *Model appropriate behavior.* Students rely heavily on instructors when someone in the class makes a potentially offensive comment. Some examples of such "triggers" (Adams, Bell, & Griffin, 1997) are the following: "I feel so sorry for people with disabilities. What a tragedy"; "Men are biologically more adapted to leadership roles"; "Homeless people prefer their life"; "People of color just blow things out of proportion"; "If women wear tight clothes, they are asking for it." Instructors need to be prepared to respond to such statements, for often not reacting to them could indicate implicit agreement. Such triggers can also be used to generate discussion (if students feel it is safe).

4. *Make it relevant.* Many students have had minimal exposure to individuals who are different. Often they do not even realize that the people they interact with or are exposed to *are* different. Socioeconomic differences are easily invisible in superficial classroom interactions, as are differences such as sexual orientation. One way to make talking about culture relevant is to tie discussion

to current events and to make local connections. If there is an American Indian reservation nearby or a national rally for gay rights or a controversy related to a minority group, the instructor can use the opportunity to educate the class about the group in question.

5. *Make it credible.* It is difficult to talk about the experiences of a group based on only your reading or secondhand experiences. For example, European American instructors are often hesitant to discuss the experiences of African Americans because they feel, sometimes correctly, that students will not consider them credible. The best thing to do is to use experts, primary sources, and the vast array of movies (*Crash, A Class Divided, What's Cooking, Mi Familia*), television shows, and musical productions. With the advent of YouTube, various short clips are easily accessible for use in class.

6. *Make it active and experiential.* Getting students involved in their learning and making class presentation more "active" have been shown to be better for student learning in a variety of situations (Bean, 1996; Warren, 2006). Providing students with ways to engage with diversity information directly is useful. Most of this book discusses such methods, including the "Who am I?" task (students illustrate their own cultural diversity by listing the ways they describe themselves), perspective-taking exercises (Watkins-Goffman, 2001), grocery shopping (in a culturally different grocery store, such as a European American student going to a Mexican American grocery store), visiting a different religion's place of worship, reflection papers for movies, book clubs on diversity (e.g., *Why Are All the Black Kids Sitting Together in the Cafeteria?*, Tatum, 2003; *Sexing the Body*, Fausto Sterling, 2004), and interviews (see Pedersen, 2004).

7. *Make it count.* If you are implementing new strategies to incorporate culture into the classroom, it is critical to assess your level of success. Measure student satisfaction with the class, and monitor if it changes from before you introduced diversity to after. Perhaps directly measure student prejudices during the course of the class (Case, 2007). Perform content analyses of student papers or choose from the many methods suggested by guides to conducting research on teaching and learning (see Gurung & Schwartz, 2009, for a review and complete guide).

Conclusions

Culture is multifaceted, influencing every aspect of life. Healthy curricula need both specialty courses and the infusion of culture into standard courses. Cultural diversity is a fact of life not yet adequately represented in academic curricula. This book provides a comprehensive review of resources and methods to optimize the integration of culture into the curriculum. Specific models of integration and best practices will provide you with the tools and material to try out new techniques immediately.

In closing, let me ask the question suggested by the title of this chapter: Have you "Got Culture"? It is important to do the following as you answer this question for yourself. Examine yourself and be cognizant of how you vary from others (e.g., sex, age, religion, family values). Examine your courses (syllabus, textbook, lectures, activities). Examine your department mission and learning outcomes, procedures and criteria for program review, merit, tenure and promotion, and the requirements for the major and minor. Examine your university mission statement, the hiring language, and the general education requirements. If you are committed to incorporating culture into the curriculum, leave none of these stones unturned.

References

Adams, M., Bell, L. A., & Griffin, P. (Eds.). (1997). *Teaching for diversity and social justice.* New York: Routledge.

American Psychological Association. (2003). Guidelines on multicultural education, training, research, practice, and organizational change for psychologists. *American Psychologist, 58,* 377–402.

Banks, J. A., & Banks, C. A. M. (Eds.) (2004). *Handbook of research on multicultural education.* San Francisco: Jossey-Bass.

Bean, J. C. (1996). *Engaging ideas: The professor's guide to integrating writing, critical thinking, and active learning in the classroom.* San Francisco: Jossey-Bass.

Branche, J., Mullennix, J., & Cohn, E. R. (Eds.). (2007). *Diversity across the curriculum: A guide for faculty in higher education.* Bolton: Anker.

Bronstein, P., & Quina, K. (Eds.). (2003). *Teaching gender and multicultural awareness: Resources for the psychology classroom.* Washington, D.C.; American Psychological Association.

Bucher, R. D. (2004). *Diversity consciousness: Opening our minds to people, cultures, and opportunities.* Upper Saddle River, NJ: Prentice Hall.

Case, K. A. (2007). Raising White privilege awareness and reducing racial prejudice: Assessing diversity course effectiveness. *Teaching of Psychology, 34,* 231–235.

Daniels, L. B. (2007). Diversity and multiculturalism in the science classroom. In J. Branche, J., Mullennix, & E. R., Cohn (Eds.), *Diversity across the curriculum: A guide for faculty in higher education* (pp. 293–297). Bolton: Anker.

Fausto-Sterling, A. (2000). *Sexing the body: Gender politics and the construction of sexuality.* New York: Basic Books.

Fowler, S. M., & Mumford, M. G. (1999). *Intercultural sourcebook: Cross-cultural training methods.* Yarmouth, ME: Intercultural Press.

Geertz, C. (1977). *The interpretation of culture.* New York: Basic Books.

Gurin, P. (1999). The compelling need for diversity in education. *Michigan Journal of Race and Law, 5,* 363–425.

Gurung, R. A. R. (2010). *Health psychology: A cultural approach* (2e). San Francisco: Cengage.

Gurung, R. A. R., & Schwartz, E. (2009). *Optimizing teaching and learning: Pragmatic pedagogy.* Malden, MA: Blackwell.

Guthrie, R. V. (2004). *Even the rat was white: A historical view of psychology.* Boston: Allyn & Bacon.

Halonen, J., et al., (2002). Report of the Task Force on Undergraduate Psychology Major Competencies: Undergraduate psychology major learning goals and outcomes. Retrieved June 2, 2005, from www.apa.org/ed/resources.html

Humphreys, D. (2000). *National survey finds diversity requirements common around the country.* Retrieved June 3, 2007, from www.diversityweb.org/digest/f00/survey.html

Johns, A. M., & Kelley Sipp, M. (Eds.). (2004). *Diversity in college classrooms: Practices for today's campuses.* Ann Arbor: University of Michigan Press.

Kees, N. (2003). Creating safe environments. In W. M. Timpson, S. S. Canetto, E. Borrayo, & R. Yang (Eds.), *Teaching diversity: Challenges and complexities, identities and integrity* (pp. 55-64). Madison, WI: Atwood.

Kitano, M. K. (1997). What a course will look like after multicultural change. In A. I. Morey & M. K. Kitano (Eds.), *Multicultural course transformation in higher education: A broader truth* (pp. 18–34). Boston: Allyn & Bacon.

Kowalski, R. M. (2000). Including gender, race, and ethnicity in psychology content courses. *Teaching of Psychology, 27,* 18–24.

Kuh, G. D., Kinzie, J., Schuh, J. H., & Whitt, E. J. (2005). *Student success in college: Creating conditions that matter.* San Francisco: Jossey-Bass.

Lorde, A. (1984). *Sister Outsider: Essays and speeches.* Freedom, CA: Crossing Press.

Matsumoto, D. (2007). Culture, context, and behavior. *Journal of Personality, 75*(6), 1285–1320.

Pedersen, P. B. (2004). *110 Experiences for multicultural learning.* Washington, DC: American Psychological Association.

Simoni, J. M., Sexton-Radek, K., Yescavage, K., Richard, H., & Lundquist, A. (1999). Teaching diversity: Experiences and recommendations of American Psychological Association Division 2 members. *Teaching of Psychology, 26,* 89–95.

Singelis, T. (1998). *Teaching about culture, ethnicity, and diversity.* Thousand Oaks, CA: Sage.

Soudijn, K. A., Hutschemaekers, G. J. M., & Van de Vijver, F. J. R. (1990). Culture conceptualizations. In F. J .R. Van de Vijver and G. J. M. Hutschemaeker (Eds.), *The Investigation of Culture: Current Issues in Cultural Psychology* (pp. 19039). Tilburg: Tilburg University Press.

Tatum, B. D. (2003). *"Why are all the Black kids sitting together in the cafeteria?" A psychologist explains the development of racial identity.* New York: Basic Books.

Timpson, W. M., Canetto, S. S., Borrayo, E., & Yang, R. (Eds.). (2003). *Teaching diversity: Challenges and complexities, identities and integrity.* Madison, WI: Atwood.

Trimble, J. E., Stevenson, M. R., & Worell, J. P. (2004). *Toward an inclusive psychology: Infusing the introductory psychology textbook with diversity content.* Washington, DC: American Psychological Association.

U.S. Bureau of the Census. (1976). *Historical statistics of the United States, Part II (series Z).* Washington, DC: U.S. Government Printing Office.

Wang, M., & Folger, T. (2004). Faculty and student diversity: A case study. In A. M. Johns & M. Kelley Sipp (Eds.), *Diversity in college classrooms: Practices for today's campuses* (pp. 133–151). Ann Arbor: University of Michigan Press.

Warren, C. S. (2006). Incorporating multiculturalism into undergraduate psychology courses: Three simple active learning activities. *Teaching of Psychology, 33,* 105–109.

Watkins-Goffman, L. (2001*). Lives in two languages: An exploration of identity and culture.* Ann Arbor: University of Michigan Press.

Whittlesey, V. (2001). *Diversity activities for psychology.* Boston: Allyn & Bacon.

Wlodkowski R. J., & Ginsburg, M. B. (1995). *Diversity and motivation: Culturally responsive teaching.* San Francisco, CA: Jossey-Bass.

3

TEACHING ABOUT DIVERSITY

Reflections and
Future Directions

Loreto R. Prieto

There are two ways of spreading light; to be the candle or the mirror that reflects it (Wharton, 1902).

In teaching students about diversity issues, my thinking has been affected by my discussions with colleagues across the country, my teaching of both graduate and undergraduate diversity courses for several years, and a national survey study I conducted (Prieto et al., in press) of teachers from high school through graduate school regarding their perceptions on teaching about diversity. These experiences have raised questions for me concerning teaching about diversity issues.

Questions on Teaching about Diversity

First, who should be responsible for teaching students about diversity issues—academicians from diverse groups or academicians from majority or more privileged groups?

Second, I have become increasingly convinced that teaching students to appreciate diversity is quite a different task than educating them on and helping them to eradicate their own personal racism, sexism, homophobia, or other oppressive views. If this is true, what does it mean for the practice of teaching about diversity?

Finally, I am convinced that teaching about diversity and oppression calls for a developmental approach and curriculum across the sum total of an educational career—from high school through graduate school, should students go that far. If this is true, how should educators implement such an education?

Who Is Responsible for Teaching About Diversity?

This is a difficult, multifaceted question. Culturally diverse teachers dealing with the inevitable resistance, fear, or confusion evoked by diversity issues have probably thought, "Why me? Why am I struggling to accomplish this? Oppression is a majority culture problem. Shouldn't a teacher that represents the majority culture be here in the classroom to fix it?" Unfortunately, this is historically not the way advances in diversity have been made in society; most advances have come from the grassroots efforts of members from oppressed groups.

Of course, this is not to say that the majority culture or demographically privileged academicians are not doing their part to teach about diversity issues. They indeed are, and they are strongly committed to their efforts. In fact, in the aforementioned national study, White American teachers in the sample were teaching diversity courses in direct proportion to their overall sample representation. In other words, faculty of color were not disproportionately teaching diversity courses as compared with their majority culture counterparts. Without question, we are all doing our part. Yet, who should be chiefly responsible for teaching about diversity?

This issue raises strong feelings on both sides, majority culture and culturally diverse academicians alike. Some tension comes from the notion that whoever made the mess should clean it up. Ironically, some tension also comes from majority culture academicians who face severe criticisms when they become involved in this area.

Some culturally diverse scholars have argued that culturally diverse persons have a proprietary right to speak to, for, and about diversity issues (see Mio & Iwamasa, 1993; Parham, 1993). Essentially, the argument is that diverse people have a better understanding of their own position in a racist/sexist/homophobic society than do majority culture academicians. Some scholars (cf. Sue & Sue, 2003) have argued that majority culture academicians have historically engaged in the study of diversity issues largely for their own benefit (i.e., publications, grants, tenure, recognition as an "expert in the area"). These scholars further argue that majority culture academicians have conducted diversity research that actually reflects majority culture biases and have failed to make any real contributions or return of investment to the diverse groups they have researched or taught about (cf. Guthrie, 1998; Parham, 1993). On other fronts, criticisms have been made against higher education in general and its traditionally European male majority culture orientation, which can preclude or discourage a focus on diversity issues for minority culture scholars who want to receive tenure (Turner & Meyers, 2000).

On the other hand, minority culture academicians can fall prey to the expectations of their colleagues or academic administrators to adopt the role of the "diversity person" on the faculty, with its attendant duties of serving on diversity-related committees, teaching diversity courses, advising diverse students, and mentoring student projects concerned with diversity issues. Saying "no" to such requests is a "damned if you do and damned if you don't" proposition. If you refuse, you seem to not care about other minority culture persons (and are counted along with those faculty who are also perceived as uncaring). If you accept these assignments, they prove to be pressures and commitments that can impinge greatly on research time, an impingement that can have serious consequences for tenure and promotion (Turner & Meyers, 2000).

As a person of color, I can attest to the fact that teaching about diversity can be a very difficult task. Over the years, I have encountered the occasional majority culture student who frustrates and frightens me with his dogged insistence that his need to become aware of his oppressive perspectives and increase his appreciation of diversity is ultimately a debatable issue. Moreover, in his eyes, it is my job to prove to him that diversity is even a worthwhile thing to consider thinking about. This type of student does not seem to care that examining these issues in himself will help both his own growth and his effectiveness with the diverse persons he will work with or encounter after graduation.

On the other hand, it has been my good fortune to have worked with an overwhelming number of students who are willing to make such self-examinations and institute changes in themselves. In fact, one of my "hard cases" has even come to a place where his ultimate commitment and efforts at personal and professional growth have been so genuine and moving that they have brought me to tears and filled me with hope that perhaps we are all moving in a fruitful direction.

I myself have been pressured to be a "diversity person." In fact, despite being interested in diversity issues since graduate school, for much of my early career I stayed close to research and activities tied to my interests in testing and assessment. I did not want to be pegged as a "one-trick pony" by doing research in the area of diversity (an area considered "weak" with respect to scholarship). It was not until I found within myself, on my own terms, the desire to express my interests in diversity issues that I began focusing most of my energy on this topic. And a major reason for that transition was having wonderful colleagues and supportive environments within which such work was valued.

In sum, regardless of how one feels about the veracity of the allegations, complaints, and concerns forwarded by both majority and minority academicians in the "who is responsible for diversity education?" argument, such polemical positions have not made teaching about diversity issues easier for anyone and can leave all interested and committed scholars from any social group unsure of how to proceed.

I believe we are all responsible for teaching about diversity issues. If our ultimate goal is to cultivate a widespread understanding and accepting environment for cultural diversity in our students, we must engage in a joint, unified effort in which academicians from both majority and diverse cultures do their part.

If such philosophical arguments do not persuade, at the very least, pragmatic empirical arguments might win out. Recent statistics (Morris, 2005) indicate that members of diverse racial and ethnic groups still constitute less than 20% of all academicians in higher education. The situation is improving for women in academia, but they are still underrepresented in the higher professorial ranks and administrative positions. A national survey of universities by the Policy Institute of the National Gay and Lesbian Task Force (Rankin, 2003) concerning various Lesbian, Gay, Bisexual, Transsexual, and Questioning (LGBTQ) issues found that only about 9% of their LGBTQ respondents were faculty members. This means that if teaching about diversity is left to faculty from diverse groups, there simply will not be enough person power to meet the teaching needs, or more importantly, to succeed in making the kind of widespread impact we seek. We need to have White American faculty teaching students about racism, men teaching students about sexism, and sexually straight academics teaching students about LGBTQ issues.

As an example, the available data for psychologists show that majority culture psychologists are doing a great deal of teaching about diversity on college campuses. The data further show that most of the students that continue to study psychology at all academic levels are persons with majority culture characteristics; for example, in our national sample, teachers reported that a full 80% or more of their high school, college, and graduate students were White American. Other academic disciplines likely have similar demographic characteristics among their faculty and student bodies.

What Is the Goal: Appreciation of Diversity or Eradication of Oppression?

The foregoing discussion leads to the next question: Is teaching about diversity supposed to enhance students' knowledge, awareness, and appreciation of different cultural worldviews and experiences or to make students aware of the oppressive historical and institutional sexist, heterosexist, and racist legacies that they represent and may perpetuate? The literature suggests that separating the concept of "appreciating diversity" from the concept of "eradication of oppressive attitudes" is not a new discussion. However, many teachers I have talked to frequently report trying to do both in their diversity courses or when they address diversity issues in class. Because expanding students' awareness of other cultures is often an easier process than having them actively examine the more personally challenging and uncomfortable aspects of the power and privilege that their particular demographic group may enjoy, I suspect that the educational path of least resistance may win out—if not for instructors, then perhaps for students.

Perhaps an easier way to convey this concern is to say that I have seen students leave a diversity course well schooled on the ways of other cultures but without having seriously considered or perhaps even recognized how their personal oppressive attitudes and cultural privileges impact their own lives and the lives of persons from oppressed groups. In short, it is quite possible for students to have gained an awareness and fact-based understanding of other cultures but still hold sexist, racist, and homophobic attitudes (and cultural privileges) as yet unexamined or unchallenged. And not just students—teachers may as well.

If these two growth areas, learning about diversity and unlearning oppression, are in fact linked, what does this mean for teaching about diversity issues? And if we have mostly majority culture faculty teaching majority culture students, how does that play into the equation?

The first step on the path of least resistance is for an instructor to simply not see diversity issues as relevant to her course. Little can be said or done about this impediment except to recognize that there is a continuing need to educate academicians about the relevancy of human diversity to all knowledge domains, as well as the educational benefits for students when they are exposed to such material.

A second obstacle concerns academicians' perceptions of whether students are interested in learning about diversity issues and will be accepting of the instructor bringing these issues into class. If a teacher does not imagine that students will be interested in or accepting of diversity issues, she will be less likely to incorporate those issues into her course content or discussions. Such concerns are somewhat understandable. Instructors are pressured enough to get through important content, and there is little time to incorporate relevant material on diversity or have an impromptu discussion with students when diversity issues come up. In addition, the great majority of academicians feel less than adequately trained to engage students in diversity-related discussions. Instructors want to protect their credibility and personal comfort.

However, is it appropriate for instructors to allow students' willingness to learn about diversity issues to guide their decisions on whether to include such issues in class? Would the English composition instructor leave it up to her students to decide if they learned the difference between the active and passive voice in writing? Would a philosopher leave the area of utilitarianism out of her survey course on ethics simply because some students might disagree with its tenets? If we leave the decision to learn about diversity up to student-based factors, will teachers recognize and receive signals of interest and acceptance when students send them? Will students even feel free to send such signals?

It is hard to imagine instruction on diversity happening with regularity in the absence of instructor initiative and support. We can also presume that brave, inquisitive, and diversity-minded students might forego sending any more signals of interest if their professors responded to those signals by saying, "You know, diversity issues aren't really relevant to what we are learning in this course."

However, instructors' level of interest in incorporating diversity issues increases when they have higher numbers of visibly diverse students in their class. Perhaps, when present in larger numbers, students of color might speak up more on diversity issues or offer more debate in class. Or perhaps the higher numbers of such students lead teachers to imagine that those students will be more interested in and accepting of diversity issues. So, yet another step on to the path of least resistance might be that when instructors are faced with class after class of largely White students, they might incorrectly assume that those students are *not* interested in or accepting of diversity issues. Instructors may actually need to see a critical mass of visibly diverse students of color before they attribute student interest in the topic. If this is so, instructors are missing prime opportunities to educate their majority culture students on diversity issues.

Even when diversity issues are integrated into courses, teachers may prefer to foster an appreciation of diversity rather than challenge students to become aware of and alter their personal oppressive attitudes. Finally, even though teachers may be quite sensitive to their students' demography when they decide whether to integrate diversity issues into their courses, they may forget to adequately account for the "stimulus value" of their own demography and its potential for enhancing students' learning about diversity.

As a male Latino, when I teach my diversity classes (or any class), if I relate my personal experiences with racism or even general facts about racism to my students, those largely White students become very attentive to what I have to say. They find the abstract idea of institutional racism more credible when they have a person of color in front of them who has experienced it firsthand and who can relate how this societal ill affects all people of color in one way or another. I also get the sense that because I am a person of color, no matter how "safe" a classroom environment might seem, it's hard for White students to admit to me that they have racist thoughts and attitudes. They believe I'll take it personally or be offended if they speak up about things they've done or said. It's easy to see how a student can perceive that as a real risk when I control the grade book or letters of recommendation.

Most interestingly, when I relate my experiences with personal (versus institutional) racism, students unfailingly hurry to give alternative possible explanations for the racist events I've experienced at the hands of individual White people. "Maybe that White person was just having a bad day"; "Could you possibly be oversensitive and looking for racism?"; "Maybe the store employees thought you were just looking around so they didn't wait on you." I think those majority culture White students want very much to deny that someone like me could be treated in such a blatantly racist fashion, and treated in that way by someone who looks like them. Ultimately, when they have exhausted their list of possible alternative explanations, they find that, because undeniably racist things happen to millions of people all the time, they are forced to give weight to the idea that racism is real. And, with that, they are one small step from also giving weight to the idea that the issue of racism directly relates to them personally as members of the majority culture.

A very different thing happens when I engage those same students as a male professor and discuss the reality of sexism and male privilege in this country. Although I do not practice misogyny or hostile sexism, I know that because I am a man raised within this sexist society, it is not a question of whether or not I am sexist. Rather, it is a question of the degree to which I have examined myself and found all the ways in which I am sexist. I also admit to students that, as a man, I have been handed an immense amount of unearned privilege and power that women do not receive. It is not a question of whether I enjoy privilege in this society; it is a matter of the extent to which I am willing to find and surrender that privilege so as to create a more equitable standing among women and men.

To foster a basic understanding of male privilege, I ask my male students: "How many of you worry about being raped when you walk to your car late at night?" Not once in over a decade of teaching has one man's hand gone up. Then I ask the women in the class the same question. Almost every time, every woman's hand goes up. I ask the men, "Can you possibly understand what it is like to constantly be having to think about your personal safety because we live in a society where men can and do abuse women at will?" The depth and type of adaptation women must undergo to survive oppression suddenly dawns on men; I can see it on their faces. The men have found a foothold (as uncomfortable as it is) in realizing the extent of their societal privilege as men. And this foothold is a good place to start, because in a classroom filled largely with White, heterosexual students, I have found that discussing sex-based oppression and privilege helps them to identify with these concepts and to use this understanding to generalize to other oppressions (racial, sexual orientation) and majority culture privileges (White privilege, straight privilege).

Many authors have adequately addressed the subject of cultural privilege, especially White privilege (a la Peggy McIntosh; Paula Rothenberg; Robert Jensen; Tim Wise). Cultural privileges (e.g., being White [of European descent], heterosexual, and male, to name a few) belong to those persons who possess implicit "norm" status in our society. These are the monolithic, unquestioned bases from which other demographic traits are explicitly judged and compared against. Privileged people also are explicitly affirmed and invested with social power because of their unqualified normative status. Finally, these cultural privileges are the direct result of societal oppressions (e.g., racism, sexism, heterosexism). For example, in describing White privilege, McIntosh (1988) states, "As a white person, I realized I had been taught about racism as something that puts others at a disadvantage, but had been taught not to see one of its corollary aspects, white privilege, which puts me at an advantage" (p. 147).

In addition to having difficulty realizing that one possesses cultural privilege, privilege holders refuse to relinquish their advantageous social position and power, mistakenly thinking that they have *earned* their positions and power based solely on their individual talent or hard work. They do not recognize (or accept) that in large part they have their positions and accomplishments because the opportunities their privileged demography afforded them were simultaneously denied to others via societal oppressions. This ignorance is linked to our societal myths that we live in a meritocracy and that we get what we deserve (earn). For example, with respect to male privilege, McIntosh (1988) states,

> I have often noticed men's unwillingness to grant that they are over-privileged, even though they may grant that women are disadvantaged. They may say they will work to improve women's status, in the society, the university, or the curriculum, but they can't or won't support the idea of lessening men's. Denials that amount to taboos surround the subject of advantages that men gain from women's disadvantages. These denials protect male privilege from being fully acknowledged, lessened, or ended. (p. 148)

It is critical to introduce and explain these cultural privileges to students, and also important for them to recognize and personally eschew these privileges. In my experience, when female students hear me, as a male professor, discuss sexism and male privilege, they are not just attentive; you can hear a pin drop. They already know all too well that sexism is not an abstract idea; it is a real, credible, daily issue for them. They already know that boys and men have had it easier and gotten more breaks than they have for their entire lives. And somehow, even though I have admitted to possessing a measure of those oppressive attitudes, paradoxically, this disclosure seems to help female students feel more comfortable in discussing their personal experiences with sexism in class. None of the hesitancy previously there during discussions of racism is present, perhaps because the women realize I will not dismiss or diminish their experiences, given my admissions and awareness. None of the women hurries to find alternative explanations for my examples of sexist behaviors; they readily recognize and accept it as sexism—the same kind of benevolent or hostile sexism they have dealt with from many other men. The women also begin to speak more frankly about the problem of sexism and male privilege, and even though I still hold all the "professorial" powers I did before (regarding grades, letters, and such), they do not seem to worry about offending me with what they have to say about men and sexism.

My open discussion of sexism and privilege also strongly affects the men in the class. They open up more about being sexist in their own ways, and these discussions too foster growth for students of both sexes. The women seem to appreciate that the men in the class are hearing from another man about men perpetuating sexism versus hearing it from a woman. They know all too well that their observations on this issue have often been dismissed, diminished, or gone unheeded. Many of the men in the class tell me (often privately) that seeing another man publicly willing to admit sexist faults and try to improve on them is a unique experience for them. More importantly, though, male students tell me that it has been particularly meaningful for them to hear another man admit to and detail the privilege and power that men enjoy in our society. Many of the privileges I mention they have not even recognized as being privileges. They can also see the connections between these privileges and societal power and the sexism they subscribe to, or at least benefit from. Moreover, they can see how these oppressive realities can easily prevent them from gaining a real understanding and appreciation of women's perspectives.

It is hard for male students to deny the reality of sexism and male privilege when one of the privilege holders, one of their own, clearly indicates that these things are a real and serious problem. It leaves little room for denial when another man shows himself willing to conduct a self-examination on these issues. The process also opens empathic doorways to students' understanding of the oppression that other groups face (racially diverse or LGBTQ sexual orientation) and the corresponding privileges that White Americans or heterosexuals possess.

Wouldn't the impact on students be astounding if all White instructors, teaching all those White students, used themselves as role models and shared their personal biases as well as their commitment to examining the problem of racism and White privilege? Such an approach might better set the stage for learning about and appreciating racially and ethnically diverse cultures. Wouldn't the impact on students be powerful if all the heterosexual instructors, teaching all those heterosexual students, voiced and accepted personal responsibility for the homophobia we are inculcated with in our anti-LGBTQ society and used themselves as models for the need to examine the problems of heterosexual privilege and discrimination against LGBTQ people? Such an approach could speak to students from all sexual orientations and help students learn about and appreciate the cultural viewpoint of LGBTQ people. The exciting part of this conception is that the science of social psychological influence supports these ideas (see discussion of the Elaboration Likelihood Model in Petty & Cacioppo, 1986).

To summarize, the answers to my first two questions are that it is up to all of us to strengthen the efforts under way for teaching about diversity issues, and for African, Asian, European, Latino, and Native Americans, straight and LGBTQ persons, and men and women to continue to work to find ways to address diversity issues in all the courses we teach. Teachers also need to differentiate between appreciating cultural diversity and recognizing and unlearning oppressive attitudes. This unlearning of oppression and foregoing of privilege are prerequisites to building any appreciation and respect for diverse cultures (see Simoni, 1996). Finally, our personal demography and privileges as instructors may have a special impact and help students be more open to unlearning oppressive attitudes. Our ability to use ourselves and the oppressive cultural legacies we may represent could be one of our most untapped teaching resources.

Teaching About Diversity Issues in a Developmental Way

In my diversity courses, I have routinely questioned students about previous diversity courses they have taken. They often say things like:

> All the diversity courses I have taken seem the same to me. You had one, you had 'em all. You always cover the four racially diverse groups, maybe learn a little about gays, and sometimes women's issues, depends on who's

teaching. You learn stuff like Asians are more interdependent and hierarchical in their family relationships. You learn Latinos suffer a lot because of language differences. You learn women have always and still make less money than men for the same work. You learn being gay is not a choice and is not pathological. And, you always have to read McIntosh's (1988) White privilege article.

From White students I also typically hear: "And don't have one of those cultural appreciation days where you make us bring in food, music, or clothes that reflect our cultural heritage; I'm a Heinz 57 mutt! I'm just plain White and I don't have the faintest idea of what my culture is! I always make brownies or cookies to take to those things!"

So, I began to wonder why the students I encountered in my diversity courses did not seem to have moved as far along in unlearning oppression and appreciating diversity as I would have expected, given their repeated exposure to the subject matter. I took as clues of this lack of growth the following ideas. If you are still without a clear racial and ethnic identification as a White American person, you still have a way to go on your racial identity journey. If you treat your knowledge of diversity as a cookbook, you're not even close to being ready for the fact that human beings are not recipes. And, with respect to privilege, McIntosh's article is only a match; perhaps the fire it was supposed to light fizzled out before a self-understanding flame had a chance to burn.

I also wondered why so many instructors from high school through graduate school choose to teach the same things in their diversity classes, despite the fact that their course may have been the second or even third diversity-oriented class a student has taken.

As I have written elsewhere (Prieto, 1999), the whole situation brings to mind Sisyphus rolling the rock up the hill. Teachers seem to start from scratch each time they instruct students about diversity. I find that even the doctoral-level students I teach continue to struggle with some basic issues related to diversity and their identity as racial and sexual beings, despite previous diversity-related course work and a genuine openness to the issues. This is not a complaint or criticism; instead, many of these students' growth areas are relevant, necessary points to work through, and their recapitulation can bring more in-depth learning.

What strikes me as odd is that many other teachers have shared with me *the very same* observations I have made regarding students' struggles surrounding diversity issues, regardless of the educational level of the students they are teaching. In other words, we end up teaching students the same basic things over and over again from high school through graduate school because students seem not to progress well in unlearning biases or understanding diversity. The rock seems to continually roll back down the hill at the conclusion of each diversity course, and each teacher starts anew to roll it back to the top.

This state of affairs might suggest that certain core content and educational processes have to be revisited for learning to take place. On the other hand, it may also indicate that educators need to move toward a more comprehensive, integrative, developmental curriculum with regard to diversity issues, a curriculum that helps students to hold on to their gains in personal growth and learning with a minimum of repetition.

Although developing and implementing any type of comprehensive, common developmental curriculum across disciplines would be a difficult task, we can establish the extent to which such a curriculum exists at this time. What similarities and differences exist in the way high school, community college, four-year, and graduate-level instructors teach students about issues of diversity? Are learning objectives logically connected across the progression of courses and the educational levels of a discipline? Do our teaching methods and processes, at successive educational levels, match students' ability to accommodate and integrate potentially "threatening" but needed information concerning diversity issues?

Taking a developmental perspective on the process involved with unlearning oppressive attitudes, foregoing privilege, and appreciating diversity is supported by major identity development theories (see Helms's White Racial and Person of Color Identity Development Models; Helms, 1995). Although these particular models focus on racial identity development, their general structure and process have also been applied to identity issues concerning women, men, LGBTQ persons, and heterosexual persons.

At earlier stages of Helms's models, where younger students (e.g., high school) with less course work and life experience might be, we find people struggling with or having difficulty accepting themselves as racial beings. Students in early stages should be helped to recognize their own minority or majority characteristics and identity status(es) so that their self-identity is strengthened before they are expected to learn about and understand the identity of others. Developing a sense of their own racial identity can help students understand how this same experience occurs for and affects others.

For those with demographic characteristics that reflect the majority culture, an understanding of cultural privileges might also be in order.

Awareness of self and other remains a key component of identity development throughout the early and middle stages of growth. Scholars also stress the importance of forestalling the tendency of this process to turn toward White, male, or heterosexual guilt—a typical majority culture reaction to realizing the cultural privilege one possesses personally or institutionally. Guilt is not a productive route for students to take, because this initial reaction can lead later to strong frustration and "backlash" attitudes.

As students move through the educational pipeline into college, Helms's models portray majority culture individuals in midrange identity statuses temporarily retreating into previously held, less open-minded attitudes because of confused or angry reactions to self-realizations concerning racial identity and privilege (i.e., backlash attitudes). In addition, they tend to embrace, in a superficial and uncritical way, an overly positive commitment to diversity. Conversely, minority culture persons may withdraw, feeling angry, suspicious, and rejecting of majority culture persons. Their realization that the world is not fair and that no matter what they do they will always been seen as "different" in our society (and often negatively) can generate a significant amount of emotion.

Instructors who integrate diversity issues into their courses should also be mindful of the vacillating and occasionally contradictory ideas that students within these midrange statuses of identity can possess. This may help instructors to be less confused by the varying amounts of openness, interest, and acceptance they sense in students surrounding diversity issues. While instructing these students, educators may find an optimal opportunity to use their own personal status as a tool for student awareness and change.

Finally, as students become clear about their own and others' racial identity and the effects of societal oppression and privilege, they can move more directly into appreciating diverse cultures. More advanced identity statuses portray individuals who are genuinely committed not only to eradicating oppression and eschewing cultural privilege but also to valuing diversity. These individuals have learned to think both critically and contextually about people as individuals, not through stereotypes or biases. Their attitudes, perceptions, and experiences are guided by a complex value base and a perspective that seeks to respect and understand people while simultaneously maintaining the integrity of their own cultural values and perspectives.

Advanced undergraduate or graduate students may be in these advanced identity statuses, and educators can seek to build within these students an in-depth knowledge about diverse cultures and culturally sensitive interaction skills. Relevant academic activities for these students might include balancing course work with practical field placements or service learning experiences that take students directly into culturally diverse community situations for extended periods of time. These experiences allow students to understand the socio-politico-economic realities that other persons face and to implement the cultural knowledge they have acquired in their courses.

In sum, teachers taking a developmental view on diversity education can foster student learning in a contextual and theory-based fashion, across the entire curriculum of their disciplines. A developmental context also provides a useful conceptual base from which to evaluate teaching interventions and assess students' progress toward eschewing oppressive perspectives and privilege, as well as valuing cultural diversity.

Closing Thoughts

We all have a responsibility to work on diversity issues. Students must eradicate their personal biases and counteract their societal privileges before they can begin to truly appreciate and respect different cultures. Teaching about diversity must be done in a developmental way to be effective and to create long-standing learning and attitude changes. Those are the simple answers to my questions. But, like most things, accomplishing these goals is easier said than done.

Regardless, exploring these questions has provided me with the impetus to seek ways to maximize my effectiveness as a teacher when it comes to diversity issues. I look forward to engaging in continuing discussions on these issues with colleagues and students, because, as with many things in life, the journey is often as meaningful as arriving at the destination.

Finally, I would like to share a personal reaction to the national survey data I was privileged to receive from educators from across the country. I was immensely encouraged by the sheer number of instructors from all backgrounds who value diversity. As a group, educators are eager to overcome obstacles and barriers, are actively looking for resources to assist in their efforts, and are willing to have tough discussions with students to address diversity issues in many different kinds of courses. This display of solidarity among educators from high school through graduate school, from both sexes, from all racial and ethnic groups, and from all sexual orientations reflects a unity that in and of itself mirrors the goal we wish to reach.

Good luck to us all as we continue on this journey together—with each other, for each other.

References

Guthrie, R. V. (1998). *Even the rat was white: A historical view of psychology* (2nd ed.). Boston: Allyn & Bacon.

Helms, J. E. (1995). An update of Helms's White and people of color racial identity models. In J. G. Ponterotto, J. M. Casas, L. Suzuki, & C. Alexander (Eds.), *Handbook of multicultural counseling* (pp. 181–198). Thousand Oaks, CA: Sage.

McIntosh, P. (1988). White privilege and male privilege: A personal account of coming to see correspondence through work in women's studies. Reprinted in M. L. Andersen & P. Hill Collins (Eds.), *Race, class, and gender: An anthology* (2nd ed.; pp. 76–87). Belmont, CA: Wadsworth.

Mio, J. S., & Iwamasa, G. (1993). To do, or not to do: That is the question for White cross-cultural researchers. *Counseling Psychologist, 21,* 197–212.

Morris, L. (2005). Dramatic changes in faculty demographics. *Innovative Higher Education, 30*(2), 85–87.

Parham, T. A. (1993). White researchers conducting multicultural counseling research: Can their efforts be "mo betta"? *Counseling Psychologist, 21,* 250–256.

Petty, R. E., & Cacioppo, J. T. (1986). The elaboration likelihood model of persuasion. In L. Berkowitz (Ed.), *Advances in experimental social psychology* (Vol. 19, pp. 123–205). New York: Academic Press.

Prieto, L. R. (1999, Spring). Issues of diversity in the psychology curriculum: Some thoughts on where to go from here. *Society for the Teaching of Psychology Newsletter (insert).*

Prieto, L. R., Whittlesey, V., Herbert, D., Ocampo, C., Schomburg, A., & So, D. (in press). Dealing with diversity issues in the classroom: A survey of the STP membership. *Teaching of Psychology.*

Rankin, S. (2003, April). *Campus climate for gay, lesbian, bisexual, and transgendered people: A national perspective.* Washington, DC: The Policy Institute of the National Gay and Lesbian Task Force.

Simoni, J. M. (1996). Confronting heterosexism in the teaching of psychology. *Teaching of Psychology, 23,* 220–226.

Sue, D. W., & Sue, D. (2003). *Counseling the culturally diverse: Theory and practice* (4th ed.). New York: John Wiley.

Turner, C., & Meyers, S. (2000). *Faculty of color in academe: Bittersweet success.* Boston: Allyn & Bacon.

Wharton, E. (1902, November). Versalius in Zante (1564). *North American Review, 175,* 625–631.

4

A METAPEDAGOGICAL APPROACH TO CULTURE IN THE CLASSROOM

Thomas N. Robinson III

One of the chief tasks of industrialized cultures in the twenty-first century is to keep pace with many of their global neighbors. For example, the United States lags behind its industrialized counterparts in the world in the fields of math and science (Mullis, Martin, Beaton, Gonzales, Kelly, & Smith, 1998; Peak, 1996; UNICEF, 2002). In order for industrialized cultures to be more educationally competitive, teachers must wed higher performance expectations in the classroom with the expectation that students become more self-reflective and globally and culturally aware.

In addition to the basic educational prerequisites, a classroom environment must cultivate in its students the tools, awareness, and experiences that will allow them to be in touch with diverse perspectives. Because most of the world is non-White and, increasingly, more of the United States is becoming non-White as well (U.S. Census Bureau News, 2004), it is critical for today's students to see diversity and the perspectives that go along with it as a complement to their intellectual and/or vocational repertoire. However, for this to happen, instructors must establish a pedagogical approach that is effective but easy enough to be a part of normal classroom operations and philosophies.

The objectives of this chapter are threefold:

1. To assist educators in developing a "metapedagogical approach" for their professional and intellectual development as well as their students' self-development
2. To help educators develop the necessary tools for cultural awareness within and beyond their respective fields of expertise

3. To provide examples that educators may use to naturally incorporate diverse themes, models, and exercises in ways that can positively sensitize students to the relevant issues of diverse populations

The Metapedagogical Approach

The metapedagogical approach (*MPA*) is an overarching teaching philosophy that is intended to be used across one's classes and also to be first applied to one's own life.[1] The MPA requires educators to become explicitly aware of their own positive and negative biases (such as in education, race, gender, or social class) and to reflect on how these personal perspectives may find their way into their instruction. In short, they must truly embrace their own "worldview": their mode of thinking that structures every aspect of their life (Belgrave & Allison, 2006). A person's worldview organizes how he or she thinks, behaves, and functions within our smaller social systems (e.g., classroom, family, and neighborhood) and the larger society. It also affects the inferences drawn from observing others' behaviors (particularly those that are ambiguous), which may lead to major (positive or negative) outcomes for the person or for others if the person is in a position of authority and/or decision making.

Developing one's MPA requires a constant introspective analysis of oneself (as educator or student) that trains one to question one's own fundamental assumptions (worldview) about the world and others. For some, it may only need to be exercised occasionally, yet for others it may initially require daily effort. In either case, doing so will naturally lead to questioning one's own place and privilege in a given society and likely to challenging one's own values and prior notions of merit-based success. Such a self-analysis may reveal that the way one was brought up to view one's own status in the world may not be how things really occurred. This type of thought process is designed to make oneself "intellectually uncomfortable" in that one may feel initially "threatened" by the notion that "I didn't really earn my position as much as I thought because I may have, instead, simply been the beneficiary of my group (e.g., gender, racial group, social class) status."

---

[1] I coined "metapedagogical awareness" as a way to impress upon educators the need to see diversity as a way of life and not a tool to arbitrarily use "just" in the classroom when political or pedagogical "correctness" warrants the situational use of "diversity" concepts. It is designed to connote the philosophy that one's personal and professional life should, overall (hence, "meta") regularly reflect and/or embrace a constant state of multicultural or diversity awareness and/or sensitivity.

Such an identity-shattering examination may eventually force people to reexamine how their worldview (old and new) may impact everything in their professional life, from the knowledge and skill sets learned during their educational training to the way they may conduct their own classroom (e.g., books chosen, theories or models chosen or ignored, and how they interact with students). In a process similar to the way the body builds muscle or the way a building is renovated, you must tear down or "gut" what has currently existed to build a sturdier, healthier foundation that will lead to a better structure. This self-examination will likely lead to the development of true openness, acceptance, and recognition of the importance of valuing cultural variation for oneself and one's students on a regular, if not constant, basis.

The chief goal of this type of initial exercise is to develop "self-knowledge." In ancient Kemet (known today as Egypt), the founding civilization responsible for virtually all bodies of scientific, religious, medical, and philosophical knowledge (ben Jochannan, 1970/1991; James, 1954/2001; van Sertima, 1994a, 1994b), one of the guiding principles was that "self-knowledge is the basis of all knowledge; self-love is the basis of all love" (Myers, 1988).[2] In other words, you must first come to terms with who you truly are (the good *and* bad "stuff") before you can know anything else substantive about life and reality. Similarly, before you can love another (platonically or intimately), you must be able to love yourself and accept your wonderful *and* "not-so-wonderful" sides. Engaging in this first step on the quest for knowledge will allow you to develop humility and to recognize that your perspective is not the only one (or necessarily the most valid one) and, thus, will allow for the *acceptance* and potential validity of other perspectives.[3]

This self-analysis can be inculcated within the student if she or he is exposed to knowledge or role models that affirm the self or the group. Thus, the student can reflect and say, "Hey, if that person, who comes from my (ethnic and/or gender and/or sexual orientation, etc.) group has succeeded, then I can too." I have had many students of color, across many different

---

[2] Many well-documented scientific and historical texts argue that Kemetic civilization was the basis on which all the Greek philosophers and scientists learned or developed their respective crafts. Texts by Yosef ben-Jochannan (1970/1991), George James (1954/2001), Ivan van Sertima (1994a, 1994b), and Robin Walker (2006) will provide interested readers with a solid basis of this evidence.

[3] I use the term *acceptance* as opposed to *tolerance* because the term *tolerance* can imply that the one who is "tolerating" is being "superior" to the one being "tolerated."

classes that I have taught, make similar statements after having been exposed to information relating to the course work that they never considered or were never taught after 12 or more years of schooling. Additionally, many of my White students generally seem to appreciate and value being given a more complete view of history, the sciences, and other subjects than what they were previously educated to believe existed.[4]

Internationally renowned multicultural educator John Howard (2006) extensively discusses the need for educators (particularly those who are White) to engage in a "personal transformation." This awareness among White educators is vital, given that they make up 90% of the teachers in public schools (National Center for Education Statistics, 2003; National Education Association, 2003) while the numbers of students of color continue to rapidly increase (Hodgkinson, 2001, 2002; National Center for Educational Statistics, 2003).

In general, Howard argues that "White educators" (and White Americans in general) cannot reasonably expect the negative impact of historical prejudice and discrimination against groups of color to be overcome until White Americans truly examine and transform their beliefs, attitudes, and actions about past and present American society. Howard further argues that White educators must expect that they will be changed by investing in engagement and dialogue with non-White groups. Thus, Howard argues that for social and educational progress to truly occur, dominant group members (White and/or male educators, in general) must expect to find that their view of the world is at least not fully reflective of non-White (or female) groups and possibly is not representative of the way the world really operates. Such an awareness is reminiscent of the movie *The Matrix* (Wachowski & Wachowski, 1999), in which Keanu Reeves's character "Neo" is faced with the decision of whether to continue naively existing in the illusion of an orderly and fair society designed by computers to control humans, or to acknowledge the "reality" of a harsh, dark world that is dangerous to the humans who dare expose the false construction of the "monster" computers. Thus, Neo is faced with the

---

[4] I am in the preliminary stages of empirical research examining the academic and psychosocial impact of presenting healthy images of women and people of color in college classrooms. The goal is to assess whether such presentations in curricula that do not "normally" present such images will increase the academic motivation of students of color, reduce stereotype threat, and further sensitize all students to the acceptance of diversity.

choice ("the blue pill or the red pill") of ignoring the *truth* about the world and living in psychological and materialistic comfort, or confronting the truth and attempting to do something about it, thus "freeing" humankind of this "techno-psychological" enslavement.

In summary, the MPA is a philosophy that starts with educators' own self-examination so that they can more effectively lead their students to a similar level of self-analysis, which then should lead all of those in the classroom to a greater acceptance of cultural differences and others from diverse backgrounds. To be maximally effective as an educator, one must try to live the MPA so that one can more effectively apply and teach it. Howard (2006) cites the words of Malcolm X: "We can't teach what we don't know, we can't lead where we won't go" (p. 6).

Examples of self-examination questions that help a person challenge her or his own worldview are the following:

- Do I get the benefit of the doubt from others because I am a member of a privileged group (e.g., male, White, heterosexual)?
- Is race (or gender) more of a factor in my personal interactions with others, or how others may perceive me, than I realize or am willing to admit?
- Do I get uncomfortable when I am in a setting in which I am "outnumbered" by others from a different racial or ethnic group?
- Are examples of television shows that I may use in class (e.g., *Friends, Seinfeld*) known or watched by my students of color?
- Are examples of music that I may use in class (e.g., the Beatles; Earth, Wind, & Fire; Bon Jovi; José Feliciano) listened to or known by my younger students?
- Before I may take exception to "Black-owned" media (e.g., *TVone; BET; Ebony magazine; Black Enterprise; The Tom Joyner Morning Show; The Michael Baisden Show*), shouldn't I consider that most popular American media (e.g., *Fox News Channel; ABC News; CBS News; NBC News; The Wall Street Journal; Forbes; Time Magazine*) may operate to primarily serve "White" American interests?

Tools for the Metapedagogical Approach

Overall, the MPA uses tools that are explicitly or implicitly familiar to most educators. The difference is that they are more than just intellectual exercises. They are tools the instructor must value, embrace, practice, and apply to himself or herself.

1. One of the first tools is to develop the "courage" to leave your own comfort zone and discuss or consider issues with which you may not have direct personal familiarity. Be willing to read materials, view documentaries, and talk to others who may possess insight about topics or controversies with which you are only vaguely familiar and/or feel uncomfortable discussing because of the controversy such issues usually entail. For example, in the area of race relations, discuss topics such as why students of color tend to prefer to sit together at lunch or other unstructured times during the school day rather than intermingle with their white peers (Tatum, 2003). A related topic is whether being "colorblind" is really a positive or negative mindset in terms of interacting with a person of color. Regardless of the topic chosen, you should be willing to get out of your mindset and truly (with as much accurate background information as possible) put yourself in the position of the "other." The other will typically be one who represents the nondominant group position (if you are a White, male, and/or heterosexual person) or in some cases may represent the dominant group position (if you are a person of color, female, and/or a homosexual person).

2. A second tool to facilitate MPA is the "Implicit Associations Test" (IAT; Greenwald, McGhee, & Schwartz, 1998). The IAT is designed to measure a person's subconscious biases for or against a variety of groups or ideologies (e.g., Black vs. White faces; women in traditionally male vs. traditionally female careers; heterosexuals vs. homosexuals). This online test measures a person's reaction time to pairings that are either consistent or inconsistent with stereotypes (e.g., Black face–"bad" adjectives vs. White face–"good" adjectives). You may take the free online test (there are over 100 different types of IAT tests) at https://implicit.harvard.edu/implicit/demo/. For example, if you mentally associate bad adjectives with Black people, your reaction time will be quicker; however, if you are presented with a Black face and a good adjective, your reaction time will be slower. This tool is very beneficial for instructors, students, counselors, employees and employers, and anyone who will come into contact with people different from themselves (whether on the basis of race, gender, religious affiliation, sexual preference, or culture). See Greenwald and Banaji and their colleagues for a discussion of the validity and reliability of the IAT (Greenwald, Nosek, Banaji, & Klauer, 2005; Lane, Banaji, Nosek, & Greenwald, 2007).

3. A third tool is to develop and practice your own critical thinking skills. Critical thinking involves solving problems by carefully evaluating the evidence of all

available perspectives (Levy, 1997). Doing so forces you to develop objectivity, particularly as it pertains to your own beliefs, as well as competing perspectives with which a person may not have any direct personal connection. The more we constantly practice this technique, the more we may reveal to ourselves and our students how biased we are. This revelation gets us closer to self-knowledge and, thus, closer to the "truth" about knowledge in general. Examples of exercises or topics one can use in the classroom to practice critical thinking and general MPA are as follows:

- Are the theories of evolution and creation really polar opposites, or can they be compatible?
- Can Greece be the origin of philosophy, science, and other wisdom as we know it when it actually persecuted its philosophers for that very thinking?
- If the definition of a "terrorist" is one who physically and/or psychologically threatens a group of people, then how should America be viewed in the eyes of Native Americans, descendants of enslaved Africans, and descendants of South and Central Americans?

Other metapedagogical awareness techniques are more straightforward:

- Always be willing to admit you don't "know it all," possibly even in your field. *Humility and honesty go a long way in gaining the trust of students and others and building a sense of integrity.*
- Make sure your students can, at least occasionally, see "themselves" (or others like them) in the material you discuss. *It is important for students, particularly for women and groups of color, to know of or "see" role models who have similar backgrounds as theirs as pioneers or important people in the content areas to which they are exposed. This will often give such students the realistic inspiration that they can succeed in such a field if others like them have come before and succeeded.*
- Even if role models are not immediately apparent, it is acceptable to preach the fundamental assumption that such role models (women, people of color) do likely exist in any field. *This assumption can inspire you, as the instructor, to work harder to find the information about role models and can inspire the students to bear some of the responsibility to search for such role models in the literature. Knowledge is much more meaningful and long-lasting if students discover or develop it themselves.*
- Do not treat women or people of color as the "sole spokespersons" for their gender or race when discussing topics directly pertaining to these groups. *Such behavior can produce a sense of "stereotype vulnerability" (Steele, 1998)*

that has been shown to cause academic underperformance and psychological disengagement from the class among the individuals of stereotyped groups.[5]

- Model and then challenge students to take a "devil's advocate" perspective of someone different from them. *Engaging in this role reversal can give students a valuable insight into how the "other side" thinks and, often more importantly,* feels. *For example, have your White students (and yourself if you are a White educator) imagine what it may be like if they attended a historically Black college or university. They may be able to better "understand" why their African American peers feel alienated and/or may choose to be around "their own" outside of class or in the dorms while attending predominantly White institutions.*

- Occasionally use examples of "non-European names" or females in test/quiz questions or assignments that may have absolutely nothing to do with one's ethnicity or gender. *For example, use names such as Aaliyah, Jamal, Raghib, and Yee Pui-san in addition to Amy, John, and Susan. Additionally, use a female's name (e.g., Susan Johnson) or an identifiably "ethnic (non-European-sounding)" name (i.e., Kareem Akbar) as president of the United States; however, DO NOT have the question be in any way related to the person's gender or ethnicity. This way, students can be introduced to the realistic notion of someone other than a White male as being president.*

Specific techniques can be used for each discipline. For those readers who teach in the area of psychology, the following are some specific additional suggestions for culturally relevant material; each can be varied for other disciplines:

- In a History and Systems of Psychology course, discuss the racist assumptions of Eugenicists and Euthenicists that were legitimized by early psychologists at American universities and the basis for current-day "IQ" and other intelligence/aptitude tests, as well as federal "Head Start" programs (Guthrie, 1976/2004).

---

[5] Stereotype vulnerability is a complex social psychological process in which people from stigmatized groups in a given society are forced (explicitly or implicitly) to become conscious of their group's stereotype. If so, they may experience a threat to their self-esteem if they exhibit any behaviors or attitudes that may even remotely cause others to view them in terms of that stereotype. If this circumstance becomes chronic, to avoid the psychological assault on their self-esteem, the person may choose to "disidentify" with the domain (i.e., specific subject area or academics altogether) and no longer hold it as a basis of their self-worth. This becomes very debilitating for the individual in the long term if the domain pertains to academics or some other area that may serve as the basis for their future success in life.

- In discussing human sexual motivation, be sure to include the evidence suggesting the significant role that biology plays in determining one's sexual orientation. *One can also use "logic" in exposing the weak argument that sexual preference is a "choice" and thus can be "changed." Ask heterosexual people to "pretend to be gay/lesbian for a day" (in every sense of the idea). It is very likely that people will see the weakness in the suggestion that sexual preference is purely a choice.*

- Use unique examples for classical conditioning that are relevant to past or present American culture. *For example, use the Confederate flag as a "conditioned stimulus" in explaining the negative reaction this symbol creates for many people, particularly African Americans and Jews. Furthermore, pair the American flag ("Old Glory"), as the second "conditioned stimulus" (referred to as* higher-order *or* second-order conditioning *in psychology), with the Confederate flag to demonstrate why some Americans may show some contempt for the American flag as well as the Confederate flag. The mental association is the many pictures (stills and videos) of Klansmen holding each flag in either hand and spewing their messages of hate and acts of violence toward specific groups.*

In summary, this chapter presents a potentially useful, easy-to-administer framework, the metapedagogical approach, to help instructors instill cultural awareness and acceptance in a classroom context. The key to the successful implementation of this technique is for instructors to become role models, not just in the classroom, but also in their personal lives. What they practice in their personal lives will more easily become reflected in their classroom demeanor as well as in the pedagogical tools they may use. The end result will be the creation of a classroom environment and student (and instructor) mindset that include diverse cultural perspectives in the "typical" classroom curricula. Educators should always remember, "What you permit, you promote." Therefore, if teachers continue to allow the often inherently sexist, racist, and/or classist status quo typical of "traditional" teaching curricula and disciplines in many cultures, their students will also subtly endorse these same cultural ideologies. However, if teachers constantly challenge this "traditional" viewpoint in the culture *and* in themselves, their students will be more likely to follow suit and develop a truly healthy sense of self and an awareness of the *need* to value other perspectives.

References

Belgrave, F. Z., & Allison, K. W. (2006). *African American psychology: From Africa to America.* Thousand Oaks, CA: Sage.

ben-Jochannan, Y. A. A. (1970/1991). *African origins of the major "western religions."* Baltimore, MD: Black Classic Press.

Greenwald, A. G., McGhee, D. E., & Schwartz, J. L. K. (1998). Measuring implicit differences in implicit cognition: The implicit association test. *Journal of Personality and Social Psychology, 79,* 1022–1038.

Greenwald, A. G., Nosek, B. A., Banaji, M. R., & Klauer, K. C. (2005). Validity of the salience asymmetry interpretation of the IAT: Comment on Rothermud and Wentura (2004). *Journal of Experimental Psychology: General, 134*(4), 420–425.

Guthrie, R. V. (1976/2004). *Even the rat was white: A historical view of psychology* (2nd ed.). New York: Allyn & Bacon.

Hodgkinson, H. (2001). Educational demographics: What teachers should know. *Educational Leadership, 58*(4), 6–11.

Hodgkinson, H. (2002). Demographics and teacher education. *Journal of Teacher Education, 53*(2), 102–105.

Howard, J. (2006). *We can't teach what we don't know: White teachers, multiracial schools* (2nd ed.). New York: Teachers College Press.

James, G. (1954/2001). *Stolen legacy: Greek philosophy is stolen Egyptian philosophy.* Chicago: African American Images.

Lane, K. A., Banaji, M. R., Nosek, B. A., & Greenwald, A. G. (2007). Understanding and using the implicit association test IV: Procedures and validity. In B. Wittenbrink & N. Schwarz (Eds.), *Implicit measures of attitudes: Procedures and controversies* (pp. 59–102). New York: Guilford Press.

Levy, D. A. (1997). *Tools of critical thinking: Metathoughts for psychology.* Boston: Allyn & Bacon.

Mullis, I. V. S., Martin, M. O., Beaton, A. E., Gonzales, E. J., Kelly, D. L., & Smith, T. A. (1998). *Mathematics and science achievement in the final year of secondary school.* Chestnut Hill, MA: Boston College, TIMSS International Study Center.

Myers, L. J. (1988). *Understanding an Afrocentric World View: Introduction to an optimal psychology.* Dubuque, IA: Kendall/Hunt.

National Center for Educational Statistics. (2003). *National assessment of educational progress. The nation's report card: 2003 mathematics and reading results.* Available online at http:// nces.ed.gov/nationsreportcard/reading/results2003/raceethnicity. asp

National Education Association. (2003, August). *Status of the American public school teacher 2000–2001.* Washington, DC: NEA Research.

Peak, L. (1996). *Pursuing excellence: A study of U.S. eighth-grade mathematics and science teaching, learning curriculum, and achievement in international context.* Washington, DC: U.S. Department of Education, National Center for Educational Statistics.

Steele, C. (1998). A threat in the air: How stereotypes shape intellectual identity and performance. In J. L. Eberhardt & S. T. Fiske (Eds.), *Confronting racism: The problem and the response* (pp. 202–233). Thousand Oaks, CA: Sage.

Tatum, B. D. (2003). *"Why are all the black kids sitting together in the cafeteria?" And other conversations about race.* New York: Basic Books.

UNICEF. (2002). *A league table of educational disadvantage in rich nations.* Florence, Italy: UNICEF Innocenti Research Center.

U.S. Census Bureau News. (2004). *Census bureau projects tripling of Hispanic and Asian populations in 50 years; non-Hispanic whites may drop to half of total population.* Retrieved November 10, 2007, from http://www.census.gov/Press-Release/www/releases/archives/population/001720.html

van Sertima, I. (Ed.). (1994a). *Egypt: Child of Africa.* New Brunswick, NJ: Transaction Publishers.

van Sertima, I. (1994b). *Blacks in science: Ancient and modern* (12th ed.). New Brunswick, NJ: Transaction Publishers.

Wachowski, A., & Wachowski, L. (Writers/Directors). (1999). *The Matrix* [Motion picture]. United States: Warner Bros.

Walker, R. (2006). *When we ruled: The ancient and medieval history of black civilizations.* London, UK: Every Generation Media.

5

LEARNING STYLES AS SELF-FULFILLING PROPHECIES

Kris Vasquez

Educators working with diverse student populations have shown a great deal of interest over the years in the construct of learning styles. Searches on Education and Psychology databases yield many recent articles about learning styles, including how learning styles are proposed to differ by gender (e.g., Campbell, 2000; Demirbas & Demirkan, 2007; Reese & Dunn, 2007), race (e.g., Bardwell & Kincaid, 2005; Fazarro & Stevens, 2004; Lincoln & Rademacher, 2006), and disability (e.g., Lisle, 2007; Mickel & Griffin, 2007). Other studies discuss the importance of learning styles as part of general teaching practice (Allison & Rehm, 2007; Chick, Tierney, & Storeyard, 2007; Choo, 2007) or explain how learning styles relate to other constructs (Ates & Cataloglu, 2007; de Jesus, Almeida, & Teixeira-Dias, 2006; Jones, Laufgraben, & Morris, 2006; Liu, 2007). Still more articles report on teacher perceptions of learning styles (Evans & Waring, 2006) or how learning styles are perceived to affect instructional strategies (Chessin, 2007; Singh Neel, 2005; Wang, Wang, & Wang, 2006).

Despite this energetic interest in the topic of learning styles, there is scant evidence that the construct is actually useful in improving the performance of teachers or students. The purpose of this chapter is to draw attention to deficiencies in the empirical literature, to outline challenges to the use of learning styles in a classroom, and to apply social psychological theory to explain why the diagnosis of student learning styles may be limiting, rather than beneficial, to the educational goal of serving diversity.

Current Evidence about Learning Styles

There are a great many articles, as already sampled, that discuss learning styles with the aim of improving student performance. However, very few researchers have conducted studies wherein some students are given learning-style-centered instruction and others are not, and then measured student performance. When such research is conducted, the findings suggest that tailoring instructional techniques to individual students' learning styles does not improve student performance (Krätzig & Arbuthnott, 2006; Neuhauser, 2002).

How, then, do educators get the impression that there is a good deal of empirical support for this construct? Work that proposes an application of learning styles—for instance, how to use learning-styles theory to teach a particular subject—often cites past studies to show efficacy, but these studies are typically problematic in design. As an example, consider recent work by Slack and Norwich (2007), who observed students who were given instruction individually tailored to their learning styles; these authors conclude that the match between student learning style and instructional method increased learning. However, without a comparison group of children who were given *mismatched* instruction (e.g., a "visual" learner being instructed in a "kinesthetic" way), there is no way to determine whether gains for the student are owing to learning-style match or some other aspect of the individualized instruction. Psychologists have known for many years that any kind of change to the environment, including observation, can change performance (e.g., the "Hawthorne Effect," Mayo, 1933).

In addition, most learning-style inventories have not published validation data, and many have been challenged as being low in statistical reliability (Harrison, Andrews, & Saklofske, 2003; Isemonger & Sheppard, 2007; Klein, McCall, & Austin, 2007; Stahl, 1999). This deficiency in documentation is problematic when dealing with measurement of something that is alleged to be vital to student success. If a student's learning style is important but measurement instruments do not reliably indicate the same style for the same student in similar contexts, then the educational decisions based on the data are suspect.

These difficulties with learning-style research have not gone unnoticed. Literature reviews seeking general patterns in learning-style research report that evidence in support of learning styles is weak at best (Cassidy, 2004; Dembo & Howard, 2007):

> The bottom line is that there is no consistent evidence that matching instruction to students' learning styles improves concentration, memory, self-confidence, grades, or reduces anxiety. An instructor may argue that he or she has found such studies. The problem is that most of these investigations are poorly designed. (Dembo & Howard, 2007, p. 106)

Practical and Theoretical Challenges

For educators, parents, and students themselves, a lack of empirical evidence in support of the educational effectiveness of learning styles may not seem like a matter of concern. The belief in the construct has produced thousands of publications, and the sheer volume of the literature may reinforce the idea that there must be something of value in the learning-styles model. Educators committed to working with students from diverse backgrounds may be particularly attracted to learning styles as a promising way to increase student success.

However, several difficulties remain for those wishing to make use of learning styles. One is that, as already discussed, the evidence is overwhelming that people believe in learning styles, but the evidence is poor that learning styles are actually useful in producing achievement. Because there is so little clear support for the overall claims about learning styles, it is nearly impossible to locate good evidence related to the use of learning styles with any specific technique, scale, topic, or group of students.

A second difficulty is figuring out which model of learning styles should be studied or used. Riding and Cheema (1991) identify over 30 frameworks used to describe different approaches to learning; Cassidy (2004) reviews 23 separate models. These models differ in core assumptions about what is important in learning and teaching. They also differ in the number of styles it is possible for a student to have. Some models have two possibilities; one (Dunn, Dunn, & Price, 1989) has 21 separate dimensions of learning styles. This is not just a matter of semantics; each of these models represents an author's belief that his or her formulation is a significant aid to student performance.

An instructor who wishes to choose the "best" model from among these candidates faces some real difficulty. With no clear consensus about which model would be most beneficial to her students, she might look to the literature to see which of the models are most frequently cited in published works. She might, as an example, encounter Entwistle and colleagues' (2000) distinction between surface, strategic, and deep processing; Kolb's (1976) distinctions between diverging, assimilating, converging, and accommodating learners; Honey & Mumford's (1992) reflector, theorist, activist, and pragmatist types; or Barsch's (1991) dimensions of visual, auditory, and kinesthetic-tactile learners. All of these models, and dozens of others, have strong proponents. But if the instructor believes that she must accommodate each of the styles to best teach her students, she will need to find a way to accommodate 3 (Entwistle et al.) x 4 (Kolb) x 4 (Honey & Mumford) x 3 (Barsch), or 144 separate learning-style combinations in her class. This is simply not feasible.

If the instructor believes that one or more of these models is important and can find no evidence as to which model that is, then she must either try to deal with this huge combination of potential styles or ignore some that might be the "right" ones. Alternatively, she could take the position that learning styles in general are important and that she must consider each student's individual style but that the particular model of learning styles she uses to do this is unimportant—a position that is hard to defend logically.

A third problem is the very idea of accommodation to a learner's style. Learning styles are often presented in recent literature as relatively fixed parts of a learner's makeup (see Cassidy, 2004). The implication is that it is important for instructors to adapt their teaching to students' characteristic learning styles. Ironically, though, this position contradicts some early work on learning styles. For instance, David Kolb says explicitly that learners should not expect to always learn in their preferred modes, because "when one perspective comes to dominate others, learning effectiveness is reduced" (Kolb, 1974, p. 41). He is also clear that learning styles develop partly in response to experience, which suggests that allowing students access to a variety of teaching methods would be beneficial, rather than detrimental or discriminatory. Thus at least one significant model of learning styles originated with the idea that students should adapt their learning strategies to the situation and would benefit from practice in doing so.

Learning Styles and Limits

Though the usefulness of individual diagnoses of learning style lacks evidential support, the construct is unlikely to be quickly abandoned. This contradiction need not be problematic; it remains possible that learning styles are useful on an aggregate level, where they might more aptly be called teaching strategies. That is, even if instructors cannot identify exactly which aspects of learning styles are important to success and cannot feasibly redesign each class to accommodate dozens of individual students' styles, there is still potential benefit to using a variety of presentation techniques. If Kolb is correct that exposure to different learning experiences will strengthen the students' repertoires of learning strategies, then using multiple modes of presentation will benefit students regardless of their initial preferences.

But an additional caution is in order. The learning-style model as currently used often involves testing students (or having them self-test) and providing them with diagnostic labels. Two social psychological theories—implicit theories and self-fulfilling prophecies—can be combined to explain how these labels may be disadvantageous to learning.

The first theory to consider is that of implicit theories (Dweck, Hong, & Chiu, 1993). According to Dweck and colleagues, people hold implicit views about personality and abilities; individualist cultures heavily endorse what are called *entity* views of intelligence and other traits. In entity views, traits are seen as a fixed component of the individual. Within academia, for example, a student may declare that she "can't do math." The logic common among those holding entity views is not to take more math classes until competent, but to steer away from everything even remotely math-related, because in an entity view a person cannot succeed in an area where she isn't innately talented.

Implicit theories are of concern in the application of learning-style models. Giving a student a label as a certain kind of learner (visual, pragmatic, assimilating, etc.) in a culture that endorses entity thinking automatically suggests to the student that her learning characteristics are an immutable part of her makeup. A student who endorses entity views and who is so labeled will not be likely to follow Kolb's advice to seek out areas of weakness to develop overall competence.

In addition to causing a person to view a quality as fixed, labels are powerful in that they shape others' perceptions of what is possible. Research on the self-fulfilling prophecy (Rosenthal, 2003; Rosenthal & Jacobson, 1996; Weinstein, 2002) shows that labeling a child as gifted or troubled generates behavior consistent with the label on the part of those who hear the label. Or consider an experiment that randomly labeled some children as hyperactive and others as not (Harris et al., 1992). The children labeled hyperactive (who were not in fact diagnosed with that condition) had less successful interactions with other children and enjoyed their work tasks less than those who had not been labeled.

A teacher reading a learning-style inventory may expect that a given student will do best when presented with material in a certain way. She may then focus her efforts on teaching in that way to that student. Her analysis of the success of her educational strategy is unlikely to be purely rational, as most humans are prone to predictable errors. She is likely, for instance, to exhibit confirmation bias (Frey & Schulz-Hardt, 2001; Snyder & Swann, 1978) in her processing of learning experiences, remembering when the student had success in a learning-style-congruent environment and when the student had difficulty in a mismatched environment. She is unlikely to intentionally put a student in an incongruent environment to see if it works as well; confirmation bias predisposes people to look only for evidence that their initial assumptions are correct. Over time, as her experiences with the student accumulate, she will become more and more certain that the student is "that kind" of learner and that the student can best succeed only in a learning-style-congruent setting. Whether she transmits her expectation overtly to the student or not, her behavior will be shaped by the initial label in ways that are most likely unintentional.

Based on these two theories, then, it is possible that putting people into seemingly benign learning-style categories will create self-fulfilling prophecies and that those processes will become self-limiting. Theoretically, if a student is told that she is a particular kind of learner and if she is reared in a culture that views abilities as fixed, the student may reasonably (but erroneously) conclude that her only hope of success is to find learning contexts that fit her strength. To put herself in a context that doesn't match her style is to risk failure. If the student believes, as Dweck argues is common for members of individualist cultures, that intelligence is an immutable trait, then failing—or even finding something moderately difficult—will not be seen as a learning experience, but rather as a diagnosis that the topic, class, or experience is simply not right for her.

Instead, this hypothetical student, motivated by Dweck's entity view and armed with a diagnostic label, will seek out experiences in which she believes she is likely to find success. That is, if she believes she is a visual learner, she will remember when she learned things smoothly by seeing them and when she was frustrated by not seeing them; most people will find it much more difficult to recall disconfirming information. She will then feel more certain that she can only succeed in the "right" learning style for her, and continue to seek educational experiences and accommodations only within that framework. The more often she filters her experience through the learning-style label, the less likely she is to seek out other strategies to learn. If her educator shares the knowledge of the label, he or she may narrow the instructional choices for the student, with the well-intentioned goal of helping her succeed. And so over time, theoretically, a person who had no more than a slight initial preference may become limited to "visual learning" through self-fulfilling prophecy.

Learning-style models are in some ways a counterargument to the idea that a student is either smart or dumb—the ultimate in entity views of intelligence—and there is nothing an instructor can do but throw information out and see who manages to pass. Certainly this "all or nothing" approach is outmoded; using a variety of teaching strategies to present material can be useful for students. The caution here is in labeling students as particular types of learners within a culture that promotes entity views. If we do this, we have traded a global entity view of intelligence for more specific, but still entity-based, categories. Given the power of labels and the educational consequences of entity thinking, this position may, in theory, limit student opportunities for growth.

Overgeneralizing Group Differences

A discussion of learning styles would not be complete without addressing the issue of proposed group-level differences. Learning-style language is often coupled with discussions of dealing with diversity in the classroom (for a review and critique, see Irvine & York, 1995). Certainly, differences in cultural backgrounds can shape some behaviors, and these behaviors can be important to academic success. However, for a researcher or an educator to conflate malleable differences rooted in experience with the construct of a learning style, an allegedly permanent personal characteristic, can hardly be seen as serving diversity. Instead, it suggests that the differences will not lessen with time and experience; the races and sexes will always be different, and therefore must always be taught differently. In other words, to argue that entire groups of people have a characteristic way of learning supports stereotypical views of racial and ethnic groups and gender differences and may lead to discriminatory educational practice (Reynolds, 1997). And when one considers the lack of evidence that a learning-style diagnosis is beneficial for a single individual, it is very difficult to justify generalizing such a diagnosis for an entire group.

One positive alternative to the use of culture-level generalizations about learning styles is proposed by Gutierrez and Rogoff (2003). These authors suggest that attending to both an individual and her cultural group in terms of patterns of engagement with cultural practice is a more sensitive and effective educational technique than assuming that behaviors are owing to traits shared by entire ethnic groups. Such a practice allows teachers to maintain a commitment to diversity and flexibility in responding to students without raising dangers of overgeneralization and labeling.

Conclusion

The construct of learning styles has more risk of limiting student achievement than promise of promoting new levels of success, at least as the construct is currently, widely used. Because of the emphasis in individualist cultures on an entity-based view of intelligence, presentations of learning-style information may leave students with the impression that they are one of a few "types" and may exaggerate the tendency for them to seek out only activities that fit their label. Students may come to believe that their label defines what is possible for them, and in an ironic self-fulfilling prophecy, become limited by a tool that is meant to offer opportunity. Moreover, perceptions of learning-style differences, when generalized for racial groups or gender, lead to potentially damaging and limiting choices in curriculum design, and are thus in the end a disservice to diversity. Given the lack of solid evidence that measuring learning styles produces any real benefit to students, as well as the risk of unintended limitations, it is time for educators to reconsider whether learning styles should be used as a pedagogical device until clear evidence of benefit is produced.

References

Allison, B. N., & Rehm, M. L. (2007). Teaching strategies for diverse learners in FCS classrooms. *Journal of Family and Consumer Sciences, 99,* 8–10.

Ates, S., & Cataloglu, E. (2007). The effects of students' cognitive styles on conceptual understandings and problem-solving skills in introductory mechanics. *Research in Science and Technological Education, 25,* 167–178.

Bardwell, G., & Kincaid, E. (2005). A rationale for cultural awareness in the science classroom. *Science Teacher, 72,* 32–35.

Barsch, J. (1991). *Barsch Learning Style Inventory*. Novato, CA: Academic Therapy.

Campbell, K. (2000). Gender and educational technology: Relational frameworks for learning design. *Journal of Educational Multimedia and Hypermedia, 9,* 131–149.

Cassidy, S. (2004). Learning styles: An overview of theories, models, and measures. *Educational Psychology, 24,* 419–444.

Chessin, D. (2007). Simple machine science centers. *Science and Children, 44,* 36–41.

Chick, C., Tierney, C., & Storeygard, J. (2007). Seeing students' knowledge of fractions: Candace's inclusive classroom. *Teaching Children Mathematics, 14,* 52–57.

Choo, K. L. (2007). Can critical management education be critical in a formal higher educational setting? *Teaching in Higher Education, 12,* 485–497.

de Jesus, H. T. P., Almeida, P. A., & Teixeira-Dias, J. J. (2006). Students' questions: Building a bridge between Kolb's learning styles and approaches to learning. *Education and Training, 48,* 97–111.

Dembo, M. H., & Howard, K. (2007). Advice about the use of learning styles: A major myth in education. *Journal of College Reading and Learning, 37,* 101–109.

Demirbas, O. O., & Demirkan, H. (2007). Learning styles of design students and the relationship of academic performance and gender in design education. *Learning and Instruction, 17,* 345–359.

Dunn, R., Dunn, K., & Price, G. E. (1989). *Learning Styles Inventory*. Lawrence, KS: Price Systems.

Dweck, C. S., Hong, Y. Y., & Chiu, C. Y. (1993). Implicit theories: Individual differences in the likelihood and meaning of dispositional inference. *Personality and Social Psychology Bulletin, 19,* 644–656.

Entwistle, N., Tait, H., & McCune, V. (2000). Patterns of response to an approach to studying inventory across contrasting groups and contexts. *European Journal of Psychology of Education, 15,* 33–48.

Evans, C., & Waring, M. (2006). Towards inclusive teacher education: Sensitizing individuals to how they learn. *Educational Psychology, 26,* 499–518.

Fazarro, D. E., & Stevens, A. (2004). Topography of learning style preferences of undergraduate students in industrial technology and engineering programs at historically Black and predominantly White institutions. *Journal of Industrial Teacher Education, 41,* 1–20.

Frey, D., & Schulz-Hardt, S. (2001). Confirmation bias in group information seeking and its implications for decision making in administration, business, and politics. In F. Butera & G. Mugny (Eds.), *Social influence in social reality: Promoting individual and social change* (pp. 53–73). Ashland, OH: Hogrefe & Huber.

Gutierrez, K. D., & Rogoff, B. (2003). Cultural ways of learning: Individual traits or repertoires of practice. *Educational Researcher, 32,* 19–25.

Harris, M. J., Milich, R., Corbitt, E. M., Hoover, D. W., & Brady, M. (1992). Self-fulfilling effects of stigmatizing information on children's social interaction. *Journal of Personality and Social Psychology, 63*, 41–50.

Harrison, G., Andrews, J., & Saklofske, D. (2003). Current perspectives on cognitive learning styles. *Education Canada, 43*, 44–47.

Honey, P., & Mumford, A. (1992). *The manual of learning styles* (3rd ed.). Maidenhead, UK: Peter Honey Publications.

Irvine, J. J., & York, D. E. (1995). Learning styles and culturally diverse students: A literature review. In J. A. Banks & C. A. M. Banks (Eds.), *Handbook of research on multicultural education* (pp. 484–497). New York: Simon & Schuster Macmillan.

Isemonger, I., & Sheppard, C. (2007). A construct-related validity study on a Korean version of the Perceptual Learning Styles Preferences Questionnaire. *Educational and Psychological Measurement, 67*, 357–368.

Jones, P. R., Laufgraben, J. L., & Morris, N. (2006). Developing an empirically based typology of attitudes of entering students toward participation in learning communities. *Assessment and Evaluation in Higher Education, 31*, 249–265.

Klein, B., McCall, L., & Austin, D. (2007). A psychometric evaluation of the learning styles questionnaire: 40-item version. *British Journal of Educational Technology, 38*, 23–32.

Kolb, D. A. (1974). Learning and problem solving: On management and the learning process. In D. A. Kolb, I. M. Rubin, & J. M. McIntyre (Eds.), *Organizational psychology* (2nd ed.; pp. 27–38). Englewood Cliffs, NJ: Prentice Hall.

Kolb, D. A. (1976). *Learning Style Inventory*. Boston: McBer.

Krätzig, G. P., & Arbuthnott, K. D. (2006). Perceptual learning style and learning proficiency: A test of the hypothesis. *Journal of Educational Psychology, 98*, 238–246.

Lincoln, F., & Rademacher, B. (2006). Learning styles of ESL students in community colleges. *Community College Journal of Reseach and Practice, 30*, 485–500.

Lisle, A. M. (2007). Assessing learning styles of adults with intellectual difficulties. *Journal of Intellectual Disabilities, 11*, 23–45.

Liu, Y. (2007). A comparative study of learning styles between online and traditional students. *Educational Computing Research, 37*, 41–63.

Mayo, E. (1933). *The human problems of an industrial civilization*. New York: MacMillan.

Mickel, J., & Griffin, J. (2007). Inclusion and disability awareness training for educators in the Kids Like You, Kids Like Me program. *Young Children, 62*, 42–45.

Neuhauser, C. (2002). Learning style and effectiveness of online and face-to-face instruction. *American Journal of Distance Education, 6*, 99–113.

Reese, V. L., & Dunn, R. (2007). Learning-style preference of a diverse freshman population in a large, private, metropolitan university by gender and GPA. *Journal of College Student Retention: Research, Theory, and Practice, 9*, 95–112.

Reynolds, M. (1997). Learning styles: A critique. *Management Learning, 28,* 115–133.

Riding, R. J., & Cheema, I. (1991). Cognitive styles: An overview and integration. *Educational Psychology, 17,* 29–49.

Rosenthal, R. (2003). Covert communication in classrooms, clinics, courtrooms, cubicles, and the truly real world. *Current Directions in Psychological Science, 12,* 151–154.

Rosenthal, R., & Jacobson, L. F. (1996). Teacher expectations for the disadvantaged. In S. Fein & S. Spencer (Eds.), *Readings in social psychology: The art and science of research* (pp. 3–9). Boston: Houghton Mifflin.

Singh Neel, K. (2005). Addressing diversity in the mathematics classroom with cultural artifacts. *Mathematics Teaching in the Middle School, 11,* 54–61.

Slack, N., & Norwich, B. (2007). Evaluating the reliability and validity of a learning styles inventory: A classroom-based study. *Educational Research, 49,* 51–63.

Snyder, M., & Swann, W. B. (1978). Hypothesis-testing processes in social interaction. *Journal of Personality and Social Psychology, 47,* 1281–1291.

Stahl, S. A. (1999). Different strokes for different folks? A critique of learning styles. *American Educator, 23,* 27–31.

Wang, K. H., Wang, T. H., & Wang, W. L. (2006). Learning styles and formative assessment strategy: Enhancing student achievement in web-based learning. *Journal of Computer Assisted Learning, 22,* 207–217.

Weinstein, R. S. (2002). *Reaching higher: The power of expectations in schooling.* Cambridge: Harvard University Press.

6

THE "WHY'S" AND "HOW'S" OF BEING A SOCIAL JUSTICE ALLY

Sandra L. Neumann

Incorporating cultural diversity into our classes is essential in our often marginalizing and isolating educational environments. But to truly serve all of our students we must go beyond teaching about diversity to becoming social justice allies. How does social justice differ from diversity? *Diversity* is often conceptualized in terms of sheer numbers on campus: "Ten percent of our students are a nontraditional age." *Multiculturalism*, another common "diversity" term, can be thought of as skills in working with a diverse group of students (e.g., multicultural competency). *Social justice* builds on our diverse campus environments and our multicultural skills and moves us into acting for social change. This is not to be confused with opposing oppression (i.e., preventing actions that do not serve a greater good). Social justice focuses on encouraging and engaging in actions that do serve a greater good (Reason & Davis, 2005).

We see this element of positive action in Washington and Evans's classic definition of a social justice ally: "a person who is a member of the 'dominant' or 'majority' group who works to end oppression in his or her personal and professional life through support of, and as an advocate with and for, the oppressed population" (Washington & Evans, 1991, p. 195). Allies work to end oppression, in part, by acknowledging their unearned privileges and power that their social identities grant them and then acting to dismantle the societal structures that support that privilege and power (Reason & Davis, 2005). This chapter will allow you to ponder and engage in positive actions as you explore your role as an ally. In it you will find questions and activities that will help you apply some of the research, theory, and ideas to your own life and work. A good place to start is by exploring the allies' behavior in the classroom. Spend some time asking yourself about your views on this issue: What first comes to mind about social justice and/or being an ally? If you were an ally, what actions would you want to engage in? Are there any specific groups of students who need allies more than others at your institution? What role does social justice play within your field? Do you know any colleagues who are allies? Students who are allies?

The Need for Allies in the Classroom

Consider the basic human desire to feel that we belong. In the classroom this translates into a need to see ourselves and our experiences reflected back at us. Such reflection helps to normalize our existence and make us feel that we belong in our campus environment (Lopez & Chism, 1993). If we as teachers don't reflect back the lives of our students from traditionally marginalized groups, these students could feel isolated and question whether they really belong on campus (Connolly, 2000). The college teacher can make or break a student's college experience. Studies with students from traditionally marginalized groups show that the teacher is an essential, if not the *most* important, part of making the student feel welcome or marginalized (Ancis, Sedlacek, & Mohr, 2000; Connolly, 2000).

It is important to spend some time thinking about and perhaps even investigating the need for allies at your own campus. Here are some questions to get you started: Is there a need for social justice allies at your campus? For any groups in particular? Ask a trusted peer who is a member of a traditionally marginalized group what the campus climate is like for him or her. If you can find students to talk with, even better. Compare your perceptions to these peoples' lived experiences. Does your campus have a nondiscrimination policy? Is it a general statement, or does it list specific groups to be protected? How easy was it for you to find? How easy would it be for students to find? In your view, or the view of marginalized others, is this policy actually adhered to? Have there been any incidents of discrimination reported on your campus? (Your campus security office might be a good place for finding answers.) Do you have a statement of respect or inclusion in your syllabus? What has been your reaction in the classroom to inappropriate comments from students?

Now try to get more specific in gathering information. Pick a group that you think may not have advocates on campus, and check into issues specific to that group. For example, if you want to focus on students with disabilities, try these questions: Do the automatic doors consistently work? Is signage on campus accessible to those with visual impairments? Are the gymnasium, theaters, and cafeteria accessible to those in wheelchairs? Does the administrative staff in the admissions office have a plan for serving students with speech impediments? How often do you lecture to the chalkboard (which would affect students who are hard of hearing)? If you don't know the answer, ask a trusted colleague to come and observe you.

Motivations of College Teacher Allies

A few researchers (e.g., Broido, 2000) have studied college students as allies. But prior to Neumann (2002), no studies expressly studied college teachers as allies. Although people serve as allies for different reasons, college teachers seem motivated by three considerations (Neumann, 2002): (1) a sense of responsibility regarding the privilege that comes with their social identities; (2) personal experiences with oppression (perhaps because, if they've been through it, they want to keep other people from going through it, too); and (3) the influence exerted by intimate others such as friends and family on how they see the world and how they act.

If you choose to be an ally, someone will inevitably ask why. This third set of questions might help you clarify your motivations: Why would you want to be an ally? Do you feel a sense of responsibility about some privileged identity? Have you experienced oppression? What was it like? Do you have students or colleagues, friends, or family members who are part of marginalized groups who could benefit from you being their ally?

Examining Our Social Identities

In order to prepare . . . students to teach in multicultural ways, we must help them change the way they perceive U.S. society and the positions they hold in that society. . . . A crucial part of this unlearning, relearning, and examining for White . . . students involves seeing themselves as racial beings, as White persons in a White-dominated society. (Lawrence & Bunche, 1996, p. 531)

This quote, which could be reworded to focus on college teachers, suggests that acknowledging dominant identities is essential to our work as allies. However, most faculty have been trained to think that they are objective fact-givers in the classroom, devoid of any personal identity, bias, or agenda. It is important to realize that we cannot leave our identities and biases out of the classroom (Bell, Washington, Weinstein, & Love, 1997; Weinstein & Obear, 1992), however much we like to think we can (Broido, 2003).

We need to be aware of our identities because they can influence what we know and how we structure our classrooms. Who chooses the texts for your classes, and using what criteria? Who picks the exam questions and fictional characters to use in an example? Members of traditionally marginalized groups tend to have more knowledge about issues of diversity (Talbot & Kocarek, 1997), perhaps because their more frequent and intimate experiences with oppression create a stronger desire to understand this phenomenon. That said, it is clearly possible for members of traditionally dominant groups to be passionate and effective allies; they have their work cut out for them. They can start by looking at their social identities (see Table 6.1).

Knowledge Versus Comfort

Broido (2003) found that having a dominant social group identity led to gaps in participants' "knowledge about diversity and oppression issues" (p. 60) and had the potential to negatively impact working with students from traditionally marginalized groups. As educators, though, we are a generally curious crowd. Acquiring knowledge (i.e., developing our multicultural competency) about oppression, privilege, and power and being an ally is the easy part. There are any number of books, articles, videos, and classes we can utilize to increase our knowledge about these topics. A resource list is provided at the end of this chapter.

What tends to be more difficult is increasing our comfort level with some of these issues and with different identity groups. Our training as academicians has not prepared most of us to deal with the emotionally charged issues and conflicts in our classrooms (Bell et al., 1997; Neumann, 2002) that often accompany teaching for social justice. Engaging in social justice education challenges our previously held worldviews and personal beliefs about people

TABLE 6.1
What Are Your Social Identities?

Some American social groups	Your identity: For each group listed, indicate your identity	How important is this identity to you? (1–5, five is high)	How valued by society is the identity you claimed? (1–5, five is high)	Are you a part of a traditionally dominant or a marginal-ized group?
Age or generation:				
Ability/disability:				
Gender and/or sex:				
Race, ethnicity, and/or country of origin:				
Religious and/or spiritual affili-ation:				
Sexual orientation:				
Social class and/or background:				

Note: Modified from a handout titled "Understanding Our Social Identities," available through the School of Graduate Studies and Continuing Education's LEARN Center at the University of Wisconsin's Whitewater campus.

(Griffin, 1997). As Frederick (1995) acknowledges in his article on effectively teaching about diversity, discussing these topics in our classrooms can be like "walking on eggs" (p. 83); this author even calls it the "dreaded diversity discussion" (p. 83).

Table 6.2 will take you through an inventory to rate your knowledge and comfort levels with certain groups of traditionally marginalized students. Use this information to help identify a group of students for whom you'd like to start being an ally. For example, some readers may choose to become an ally for the group about which they are most knowledgeable. Others may start with the group with which they have the least comfort. Everyone is different; focus on what feels right to you.

TABLE 6.2
What Are Your Knowledge and Comfort Levels?

Instructions:
Rate your knowledge of the specific educational needs of the groups of students listed below. Next rate your comfort level in working with these various groups. Remember that no one but you will see your answers. Be honest. This is where the real work begins.

(low)   1   2   3   4   5   (high)

Older/Returning/Nontraditional age	Knowledge: _____	Comfort: _____
Students with learning disabilities	Knowledge: _____	Comfort: _____
Students with physical disabilities	Knowledge: _____	Comfort: _____
Female	Knowledge: _____	Comfort: _____
Transidentified	Knowledge: _____	Comfort: _____
African American	Knowledge: _____	Comfort: _____
Asian American	Knowledge: _____	Comfort: _____
Hispanic/Latino/Chicano	Knowledge: _____	Comfort: _____
Middle Eastern descent	Knowledge: _____	Comfort: _____
Native American/Pacific Islander/Native Alaskan	Knowledge: _____	Comfort: _____
Atheist	Knowledge: _____	Comfort: _____
Jewish	Knowledge: _____	Comfort: _____
Muslim	Knowledge: _____	Comfort: _____
Gay, Lesbian, and Bisexual	Knowledge: _____	Comfort: _____
From working-class or poor families	Knowledge: _____	Comfort: _____

Getting Specific

Wilkerson (1992) suggests that the primary obstacle to making our classrooms more inclusive is not the acknowledgment that such actions are needed; rather, it is not knowing where to start. Connolly (2000) suggests that we should modify our teaching methods as well as the course content. Making such modifications may feel like simply diversifying your classroom. But, to the extent that "doing diversity" will allow you to engage in dialogue with your students and create opportunities for advocacy, you are also being an ally.

Our methods of teaching can show students that we are social justice allies. Addressing explicit and veiled discriminatory remarks in class, challenging the assumptions of our students (and ourselves), creating a nondiscrimination policy in the syllabus that sets an inclusive atmosphere from the first day, and using different groups in examples are all things we can do to demonstrate our commitment to teaching inclusively. For example, why not say, "Javier was walking down the street" instead of "John"? Even those of us who do not teach social science courses, where inclusivity is perceived to be easier, can still reflect our students' lives back at them. For example, I've used questions on a statistics quiz that included issues of sexual diversity (e.g., "Bill has a 50% of getting a date with Sue on Friday and a 75% chance of getting a date with Dan. What is the probability that Bill will have at least one date on Friday night?") We are limited only by our creativity.

Modifying our class content may take a bit more time and energy. But with a little effort, we can begin to incorporate a host of diverse topics into our assignments, in-class activities, and lectures. For example, Johnson (2006) suggests an assignment that asks students to imagine waking up one morning as another gender. DeWelde and Hubbard (2003) ask students, the majority of whom are heterosexual, to write a coming out letter to an important person in their lives. Colwell (2003) invites music therapy students to take part in a disability simulation to raise awareness about issues faced by people with physical disabilities. Porta (2002) discusses how students are influenced by being exposed to racial diversity among biomedical scientists. These topics may allow students to examine their perceptions of different groups, illustrate unearned privileges, and demonstrate how marginalized group members are treated by society. Additionally, there are many books on diverse teaching strategies (cf. Cole, 2001), and many discipline-specific teaching journals routinely publish articles on teaching about diversity. This next set of questions challenges you to think about your teaching endeavors in more inclusive terms: What groups of students do you most often leave out? What can you do to make your classroom more inclusive? Where and how do diversity and social justice fit into your teaching activities? Think about your favorite lecture topic. What is one way you could modify either the content or your method of delivery to be more inclusive? Write an exam question that is inclusive of religious diversity; create a research assignment that addresses economic inequality. Find out if your colleagues are doing any diversity and/or social justice in their classrooms and use their ideas!

Last, being an ally can even reach beyond our own classrooms and into the wider college community. For example, Evans (2002) discusses in poignant detail the significant impact of having a lesbian, gay, bisexual, and transgender (LGBT) safe zone project in place for both LGBT and hetero-sexual members of one campus community.

Maintaining Your Commitment

Doing social justice work is extremely rewarding, especially if you have patience (Ayvazian, 2004) and colleagues to support you (Griffin, 1997). Unfortunately, this work can also come at a cost (Bell et al., 1997).

Neumann (2002) found three primary problems that teachers encounter when taking a social justice perspective in the classroom. The first was resist-ance from students, which may come from those who represent both domi-nant and marginalized social groups. Indeed, Thompson (1991) asks, "Can White heterosexual men understand oppression?" Being a part of a domi-nant, traditionally oppressing group may lead others (and yourself) to question your credibility (Broido, 2003). If you seek help in resolving this resistance, you may face another difficulty: lack of support from peers and supervisors. This then could lead to the third type of problem, internalized doubts about your commitment to social justice advocacy.

Appropriately so, Ayvazian (2004) advises us to prepare for the "long haul" (p. 603) when walking the path of an ally. She suggests that we look for support from others, learn to be at peace knowing that we may never see the fruits of our labor, and remember that there is no such thing as a perfect ally. Even in the statistics question I posed about Bill, Sue, and Dan, all the names reflect European American ancestry. Although they may challenge students' heterosexist perceptions, they leave intact perceptions of living in a White world. But I find comfort in the words of Ayvazian's colleague Kenneth Jones: instead of trying to be perfect, we should strive instead to be "consistently conscious" (p. 603).

Is this work really worth it? Only you can answer that question. On a pos-itive note, there are good days, there are students who appreciate what we do, and there are peers who are inspired by our actions. "Even if I don't change the world for me, I have faith that my work can contribute to a better world for the generations yet to come. That's what keeps me doing it, keeps me grounded, being grateful and knowing that my little part helps" (Bell et al., 1997, p. 310). The last set of questions for you to ponder addresses what you need to maintain your commitment: If you have already experienced or anticipate experiencing resistance to your social justice efforts, what do you need to persevere? Where can you find these resources? List one person to whom you have ready access who will be a support, sounding board, or cheerleader for you. If you have previously tried diversifying your classroom, what were student reactions? Reactions from a colleague's efforts? Make connections with different people on campus who *may* (or may not) act as supports. For example, meet someone in your campus disability office or from student diversity groups. Campus student affairs offices are also good places to find like-minded people.

Conclusion

Being a social justice ally is about more than just acknowledging diverse people and being multiculturally competent. Although these two pieces are generally necessary for social justice work, they are not sufficient. As you imagine yourself as an ally, remember that your efforts will rightfully dismantle the often isolating and marginalizing state of affairs for students who come from nondominant backgrounds. Your efforts will also challenge the often uninformed perceptions of students who come from dominant backgrounds. Instead of tokenizing and patronizing the nondominant students who enter your classroom, you are inviting them to take their place at the academic table. When you do that, you will be serving the greater good by being a teacher for all of your students.

References

Ancis, J. R., Sedlacek, W. E., & Mohr, J. J. (2000). Student perceptions of campus cultural climate by race. *Journal of Counseling and Development, 78,* 180–185.

Ayvazian, A. (2004). Interrupting the cycle of oppression: The role of allies as agents of change. In P. S. Rothenberg (Ed.), *Race, class, and gender in the United States: An integrated study* (6th ed., pp. 598–604). New York: Worth.

Bell, L. A., Washington, S., Weinstein, G., & Love, B. (1997). Knowing ourselves as instructors. In M. Adams, L. A. Bell, & P. Griffin (Eds.), *Teaching for diversity and social justice: A sourcebook* (pp. 299–310). New York: Routledge.

Broido, E. M. (2000). The development of social justice allies during college: A phenomenological investigation. *Journal of College Student Development, 41,* 3–18.

Broido, E. M. (2003). Practicing praxis: Identity in diversity education. *Inquiry: Critical Thinking across the Disciplines, 22,* 57–63.

Cole, R. W. (Ed.). (2001). *More strategies for educating everybody's children.* Alexandria, VA: Association for Supervision and Curriculum Development.

Colwell, C. M. (2003). Integrating disability simulations into a course for student music therapists. *Music Therapy Perspectives, 21,* 14–20.

Connolly, M. (2000). Issues for lesbian, gay, and bisexual students in traditional college classrooms. In V. A. Wall & N. J. Evans (Eds.), *Toward acceptance: Sexual orientation issues on campus* (pp. 109–130). Lanham. MD: University Press of America.

DeWelde, K., & Hubbard, E. A. (2003). "I'm glad I'm not gay": Heterosexual students' emotional experience in the college classroom with a "coming out" assignment. *Teaching Sociology, 31,* 73–84.

Evans, N. J. (2002). The impact of an LGBT safe zone project on campus climate. *Journal of College Student Development, 43,* 522–539.

Frederick, P. (1995). Walking on eggs: Mastering the dreaded diversity discussion. *College Teaching, 43,* 83–92.

Griffin, P. (1997). Facilitating social justice education courses. In M. Adams, L. A. Bell, & P. Griffin (Eds.), *Teaching for diversity and social justice: A sourcebook* (pp. 279–298). New York: Routledge.

Johnson, A. G. (2006). *Privilege, power and difference* (2nd ed.). Boston: McGraw-Hill.

Lawrence, S. M., & Bunche, T. (1996). Feeling and dealing: Teaching White students about racial privilege. *Teaching and Teacher Education, 12,* 531–542.

Lopez, G., & Chism, N. (1993). Classroom concerns of gay and lesbian students: The invisible minority. *College Teaching, 41,* 97–103.

Neumann, S. L. (2002). *Allies in the classroom: Understanding the commitment to and essence of social justice among preparing future faculty scholars.* Unpublished doctoral dissertation. Miami University.

Porta, A. R. (2002). Using diversity among biomedical scientists as a teaching tool: A positive effect of role modeling on minority students. *American Biology Teacher, 64,* 176–182.

Reason, R. D., & Davis, T. L. (2005). Antecedents, precursors, and concurrent concepts in the development of social justice attitudes and actions. *New Directions for Student Services, 110,* 5–15.

Talbot, D. M., & Kocarek, C. (1997). Student affairs graduate faculty members' knowledge, comfort, and behaviors regarding issues of diversity. *Journal of College Student Development, 38,* 278–287.

Thompson, C. (1991, Winter/Spring). Can White heterosexual men understand oppression? *Changing Men, 22,* 14–17.

Washington, J., & Evans, N. J. (1991). Becoming an ally. In N. J. Evans & V. A. Wall (Eds.), *Beyond tolerance: Gays, lesbians, and bisexuals on campus* (pp. 195–204). Washington, DC: American College Personnel Association.

Weinstein, G., & Obear, K. (1992). Bias issues in the classroom: Encounters with the teaching self. In M. Adams (Ed.), *Promoting diversity in the college classroom: Innovative responses for the curriculum, faculty, and institutions* (pp. 39–50). San Francisco: Jossey-Bass.

Wilkerson, M. B. (1992, January/February). Beyond the graveyard: Engaging faculty involvement. *Change, 24,* 59–63.

Resource List

Becoming an ally . . . one step at a time. Retrieved June 8, 2007, from the University of New Hampshire's Office of Residential Life's Web site: http://www.unh.edu/ residential-life/diversity/index.html

Brandyberry, L. J. (1999). Pain and perseverance: Perspectives from an ally. *Journal of Counseling and Development, 77,* 7–9.

Diversity Resources. (n.d.). Retrieved June 8, 2007 from The Ohio State University's Fisher College of Business' Web site: http://fisher.osu.edu/offices/diversity/ diversity-resources

Hardiman, R., & Jackson, B. W. (1997). Conceptual foundations for social justice courses. In M. Adams, L. A. Bell, & P. Griffin (Eds.), *Teaching for diversity and social justice: A sourcebook* (pp. 16–29). New York: Routledge.

Issue specific resources. (n.d.) Retrieved June 8, 2007, from University of Maryland's Diversity Database Web site: http://www.development.umd.edu/Diversity/Specific/

Lockhart, J., & Shaw, S. M. (n.d.). Writing for change: Raising awareness of difference, power, and discrimination. Retrieved June 21, 2007, from the Tolerance.org Web site: http://www.tolerance.org/teach/web/wfc/index.jsp

Tatum, B. D. (2000). The complexity of identity: "Who am I?" In M. Adams, W. J. Blumenfeld, R. Castaneda, H. W. Hackman, M. L. Peters, & X. Zuniga (Eds.), *Readings for diversity and social justice: An anthology on racism, antisemitism, sexism, heterosexism, ableism, and classism* (pp. 9–14). New York: Routledge.

7

THE DIVERSITY MONOLOGUES

*Increasing Understanding
and Empathy, Decreasing Stereotypes and Prejudice*

Amy Hackney

> *I think gender discrimination is a thing of the past.*
> *Feminists are just trying to cause trouble.*
> (White male student responding to the question:
> Are women discriminated against in the workplace?)
> *I'm so tired of Blacks complaining about discrimination. America is the land*
> *of opportunity. Today Blacks have just as many rights as Whites.*
> *A lot of them are just making excuses.*
> (White male student responding to the question:
> Is racial discrimination still a problem today?)
> *I am disgusted and in shock. I can't believe those people think they have a right*
> *to have children. And to pretend that they are religious. . . . I am a Christian*
> *and the Bible says that homosexuality is an abomination. It is a sin.*
> (White female student responding to a film that depicted
> gay and lesbian couples and their children)

These comments were written by students early in the semester in a psychology of gender course. The first two comments reflect stereotypes about feminists and African Americans and a lack of understanding about gender and racial discrimination; the third comment illustrates blatant prejudice against gays and lesbians. It is noteworthy that I had taught two of these students in previous classes, and I knew them to be kind and intelligent. So how could they hold such negative thoughts and feelings about others? More importantly, could I change these attitudes through a course project? This chapter first briefly reviews the literature on stereotype and prejudice development and maintenance to show that common cognitive and psychological processes can cause intelligent and caring people to have erroneous, negative, and hurtful attitudes toward others. After reviewing the literature on stereotype and prejudice reduction, it concludes with a class project I developed to help my students decrease their negative thoughts and feelings toward outgroups and increase their commitment to equality and diversity education.

Where Do These Negative Attitudes Come From?

Although stereotypes, prejudice, and discrimination are separate components of attitudes toward an outgroup, they are closely related. Stereotypes are the cognitive component, prejudice is the affective component, and discrimination is the behavioral component of an outgroup attitude. Often the development of one component leads to the development of the others. Here I review some of the most common pathways to the development of stereotypes and prejudice.

Categorization.   Many researchers have posited that stereotypes are initially formed through social categorization, the process of matching a target person to a past social category (e.g., Allport, 1954; Fiske & Neuberg, 1990; Tajfel & Billig, 1974; Tajfel & Forgas, 1981; Taylor, 1981). When social category labels (e.g., Black; feminist) are activated, stereotypes (e.g., lazy; man-hating), being the traits that are linked to social category labels in semantic memory, are also activated. The basic function of stereotypes is cognitive efficiency; they reduce the amount of information to which perceivers must attend. People who have been grouped into one category can be treated as equivalent, so that the perceiver does not have to spend time analyzing specific information about each person. This cognitive efficiency, however, causes one to make biased or faulty decisions about people (e.g., Howard & Rothbart, 1980).

Illusory Correlations.   A process that seems to play a major role in the formation of negative stereotypes of minority group members is the "illusory" correlation between two distinctive and infrequent events (Hilton &

von Hippel, 1996). One of these events is Whites' observation of and interaction with Blacks. Similarly, undesirable (nonnormative) behavior is statistically less frequent than desirable behavior and is therefore distinctive. Because these two events are distinctive, Hamilton and Gifford (1976) found that the typical White observer infers that they co-occur more frequently than they actually do.

Self-Fulfilling Prophecies.   Once a majority group member (White) associates a negative trait with a minority group member (Black), as, for example, occurs in an illusory correlation, this trait can be confirmed through self-fulfilling prophecies, providing a second basis for the formation of specific stereotypes. Self-fulfilling prophecies occur when a perceiver holds expectations about another that influence the way that he or she acts toward the other person. This action, in turn, encourages behavior from that other person that confirms the perceiver's initial expectation. Devine (1995) provides the following example. A White person associates hostile behavior with Blacks. Upon encountering a Black person, expecting that person to be hostile, the White person may act in a cold, distant manner. The Black person, responding to the White person's aloof behavior, behaves in a rather hostile manner, confirming the White person's initial expectation. Research on self-fulfilling prophecies (Word, Zanna, & Cooper, 1974) supports this example and also shows that a perceiver can create confirming evidence of a stereotype in a target automatically, without any conscious intent, expectancies, or awareness (Chen & Bargh, 1997).

Faulty Attributions.   A third basis for negative stereotypes is faulty attributions. The fundamental attribution error (Heider, 1958; Ross, 1977) or, as it is also known, the correspondence bias (Jones, 1979), refers to the tendency to underestimate the impact of the situation and overestimate the impact of personal disposition when explaining an actor's behavior. An extension of the fundamental attribution error, called the "ultimate attribution error" (Pettigrew, 1979), refers to the tendency to make this error more in relation to outgroup members than to ingroup members. Conversely, positive acts performed by outgroup members are more likely to be explained by nondispositional factors (e.g., luck, the situation) than if the acts were performed by an ingroup member. Both the fundamental attribution error and the ultimate attribution error are likely to contribute to the specific content of the Black stereotype (Mackie, Hamilton, Susskind, & Rosselli, 1996).

Psychological Functions of Stereotypes and Prejudice

Understanding the functions of stereotypes and prejudice, that is, "why" people have negative thoughts and feelings about outgroup members, is essential to understanding their enduring nature. As previously noted, stereotypes serve a cognitive function in that they are efficient. But as the following paragraphs explain, they also serve important psychological functions.

Self-Affirmation.   Fein and Spencer (1997) investigated the role of self-affirmation in stereotyping and prejudice. They hypothesized that the motivation to maintain a feeling of self-worth and self-integrity could account for some instances of stereotyping and prejudice. In a series of three experiments, the experimenters investigated both the roles of self-affirmation and self-image threat in influencing stereotype use and the role of stereotypes and prejudice in helping individuals restore their self-worth. Results showed that self-affirmation reduced the likelihood that individuals negatively stereotyped minority group members; furthermore, when self-image was threatened, individuals discriminated more against a stereotyped target, which led to an increase in self-esteem.

Justification of the Status Quo.   Another function of stereotypes is that they provide a rationale for and justification of group status differences, or a justification of the status quo. Jost and Banaji (1994) proposed that, in addition to ego justification (e.g., self-affirmation), there is a process they term "system justification," which preserves "existing social arrangements even at the expense of personal and group interest" (p. 1). The authors proposed that system justification plays a dominant role in the maintenance of stereotypes, as, over time, the biases of people with power (ingroup members) reinforce social hierarchies and inequality. Goodwin, Operario, and Fiske (1998) proposed an expanded model of system justification based on their program of research. They specified that both power (situation control) and dominance (desire for control) promote stereotyping, which leads to the unfair distribution of valuable resources, which, across people and over time, leads to the justification of the status quo. They also hypothesized that (1) individuals with power stereotype subordinates by both ignoring counterstereotypic information and paying more attention to the subordinates' stereotypic traits; (2) dominant individuals stereotype subordinates in this same cognitively biased manner if there is potential for outcome control; and (3) individuals high in power and dominance express more stereotypic impressions as a result of their biased information processing. A series of six experimental studies provided support for all hypotheses, demonstrating that situational power and need for control promote stereotyping, which functions to maintain the status quo.

In summary, multiple and interacting methods and processes are involved in the formation and maintenance of stereotypes and prejudice. Stereotypes are formed through social categorization, with the specific stereotype content being influenced by processes such as illusory correlations, self-fulfilling prophecies, and faulty attributions. Stereotypes and prejudice are also strengthened and maintained through the psychological functions they serve. The research described also alludes to another means of stereotype maintenance—their automatic nature. Many studies have demonstrated the automatic activation of stereotypes (e.g., Chen & Bargh, 1997; Devine, 1989; Perdue & Gurtman, 1990). Research confirms that stereotypes can be activated and used automatically, without the perceiver's conscious intention or awareness (e.g., Banaji & Greenwald, 1995; Dovidio, Kawakami, Johnson, Johnson, & Howard, 1997; Kawakami & Dovidio, 2001). Thus, the automatic nature of stereotype activation and application is another factor in the maintenance of stereotypes.

Reducing Stereotypes and Prejudice

Although stereotypes and prejudice result from many common cognitive and psychological processes, there is recent evidence that they may be reduced or eliminated given the right set of circumstances. The following paragraphs review the research on techniques that seem to be effective in reducing intergroup stereotypes and prejudice.

Increasing Intergroup Contact. Allport (1954) was the first to specify the conditions under which intergroup contact would lead to a reduction in intergroup stereotyping and prejudice. Specifically, he hypothesized that four elements were crucial for positive intergroup contact to occur:

equal status among group members, common goals, intergroup cooperation, and the support of authorities, laws, or social norms. Amir (1969) added two more variables: a favorable climate for intergroup contact and intimate, rather than casual, contact between group members. Pettigrew (1998) reviewed the literature and determined that four related processes affect the relationship between increased contact and decreased prejudice: "learning about the group, changing behavior, generating affective ties, and ingroup reappraisal" (p. 70). Pettigrew reformulated the contact theory as a longitudinal process that allows intergroup friendships to develop. This process initially involves decategorization, in which ingroup versus outgroup categorization is minimized; for example, White students should get to know Black students on an individual basis, learn that they have similar attitudes and interests, and feel comfortable interacting with them so that feelings of anxiety are diffused. The next step involves "salient categorization," in which people recognize that the individual they have come to like is a member of the outgroup (Blacks). This is optimally accomplished by the outgroup member relating an experience of being a victim of prejudice. White students then realize that their friend has been hurt by racial prejudice and discrimination. The feeling of empathy is key to this process.

Many researchers have noted the limits of cognitive processes in prejudice reduction. People develop subtypes as a cognitive means to maintain general stereotypes for a group as a whole while allowing that there are certain exceptions (Fiske, 1998). Subtyping occurs when ingroup members have minimal knowledge of outgroup members. From the perception of a White individual, other Whites are members of the ingroup, and Blacks are members of the outgroup. Although there has been relatively little social psychological research on racial subtype content, research demonstrates that in addition to the "Black" stereotype, there are also subtypes of the Black "athlete," "businessman," and a combination of "from the ghetto, streetwise, and on welfare" (Devine & Baker, 1991). A White individual, for example, may encounter a Black individual who does not fit his or her generic Black stereotype. Instead of changing the general stereotype, this individual is more likely to form a separate subcategory, such as "Black businessman or Black student." In this manner, subtypes function to preserve the existing general stereotype of the outgroup. However, if the White individual has a feeling of empathy, instead of reclassifying the outgroup individual, his or her feelings of sympathy and identity should generalize to other members of the outgroup (all or most Blacks). Finally, Pettigrew proposes that the third step to prejudice reduction is recategorization, in which the individuals adopt a unified common identity.

The Importance of Empathy.   There are different types of the important emotion of empathy. Stephan and Finlay (1999) describe three types of empathy: cognitive empathy and two types of emotional empathy. Cognitive empathy involves cognitively putting yourself in the shoes of another, which Davis (1994) refers to as perspective taking; for example, a multicultural program might emphasize the history, values, and behaviors of different groups. Cognitive empathy may reduce stereotypes and prejudice because it leads people to see that outgroup members have similar attitudes and goals to ingroup members, but it may also result in subtyping. Parallel empathy is an emotional empathy that involves having the same feelings as the target. For example, if you feel outrage when you hear someone maligning gays, you are experiencing parallel empathy. According to Finlay and Stephan (2000), parallel empathy can reduce prejudice by activating outrage at injustice. Reactive empathy is an emotional empathy that involves feelings of sympathy for the target. If you feel sympathy and pain for the target of the sexual slur, you are experiencing reactive empathy. Batson et al. (1997) propose that reactive empathy can lead to a reduction in prejudice by producing generalized positive feelings and concern for the welfare of outgroup members. Overall, research indicates that empathy is related to many positive feelings and behaviors, whereas a lack of empathy is associated with negative feelings and behaviors (e.g., Batson, 1991; Batson et al., 1997; Hackney-Hansen, Mullins, & Maze, 2007).

Whereas the studies just reviewed have measured the reduction of explicit stereotypes and prejudice, Rudman, Ashmore, and Gary (2001) have experimental evidence that implicit or automatic prejudice and stereotypes may also be unlearned. In two experiments students enrolled in a prejudice and conflict seminar showed reduced implicit and explicit levels of prejudice in comparison to students in control conditions. Rudman et al. found that the reduction of explicit stereotypes and prejudice was associated with an increased understanding of outgroups and an awareness of one's own biases; implicit stereotypes and prejudice were associated with an increased feeling of positivity and a decreased feeling of fear toward the outgroup. This research provides further support that reactive and parallel empathy may be more important than cognitive empathy in the reduction of prejudice.

The Diversity Monologues

The project I developed has been used twice as a final course project in a psychology of gender course. However, the project should easily be adaptable to any class hoping to promote diversity and decrease stereotypes and prejudice. In a typical college classroom, many of the requirements for successful intergroup contact (Pettigrew, 1998) may by lacking and will need to be facilitated by the instructor. For example, most students have been socialized to view the classroom as a competitive environment in which the goal is individualistic: to win the instructor's favor and to perform better than other students on assignments and exams. One way to focus on common goals and intergroup cooperation would be to emphasize in the course syllabus that a major objective in the course is to achieve an understanding of the relationship between the self and others and to increase positive relationships among people of different ethnic, racial, gender, sexual orientation, age, and social class groups.

We started the semester with an opportunity for students to express their thoughts and feelings regarding a range of topics related to the course. I assessed students' attitudes regarding gender and racial discrimination and feelings about gays and lesbians. Although the majority of students indicated egalitarian beliefs, many felt that discrimination was a thing of the past, and several expressed disgust or disapproval regarding homosexuality.

Following Pettigrew's (1998) reformulated contact theory, I devised activities to give students the opportunity to get to know one another as individuals and to become friends. I asked students to generate questions relevant to the course and assigned them to discuss the answers with others. To get them started, I asked these questions: "What are you curious about? What have you always wanted to ask, but were afraid to? What do you wish others understood about you?" Students generated the following questions: "When was the last time you cried? How do you feel about your body? Is there anything difficult about being a man?" Students wrote their answers down on paper, and then they were paired with a fellow student. When possible, I tried to encourage the pairing of intergroup members (e.g., males and females; straight students and gay students, etc.). These writing and sharing activities were interspersed with lectures and other class activities throughout the semester. The sharing of common experiences, such as low body-esteem, should result in decategorization (Pettigrew, 1998).

Around the 10th week of class, students received the instructions for their final course project. They were instructed to write in-depth on five topics related to the course and to also interview five diverse others on these topics. Examples of topics included being a victim of prejudice or discrimination, the aging process, and feelings about one's body. In writing their personal monologues, students were instructed to be specific and detail oriented; to explore *why* their feelings, beliefs, or behaviors existed; and to examine any psychological, social, or cultural influences. For interviewing others, students were given interviewing tips and practiced probing for details and underlying processes with a partner in class. Students electronically turned in the monologues and interviews approximately 10 to 14 days before the end of the semester. I then collated the monologues by question, chose one monologue per student to be shared with the class, wrote a brief narration for each monologue, and developed a program for the performance of the diversity monologues.

The diversity monologues were performed in class during the two-hour final examination period at the end of the semester. This performance was inspired by the plays based on Eve Ensler's *The Vagina Monologues* (2000). To increase empathic responses, students were explicitly instructed to identify with their interviewees and classmates as they listened to their stories. They were instructed to focus on the thoughts and feelings of the other and to be aware of their emotional responses to the situation (Stephan & Finlay, 1999). The following are excerpts of two of the monologues performed by my students. The first was written by a Latina:

> There was a time where I wished so much that I was White. I remember being in the 6th grade and doing a group assignment in class. I got paired with two of the more popular kids. I don't remember why, but one of the boys started to push things off his desk and told me to "clean it up, wetback. That's all you're good for." . . . He kept on calling me names and even threw things at me, telling me to pick it up or "go pick some more onions." . . . Tears rolled down my face and the other girl in

my group did nothing. At first I wondered why she didn't say anything. But I knew why. She didn't want to be ridiculed for sticking up for the "wetback."

The second was written by a middle-aged European American female:

My father was not pleased because I was a girl. He had wanted a boy and somehow I was responsible for disobeying him. When I wanted to do something, he would point out that I was a girl. He would say, rather often it seems, if you were a boy, you could go there, or you could do this, but since you are a girl, you need to stay home and help your mother (do housework). I was taught to be submissive. We children were not allowed to express anger (not even argue with each other). We would get a whipping for that—so I learned not to stand up for myself . . . I learned that girls were inferior to boys. Boys were allowed to do fun things and allowed to mess up. Girls were expected to stay home and clean up. I did well in school and had big dreams. . . . I loved chemistry and biology and liked using the microscope. I wanted to work in the medical research field. That was where I ran into a brick wall. I didn't know how to get the necessary funding. My father thought that a high school education was good enough for a girl. (I wonder how many times I've heard that—that is "good enough" for you.) He said I didn't need higher learning. A woman's place is in the home. . . . I have spent so much time trying to be a "good girl," to not make waves, and fit into the mold of what other people think I should be, that sometimes I'm not sure of who I am.

By the time these monologues were read, students knew each other and felt comfortable around each other. Many students cried in reaction to the older woman's experience of gender discrimination. According to Pettigrew (1998), the students should have been experiencing salient categorization, in which they realized that their classmates and friends were members of groups that are victims of stereotypes, prejudice, and discrimination. This situation should lead to both reactive and parallel empathy, as well as to a generalized reduction in stereotypes and prejudice. Finally, to end the diversity monologues, the class read in unison a monologue that attempted to create a recategorization of a unified group committed to decreasing stereotypes and prejudice. The following is an excerpt.

I believe that negative thoughts, feelings, and actions compromise my values and my well-being, and I commit to thinking, speaking, and acting positively about myself and others, regardless of their age, gender, race, ethnicity, sexual orientation, religion, size, or ability. . . . I believe that all men and women have hopes, fears, joys, sadness, strengths, and weaknesses, and I commit to their full expression. . . . I believe in the power of the individual. That if I speak up when I witness injustice, others will listen and follow, and I commit to this cause. I believe in our power to eliminate stereotypes, prejudice, and discrimination and to increase peace and harmony, and I commit to this cause.

References

Allport, G. W. (1954). *The nature of prejudice.* Reading, MA: Addison-Wesley.

Amir, Y. (1969). Contact hypothesis in ethnic relations. *Psychological Bulletin, 71*(5), 319–342.

Banaji, M. R., & Greenwald, A. G. (1995). Implicit gender stereotyping in person judgment. *Journal of Personality and Social Psychology, 65,* 272–281.

Batson, C. D. (1991). *The altruism question: Toward a social psychological answer.* Hillsdale, NJ: Erlbaum.

Batson, C. D., Polycarpou, M. P., Harmon-Jones, E., Imhoff, H. J., Mitchener, E. C., Bednar, L. L., Klein, T. R., & Highberger, L. (1997). Empathy and attitudes: Can feeling for a member of a stigmatized group improve feelings toward the group? *Journal of Personality and Social Psychology, 72,* 105–118.

Chen, M., & Bargh, J. A. (1997). Nonconscious behavioral confirmation processes: The self-fulfilling consequences of automatic stereotype activation. *Journal of Experimental Social Psychology, 33,* 541–560.

Davis, M. H. (1994). *Empathy: A social psychological approach.* Madison, WI: Brown and Benchmark.

Devine, P. G. (1989). Stereotypes and prejudice: Their automatic and controlled components. *Journal of Personality and Social Psychology, 56,* 5–18.

Devine, P. G. (1991). Measurement of racial stereotype subtyping. *Personality and Social Psychology Bulletin, 17,* 44–50.

Devine, P. G. (1995). Prejudice and out-group perception. In A. Tesser (Ed.), *Advanced social psychology* (pp. 467–512). New York: McGraw-Hill.

Dovidio, J. F., Kawakami, K., Johnson, C., Johnson, B., & Howard, A. (1997). On the nature of prejudice: Automatic and controlled processes. *Journal of Experimental Social Psychology, 33,* 510–540.

Ensler, E. (2000). *The vagina monologues.* New York: Villard.

Fein, S., & Spencer, S. (1997). Prejudice as self-image maintenance: Affirming the self through derogating others. *Journal of Personality and Social Psychology, 73,* 31–44.

Finlay, K. A., & Stephan, W. G. (2000). Improving intergroup relations: The effects of empathy on racial attitudes. *Journal of Applied Social Psychology, 30,* 1720–1737.

Fiske, S. T. (1998). Stereotyping, prejudice, and discrimination. In D. T. Gilbert, S. T. Fiske, & G. Lindzey (Eds.), *The handbook of social psychology* (pp. 357–411). Boston: McGraw-Hill.

Fiske, S. T., & Neuberg, S. L. (1990). A continuum of impression formation, from category-based to individuating processes: Influences of information and motivation on attention and interpretation. In M. Zanna (Ed.), *Advances in experimental social psychology* (Vol. 23, pp. 1–74). San Diego, CA: Academic Press.

Goodwin, S. A., Operario, D., & Fiske, S. T. (1998). Situational power and interpersonal dominance facilitate bias and inequality. *Journal of Social Issues, 54*(4), 677–698.

Hackney-Hansen, A. A., Mullins, T. D., & Maze, H. (2007). The relationships between empathy, belief in a just world, and homophobia. Unpublished manuscript.

Hamilton, D. L., & Gifford, R. (1976). Illusory correlations in interpersonal perception: A cognitive basis of stereotypic judgments. *Journal of Experimental Social Psychology, 12,* 392–407.

Heider, F. (1958). *The psychology of interpersonal relations.* New York: Wiley.

Hilton, J. L., & von Hippel, W. (1996). Stereotypes. *Annual Review of Psychology, 47,* 237–271.

Howard., J. W., & Rothbart, M. (1980). Social categorization and memory for ingroup and out-group behavior. *Journal of Personality and Social Psychology, 38*(2), 301–310.

Jones, E. E. (1979). The rocky road from acts to dispositions. *American Psychologist, 34,* 107–117.

Jost, J. T., & Banaji, M. R. (1994). The role of stereotyping in system-justification and the production of false consciousness. *British Journal of Social Psychology, 33,* 1–27.

Kawakami, K., & Dovidio, J. F. (2001). The reliability of implicit stereotyping. *Personality and Social Psychology Bulletin, 27*(2), 212–225.

Mackie, D. M., Hamilton, D. L., Susskind, J., & Rosselli, F. (1996). Social psychological foundations of stereotype formation. In C. N. Macrae, C. Stangor, & M. Hewstone (Eds.), *Stereotypes and stereotyping* (pp. 41–78). New York: Guilford Press.

Perdue, C. W., & Gurtman, M. B. (1990). Evidence for the automaticity of ageism. *Journal of Experimental Social Psychology, 26*(3), 199–216.

Pettigrew, T. W. (1979). The ultimate attribution error: Extending Allport's cognitive analysis of prejudice. *Personality and Social Psychology Bulletin, 5,* 461–476.

Pettigrew, T. F. (1997). Generalized intergroup contact effects on prejudice. *Personality and Social Psychology Bulletin, 23*(2), 173–185.

Pettigrew, T. F. (1998). Intergroup contact theory. *Annual Review of Psychology, 49*, 65–85.

Ross, L. (1977). The intuitive psychologist and his shortcomings. In L. Berkowitz (Ed.), *Advances in experimental social psychology* (Vol. 10, pp. 173–220). New York: Academic Press.

Rudman, L. A., Ashmore, R. D., & Gary, M. L. (2001). "Unlearning" automatic biases: The malleability of implicit prejudice and stereotypes. *Journal of Personality and Social Psychology, 81*(5), 856–868.

Stephan, W. G., & Finlay, K. A. (1999). The role of empathy in improving intergroup relations. *Journal of Social Issues, 55*(4), 729–744.

Tajfel, H., & Billig, M. (1974). Familiarity and categorization in intergroup behavior. *Journal of Experimental Social Psychology, 10*, 159–170.

Tajfel, H., & Forgas, J. P. (2000). Social categorization: Cognitions, values, and groups. In C. Stangor (Ed.), *Stereotypes and prejudice: Essential readings* (pp. 49–63). New York: Psychology Press.

Taylor, S. E. (1981). A categorizing approach to stereotyping. In D. L. Hamilton (Ed.), *Cognitive processes in stereotyping and intergroup behavior.* (pp. 83–114). Hillsdale, NJ: Erlbaum.

Word, C. O., Zanna, M. P., & Cooper, J. (1974). The nonverbal mediation of self-fulfilling prophecies in interracial interaction. *Journal of Experimental Social Psychology, 10*, 109–120.

8

INFUSING CROSS-CULTURAL EXPERIENCES INTO THE CLASSROOM

Craig Abrahamson

As an American Caucasian male growing up in a far Northwest community, I did not recognize my privileged condition until, as a teenager and college student, I began interacting with Native Americans on their reservations and realized that diversity goes way beyond the primary dimensions of racial orientation. I heard Native Americans "tell their stories" during their pow-wows. I participated in "archeological diggings" on a reservation; learned about their perspectives on life, including spiritual beliefs, family values, and roles of individuals depending on their age, sex, and physical characteristics; and learned how these characteristics impacted Native Americans' "present life" through the stories that their elders would share.

During the thirty years I have been teaching in higher education and mirroring a national movement along the same lines, I have incorporated elements of diversity into course content and assignments. Because people cognate their experiences, their culture, and their world within their own unique perspectives, it is difficult for them to see beyond their own perspectives, and this characteristic limits their learning substantially, whether the learning occurs inside or outside the academy. However, my students learned to incorporate these elements of diversity into their class work. Instructors in any discipline can adapt for their courses the lectures, class assignments, and field research I gave to my students. These scholarly activities can provide all students with experiences in diversity.

Storytelling

Native American storytellers I listened to in college taught me the power of storytelling as a teaching tool. As the story begins, the storyteller captures the attention and interest of the audience, thus setting the stage for learning (Hodge, Pasqua, Marquez, & Geishirt-Contrell, 2002). As the story unfolds, the listeners are compelled to draw their own conclusions and do their own unique cognitive processing, which in turn creates their own sense of reality and secures it in memory (Wilson, 2007). Stories are effective because they present essential ideas and values that pertain to specific course content in a simple, entertaining form (Abrahamson, 1998). As a professor, I include personal stories, rooted in my own experiences, in lectures to students. The feedback that I received from student evaluations indicated that, indeed, my "stories," interwoven into course content, helped student relate my experiences to their own, especially since the "stories" are specific examples of course material. Storytelling is a comfortable way for students from diverse backgrounds to discuss openly and easily their own unique perspectives in class discussions. It is an effective way of creating a mutual bond between students and their instructor and also a method that helps students to connect to course content from different perspectives.

Cross-Cultural Field Work

However, cross-cultural field experiences add another dimension to student learning outcomes. These activities give students "hands-on" exposure to some of the important aspects of cultural diversity that can and do relate to course content. One way to infuse course work with these experiences is to participate in the Semester at Sea Program, directed by the University of Pittsburgh until 2006 and now operated by the University of Virginia. The one-semester "experience" is designed to create a life-altering experience; students and faculty have the mobility of a floating university and the opportunity to observe and participate with extremely diversified cultures.

Many disciplines were represented in the syllabi developed for the Semester at Sea Program for fall 2005. The professors on the voyage represented the disciplines of anthropology, biological sciences, business administration, communication arts, economics, English, geology, music, political science, philosophy, religious studies, sociology, and theater arts. They came from universities and colleges from all over the world, public and private: Africa University in the Eastern Highlands of Zimbabwe, California State University (Chico, East Bay, Long Beach, and San Bernardino campuses), Colorado State University, Franklin and Marshall University, La Trobe University in Melbourne, Australia, Indiana University at South Bend, Millikin University, Pennsylvania State University, Towson State University, University of California at Berkeley, University of Houston, University of Missouri, University of the Pacific, University of Pittsburgh (Jonestown and Pittsburgh campuses), University of St. Thomas, University of Victoria in British Columbia, and Wabash College.

The faculty developed assignments for their three shipboard courses that included class readings as well as on-site field experiences. The syllabi, regardless of the discipline, reflected the integration of human diversity, especially from a cross-cultural orientation.

I participated in this fall 2005 voyage and, along with the other faculty members, infused course work with the field experience of the ten different port countries and even more diverse cultures that both students and faculty members would encounter during the approximately 100 days of the semester. While at sea, the daily classroom contact emphasized maximum student involvement. Class size averaged between 20 and 30 students. While at sea we lived as one community both day and night. This closeness enabled students to feel comfortable while assimilating into divergent cultures. Most professors on board had lived or traveled in the countries on the itinerary and could therefore facilitate their students' integration into the different societies.

Lecturers joined the ship at one port and sailed to another port with the Semester at Sea community. These educational, government, and business officials presented seminars about their countries, joined informal discussions, and participated in a variety of classes, thus helping students and faculty alike to integrate diversity into the learning process.

An obvious benefit of participating in the Semester at Sea Program is the international field experiences, which account for 20% of the credit hours needed for each onboard course. Field activities are transformed into an academic laboratory. These experiences, designed and often led by faculty members who draw on their own diversified international experiences, can include such encounters as observing and interacting with children in the Cultural Mobilization Project for Children in Danger representing the Axe Opo Afonja Candomble Terreiro in Brazil; participating in a Feeding Ceremony in Myanmar; talking with musicians from a township shabeen in South Africa; observing healthcare workers in India or Nike manufacturers in Vietnam; and perhaps participating in a lecture given by a native anthropologist in Taiwan's Taroko National Park regarding the cultural utilization of 200-million-year-old fossils. These types of international experiences, coupled with stimulating onboard classroom environments, can create exceptional opportunities for students to integrate diversity into their academic cross-cultural journey.

While out at sea, the shipboard faculty shared the teaching techniques they used with their students as the students completed written assignments to maximize the learning outcomes. I developed course syllabi for my three shipboard classes (Abnormal Psychology, Social Psychology, and Topics in Social Psychology: Community Psychology in Developing Societies). The following is a brief synopsis and overview of typical field experience assignments required in the courses. In each course, students had to choose from several assignments and write up their experiences, linking them with concepts from required readings and class lectures. Their papers were a minimum of five pages.

Field-Directed Practicum Assignment

The field-directed practicums involved (1) observations of parents and children from two different cultures or ports and (2) observations of adults from two different cultures or ports—for a minimum of 60 minutes. Students in these field-directed practicums compared levels of physical touch in these two cultures with the levels of physical touch in their own culture of origin, utilizing the reliability and validity assessment models discussed in class and outlined in the textbook.

Reception Assignments

The observations at the welcoming receptions were a minimum of 90 minutes. Several assignments were framed around the receptions that the students attended. One assignment required students to identify three behaviors that were demonstrated at each reception that might be regarded as being normal from their cultural perspective. They described the two different cultural settings and each of the behaviors they observed. Then they discussed their personal reactions to the behaviors, using reliability and validity assessment models to explain how their "norms" from their "immediate" culture of origin would view these behaviors.

For another assignment involving a reception, students had to compare the cultural roles and beliefs that influence group membership and interaction and describe their personal reactions to their observations. They then related four course concepts to the observations they made.

A third assignment of this type was for students to compare the cultural roles and beliefs that influence group interaction. Students had to elaborate on the following dynamics: ways in which behavior is affected by the presence of others, social loafing, deindividuation, group polarization, groupthink, and the influence of the minority. They gave two examples for each dynamic of how the behaviors related to the social psychological constructs.

Home Visit Assignments

The home visit was for a minimum of two days and one night during a port visit. One assignment was to write a paper from behavioral, cognitive, and sociocultural perspectives utilizing the "standardized" definitions of these perspectives. Students gave an overview of five familial interactions that they observed; explained the causes of the behavior from each of the three different perspectives; and identified and discussed three similarities and three differences as they related to the students' culture of origin.

Another assignment on human behavior required students to write an overview of three separate observations (for a minimum of 45 to 60 minutes each and in three different cultures or ports) of one or more individuals whose behavior would be labeled as "normal" or "abnormal" by the culture in which the behavior(s) took place. Each "overview" included the following: description of individual(s); description of cultural setting and the behavior observed; and the students' interpretations of how these different cultures would label these specific behaviors as normal or abnormal from one of the following standards: norm violation, statistical rarity, personal discomfort, maladaptive behavior, or combined standard, as defined in our text.

A third assignment required the students to write a paper on the concepts of behavior and attitudes, addressing three behavioral influences on behavior habits and discussing three ways that attitudes affect behavior.

Still other students wrote about how a family in a developing society coped with the conflicts and instability in their culture as it strove for human rights and democratic rule. The students gave examples of how these topics affected interaction within the household.

Educational Setting Assignments

For an assignment on gender dynamics, the students visited at least two schools and observed the roles of women, men, girls, and boys for a minimum of 90 minutes for each visit. In their papers they discussed how five of the following social characteristics related to their observations: culture and behavior; social roles, independence versus connectedness; social dominance; aggression; sexuality; gender-role variations; and the effects biology has on behavior. They also gave examples of how the five selected social characteristics were manifested in their observations.

For an assignment on educational environment, the students visited two schools in two different cultures (a minimum of 90 minutes for each observation) and compared the two school styles and atmospheres in their papers. They discussed how these educational environments might be affected by the conflicts and instability in the culture as it strove for human rights and democratic rule.

Student Outcomes

The student papers were of high quality from a cross-cultural perspective. Each paper had five interrelated components, and each component was worth a specific number of earned points. The high quality of these papers was due in part to students being required to relate course content to different cultural contexts, which increased their "ownership" of the assignment. The various "in port" assignments gave students an "academic mission" to interact with the local peoples instead of exhibiting the "typical tourist behavior" when visiting another country. After reading the transcriptions of their experience, I concluded that their observations and resulting interactions had a profound effect on their understanding of diversity from a "cross-cultural" perspective. An example of a typical student comment was: "I found myself being directly involved with this course by being required to relate course content to the observations that I made of people interacting."

At the end of the fourth week of the semester, students turned in their first paper. I could tell from class discussions that something had changed in many of the students' perspectives regarding their appreciation of diversity. They no longer labeled differences as "inferior" to their own attitudes and behaviors. The assignments definitely challenged their ethnocentricity and encouraged them to go beyond just "viewing" observational differences. As the students interacted directly with the peoples of diverse cultures, they had opportunities to examine their own behaviors in new ways. I had never before had such an opportunity to integrate cultural diversity into students' understanding of course content.

Return to Home University

Throughout the 2005 fall semester, I had mentally explored ways in which I could implement at my home campus some aspects of the Semester At Sea assignments. Upon my return to my home university in spring 2006, the real challenge began, for I was committed to my students' "discovering" diversity from within their own immediate cultural arenas and to sharing with my colleagues the application of cross-cultural concepts to their programs of study. Courses in the General Education Program seemed most suitable for cross-cultural field work, since, like the Semester at Sea Program, they were taught by faculty from multiple disciplines and were taken by students with many different majors.

I was able to utilize the framework of the assignments written for the voyage in my general education courses. For example, in one class, sophomores were to discuss a cross-cultural experience in their community. An Early Childhood Special Education major wrote about attending a Catholic mass spoken in Spanish, "to see how out of place I would feel." She developed empathy for "a person who speaks another language in this country. I was able to see how frustrating, aggravating, and tiring it can be to struggle to understand what everyone around you is saying." For a group project in another class, students chose a break-dancing club with which none of them had interacted before. After completing their papers, the students invited club members to talk about their love of break-dancing and its origins and to perform for the class.

Students indicated that, in identifying aspects of their own culture and themselves in particular, they become aware of the dynamics that they had taken for granted. When they looked for subcultures different from their own, they were often surprised to find them either on campus or within their communities. They indicated that they had not been aware that these cultural diversities existed before they actually had to "find" them.

Many of my colleagues in the hard sciences at my university have implemented some aspects of the teaching methods that I shared with them. They told me that this process and ones related to it have helped students understand the differences in cultural interpretations of empirical research results.

Conclusion

Glen Gish (1979) extended Lawrence Kolb's experiential learning theory in his statement that although there is value in traditional learning, learning "can be seen as a process in which a person experiences something directly (not vicariously), reflects on the experience as something new or as related to other experiences, develops some concept by which to name the experience and connect it with other experiences, and uses the concept in subsequent actions as a guide for behavior" (pp. 2–3). Because of the pluralistic culture in the United States, it is the responsibility of the educator to provide students with ample opportunities to explore various subcultures through "interactive" writing experiences that foster interdisciplinarity. Our educational system needs to give both teachers and students the opportunities for experiencing many aspects of diversity as part of the foundation for learning. It is imperative that the realities of diversity be interwoven into the content of a course. Cross-cultural writing assignments can help implement the process.

Finally, with the rapid onset of globalization, creating an awareness of how diversity is impacting the "global community" is essential to the mission of the educational process. Through appropriate writing assignments, both on campus and aboard a floating university, students can experience diversity as they reflect on their course content through activities that enhance their learning outcomes. If the university community explores our academic realms, not only will we find cultural diversity in abundance, but we will also use it to increase our students' understanding of the cross-cultural diversity that exists in their own communities.

References

Abrahamson, C. E. (1998). Storytelling as a pedagogical tool in higher education. *Education, 118*(3), 440–451.

Gish, G. (1979). The learning cycle. *Synergist, 8,* 2–7.

Hodge, F., Pasqua, A., Marquez, C., & Geishirt-Cantrell, B. (2002). Utilizing traditional storytelling to promote wellness in American Indian communities. *Journal of Transcultural Nursing, 13,* 6–11.

Wilson, M. (2007). Native American storytelling: A reader of myths and legends. *Journal of Transatlantic Studies, 5,* 107.

9

TEACHING ABOUT THE SOCIAL PSYCHOLOGY OF DISABILITY

Issues of Being, Not Becoming

Dana S. Dunn

There is nothing either good or bad, but thinking makes it so.
—Hamlet, Act II, scene ii

I f there is a summary lesson for teaching about disability and the culture of disability, this oft-cited quote by Shakespeare fits the bill. In fact, this epigraph does double duty in the context of disability: How people with disabilities think about themselves and how nondisabled people think about them matters a great deal. The latter focus has primacy in this chapter, as teaching about disability is most likely designed to educate nondisabled audiences in ways that challenge and reform their expectations about what disability must be like.

Arguably, the social psychology of disability begins with the fact that people with disabilities attract attention in most social contexts. If there is a perceptual-social-cognitive explanation for this, it is simply that the appearance and behavior of people with disabilities trigger dispositional analyses (Gilbert & Malone, 1995; Ross, 1977). In other words, personality is often erroneously deduced from behavior. What renders disability a different case, however, is that nondisabled perceivers often go beyond a dispositional analysis by presuming what having a disability (e.g., tetraplegia) must necessarily be like, a psychological interpretation known as the *insider-outsider distinction* (Dembo, 1969; Shontz, 1982; Wright, 1991).

Briefly, able-bodied observers (*outsiders*) assume that disability is a life-changing, all-encompassing quality that causes individuals with disabilities (*insiders*) to be completely preoccupied with their physical or mental states, especially those things they cannot do, and to have a concomitantly lowered quality of life, one devoid of pleasure or opportunity. Preferring to focus on what they can do, insiders know what outsiders do not: namely, that disability is not central to identity and that leading a normal—a pleasant and interesting—life is entirely possible (Dunn, in press; Dunn, Elliott, & Uswatte, in press; Ubel, Loewenstein, Hershey, Baron, Mohr, Asch, & Jepson, 2001).

A motivation for outsiders' misperceptions is the *fundamental negative bias*, the frequent tendency to give more attention to pessimistic information concerning disability than to optimistic—even diagnostic—information (Wright, 1988, 1991); bad news can indeed be stronger than good news (Baumeister, Bratlavsky, Finkenauer, & Vohs, 2001). Perhaps, too, observers confuse the state of *being* disabled (an ongoing process subsumed among other processes of daily living) with *becoming* disabled (often an acute and traumatic event) (Dunn, in press; Kahneman, 2000).

The main message of this chapter is that when teaching about disability, teachers must convey to students that living with disability—being rather than becoming—is different from their presumptions, that observers' expectations neither conform to nor confirm the actual experience of affected individuals. To help instructors defy such preconceptions, I offer ways to define disability, discuss its relationship to prejudice and stereotyping, recommend accounts and empirical research chosen to make the experience of disability phenomenally real for students, and identify resources for introducing the culture of disability in the classroom.

Defining and Construing Disability

The term *disability* can be a loaded one, especially if one wants to define it as the "absence of some mental or physical ability" that is seen as integral to "normal functioning" or "quality of life" or the like. Although disabilities do entail mental or physical distinctions or differences (or some combination of both), a better way to think of disability is as a social construction, one involving ingroup and outgroup processes or minority-majority relations, as well as identification and explication of some condition (e.g., amputation, brain injury, multiple sclerosis, spinal cord injury, mental illness) (Peterson & Elliott, in press; World Health Organization, 2001).

Who has a disability? Approximately 20% of the U.S. population can be characterized as having a disability (LaPlante & Carlson, 1996). Chances are that either you already have some disability (e.g., vision impairment, although you may not label it as "disabling") or will acquire one at some point in your life (e.g., hearing loss). Disability is not an all-or-nothing state, then; it is really more a matter of degree and, of course, perception (usually that of outsiders). Despite the fact that most people probably think of disability in rather straightforward and salient—even simple—terms (e.g., being blind or deaf), the culture of disability is a rather large and heterogeneous one. Disabilities come in myriad forms—some congenital, others acquired via disease or trauma. Some are obvious, and others are subtle, occurring without notice by either the possessors or those interacting with or otherwise observing them.

More to the point, disability is a function of the relationship between the person with the disability and the environment in which he or she lives (e.g., Wright, 1983). Situational factors, especially environmental constraints (e.g., no ramps or elevators, absence of Braille signage), pose more problems for people with disabilities than the disabilities themselves (Dembo, 1982; Meyerson, 1948; Wright, 1983). Outsiders, guided by their expectations, however well intentioned, also constitute situational effects impinging on people with disabilities.

Disability, Prejudice, and Stereotyping

Inevitably, interest in disability turns to issues of prejudice and stereotyping. I want to caution teachers at the outset that although understanding and combating antisocial beliefs about disability is important, this topic should not be the main focus—students will benefit from receiving a more nuanced and balanced presentation, one that includes a variety of topics besides prejudice. Much relevant literature falls under the heading of attitudes toward persons with disabilities (e.g., Antonak & Livneh, 2000; Yuker, 1988). The main finding is easily summarized: Nondisabled individuals tend to hold negative attitudes toward people with disabilities (e.g., Yuker, 1988, 1994; but see Soder, 1990). Regrettably, with few exceptions, the voluminous literature on prejudice from social psychology makes little reference to disability (e.g., Esses & Beaufoy, 1994; Snyder, Kleck, & Strenta, 1979), but the social-cognitive processes applied to other minority groups (e.g., Dovidio, Glick, & Rudman, 2005) no doubt apply to attributions directed at people with disabilities.

As already noted, people with apparent disabilities are salient—their distinctiveness and differences attract observers' curiosity and trigger social judgments. Expectations associated with disability create prejudice in two forms, one negative and one positive. Negative prejudice is familiar and commonsensical: Outsiders presume that the presence of some disability significantly detracts from a person's life, adversely affecting their happiness and well-being. Beyond the aforementioned fundamental negative bias, so-called *spread effects* can occur, in which outsiders erroneously anticipate that an insider's disability in one domain (e.g., a speech impediment) necessarily portends deficiencies in others (e.g., mobility, intelligence) (Dembo, Leviton, & Wright, 1956). Insiders know such views are patently false and prejudicial; a single quality, whether weakness or strength, does not define a person.

Social judgments concerning the cause of a disability can also be a source of prejudice. For example, many perceivers subscribe to the *just world hypothesis* (Lerner, 1980), assuming that the nature of people's actions (good or bad, constructive or destructive) are causally connected to fate and just rewards. Thus, when a negative event occurs (e.g., a driver is paralyzed following a car accident), some observers conclude that the afflicted individual is duly responsible for and somehow deserving of his disability (see also Janoff-Bulman, 1992; Weiner, 2006). Regrettably, upholding such a consistent worldview of distributive justice sometimes encourages perceivers to derogate or devalue people with disabilities.

But what about favorable forms of prejudice, such as those situations in which persons with disabilities are praised for their ability to "rise above" their impairments or infirmities? Aren't such social judgments beneficial or at least benign? Not necessarily. Above all else, perhaps, people with disabilities want to be treated the same as others by having their strengths, weaknesses, and common humanity recognized and accepted. Having a disability is a descriptor, a single characteristic among many, one that is neither ennobling nor tragic. Admiring someone for overcoming a physical or mental disability, for example, or seeing "virtue in suffering," represent atypical forms of stigma, but such views can still lead to differential social treatment and the maintenance of social barriers (Wright, 1991).

Reducing Prejudice: Individuation and the Role of Contact

What factors reduce people's proclivity to prejudge what having a disability must necessarily be like? Two key ideas are especially relevant. First, language issues, such as referring to people as people, not objects, matter. Researchers and therapists long ago adopted the strategy of *individuation*, preferring to refer to people as individuals in everyday encounters and discourse ("Karen, who has tetraplegia") and not monolithic, homogeneous terms ("tetraplegics," "the handicapped," "the disabled"). The recurrent phrase "people with disabilities" is not idly chosen (for a detailed discussion of this issue, see Dunn & Elliott, 2005; Wright, 1983). Placing "people first" is not mere "political correctness" but a straightforward way to treat them with dignity and integrity.

Second, social psychologists appeal to what is commonly referred to as the *contact hypothesis*, the idea that sustained, meaningful contact between nondisabled individuals and persons with disabilities can reduce or even eliminate the more common forms of prejudice (Langer, Bashner, & Chanowitz, 1985). The contact hypothesis is representative of a larger literature illustrating that consequential, equal-status, intergroup contact, including cooperative ventures, can reduce prejudice (Brewer & Brown, 1998; Brown & Hewstone, 2005; Pettigrew & Tropp, 2006). Moreover, learning about individuation and intergroup contact can promote a more accurate understanding of the experience of disability.

The Experience of Disability: Using Subjective and Empirical Accounts

Narratives can be powerful teaching tools and research methods (e.g., Couser, 1997, 2006; Josselson, Lieblich, & McAdams, 2002; McAdams, 2001). In order to approach some understanding of disability, students need to learn from people with disabilities themselves. The extant literature on the experience of disability does not ask "what does it mean to *be* different?" or "how *will* I live my life now?" so much as it asks "what does it mean to be *perceived* as different?" and "how *do* I live my life?" Many first-person testimonials emphasize that living with a disability is not a defining quality but rather one among many, that any adjustment is best described as normative (e.g., Cole, 2004; Johnson, 2003, 2005a; Kingsley & Levitz, 1994; Murphy, 2001; see also Berube, 1998; Elliott & Kurylo, 2000).

These personal stories raise a broad and important question that has received little empirical examination heretofore: How does having a disability shape the development (and developmental course) of a positive identity (Olkin, 1997)? Johnson (2006), for example, wrote a semi-autobiographical, coming-of-age novel about Jean, a 17-year old girl who has cerebral palsy. Written for a young adult audience, the book portrays the "crip" campers at "Camp Courage" as recipients of benign condescension from able-bodied counselors and benefactors who try to approximate "a normal summer camp experience." As Jean's consciousness is raised, so is the reader's, and disability is treated as socially and politically empowering rather than a matter for pity or objectification.

In the absence of actual social interactions between people with disabilities and students, how can teachers ensure that such first-person accounts of disability serve as a proxy method of contact? One approach is to have students react to these sorts of narratives by doing in-class writing (Dunn, 2005). Both psychologists (e.g., Niederhoffer & Pennebaker, 2002; Pennebaker, 1991, 1997) and writing teachers (e.g., Elbow, 1986) argue that nondirected writing is an effective way for people to find meaning by linking their self-perspectives to course material (see Dunn, 2005, for suggestions).

Such first-person, subjective accounts can be supplemented with empirical studies from psychology illustrating that individuals adjust to life's vagaries, including disability (e.g., Brickman, Coates, & Janoff-Bulman, 1978; Bulman & Wortman, 1977; Dunn, 1996; Heinemann, Bulka, & Smetak, 1988). What remains to be demonstrated—and can serve as an excellent discussion point—is whether such adjustment defies the forecasts of those affected by the onset of disability, as considerable evidence indicates people do not predict their future feelings very well at all (Kahneman, 2000; Wilson & Gilbert, 2003, 2005). After the onset of disability, for example, are insiders surprised at their hedonic adjustment? Should outsiders be incredulous when faced with claims of insider coping? Similarly, unaffected observers underestimate the quality of life of individuals who have chronic health issues (Brickman et al., 1978; Ubel et al., 2001). A review of autobiographical and empirical studies can also provide students with the opportunity to critically consider the "benefit finding" reported by some individuals after becoming disabled (e.g., McMillen & Cook, 2003; McMillen & Curtis, 1998; see also Elliott, Kurylo, & Rivera, 2002).

Broader psychosocial perspectives on disability, too, are available in classic (Wright, 1983; see also Dunn & Elliott, 2005) and contemporary sources (Frank, Caplan, & Rosenthal, in press; Vash & Crewe, 2004). These sources embrace a Lewinian field theory perspective by which behavior is a function of the person and his or her real as well as perceived environment (e.g., Lewin, 1935), reinforcing the idea that disability is a social, psychological, and environmental construct as much as it is a physical one (e.g., Brandt & Pope, 1997; Pope & Tarlov, 1991). Disability has links to the burgeoning positive psychology movement (Dunn & Dougherty, 2005), even with the teaching of research methods (Woolf & Hulsizer, 2007). Finally, current empirical research and literature reviews are available in the journal *Rehabilitation Psychology,* and selected readings on a variety of rehabilitation issues in psychology can be found at http://www.apa.org/divisions/div22/readings.html.

Resources for Teaching About Disability Culture

Not so long ago, attempts to teach students about disability identity were accomplished through identification exercises. Although well-intentioned, blind-folding students to "mimic" blindness or driving them around campus in a wheelchair so as to "identify with what it's like to be handicapped," for example, are overly simplistic, vaguely offensive, and doomed to failure. At best, such antics are poor proxies for the experience of disability; at worst, they caricature people's conditions and how they live. By eschewing such activities, students must be taught that disability is as much about social and political rights as it is about issues of psychological well-being, which leads to the study of disability culture.

By "disability culture," I am referring to disability as a way of life for many people, one that must be understood in historical, political, and academic terms (e.g., Longmore & Umansky, 2001). Until late in the twentieth century, people with disabilities were ignored, if not institutionalized; they lacked social power, political capital, general acceptance, and even legitimacy. Significant social progress and intentional activism have reduced discrimination and shifted focus to issues of integration: education, employment, and full participation in the sacred and mundane aspects of daily life (Nagler, 1993; see also Olkin & Pledger, 2003). As Gill (1995) wrote:

> It is not simply the shared experience of oppression. . . . The elements of our culture include, certainly, our long standing social oppression, but also our emerging art and humor, our piecing together of our history, our evolving language and symbols, our remarkably unified worldview, beliefs and values, and our strategies for surviving and thriving. (p. 18)

In fact, the recent history of the disability rights movement in the United States, which includes the groundbreaking Americans With Disabilities Act (1990), is one of political and social activism (Charlton, 1998). One wing of the disability movement is academic, the area of inquiry known as disability studies, which posits that disability is a universal quality of humanity (see, for example, Albrecht, Seelman, & Bury, 2001; Barnes & Mercer, 2003; Davis, 2002, 2006; Oliver, Barton, & Barnes, 2002). Disability studies argue that people with disabilities have been marginalized like many other minorities, and the community's radical reactions to cultural prejudice and discrimination match some of the social patterns established by feminism, the women's rights movement, the civil rights movement for African Americans, and the mainstreaming of gay and lesbian issues. Although the study of disability and rehabilitation in the discipline of psychology is only one part of the larger culture of disability, students will benefit from learning that psychologists and other social scientists are learning from this progressive movement by relying less on a traditional medical model and more on a sociopolitical one (e.g., Olkin & Pledger, 2003). By adopting the latter model, those who do research or therapy with people with disabilities can consider the impact of economic, environmental, legal, and social policy issues that affect health and well-being (see also Dunn & Dougherty, 2005; Elliott, 2002).

Most recently, the ethics of life with a disability and who should have the right to choose or to (dis)continue medical treatment has been a national discussion (e.g., the right to die issues surrounding the Terri Schiavo case, the medical intervention designed to take care of a child with profound intellectual disabilities known only as "Ashley" easier by preventing her puberty and growth to maturity). These and other debates involve a variety of philosophical and ethical issues (e.g., Singer, 2007), as well as matters of rights for persons with disabilities and the nondisabled (e.g., Johnson, 2005b). The issues are complex and the answers are not easy; therefore, I encourage teachers to make certain their students understand the idea of disability rights and activism, notably why many people with disabilities deride the "telethon mentality" that often accompanies consideration of their medical, legal, social, political, and ethical standing (e.g., Johnson, 2005a, 2006).

(Im)Parting Wisdom

Distinguishing self from other is an early developmental milestone, one that repeats itself later, albeit with greater complexity, when we learn that our view of the world is distinct, even unique, from that of others. If we are fortunate, a final maturing occurs when we recognize that our own culture, however rich and varied it may be, is not superior to any other; it's just different. One goal of teaching about disability and disability culture is to help students realize that the experience of disability is not what they expect it to be, that the phenomenal experience of insiders can be both positive and "normal," that outsiders may well be misperceiving the situation (Dunn, 2005). Fine and Asch (1988, p. 11) may have unintentionally paraphrased Hamlet when they wrote that, "while never wished for—[disability] may simply not be as wholly disastrous as imagined."

References

Albrecht, G. L., Seelman, K. D., & Bury, M. (Eds.). (2001). *Handbook of disability studies*. Newbury Park, CA: Sage.

Americans With Disabilities Act of 1990, Pub. L. No. 101–336, 104 Stat. 328 (1991).

Antonak, R. F., & Livneh, H. (2000). Measurement of attitudes towards persons with disabilities. *Disability and Rehabilitation, 22,* 211–224.

Barnes, C., & Mercer, G. (2003). *Disability.* Malden, MA: Blackwell.

Baumeister, R. F., Bratlavsky, E., Finkenauer, C., & Vohs, K. D. (2001). Bad is stronger than good. *Review of General Psychology, 5,* 323–370.

Berube, M. (1998). *Life as we know it: A father, a family, and an exceptional child.* New York: Vintage.

Brandt, E. N., & Pope, A. M. (Eds.). (1997). *Enabling America: Assessing the role of rehabilitation science and engineering.* Washington, DC: National Academy Press.

Brewer, M. B., & Brown, R. J. (1998). Inter-group relations. In D. T. Gilbert, S. T. Fiske, & G. Lindzey (Eds.), *Handbook of social psychology* (4th ed., Vol. 2, pp. 554–594). New York: McGraw-Hill.

Brickman, P., Coates, D., & Janoff-Bulman, R. (1978). Lottery winners and accident victims: Is happiness relative? *Journal of Personality and Social Psychology, 37,* 917–927.

Brown, R., & Hewstone, M. (2005). An integrative theory of intergroup contact. In M. P. Zanna (Ed.), *Advances in experimental social psychology* (pp. 255–343). San Diego, CA: Elsevier.

Bulman, R. J., & Wortman, C. B. (1977). Attributions of blame and coping in the "real world": Severe accident victims react to their lot. *Journal of Personality and Social Psychology, 35,* 351–363.

Charlton, J. I. (1998). *Nothing about us without us: Disability oppression and empowerment.* Berkeley: University of California Press.

Cole, J. (2004). *Still lives: Narratives of spinal cord injury.* Cambridge, MA: MIT Press.

Couser, G. T. (1997). *Recovering bodies: Illness, disability, and life writing.* Madison: University of Wisconsin Press.

Couser, G. T. (2006). Disability, life narratives, and representation. In L. J. Davis (Ed.), *The disability studies reader* (2nd ed.). New York: Routledge.

Davis, L. J. (2002). *Bending over backwards: Disability, dismodernism, and other difficult positions.* New York: New York University Press.

Davis, L. J. (2006). *The disability studies reader* (2nd ed.). London: Routledge.

Dembo, T. (1969). Rehabilitation psychology and its immediate future: A problem of utilization of psychological knowledge. *Rehabilitation Psychology, 16,* 63–72.

Dembo, T. (1982). Some problems in rehabilitation as seen by a Lewinian. *Journal of Social Issues, 38,* 131–139.

Dembo, T., Leviton, G. L., & Wright, B. A. (1956). Adjustment to misfortune: A problem of social-psychological rehabilitation. *Artificial Limbs, 3*(2), 4–62.

Dovidio, J. F., Glick, P., & Rudman, L. A. (Eds.). (2005). *On the nature of prejudice: Fifty years after Allport.* Malden, MA: Blackwell.

Dunn, D. S. (1996). Well-being following amputation: Salutary effects of positive meaning, optimism, and control. *Rehabilitation Psychology, 41,* 285–302.

Dunn, D. S. (2005). Negotiating realities to understand others: Teaching about meaning and well-being. *Journal of Social and Clinical Psychology, 24,* 30–40.

Dunn, D. S. (in press). The social psychology of disability. To appear in R. G. Frank, B. Caplan, & M. Rosenthal (Eds.), *Handbook of rehabilitation psychology* (2nd ed.). Washington, DC: American Psychological Association.

Dunn, D. S., & Dougherty, S. B. (2005). Prospects for a positive psychology of rehabilitation. *Rehabilitation Psychology, 50,* 305–311.

Dunn, D. S., & Elliott, T. R. (2005). Revisiting a constructive classic: Wright's *Physical Disability: A Psychosocial Approach*. *Rehabilitation Psychology, 50,* 183–189.

Dunn, D. S., Elliott, T. R., & Uswatte, G. (in press). Happiness, resilience and positive growth following disability: Issues for understanding, research, and therapeutic intervention. To appear in S. J. Lopez (Ed.), *Handbook of positive psychology* (2nd ed.). New York: Oxford University Press.

Elbow, P. (1986). *Embracing contraries: Explorations in learning in teaching.* New York: Oxford University Press.

Elliott, T. R. (2002). Defining our common ground to reach new horizons. *Rehabilitation Psychology, 47,* 131–143.

Elliott, T., & Kurylo, M. (2000). Hope over disability: Lessons from one young woman's triumph. In C. R. Snyder (Ed.), *The handbook of hope: Theory, measurement, and interventions* (pp. 373–386). New York: Academic Press.

Elliott, T. R., Kurylo, M., & Rivera, P. (2002). Positive growth following acquired physical disability. In C. R. Snyder & S. J. Lopez (Eds.), *Handbook of positive psychology* (pp. 687–699). New York: Oxford University Press.

Esses, V. M., & Beaufoy, S. L. (1994). Determinants of attitudes toward people with disabilities. *Journal of Social Behavior and Personality, 9,* 43–64.

Fine, M., & Asch, A. (1988). Disability beyond stigma: Social interaction, discrimination, and activism. *Journal of Social Issues, 44,* 3–21.

Frank, R. G., Caplan, B., & Rosenthal, M. (Eds.). (in press). *Handbook of rehabilitation psychology* (2nd ed.). Washington, DC: American Psychological Association.

Gilbert, D. T., & Malone, P. S. (1995). The correspondence bias. *Psychological Bulletin, 117,* 21–38.

Gill, C. J. (1995). A psychological view of disability culture. *Disability Studies Quarterly, Fall,* 16–19.

Heinemann, A. W., Bulka, M., & Smetak, S. (1988). Attributions and disability acceptance following traumatic injury: A replication and extension. *Rehabilitation Psychology, 33,* 195–206.

Janoff-Bulman, R. (1992). *Shattered assumptions: Towards a new psychology of trauma.* New York: Free Press.

Johnson, H. M. (2003, February 16). Unspeakable conversations. *New York Times Magazine, 50* (5), 74–79.

Johnson, H. M. (2005a). *Too late to die young: Nearly true tales from a life.* New York: Henry Holt.

Johnson, H. M. (2005b, March 23). Not dead at all: Why Congress was right to stick up for Terri Schiavo. *Slate.* Retrieved March 9, 2007, from http://www.slate.com/id/2115208/ on March 9, 2007

Johnson, H. M. (2006). *Accidents of nature.* New York: Henry Holt.

Josselson, R., Lieblich, A., & McAdams, D. P. (Eds.). (2002). *Up close and personal: The teaching and learning of narrative research.* Washington, DC: American Psychological Association.

Kahneman, D. (2000). Experienced utility and objective happiness: A moment-based approach. In D. Kahneman & A. Tversky (Eds.), *Choices, values, and frames* (pp. 673–692). New York: Russell Sage Foundation and Cambridge University Press.

Kingsley, J., & Levitz, M. (1994). *Count us in: Growing up with Down Syndrome.* New York: Harcourt.

Langer, E. J., Bashner, R., & Chanowitz, B. (1985). Decreasing prejudice by increasing discrimination. *Journal of Personality and Social Psychology, 49,* 113–120.

LaPlante, M. P., & Carlson, D. (1996). *Disability in the United States: Prevalence and causes,* 1992 (Disability Statistics Rep. No. 7). Washington, DC: U.S. Department of Education, National Institute on Disability and Rehabilitation Research.

Lerner, M. J. (1980). *The belief in a just world: A fundamental delusion.* New York: Plenum.

Lewin, K. A. (1935). *A dynamic theory of personality.* New York: McGraw-Hill.

Longmore, P. K., & Umansky, L. (Eds.). (2001). *The new disability history: American perspectives.* New York: New York University Press.

McAdams, D. P. (2001). The psychology of life stories. *Review of General Psychology, 5,* 100–122.

McMillen, J. C., & Cook, C. L. (2003). The positive by-products of spinal cord injury and their correlates. *Rehabilitation Psychology, 48,* 77–85.

McMillen, J. C., & Curtis, R. H. (1998). The Perceived Benefits Scales: Measuring perceived positive life changes after negative events. *Social Work Research, 22,* 173–186.

Murphy, R. F. (2001). *The body silent: The different world of the disabled.* New York: Norton.

Meyerson, L. (1948). Physical disability as a social psychological problem. *Journal of Social Issues, 4,* 2–10.

Nagler, M. (Ed.). (1993). *Perspectives on disability* (2nd ed.). Palo Alto, CA: Health Market Research.

Niederhoffer, K. G., & Pennebaker, J. W. (2002). Sharing one's story: On the benefits of writing or talking about emotional experience. In C. R. Snyder & S. J. Lopez (Eds.), *Handbook of positive psychology* (pp. 573–583). New York: Oxford University Press.

Oliver, M., Barton, L., & Barnes, C. (Eds.). (2002). *Disability studies today.* Malden, MA: Blackwell.

Olkin, R. (1997). Human rights of children with disabilities. *Women and Therapy,* *20,* 29–42.

Olkin, R., & Pledger, C. (2003). Can disability studies and psychology join hands? *American Psychologist, 58,* 296–304.

Pennebaker, J. W. (1991). Self-expressive writing: Implications for health, education, and welfare. In P. Belanoff, P. Elbow, & S. I. Fontaine (Eds.), *Nothing begins with n: New investigations of freewriting.* Carbondale and Edwardsville, IL: Southern Illinois University Press.

Pennebaker, J. W. (1997). *Opening up: The healing power of expressing emotions* (rev. ed.). New York: Guilford.

Peterson, D. B., & Elliott, T. R. (in press). Advances in conceptualizing and studying disability. To appear in R. Lent & S. Brown (Eds.), *Handbook of counseling psychology* (4th ed.). New York: Sage.

Pettigrew, T. F., & Tropp, L. R. (2006). A meta-analytic test of intergroup contact theory. *Journal of Personality and Social Psychology, 90,* 751–783.

Pope, A. M., & Tarlov, A. R. (Eds.). (1991). *Disability in America: Toward a national agenda for prevention.* Washington, DC: National Academy Press.

Ross, L. (1977). The intuitive psychologist and his shortcomings: Distortions in the attribution process. In L. Berkowitz (Ed.), *Advances in experimental social psychology* (Vol. 10, pp. 174–221). New York: Academic Press.

Shontz, F. C. (1982). Adaptation to chronic illness and disability. In T. Millon, C. Green, & R. Meagher (Eds.), *Handbook of clinical health psychology* (pp. 153–172). New York: Plenum Press.

Singer, P. (2007, January 26). A convenient truth [op-ed]. *New York Times,* p. A21.

Snyder, M. L., Kleck, R. E., & Strenta, A. (1979). Avoidance of the handicapped: An attributional ambiguity analysis. *Journal of Personality and Social Psychology, 37,* 2297–2306.

Soder, M. (1990). Prejudice or ambivalence? Attitudes toward people with disabilities. *Disability, Handicap, and Society, 5,* 227–241.

Ubel, P. A., Loewenstein, G., Hershey, J., Baron, J., Mohr, T., Asch, D., & Jepson, C. (2001). Do nonpatients underestimate the quality of life associated with chronic health conditions because of a focusing illusion? *Medical Decision Making, 21,* 190–199.

Vash, C. L., & Crewe, N. M. (2004). *Psychology of disability* (2nd ed.). New York: Springer.

Weiner, B. (2006). *Social motivation, justice, and the moral emotions: An attributional approach.* Mahwah, NJ: Lawrence Erlbaum.

Wilson, T. D., & Gilbert, D. T. (2003). Affective forecasting. In M. P. Zanna (Ed.), *Advances in experimental social psychology* (Vol. 35, pp. 345–511). San Diego, CA: Academic Press.

Wilson, T. D., & Gilbert, D. T. (2005). Affective forecasting: Knowing what to want. *Current Directions in Psychological Science, 14,* 131–134.

Woolf, L. M., & Hulsizer, M. R. (2007). Understanding the mosaic of humanity through research methodology: Infusing diversity into research methods courses. In D. S. Dunn, R. A. Smith, & B. C. Beins (Eds.), *Best practices in teaching statistics and research methods in the behavioral sciences* (pp. 237–256). Mahwah, NJ: Lawrence Erlbaum.

World Health Organization. (2001). *International classification of functioning, disability, and health.* Geneva, Switzerland: Author.

Wright, B. A. (1983). *Physical disability: A psychosocial approach* (2nd ed). New York: Harper & Row.

Wright, B. A. (1988). Attitudes and the fundamental negative bias: Conditions and corrections. In H. E. Yuker (Ed.), *Attitudes towards persons with disabilities* (pp. 3–21). New York: Springer.

Wright, B. A. (1991). Labeling: The need for greater person-environment individuation. In C. R. Snyder & D. R. Forsyth (Eds.), *Handbook of social and clinical psychology: The health perspective* (pp. 469–487). New York: Pergamon Press.

Yuker, H. E. (Ed.). (1988). *Attitudes toward persons with disabilities.* New York: Springer.

Yuker, H. E. (1994). Variables that influence attitudes toward people with disabilities: Conclusions from the data. *Journal of Social Behavior and Personality, 9,* 3–22.

10

FOREIGN LANGUAGE LEARNING

A Different Form of Diversity

Paul C. Smith

Incorporating diversity into the curriculum usually involves giving students the opportunity to take course work in ethnic studies, gender studies, or racial issues. However, there are other ways to give students the benefits of diversity. Foreign language study can help students to understand key processes underlying learning. At the same time, it can expose students to an aspect of diversity familiar to much of the world but still given relatively little attention in the United States.

When I studied Spanish and French in high school and college, I never imagined that I would one day have the opportunity to travel to a Hispanophone or Francophone country. When I finally did get the opportunity for international travel, I found my interest in languages rekindled and soon burning strongly. When I had my first sabbatical, I spent five weeks at a language school in Aix-en-Provence in southern France, staying with French families. I have since returned to that school a few more times, and I've also done some short language immersion study trips to schools in Quebec and Costa Rica to study French and Spanish. During those trips I learned about the culture and day-to-day life of the places where I stayed, and I also had a great opportunity to watch the efforts of other students from all over the world as they tried to learn languages.

In watching those efforts while reflecting on my own, I saw a unique opportunity to understand the experiences of those whose circumstances require them to learn a language other than their native one. Students in the

United States are not usually required to learn a second language, though increasing numbers are electing to do so (Furman, Goldberg, & Lusin, 2007). However, according to the 2000 census, 18% of Americans five years old or older speak a language other than English in their homes (United States Census Bureau, 2003). Most of those report also speaking English "very well." The experience of learning a second language is common in the European Union (EU), and in 2003 the European Commission issued an action plan calling for all EU citizens to learn two languages in addition to their native language (European Commission, 2003). A recent survey showed that 56% of EU citizens already speak one language other than their native one, and 28% speak two additional languages (European Commission, 2006). Both globally and in the United States, multilingualism crosses economic class boundaries, and learning a second language is a significant part of the experience of a wide variety of people in all parts of the world. Sharing that experience should be a goal for students pursuing an understanding of the diversity of human experience.

Explaining Differences in Learning

Progress in language ability is more apparent to a learner and to her peers than is progress in most other academic disciplines, where performance may be more private and difficult to assess. As a result, students of foreign languages tend to be actively curious about differences among learners and among learning tasks. Why are some students quicker than others at learning vocabulary? Why are some words easier to remember than others? Why are some languages easier to learn than others? These questions provide an excellent context for discussions of the dramatic effects on learning of different kinds of prior knowledge.

Prior Knowledge of the Foreign Language

The effect of prior knowledge of a language provides a solid illustration of a learning principle: "the rich get richer." In the context of learning to read in one's native language, Stanovich (1986) labeled this the "Matthew Effect." He suggested that it reflects a "bootstrapping" phenomenon, in that better readers read more, resulting in a reciprocal relationship between reading and learning to read. This effect also occurs in foreign language learning: The more you know of a language, the easier it is to learn new grammar and vocabulary. The important underlying mechanism is probably that existing knowledge provides multiple cues to newly learned information. All of our knowledge about a topic is interconnected, and our ability to work with that knowledge—to recall a particular fact or bring the correct skill into play at the right moment—depends on moment-by-moment situational cues. The improved cue accessibility that comes with having significant prior knowledge of a language makes it more likely that the information—the appropriate vocabulary word—will be retrieved from long-term memory when needed.

The Matthew Effect can also be attributed in part to the fact that once we have learned a subject well enough, we can shift our attention to new learning tasks. We have plenty of space in memory for all of the facts, rules, and skills involved in learning a subject, but we can pay attention to only a few things at any one time. The process of learning makes significant demands on that attention, both as we take in and process new information and as we try to retrieve what we have already learned. With practice in a subject, though, we can make retrieval of information automatic. For example, a learner who knows vocabulary well enough for automatic retrieval doesn't have to consciously search for the meaning of a particular word and can pay attention to other simultaneous learning tasks such as puzzling out the meanings of other words or properly applying a newly learned grammatical rule. Whenever a cognitive task can be done without using attentional resources, more of that attention is freed up for the other cognitive tasks involved in learning.

These two principles—that multiple cues enhance recall and that automating a learning task frees resources for other learning tasks—are among the most important principles in the study of the learning process. Learning a foreign language and being around other language learners provides students with numerous clear illustrations of these principles.

Prior Knowledge of One's Native Language

Prior knowledge of one's native language also affects the pace of learning of foreign language vocabulary. Because English words often share roots with words in other languages, native English speakers have a head start with respect to those languages, as many of the foreign words resemble the English words with the same meanings. For example, while English speakers learning Spanish would not guess that *perro* means "dog," they would probably guess that *instrucciones* means "instructions." In the context of foreign language study, these matched pairs of words are referred to as "cognates" (linguists use the term differently, referring to pairs of words having common origins rather than to pairs of similar words sharing a meaning).

Pairs of words with similar spellings but different meanings in two languages are commonly referred to as "faux amis" ("false friends": again, though, this is a colloquial usage not shared by linguists). For example, native English speakers learning Spanish could be expected to mistranslate *dirección* in the phrase "cual es su dirección" as "direction" when instead it means "address." Cognates show that we do not begin as "blank slates" with respect to a topic, while faux amis show that prior knowledge sometimes interferes with rather than enhances learning, a fact often lost in sometimes overly enthusiastic exhortations to help students "connect with what they already know."

General Prior Knowledge

Knowledge of a language is not the only kind of prior knowledge that has an impact on language learning: general background knowledge is important as well. On a trip in Provence a few years ago, I rode with my classmates through Lourmarin, the town where Albert Camus was buried after his death in an automobile accident in 1960. Our guide described Camus' life and death, in French, of course. Afterwards I asked one of the beginning students how much she had understood, and she replied that she heard him using the word *connue,* the past participle of *connaître.* I explained that he hadn't said "connue," but instead was talking about Camus, and she said she had never heard of him. She had been trying to make sense of our guide's French and had failed not because of her lack of background with the language but because of her lack of relevant cultural knowledge. General cultural, historical, and geographical knowledge can be strong contributors to progress in learning a foreign language, and conversely, a person's lack of progress in learning a foreign language may be due to a lack of familiarity with cultural reference points.

Improving One's Own Learning

Differences in various kinds of prior knowledge help to explain individual differences in the pace of learning. However, students' experience in learning a foreign language can go beyond description and explanation to developing strategies to improve their learning. The full range of prescriptions for learning (e.g., spaced practice, active learning, and contrasting cases: National Research Council, 1999) can apply to language learning, and because language learning has such tangible results, it provides an excellent context for students to try new learning methods.

Testing Effect

Much of language learning involves retrieving memorized information: words, verb endings, irregular verb forms. Pure memorization has largely fallen out of favor in higher education, but the ability to memorize and easily retrieve information remains a valuable tool. It is natural to assume that one memorizes best by simple repetition, reading the material over and over again, with only occasional testing. But in fact learning is more efficient when you test yourself more often (Roediger & Karpicke, 2006). This "testing effect" occurs because memory retrieval is a skill that improves with practice. Cues to retrieval—the little hints, sometime unconscious, that remind us of the next word—become easier to find if you practice finding them.

Memorizing foreign language literature and especially foreign language poetry provides a wonderful opportunity to experience this, as we are often aware of some of the hints we use, such as odd word sounds or the slightly alien "music of language" we find in foreign literature. The last time that I attended language school in Provence, I gave a presentation about the psychology of learning, including a brief piece about rote memorization. In response, the professor decided to assign our class poetry to memorize over the weekend. I memorized Victor Hugo's *Demain de l'aube*, relying on the testing effect to guide my practice. I was surprised at how effective study interspersed with regular testing was, and my professor and class were surprised to hear me recite the piece from start to finish with no more than a few hesitations the following Monday morning.

Problem Representation

I learned early in my language immersion experience that my language teachers hated bilingual dictionaries. A number of students came to language classes with French-English dictionaries that they parked in their laps, only occasionally looking up as they spoke in class. When they tried to answer questions orally, they were frequently stumped, frantically paging through the dictionary to find the proper French word for what they wanted to say. As the directeur pédagogique of the school in Provence scoldingly pointed out, this is not learning to speak a foreign language; it is learning to use a dictionary.

In my discipline of psychology we might refer to this as a matter of problem representation. Many students learning a foreign language represent the problem as one of *finding the right words to express what they want to say*. However, it is more useful to represent the problem as one of *expressing what you want to say using the limited stock of words that you already have*. The ability to express oneself with a limited vocabulary is the only skill that really matters to non-native speakers of a language. Because it is very unlikely that a student of a second language will develop the vocabulary of a native speaker, it is necessary to also practice the uncomfortable skill of finding ways to say what one wants to say using the wrong words. Consciously contrasting these two ways to think about the problem of learning a language provides a concrete illustration of the importance of problem representation.

Theories of Intelligence

Earlier I mentioned that my language immersion classmates were surprised that I was able to complete an assignment to memorize a piece of French poetry. In fact, only one of my fellow students had even worked on the assignment: the rest simply assumed that they could not memorize a poem in French and did not even try. Carol Dweck and Ellen Leggett (1988) present a "social-cognitive" theory suggesting that a student's belief about her ability to learn a skill affects her persistence at learning that skill. Dweck and Leggett found that students (and often teachers and parents) implicitly hold one of two theories of intelligence in a discipline: an Entity Theory, or an Incremental Theory. A student holding an Entity Theory believes that intelligence is a fixed entity: you either have it or you don't. These students tend to set "performance goals," demonstrating their intelligence through successful performance and avoiding experiences in which they risk demonstrating a lack of intelligence. As long as everything is going well, such a student will attend and participate eagerly, following a "mastery-oriented" pattern of learning behaviors. However, when she suffers a setback, these "performance goals" cause her to shift from the mastery orientation to a helpless response, "characterized by an avoidance of challenge and a deterioration of performance in the face of obstacles" (p. 256). A student who holds performance goals will take these experiences as failures, signs of a lack of innate ability in the study of French and as reason to avoid those tasks in the future. Besides this avoidance of challenge, Dweck and Leggett (1988) detail a number of other emotionally laden responses that students with an Entity Theory have to learning setbacks. These include excessively worrying about results and an inability to concentrate on the learning tasks.

Students holding the contrasting Incremental Theory believe that intelligence is not a fixed characteristic, but rather is developed by working hard in a certain field over a long period of time. A student who holds an Incremental Theory will set mastery of the material as her learning goal. According to Dweck and Leggett, such a student will seek out challenging tasks and work effectively at them even while failing to perform. It is because they continue to work even after failure that these students do the work necessary to eventually succeed at a learning task.

I have caught myself slipping into the assumption that poor performance reflects a lack of innate ability. Around the time that I first read about implicit theories of intelligence, I made my first visit to Avignon, where I found myself fascinated by some handmade tiles. When I returned home, I bought some terra cotta and tried to make some myself. After about an hour's work produced nothing but some ugly lumps, I was completely frustrated and convinced that I have no artistic talent. I later realized that I had made the same mistake I had read about in Dweck's article. I had put almost no effort into learning to work with terra cotta—I had not even looked at a book on the subject—and yet rather than taking that setback as a sign that I needed to make a more disciplined effort, I took it as proof that I lacked innate artistic ability and simply could not learn the skills involved.

Understanding Others' Experiences

Discussions of the relationship between foreign language learning and learning about diversity have typically focused on what students learn about a particular target culture or on changes in their attitudes about that culture and its members (e.g., Holmquist, 1993; Wright, 1999). Not surprisingly, while learning a foreign language seems to have an overall positive effect on knowledge of and attitudes about a culture, the strength of that effect is dependent on the way that culture is presented along with language in the program, and is not something that inevitably emerges from language learning (Wright, 1999).

However, language learning does have another, more distinct contribution to the development of students' appreciation for diversity. As Thomas Friedman pointed out (Friedman, 2005), a variety of technologies make it possible for work to move across national and linguistic boundaries. Consequently, our students are increasingly likely to interact in their work and personal lives with people in a language that is not native to some of those people. Because communication is so central to experience, learning a second language is a significant formative experience for those who do so. Most dimensions of diversity are defined by fixed characteristics; we cannot change our ethnicity or cultural background. But any of us can choose to have the experience of learning a second language. Students who choose to do so give themselves a rich experience in diversity.

References

Dweck, C. S., & Leggett, Ellen L. (1988). A social-cognitive approach to motivation and personality. *Psychological Review, 95,* 256–273.

European Commission. (2003). *Promoting language learning and linguistic diversity: An action plan 2004–2006.* Retrieved December 25, 2007, from http://ec.europa.eu/education/doc/official/keydoc/actlang/act_lang_en.pdf

European Commission. (2006). *Europeans and their languages.* Retrieved December 26, 2007, from http://ec.europa.eu/public_opinion/archives/ebs/ebs_243_sum_en.pdf

Friedman, T. L. (2005). *The world is flat.* New York: Farrar, Straus and Giroux.

Furman, N., Goldberg, D., & Lusin, N. (2007). *Enrollments in languages other than English in United States institutions of higher education* (Fall 2006). Retrieved December 25, 2007, from http://www.mla.org/pdf/enrollmentsurvey_final.pdf

Holmquist, J. (1993). Social and psychological correlates of achievement: Spanish at Temple University. *Modern Language Journal, 77,* 34–44.

National Research Council. (1999). *How students learn: Brain, mind, experience, and school.* Washington DC: National Academy Press.

Roediger, H. L., & Karpicke, J. D. (2006). The power of testing memory: Basic research and implications for educational practice. *Perspectives on Psychological Science, 1,* 181–210.

Stanovich, K. E. (1986). Matthew effects in reading: Some consequences of individual differences in the acquisition of literacy. *Reading Research Quarterly, 21,* 360–406.

United States Census Bureau. (2003). *Language use and English speaking ability: 2000.* Retrieved December 25, 2007, from http://www.census.gov/prod/2003 pubs/c2kbr-29.pdf

Wright, M. (1999). Influences on learner attitudes towards foreign language and culture. *Education Research, 41,* 197–208.

SECTION TWO

FEMINISM AND DIVERSITY EDUCATION

11

TEACHING GENDER DIVERSITY THROUGH DIVERSE LENSES

Janet E. Kuebli, Accalia R. Kusto, and Karen Wilson

S uppose you began class one day by asking students to imagine themselves in the following scenario:

> You live in a society that is deeply and pervasively gender-structured. Males and females have different roles, separate responsibilities, and distinct opportunities and expectations. Differences are the rule for females and males throughout the society's institutions—its schools, churches, government, politics, defense, the arts and entertainment, leisure and recreation, communications, technology, and healthcare—and in private life, including customs and practices associated with personal and family life and interpersonal relationships.

> Now, assume that you are appointed to a special committee charged with designing a new society that is grounded in principles of justice and fairness. Specifically, the committee must restructure the society and eliminate all gender-based inequities. To ensure that the committee has no vested interests in the outcomes of its deliberations, none of its members will know whether in the new society they will be female or male. Therefore, this one "veil of ignorance" means that no one will be able to tailor the principles that the committee develops to his or her personal advantage.

This exercise is called the *Original Position Exercise*. One of us (Kuebli) has used it with undergraduate and graduate students. At this point, the class is divided into small groups with the instruction to brainstorm ideas. Each time, stunned silence ensues as students struggle to shed old habits of mind in order to see the world differently. The exercise requires students to think systematically about the prospects, good and bad, of living in a society as someone of the opposite sex.

Credit for the Original Position Exercise goes to Susan Moller Okin, a political scientist whose feminist critique of modern political theory was detailed in her 1989 book *Justice, Gender, and the Family*. Okin cited philosopher John Rawls's theory of justice as her inspiration; but she took Rawls to task. Although other diversity variables (e.g., social status) were concealed, Rawls had neglected to make the committee members ignorant of their sex in the new society. Fortunately, Rawls's oversight yields a valuable class exercise in perspective-taking, among other critical-thinking skills. In effect, students practice seeing the world through a different lens.

Much scholarship and pedagogy on diversity have relied on the "through the lens" metaphor (Harris, 2000). The lens highlights seeing and thinking about what is familiar to us in fresh and sometimes unanticipated ways.

As this book illustrates, lenses through which to understand diversity have proliferated, expanding beyond the classic variables of race, ethnicity, and gender. Notions of diversity itself have become more diverse, complicated, and sophisticated (deAngelis, 2007). Calls for more internationally oriented lenses are responses to emerging global trends, issues, and tensions.

Helping students exchange well-worn lenses for newer ones has many advantages. Multiplying the lenses through which students engage with the world can help dispel harmful stereotypes, foster attitudes of respect and fairness, and develop critical-thinking skills and cultural competence, as well as promote civic values and social justice. Combining two or more lenses expands students' understanding of diversity within groups. For example, studying diversity through the double lenses of disability and ethnicity or gender and immigration status underscores intragroup variability. Although traditional diversity variables remain core elements of diversity education, new theory and research suggest ways to modify traditional approaches to teaching about race, ethnicity, and gender.

This chapter describes how lenses derived from social, feminist, and developmental psychology can enhance teaching about gender diversity. We recommend using these lenses to gauge student readiness for gender diversity lessons. Student *unreadiness* can impede learning about diversity and acquiring new multicultural competencies. Before teaching diversity lessons, instructors should first strive to understand the presuppositions that students bring into the classroom. Introducing gender diversity concepts, lessons, and activities without first assessing students' readiness is like giving them new glasses without a thorough prior eye examination. Specifically, this chapter discusses several aspects of students' initial ways of thinking that may frame their engagement with social issues of sex, gender, and power. Suggestions for several exercises are also provided.

Using the Lens of Social Psychology

Social psychological research sheds light on students' possible resistance to examining gender diversity and provides useful tips for classes across disciplines. Understanding students' gender-related attitudes can help instructors predict how discussions of diversity might play out in the classroom and to manage the "hot moments" that often arise when we ask students to look at the world through new lenses. Sexist beliefs are among the attitudes that students are likely to bring with them to the classroom. Even students with positive course expectations may have difficulties with discussions of gender diversity. Ambivalent sexism and modern sexism (Swim, Aiken, Hall, & Hunter, 1995) are two well-established social psychological theories that examine sexist beliefs.

Glick and Fiske (1996) proposed two forms of ambivalent sexism. *Hostile sexism* consists of sexist antipathy, negative and resentful feelings about women's abilities and values. *Benevolent sexism*, on the other hand, refers to positive but patronizing attitudes toward women. Glick and Fiske (2001) reported that U.S. participants were lower in hostile and benevolent sexism than individuals in other countries. Nevertheless, men and women both showed moderate levels of hostile and benevolent sexism, with men being slightly higher overall. Awareness of these common belief patterns can inform instructors as they prepare readings, activities, or assignments on gender diversity.

Modern sexist attitudes (Swim, Aiken, Hall, & Hunter, 1995) are characterized by denial of discrimination toward women, antagonism toward women's demands, and a lack of support for policies benefiting women. Individuals scoring low in modern sexism still habitually use sexist language, underscoring how self-reported attitudes may not always be in line with actual behavior. Thus, students may engage in sexist behaviors despite wanting to be fair-minded. This may also explain some students' resistance to reflecting upon their attitudes toward men and women. Indeed, these beliefs are usually apparent in some student reactions to the Original Position Exercise.

Self-report measures alone may not be adequate to assess attitudes and stereotypes because of social desirability concerns. Implicit measures that tap into unconscious processes assess attitudes that individuals may not be willing or able to express. The Implicit Association Test (IAT; IAT corp., 2007) is a common measure of implicit attitudes, assessing how fast associations are made between an attitude object (e.g., a female face/name) and descriptors of the attitude object. The IAT can illustrate one of the assumptions of theories like ambivalent and modern sexism: that sexist attitudes are well learned and automatic. For example, Banaji and Greenwald (1995) found that both men and women were faster to associate fame with male names than with female names. Nosek, Banaji, and Greenwald (2002) found that people were more likely to associate math with being male than with being female. Additionally, women who had stronger associations of math with being male were less likely to associate themselves with math. A more recent study (Kiefer and Sekaquaptewa, 2007) demonstrated that implicit math stereotyping and gender identification predicted performance in college math courses. Women with high gender identification and high implicit stereotyping performed worse on a final exam and were less inclined to pursue math-based careers than women low on gender identification and implicit stereotyping. These findings suggest that it is likely that some students (and teachers), despite professing positive explicit attitudes, will have implicit stereotypes that underlie either receptivity or resistance to learning about gender diversity.

Instructors in any discipline can directly use the social psychological literature to help students understand their own gender-related attitudes, as well as the attitudes of their peers. Classes can discuss studies such as those already mentioned as examples of research on sexist attitudes. Teachers can also create assignments in which students take the IAT, available freely on the Internet, and discuss their reactions to the test. For example, based on the results of fame judgments by Banaji and Greenwald (1995), students could write down all the names they associate with famous people and examine the proportion of male versus female names mentioned. When one of us

(Wilson) did this in a general psychology class, more male than female names were listed. Students can also complete measures such as the Ambivalent Sexism Inventory and Modern Sexism Scale (Glick & Fiske, 1996; Swim et al., 1995) and then analyze their attitudes and explore where these attitudes may have originated. Such activities not only help students understand their own attitudes but also help the instructor understand the students.

Using a Feminist Lens

It is common for students to hold essentialist views of gender, namely, that members of a group must possess certain properties associated with that group in order to belong to the group. Women and men, therefore, are simply the composite of the characteristics associated with their respective sex. In this framework, gender differences become fixed individual traits that do not change over time. The focus is on objectively discovering those differences.

The essentialist perspective on gender is reinforced by many college textbooks. A decade ago, Hurd and Brabeck (1997) examined discussions of gender in textbooks dealing with human development, adolescent psychology, and psychology of women. They compared textbooks written before and after Carol Gilligan's 1982 work *In a Different Voice*, which challenged the androcentricism of psychological theories of development by analyzing and illuminating women's voices and experiences. From 1970 through 1990, discussions of gender increased over time; yet Hurd and Brabeck further found that the presentation of the construct remained in simple terms. Disappointingly, current textbook discussions of most forms of diversity remain inadequate (Smith, 2001; Tomes, 2005).

Hurd and Brabeck recommended an alternative way of conceptualizing gender: "To present the most accurate view of women, we suggest that those using college textbooks adopt an explicitly feminist lens" (1997, p. 164). Feminism refers both to a theoretical position and a form of political activity (Zalta et al., 2004). Feminism generally holds that injustices against women exist and that a moral standard regarding appropriate treatment of women is desirable and attainable (Zalta et al., 2004). Feminist organization and political activism strive to enact social change in political and economic realms and those addressed in the Original Position Exercise that will rectify the perceived injustices. According to Hurd and Brabeck, a feminist perspective also supports more in-depth and complex understandings of gender because its scholarship strives for more accurate portrayals of the differences *and* similarities between men and women. Among the more general and lasting principles to emerge from feminist-inspired research is that variability in behavior is often greater within each sex than between women and men (e.g., Maccoby, 1998).

Social constructionism is a complex theoretical account of gender that uses a feminist lens. Social constructs like gender are regarded as developing through people's participation in behaviors that are based on their interpretations of reality, which become traditions and artifacts of cultures and societies. Rather than social constructs being a product of naturally occurring categories, as in essentialism, constructs such as gender are viewed as dynamic products of social interaction with particular meanings in certain social contexts. When this lens is applied, gender comes to be viewed as what we do rather than who we are.

Introducing students first to social constructivist thinking about gender can help prepare them to learn more from exercises such as the Original Position Exercise. Students' understanding of social constructionism and its implications can be strengthened with in-class activities, such as the *Who am I?* exercise. Students begin by listing 10 qualities in response to the question "Who am I?" (Moradi & Yoder, 2001). The instructor reads students' lists aloud. The class then guesses the gender of the respondent upon hearing each description. Students' high success rate (typically better than chance) can be used to discuss what it means to "do gender" and how that is reflected in our self-descriptions. The *Who am I?* exercise also illustrates the contrast with essentialist views on gender. The fluidity of gender boundaries and variance within and between men and women is demonstrated in the variety of ways students describe themselves.

The distribution of power among men and women is another feminist example of "doing gender." Activities like the Original Position Exercise permit students to think about how "doing gender" is affected by the way power is assigned to various social roles (Collins, 2000). Another exercise starts with students rating men and women on a list of characteristics that are associated with people in dominant and subordinate roles (e.g., physically abled versus disabled individuals, or adults versus children). The class then watches the video *Quiet Rage*, which depicts the Stanford Prison Experiment (Haney, Banks, & Zimbardo, 1973). In this classic psychological study, a mock prison was set up and undergraduate volunteers were randomly assigned to guard or prisoner roles. As the participants conformed to their roles, their behavior quickly became potentially physically and psychologically dangerous, with guards ensuring humiliation and degradation of prisoners and prisoners displaying learned helplessness in the face of this treatment. After watching actual footage of this behavior, students rate the guards and prisoners using the same list of characteristics. Students' ratings for men and guards are usually similar, as they are for women and prisoners. The activity shows students that men who are placed in a position of subordination will display behaviors typically associated with what women "do" (e.g., show passivity, act emotionally). Instructors can facilitate discussion concerning how situations containing power differentials between groups or individuals generally affect behavior. The relationship of power to social roles, and specifically gender roles, can also be emphasized. For example, traits usually associated with masculinity (e.g., ambition) are typically those behaviors valued by our society (over feminine ones such as nurturing). This activity can be further extended in ways that support students' reflections on their own values and attitudes. Thus, discussion could address the assignment of blame and responsibility in situations where power is abused, specifically those relevant to gender roles (e.g., domestic violence) (Collins, 2000).

Using a Developmental Lens

Both social psychological and feminist perspectives offer students alternative means of perspective-taking, a key to critical thinking. In addition to fostering appreciation for competing viewpoints, teaching about gender diversity builds other critical-thinking skills. For example, attention drawn to diverse perspectives often heightens students' awareness of their own preconceptions, assumptions, and values, thereby fostering development of metacognitive abilities. Additionally, instructors should urge students to examine and evaluate the sources of their own and others' beliefs about men and women. Students can practice detecting critical-thinking errors and logical fallacies in everyday conceptions of women's and men's behaviors. A simple example is the fundamental attribution error. Students may more readily attribute gender differences in salaries to dispositional factors, such as women's indifference to money or men's competitiveness, and neglect situational explanations. Guiding students to consider rival causes in the social environment (e.g., business practices) may help them to recognize this common critical-thinking error. Instructors should also teach students to use evidence to test or support claims about gender differences. For example, students might consider the results of a recent study (Mehl, Vazire, Ramirez-Esparza, Slatcher, & Pennebaker, 2007) that challenge the everyday notion that women talk more than men. Despite large individual differences, this study showed that average daily use was around 16,000 words for both women and men who attended college. In general, diversity exercises lend themselves to development of higher-order thinking skills when teachers give students opportunities to reflect upon, analyze, and evaluate their own and others' thinking.

However, a word of caution is in order. Classroom experience indicates that critical thinking does not come easily to many people. Instructors need to also consider students' developing capacities for critical thinking and reflective thought about diversity. Evidence suggests that critical thinking develops in a stage-like manner. Several models and theories describing progressive changes in college-aged students' thinking provide insight into students' readiness for diversity exercises. The classic perspective on knowledge and epistemological development is Perry's (1999) description of four periods in college students' thinking. Chickering (1993) and Baxter-Magolda (1992) provide different but related insights. Perhaps best known and most empirically tested is King and Kitchener's (1994, 2004) model of cognitive development during late adolescence and early adulthood.

All of these writers posit similar developmental shifts in students' thinking. King and Kitchener describe early thinking as *prereflective*. During this stage, resistance to multiple perspectives stems from absolutist assumptions about "Truth" as singular and about perspectives as either right or wrong. Students rely on authorities to deliver knowable facts and neglect to test assumptions or justify claims in light of evidence. Prereflective thinking often gives way to *quasi-reflective* reasoning. Students begin to acknowledge uncertainty about what is known or knowable and to accept multiple viewpoints. However, evidence-based evaluation is still underdeveloped, so students regard diverse perspectives as "mere" opinions that are all equally valid. The quasi-reflective thinker may not see any value in understanding the world through different lenses, since one is as good as another. Some students will in time progress to *reflective* thought stages. Higher-order critical thinking becomes apparent in these students' ability to manage uncertainty and complexity when encountering a novel view of life through a different lens and to use criteria more systematically when evaluating claims pertaining to others' experiences. The reflective student also takes into account the extent to which knowledge is actively constructed, based on context, and subject to interpretation.

The main point for instructors is to strive to determine in advance the critical-thinking skills and reflective judgment that students possess. This assessment of students' readiness can then inform lectures, reading selections, and the design of exercises and assignments. Instructors can then better coordinate the levels of thinking emphasized in their teaching with the thinking skills they wish students to develop. In conclusion, more attention to the development of students' thinking and a better understanding of the gender-related attitudes and assumptions students already hold will enhance students' learning about gender diversity.

References

Banaji, M. R., & Greenwald, A. G. (1995). Implicit gender stereotyping in judgments of fame. *Journal of Personality and Social Psychology, 68,* 181–198.

Baxter-Magolda, M. B. (1992). Students' epistemologies and academic experiences: Implications for pedagogy. *Review of Higher Education, 15*(3), 265–287.

Chickering, A. W. (1993). *Education and identity* (2nd ed.). San Francisco: Jossey-Bass.

Collins, L. H. (2000). Creating gender role behavior: Demonstrating the impact of power differentials. *Teaching of Psychology, 27,* 37–40.

deAngelis, T. (2007). An expanding notion of diversity. *GradPSYCH, 5*(2), Retrieved June 21, 2007, from http://gradpsych.apags.org/mar07/cover-notion.html

Gilligan, C. (1982). *In a different voice: Psychological theory and women's development.* Cambridge: Harvard University Press.

Glick, P., & Fiske, S. T. (1996). The Ambivalent Sexism Inventory: Differentiating hostile and benevolent sexism. *Journal of Personality and Social Psychology, 70,* 491–512.

Glick, P., & Fiske, S. T. (2001). Ambivalent sexism. In M. P. Zanna (Ed.), *Advances in experimental social psychology* (Vol. 33, pp. 115–188). New York: Academic Press.

Haney, C., Banks, C., & Zimbardo, P. (1973). Interpersonal dynamics in a simulated prison. *International Journal of Criminology and Penology, 1,* 69–97.

Harris, N. (2000). Practice through a lens: A metaphor for planning theory. *Journal of Planning Education and Research, 19,* 309–315.

Hurd, T. L., & Brabeck, M. (1997). Presentation of women and Gilligan's ethic of care in college textbooks, 1970–1990: An examination of bias. *Teaching of Psychology, 24,* 159–167.

IAT corp. (2007). Project Implicit. Retrieved July 22, 2007, from https://implicit.harvard.edu/implicit/

Kiefer, A. K., & Sekaquaptewa, D. (2007). Implicit stereotypes, gender identification, and math-related outcomes: A prospective study of female college students. *Psychological Science, 18*(1), 13–18.

King, P. M., & Kitchener, K. S. (1994). *Developing reflective judgment: Understanding and promoting intellectual growth and critical thinking in adolescents and adults.* San Francisco: Jossey-Bass.

King, P. M., & Kitchener, K. S. (2004). Reflective judgment: Theory and research on the development of epistemic assumptions through adulthood. *Educational Psychologist, 39*(1), 5–18.

Maccoby, E. E. (1998). *The two sexes: Growing apart, coming together.* Cambridge: Belknap Press/Harvard University Press.

Mehl, M. R., Vazire, S., Ramirez-Esparza, N., Slatcher, R. B., & Pennebaker, J. W. (2007). Are women really more talkative than men? [Electronic version]. *Science, 317*(5834), 82.

Moradi, B., & Yoder, J. D. (2001). Demonstrating social constructionism in psychology courses: The "Who am I" exercise. *Teaching of Psychology, 28,* 201–203.

Nosek, B. A, Banaji, M. R., & Greenwald, A. G. (2002). Math = male, me = female, therefore, math ≠ me. *Journal of Personality and Social Psychology, 83,* 44–59.

Okin, S. M. (1989). *Justice, gender and the family.* New York: Basic Books.

Perry, W. (1999). *Forms of intellectual and ethical development in the college years: A scheme.* San Francisco: Jossey-Bass.

Smith, D. (2001). A primer on diversity. *Monitor on Psychology, 32*(10). Retrieved June 21, 2007, from http://www.apa.org/monitor/nov01/primer.html

Swim, J. K., Aiken, K. J., Hall, W. S., & Hunter, B. A. (1995). Sexism and racism: Old-fashioned and modern prejudices. *Journal of Personality and Social Psychology, 68,* 199–214.

Tomes, H. (2005). Diversity's unmet needs. [Electronic version]. *Monitor on Psychology, 36*(8), 37.

Zalta, E. N., et al. (Eds.). (2004, March 15). Topics in feminism. In *Stanford encyclopedia of philosophy.* Retrieved May 15, 2007, from http://plato.stanford.edu/entries/feminism-topics/

12

PEDAGOGICAL INTERSECTIONS OF GENDER, RACE, AND IDENTITY

Signs of a Feminist Teacher

Karlyn Crowley

"I hate the circle," Kate said.[1] "What?" I asked incredulously. "I hate the circle," she repeated. "None of my other classes meet in a circle and I want to look at you—the professor—not my other classmates. I want to talk to you," she finished pleadingly. My Introduction to Women's and Gender Studies class was, of course, sitting in a circle rather than in lecture-style arrangement with desks in a row and the teacher behind a podium. Her bold statement of disinterest in her classmates made me realize two things: one, how much I have normalized basic feminist pedagogical principles that not too long ago were seen as radical changes to the classroom; and two, how powerful those principles still are. The simple act of sitting in a circle upends conventions about the professor being the locus and dispenser of knowledge, the students passive recipients. No wonder Kate hated the circle: its democratic, participatory approach to knowledge demanded that she play a more active role in her education, something that some students can at first find frightening (or a tiresome interruption to their text messaging), but which they later usually embrace.

Like other successes of feminism, much in feminist pedagogy has now become widespread. Many teachers have their classes sit in circles, and I doubt they all realize that they are implementing a basic feminist pedagogical tool.

---

[1]Student name changed for issues of privacy.

Indeed, part of my impetus for this essay is to celebrate the feminist roots of a pedagogical approach that has transformed the academy enough that in some circles (pun intended), this kind of teaching is seen, remarks Caryn McTighe Musil, as "simply good teaching" (2004/2005, par. 1). Furthermore, I want to identify succinctly the core tenets of feminist pedagogy and offer concrete suggestions for implementing them to become a more effective teacher. The tools of a feminist teacher are not gender-specific; rather, they are a set of beliefs and practices, informed by a gendered awareness of power, that anyone can enact.[2] While putting a class in a circle is not proprietary to feminist teachers, having students sit in a circle reveals several key components of feminist approaches to teaching and knowledge, especially as these reflect power and privilege.

Feminist approaches to authority tend to challenge assumptions that more traditional classrooms are based on, such as the following:

- Professors have all the knowledge.
- Knowledge is best conveyed as either a one- or two-way exchange.
- Student peers have nothing to contribute to knowledge production.
- Community building in a classroom does not contribute to knowledge building.

This list corresponds to Paulo Freire's famous description of "banking education": the paradigm of education in which the teacher teaches and the students are taught; the teacher knows everything and the students know nothing; and the teacher chooses the program content and the students (who were not consulted) adapt to it (2000, p. 73). As Peter McLaren says, this kind of normative pedagogy "mirrors oppressive society as a whole" because it maintains and perpetuates the power relations of those in control (teachers) and those who are docile (students) (2003, p. 86). McLaren concludes that such pedagogical practices "prepare students for dominant or subordinate positions in the existing society" (2003, p. 86). In contrast to these approaches, McTighe Musil explains that feminist pedagogy believes in "cultivating student voice and empowerment, endorsing students as creators and not merely receivers of knowledge, de-centering the classroom to promote more active and collaborative learning, engaging in dialogue across differences, and applying knowledge to address real world issues" (2004/2005, par. 1). While feminist pedagogy is not often given the appropriate

[2]See Schacht, S. (2000). Using a feminist pedagogy as a male teacher: The possibilities of a partial and situated perspective. *Radical Pedagogy, 2*(2). Retrieved May 1, 2008, from http://radicalpedagogy.icaap.org/content/issue2_2/schacht.html

credit for this shift in thinking about teaching, it nonetheless appears under different names that signal teaching excellence, such as "active learning," "collaborative learning," and "civic engagement." I argue further that by learning how to describe feminist pedagogical practices, teachers will not only make their purpose clearer, but will also make their classroom more powerful.

Signs of a Feminist Teacher

(1) Feminist Teachers Are Self-Reflective and Attempt to Make Teaching Transparent

Feminist teachers let students peak behind the *Wizard of Oz* curtain and help them understand how the university institution works and how teachers work within it. By reflecting on power, by highlighting how classrooms "work," and by showing how the process of learning is as important as the content, feminist teachers make students aware that *what* they are learning and *how* they are learning are not transhistorical or without ideological biases. How is that done? Teachers carefully and self-consciously break the frame of the classroom and ask the class to be self-critical—to think about itself as a group and to think about themselves as learners. They ask basic questions like "How are we communicating?" "How are we pushing ourselves?" In turn, they self-reflect: "How am I taking risks in the classroom?" "Am I willing to examine difficult topics?" They highlight the construction of the classroom to critique the process of learning generally and reveal the rules and history of higher education learning. For example, I typically assign readings that ask students to reflect on (a) their role as students, (b) the goals and purpose of education, and (c) the historical context of their education. Students read Adrienne Rich's "Claiming an Education," the canonical essay on women and education, which challenges students to move from a passive to an active stance as thinkers (1979, p. 234). Combined, these teaching strategies move students away from seeing learning as a prepackaged commodity that they pick up at the university store, to participating in the construction of knowledge.

(2) Feminist Teachers Appreciate and Encourage Student Voice in Order to Foster a More Inclusive, Less Hierarchical Learning Community

In the 1960s, when women's studies professors first began incorporating student voice and experience in the classroom, it was a revolutionary idea. To even imagine that student experience might count as legitimate knowledge meant breaking with ancient university models. Today, while many teachers try to incorporate student voice, it often remains peripheral rather than integral to class planning. By envisioning student voice on a continuum, teachers might understand how it is not simply a matter of students either speaking up or not speaking up, but how much student voice can be nurtured:

Silent	Speaks Occasionally	Speaks Often	Speaks With Leadership	Speaks as Scholar	Speaks as Equal	Speaks as Innovator

Teachers must do more than just encourage discussion; they must allow students to produce new knowledge by fundamentally shaping the discussion.

Studies indicate that students move most quickly from receptacles of knowledge to producers of knowledge when you teach the skill of how to ask a good question. In *What the Best College Teachers Do*, Ken Bain says that "people learn best when they ask an important question that they care about answering" (2004, p. 31). When students are forced to ask good questions because the class requires it and their grade is enhanced by it, they also slowly start to develop argumentative and critical skills.

Consider focusing on this skill in these ways:

- Examine a short passage from a text. Challenge students to ask only questions about the passage—again, real questions to which they do not know the answers. While students are uncomfortable at first, they soon feel liberated by not having to know any answers and start asking great questions.
- Use a class e-mail list as a way for them to post their questions about texts to the entire class, thereby starting a conversation before the next class period. Encourage students to build their essays from their e-mail questions.

As students realize that the "answers" to questions are not locked in a secret vault where the teacher has the key, the classroom develops the climate of asking and responding to questions that really matter. Students realize that good questions spark never-ending conversations.

(3) Feminist Teachers Take Gender Seriously as a Category, in Both Content and Process

Carolyn Shrewsbury suggests that "at its simplest level, feminist pedagogy is concerned with gender justice and overcoming oppressions" (1993, p. 9). One challenge is producing inclusive curricula, which means including texts that privilege women's voices. While such curricular reform is fairly straightforward, a teacher's awareness of gender as part of the process—that is, being aware of how women act and are treated differently in classrooms—is more subtle. I find Bernice Sandler's classic work on the "chilly classroom climate for women" essential reading for getting gender dynamics and oppression in the classroom out on the table.[3] Sandler lists the ways that women and men may be treated differently in the classroom, from who speaks to who perpetuates gender bias by affirming the validity of certain ideas and dismissing others (Sandler, Silverberg, & Hall, 1996, p. 21).

Since the advent of the field of Women's and Gender Studies 40 years ago, scholars have pinpointed very specific ways that women suffer in educational settings, even as record numbers of female students enroll in higher education. In 1977, Adrienne Rich made the case that women usually do not take themselves seriously as scholars because there are virtually no intellectual role models, and that gender socialization insists that "women should be nice, play safe, have low professional expectations, drown in love and forget about work, live through others, and stay in the places assigned to us" (1979, p. 234). In 2003, Anna Quindlen still observed this phenomenon when commenting on how female undergraduates responded to a Duke University survey: "They're expected 'to hide their intelligence in order to succeed with their male peers.' 'Being "cute" trumps being smart for women in the social environment,' the report concludes. That's not postfeminist. That's prefeminist" (2003, par. 2–4).[4] Because discrimination may often be covert and is frequently internalized, teachers need to realize how crucial it is to highlight these discrepancies for students.

---

[3]See also http://www.bernicesandler.com/
[4]See Sax, Linda J. (2007). College women still face many obstacles in reaching their full potential. *The Chronicle of Higher Education, 54*(5), B46; Duke University Women's Initiative Study: http://www.duke.edu/womens_initiative/report_report.html

(4) Feminist Teachers Know That Creating Community Helps to Increase Students' Ability to Learn

As one of my own professors once said, "The classroom should be the safest place because it is the riskiest place." In other words, the classroom must be a safe place because expressing ideas is a risky business, especially for women. To create this "safe place," I have students in a class discuss expectations for supporting and challenging one another in civil debate. I often ask them to think of a recent great conversation, a vigorous debate, or a classroom discussion that really worked, and to share the qualities that made those experiences successful. Once students have completed this task, the class creates guidelines for the semester, with both expectations of one another and of the professor. During this discussion, teachers must help students flesh out vague statements like "we need to listen well" and insist that they speak concretely about what that might look like. When students feel safe and respected, they tend to understand and retain content material more effectively. Because of the sensitive subject matter of teaching diversity, it is imperative that the classroom be as safe as possible. Therefore, I often use subject-relevant "icebreakers," not only as a way to warm up the class, but also to continue helping students build connections for better learning.

(5) Feminist Teachers Believe That Knowledge Is Not Value-Neutral but Exists in Time and Space

While debates about the objective nature of knowledge will continue, scholars now rarely claim that they teach from a purely objective stance. Still, universities have been founded for thousands of years on the notion that objectivism and rationality are signs of authentic knowing. But who is served by these illusions of objectivity? As Julie Brown argues about the feminist critique of so-called value-neutral higher education, "feminists would argue that, historically, placing the emphasis on quality (whose definition?) and progress (toward what ideal?) has only served to marginalize certain groups of students, namely women and minorities" (1992, p. 53). In turn, Johnnetta Cole suggests that in contrast to the claim that "liberal arts education is an objective, value-free exploration of the range of human history, activity, knowledge, and creativity . . . the reality is that this education is based on a Eurocentric perspective of the world, reflecting a racial, gender, and class bias" (2004, p. 23). Cole suggests "five challenges" to higher education that defend the place of Black Studies in the liberal arts curriculum: "Black Studies challenges what is taught in the liberal arts curricula of America's colleges and universities; to whom and by whom it is taught; how it is taught; and why it is taught" (2004, p. 23). Teachers should highlight the conditions of the modern college or university, the state of the field of their discipline, the makeup and challenge of a particular classroom, and the impetus behind privileging the construction of knowledge in the first place. It is a big task but an essential one.

(6) Feminist Teachers Use Practices That Level Power Imbalances Rather than Accentuate Them

Teachers need to recognize that they have power as professors, and while accepting that power, they must neither abuse it nor try to increase it. This means relinquishing traditional forms of patriarchal power, a practice that is at times difficult for both professor and student (e.g., Kate's discomfort with the circle). In an attempt to reduce power imbalances, McTighe Musil explains how "typically, feminist teachers redesigned seating arrangements, lectured less, had students participate more, devised tools for ensuring all students spoke, used journals and group projects, validated experiential knowledge, engaged students in addressing pressing problems, and created assignments that required students to act" (2004/2005, par. 5). bell hooks suggests that "one simple way to alter the way one's 'power' as teacher is experienced in the classroom is to elect not to assume the posture of all-knowing professors" (1989, p. 52).

However, when female professors, in particular, begin to decentralize power, they may face a cost: subtle disrespect. It is essential to frame feminist pedagogical techniques to let students know that teachers are sharing power, not abnegating it. For instance, I sometimes make the following statements in class: "Studies indicate that active learning and engaged pedagogy produce the best results. Thus you will not find me at the podium, but in the circle beside you." Lynne Webb, Myria Allen, and Kandi Walker note how feminist pedagogy "offers both the professor and students new relational roles" (2002, p. 68), and, like any new role, it can be frightening, empowering, baffling, or infuriating to occupy; more often than not it is all of the above.

(7) Feminist Teachers Encourage Both
Personal and Cultural Transformation

We all know that education is transformational. Feminist pedagogy, however, has often taken such transformation a step further to say that learning should be revolutionary. The personal becomes political. Classroom revolution occurs when students see themselves as creators of knowledge who grasp how that knowledge is essential to their life outside the classroom. As Marilyn Jacoby Boxer notes about the history of feminist pedagogy, "The women's studies students who speak out clearly express this sense of seeking to integrate their intellectual understanding into their personal lives" (1998, p. 89). Lee Anne Bell, Sharon Washington, Gerald Weinstein, and Barbara Love suggest that professors should further this integration process by "sharing our own struggles" to give "permission for our students to engage in the difficult process of doing so themselves" (2003, p. 474).

In my class, we read Jennifer Baumgardner and Amy Richard's classic piece "A Day Without Feminism," which briefly describes what a day might look like if we turned back the clock.[5] Students recognize the personal and political implications of what they are undertaking. Some critics might argue that feminist pedagogy can veer in the direction of indoctrination, but I think it is important to remember that feminist pedagogy does not lecture about how things should be, but rather encourages students to ask questions about how they are, why they are, and whose advantage they serve. The more students see the relevance of their learning to themselves and the world around them, the greater responsibility they take for their own learning goals. I encourage students to make learning their own by creating contexts in which the learning *really matters*. In my experience, I have found that giving students real occasions for writing—a letter, something to be published, an important document for a needy organization—prompts them to write powerfully for real goals.

---

[5]See Baumgardner, J., & Richards, A. (2000). *Manifesta: Young Women, Feminism, and the Future.* New York: Farrar, Straus and Giroux.

(8) Feminist Teachers Are Aware of Multiple Intersecting Identities, Oppressions, and Realities as They Appear Both in the Classroom and in Their Material

One of the most profound challenges of feminist pedagogy is to be attuned to how intersecting theories of power, privilege, and oppression play out practically and theoretically in the classroom. For example, in one of the initial conversations my Women's and Gender Studies class had about lesbian, gay, bisexual, and transgender (LGBT) issues, many women in the class discussed how much they loved their "gay male best friends." After class, another student said to me, "I felt like they were talking about their dogs or dollies." In other words, students were unknowingly fetishizing their gay male friends. What to do? If I discussed this issue, especially at the beginning of the semester when I barely knew the students, they might hear it as a finger-wagging punishment. If I did not discuss it, I risked alienating any LGBT students in the classroom who may not have felt comfortable speaking up. This conundrum—how to negotiate difference—is a daily experience in most Women's and Gender Studies classes. Gail Cohee argues that feminist pedagogy is "more complex than the idea that teachers and students simply share power or that arranging chairs in a circle makes a classroom feminist. How a classroom is arranged physically might—or might not—matter but who is or is not in the classroom, who is spoken or listened to, who is spoken about, do matter" (2004, par. 6). Even though new theories have challenged "identity politics," suggesting that our identities are not the only determinant of who speaks or understands certain experiences, identities still clearly matter.

---

[6]See Crabtree, R., & Sapp, D. (2003). Theoretical, political, and pedagogical challenges in the feminist classroom: our struggles to walk the walk. *College Teaching, 51*, 131–140.

[7]To testify to how deeply ingrained the "professor archetype" is culturally, here are just a few of the hundreds of cinematic representations: *Goodbye Mr. Chips* (1939), *Ball of Fire* (1941), *The Absent-Minded Professor* (1961), *My Fair Lady* (1964), *Who's Afraid of Virginia Woolf* (1966) *Educating Rita* (1983), *Dead Poets Society* (1989), *School Ties* (1992), *Oleanna* (1994), *Good Will Hunting* (1997), *Wonder Boys* (2000), *Finding Forrester* (2000), *A Beautiful Mind* (2001), *The Emperor's Club* (2002), *Stranger Than Fiction* (2006), and *The History Boys* (2006).

[8]See Anderson, K., & Miller, E. (1997, June). Gender and student evaluation of teaching. *Political Science and Politics, 30*(2), 216–219. They claim that "several studies found that if a professor displays a mix of feminine and masculine characteristics, student evaluations will be higher than for those who only show one or the other" (p. 218).

Conclusion

While my hope in this essay is to provide strategies for incorporating feminist pedagogy, I am also acutely aware that feminist pedagogy is far from a utopian practice.[6] Students often expect professors to be White male, tweed-wearing, all-knowing, lecture-giving Mr. Chips sorts.[7] Deviations from this authoritative White ideal may be seen as "less than" professorial. JoAnn Miller and Marilyn Chamberlin claim that "if a woman at a research university uses a teaching strategy that reminds third and fourth year university students of their high school learning experiences, it is possible that students will misperceive the 'professor' to be a 'teacher'" (2000, p. 295). Laura I. Langbein suggests that "female faculty are rewarded relative to men, for supportive, nurturing behavior, but they are punished relative to men, for objective, authoritarian behavior that is role inconsistent" (1994, p. 551). This impossible dilemma of having to occupy two gender roles simultaneously and perfectly is characterized as "the double bind."[8] Roxanna Harlow notes how race further complicates this "double bind" for female African American professors who "do not fulfill the 'motherly' expectation" but have a "businesslike approach": students are likely to interpret them as Black women who "are angry and have an attitude" (2003, p. 357).

When students resist those who do not abide by the professor archetype, they may participate in "contrapower harassment," which is defined by Katherine Benson as "the harassment of those with more organizational power by those with less" (Buchanan & Bruce 2004/2005, par. 6). In other words, "while a female professor may have more formal power than a male student, because society still conveys more power and authority to men, the male student has more informal power due to his gender" (Buchanan & Bruce, 2004/2005, par. 6). Contrapower harassment may play out through "suggestive looks, body language, physical harassment, or verbal remarks directed towards a professor by a student" (Buchanan & Bruce, 2004/2005, par. 8). My own experience of contrapower harassment ranges from mild boundary crossing to hostile physical intimidation and has made me acutely aware of the dance that must be done to share my power without seeming to give it all away—a dance that many male professors rarely need worry about. Susan Basow notes in a helpful list how concerns of dress, credentialing, teaching style, and availability all determine one's teaching evaluations and must be handled with political savvy as well as integrity (1998, p. 151).

Coda: Returning to the Circle with Deeper Meaning

I first encountered classrooms in a circle at my alma mater, Earlham College, a Quaker college where most classes were conducted in a circle to reflect the Quaker belief that all are equal and have equal access to the Inner Light. At the time, I did not understand the spiritual, pedagogical, and political significance of being in a circle, but I did sense that the community recognized me and gave me full participation in that place. This is our job as feminist teachers—to allow our students full participation through our daily classroom practice. Our job is to make it possible for feminist pedagogy and "simply good teaching" to be both synonymous and yet different: one implies change, while the other focuses on a noble project, but not necessarily a revolutionary one. Just as "academic feminism in any national scene can never stand as a whole," as Robyn Wiegman has noted, feminist pedagogy is not singular, but multiple and growing (2005, p. 56). Still, there are ongoing feminist pedagogical themes that I have tried to name and explain here. To create a richer classroom experience, we must, as Joni Mitchell claims, not only "look behind from where we came" and "go round in the circle game," but also expand circles of democracy, justice, and academic excellence through feminist pedagogy.

References

Bain, K. (2004). *What the best college teachers do*. Cambridge: Harvard University Press.

Basow, S. (1998). Student evaluations: The role of gender bias and teaching styles. In L. Collins, J. Chrisler, & K. Quina (Eds.), *Arming Athena: Career strategies for women in academe* (pp. 135–156). London: Sage.

Bell, L., Washington, S., Weinstein, G., & Love, B. (2003). Knowing ourselves as instructors. In A. Darder, M. Baltodano, & R. D. Torres (Eds.), *The critical pedagogy reader* (pp. 464–478). New York: Routledge.

Brown, J. (1992). What exactly is feminist pedagogy? *Journal of General Education, 41*, 51–63.

Boxer, M. J. (1998). *When women ask the questions: Creating women's studies in America*. Baltimore: Johns Hopkins University Press.

Buchanan, N., & Bruce, T. (Fall 2004/Winter 2005). Contrapower harassment and the professorial archetype: Gender, race, and authority in the classroom. *On Campus With Women, 34*(1–2). Retrieved May 1, 2008, from: http://www.aacu.org/ocww/volume34_1/feature.cfm?section=2

Cohee, G. (2004). Feminist pedagogy. *The teaching exchange.* September. Retrieved May 1, 2008, from Brown University: http://www.brown.edu/Administration/ Sheridan_Center/pubs/teachingExchange/sept2004/02_cohee_feminist.shtml

Cole, J. (2004). Black studies in liberal arts education. In B. Jacqueline, C. Hudley, & C. Michel (Eds.), *The black studies reader.* New York: Routledge.

Freire, P. (2000). *Pedagogy of the oppressed.* New York: Continuum.

Harlow, R. (2003). Race doesn't matter, but . . . : The effect of race on professors' experiences and emotion management in the undergraduate college classroom. *Social Psychology Quarterly, 66*(4), 348–363.

hooks, b. (1989). Toward a revolutionary feminist pedagogy. In *Talking back: Thinking feminist, thinking black.* Boston: South End Press.

Langbein, L. I. (1994). The validity of student evaluations of teaching. *PS Political Science and Politics, 27*(3), 545–553.

McLaren, P. (2003). Critical pedagogy: A look at the major concepts. In A. Darder, M. Baltodano, & R. D. Torres (Eds.), *The critical pedagogy reader* (pp. 151–184). New York: Routledge.

McTighe Musil, C. (2004 Fall/2005 Winter). Feminist pedagogy: Setting the standard for engaged learning. *On Campus With Women, 34* (1–2). Retrieved May 1, 2008, from the Association of American Colleges & Universities: http://www.aacu.org/ocww/volume34_1/director.cfm

Miller, J., & Chamberlin, M. (2000, October). Women are teachers, men are professors: A study of student perceptions. *Teaching Sociology, 28*(4), 283–298.

Quindlen, A. (2003, October 12). Still needing the F word. *Newsweek.* Retrieved May 1, 2008, from http://www.newsweek.com/id/61881

Rich, A. (1979). *On lies, secrets, and silence: Selected prose 1966–1978.* New York: W.W. Norton.

Sandler, B., Silverberg, L., & Hall, R. (1996). *The chilly classroom climate: A guide to improve the education of women.* Washington, DC: National Association for Women in Education.

Shrewsbury, C. (1993). What is feminist pedagogy? *Women's Studies Quarterly, 20,* 8–15.

Webb, L., Allen M., & Walker, K. (2002, March). Feminist pedagogy: Identifying basic principles. *Academic Exchange Quarterly, 6*(1), 67–72.

Wiegman, R. (2005). The possibility of women's studies. In E. Kennedy & A. Beins (Eds.), *Women's studies for the future: Foundations, interrogations, politics* (pp. 40–60). Rutgers University Press.

SECTION THREE

THE INCLUSIVE CLASSROOM

13

DEVELOPING DEMOCRACY

Encouraging Multiple Viewpoints and Community in Classrooms

Kathie E. Shiba

Responsible citizenship in a democratic society involves the ability to listen and communicate with individuals whose viewpoints are diverse (e.g., Cohen, 1999; Dewey, 1997; Harwood & Hahn, 1990; Nelson Laird, Engberg, & Hurtado, 2005; Umbach & Kuh, 2006). Institutions of higher education, especially those that focus on the liberal arts, strive to develop critical thinkers who are willing to examine issues from multiple perspectives and disciplines. As an educator, I challenge myself to facilitate and model for students the skills needed to listen, critically analyze, and discuss a variety of ideas, especially those that may be very different from their own.

Incorporation of diverse perspectives and open discussions can bring about a variety of responses in students, including anger, resentment, detachment, anxiety, curiosity, excitement, and epiphany (Torres, Howard-Hamilton, & Cooper, 2003). If negative responses are not handled appropriately, they can lead to a classroom climate that is not conducive to learning and is detrimental to relationships. When this happens, instructors may avoid topics that they know will cause such reactions, may lose focus and become emotionally aroused or emotionally drained, may dread teaching a class, or may even lose confidence in themselves (Harwood & Hahn, 1990; Palmer, 1998).

In my experience, it is worth taking the time to develop a classroom climate that promotes a sense of community. In a trusting environment, students are willing to listen respectfully to others, to participate in discussions more frequently, to examine issues more critically, to feel committed to the class, and to report feeling connected to others (e.g., Umbach & Kuh, 2006). Empirical studies have found that students of all ages value classrooms that encourage trust and community building. For example, Rogers and Freiberg (1994) interviewed hundreds of elementary, middle, and high school students across the United States and found a common thread regarding what students wanted. They wanted classrooms that encouraged caring, community building, trust, and respect. Rogers and Freiberg concluded from their literature review of research that healthy learning environments have a positive effect on learning. A decade later, Buskist and Saville (2001) interviewed students at Auburn University in the United States who were enrolled in undergraduate introductory psychology courses. They found that students reported increased motivation to attend, participate, and pay attention in class, as well as increased enjoyment in classes where teachers created rapport in their classrooms. The research gathered from students' experiences supports the conclusion that developing a sense of community is worth the time and effort and is a necessary step toward encouraging a diversity of perspectives in the classroom.

Two models in education that give theoretical support for building trust, promoting community, and increasing opportunities for multiple viewpoints in classrooms are the learning-communities approach and Integrated Thematic Instruction (ITI). A learning-communities approach uses a multicultural argument that suggests that successful students need to learn to interact with people from diverse backgrounds, perspectives, and experiences (Bielaczyc & Collins, 1999). In addition, it incorporates a Vygotskian social-constructivist perspective that the construction of knowledge occurs best with the assistance and support of others. Furthermore, a learning-communities approach is integrative and holistic by nature and encourages examination from multiple perspectives, collaborative problem solving, collective-knowledge formation, and a valuing of differences. Every student is a potential learning resource in this type of classroom, and therefore building trust and promoting community are necessary to the success of developing collective knowledge in a class.

Another educational model, Highly Effective Teaching (HET, formerly known as Integrated Thematic Instruction), focuses on the development of responsible citizens who can function in a democratic society that realizes the importance of working with diverse people (Kovalik & McGeehan, 1999). HET is based on learning theory research, memory research, brain research, and Howard Gardner's theory of multiple intelligences. Teaching strategies, classroom environments, and involvement of parents are all used to build productive classroom and school communities. HET acknowledges and supports the interrelationship between family and school in the development of student citizens. Furthermore, "Lifelong Guidelines" and "LIFESKILLS" are HET community-building tools that are specifically used to develop relationships and expectations for behavior (Kovalik & McGeehan, pp. 382–385). Therefore, community building and trust are at the heart of HET.

How do facilitators of learning establish communities in classrooms and encourage multiple perspectives? Murphy and Valdez at the Instituto Tecnologico y de Estudios Superiores de Monterrey in Mexico (2005) developed a model that they called the Resistance Breaking Process (RBP). RBP focuses on three interrelated phases that build rapport and are important to establish prior to using collaboration in the classroom. During the first phase, teachers encourage an examination of the self, as students begin to become acquainted with their fellow classmates. Phase two involves finding connections and shared experiences with others in the class. Finally, the third phase involves the sharing of more intimate information with classmates. Murphy and Valdez suggest that RBP is ideal to use with classes that are resistant to collaboration because it helps students develop trusting relationships across time.

Buskist and Saville (2001) suggested that rapport could be created in many ways—by using personally relevant examples in class, recognizing students by their names, being available to students outside of class, and exhibiting characteristics such as humor, respect, and enthusiasm. Rogers and Freiberg (1994) suggested that teachers need to respond to the feelings of students, emphasize creative methods of learning, and encourage cooperation in the classroom. Hansen (1998) and Harwood and Hahn (1990) urged teachers to encourage quieter students to challenge themselves by speaking up in class, while talkative students are challenged to wait their turn; this practice creates maximum opportunities for sharing multiple perspectives. Glynn (2001), who has studied the psychology of teaching in the United States, reported that exemplary teachers exhibit psychological characteristics of commitment, enthusiasm, and interpersonal warmth with their students. Torres et al. (2003) suggested that students could write their own stories as a way to share their cultural backgrounds and talk about how their experiences might impact their responses to discussions or assignments during the semester. Finally, Mildred and Zuniga (2004) stated that the creation of a safe and supportive classroom requires developing guidelines for discussions, acknowledging that learning is a process, and monitoring class discussions.

I have found that the first day of class sets the stage for the rest of the semester. One method that I use to remember students' names is to take their photos on the first day of class (either alone or in pairs) and have each student sign his or her name in the same order as I have taken their photos. Later, I either print a class chart with their names listed below their picture or I print each photo separately with their names on the back (like flash cards) and then study them. By the second day of class, I am usually able to address many of my students by name. Students know that they cannot remain anonymous in my classes.

In my cross-cultural psychology course, I have students develop cultural genogram maps of their families across three generations. They examine areas such as religiosity, employment, ethnicity, marital status, and political affiliation. We use these to honor our diversity in the class and to consider how these issues might affect our classroom interactions.

Another activity that I use on the first day of class involves student participation in a continuum lineup; this gives them an opportunity to quickly learn more about each other. I ask them to form a line in front of the class so that they group themselves by birth order (oldest, middle, youngest, only child, etc.). I then ask them to brainstorm their stereotypes regarding the oldest sibling and request that the oldest not say anything in response. I remind them that stereotypes are generalizations that we make about members of a group based on our interpretations that we have learned as a result of being a member of our society (Jones, 1997). Once they are finished, I give the oldest siblings an opportunity to respond from their personal experiences. We then focus on the middle, youngest, and so forth, until all have had an opportunity to contribute. I then ask them to consider how this experience might affect interactions in our class. This gives the students a chance to talk about stereotypes and diversity of experiences, as well as to listen to each other respectfully. Another activity is to have them step forward (or to raise their hand) if they have had, or currently have, anything that they consider a disability (I modify this as needed by the makeup of the class). I invite them to share this with the group, if they like, and we also engage in a discussion regarding accessibility issues, as well as the emotional and psychological impact of discrimination and accessibility.

Other topics that I have used with the continuum lineup activity are gender, length of time in region (which lends itself to discussions of insider/outsider experiences, language differences, etc.), and birthplace. Topics that are a bit more revealing or controversial include economic background (i.e., had enough, did not have enough, or had plenty when growing up), ethnic or racial identity, and sexual orientation (e.g., how many people you consider close to you have told you that they are gay, lesbian, bisexual, transgender, or questioning?). When doing this continuum lineup activity, I have found that it is best to begin with less controversial topics and then move to ones that require more disclosure and are more controversial. Also, I usually do this across several different class periods. Other questions that could be used to prompt discussions are the following: What surprised you about this exercise? What benefits did you see that you enjoy just because you belong to some groups? What problems or barriers do you face because you belong to some groups? How do you think this will affect our class community?

One activity that promotes community building and encourages listening and speaking involves discussing an issue with a partner. I ask students to find a partner whom they do not know very well and to spend four minutes talking about an assigned topic while their partner listens attentively without responding. After two minutes, I encourage the speakers to delve more deeply into what they are discussing, until the end of the four minutes. Then they switch roles and spend four minutes in their new roles. I use topics that are related to the course, especially where it is helpful to learn about different experiences. For example, in psychology of adolescence, I ask them to talk about a high point in their own adolescence (e.g., what were you especially proud of during your adolescence?). Then I give students an opportunity to share with the entire class what they learned about the topic and about the process of the activity. They are able to learn more about their classmates and to see similarities and differences in experiences and perceptions. In addition, we address possible explanations for the similarities and differences and consider whether these explanations support research and theory.

Sometimes issues discussed in class are controversial or emotionally arousing. When this occurs, one method that I use is to have my students write a five-minute journal entry in which they jot down not only the main points learned about the issue but also the emotions they are feeling. I also ask them to list additional issues that arose for them, to consider how their past experiences affect their feelings or perceptions, and/or to consider how people their same age 20 years ago might have responded. Other questions could be included that allow for reflection, comparisons, and analysis. When the journal writing is completed, I either have the students share what they wrote with a partner, or I offer students the opportunity to share what they wrote aloud to the entire class, and I connect it with the topic or issues that I consider important for them to think about. This has been successful because it gives all of the students an opportunity to voice their emotions through their writings. In addition, if they choose to share verbally with the class, they have the opportunity to hear multiple perspectives. Finally, it demonstrates to the class appropriate ways to deal with emotions and the variety of ways that we feel about the same situation or issue (Torres et al., 2003).

In the event that there is an angry outburst from a student, there are many ways to deal with it. Worchel, Coutant-Sassic, and Wong (1998) remind us that conflict often is the impetus for self-examination, creative thinking, personal growth, and reinvigoration of relationships. It is our reaction to the conflict that may be problematic. One way to deal with a negative reaction would be to acknowledge the emotion that the student is exhibiting and to ask the student to reflect on *why* he or she is feeling such strong emotions (e.g., a personal experience may have caused the aroused emotions). It is through reflection that we often are able to grow and understand ourselves (Cohen, 1999). If the time is not right for the discussion, the student could be encouraged to speak with the instructor after class, who should then ensure that this happens. Another response might be to remind the student to take the time to listen to the other perspective and to repeat what he or she heard the other person say (i.e., to deal with the reaction as a communication issue). However, when the reaction is due to differences in perspectives, each side could be given the opportunity to explain its position to the class. Then the rest of the class can discuss areas where they see agreements. Through this intentional process, students who initially believe that they have very different positions can begin to see where they can agree. The important thing is to deal with the outburst immediately, so that all the students see that the instructor is willing to listen, is striving to maintain a safe environment, and is willing to work with students to figure out ways to deal with topics that elicit strong emotional responses.

As facilitators of learning, instructors are challenged daily to call upon characteristics and strengths within themselves, from their own "professional training, intellect, courage, responsiveness, determination, flexibility and faith in the very idea that people can grow and develop" (Hansen, 1998, p. 392). Students depend upon instructors who are willing to model risk taking, reflection, and flexibility in building community and trust in their classes (e.g., Logue, 2001; Price, 2001; Rogers & Freiberg, 1994). In addition, instructors need to be aware of their past experiences and histories and how these might affect interactions with students, who likewise have their own histories and past experiences that influence their behaviors and perceptions (Cohen, 1999). Instructors need to model the ability to tolerate and encourage a variety of views, thereby creating an intellectually safe environment for discussion (Harwood & Hahn, 1990). Another important quality in teachers is the ability to be aware of nonverbal communication in students; in other words, instructors need to be sensitive to social cues (e.g., Cohen, 1999; Hansen, 1998). In doing this work, it is important to offer support and professional growth opportunities by sharing teaching strategies and giving and obtaining emotional support from colleagues through workshops, conferences, and study groups.

The benefits and challenges of encouraging multiple perspectives in the classroom are numerous. The ability and willingness of instructors to form strong classroom communities impact relationships with students, both in and out of the classroom. Barton (2001) suggests that effective teachers are able to forge strong, honest relationships in which students "can learn to respect that even an educator can be 'wrong' or struggle through problem-solving" (p. 220). Through a willingness to take risks and to be flexible, by demonstrating and encouraging recognition of our own mistakes and how to handle them, and through an acknowledgement and passion for the value of multiple perspectives, instructors also have the long-term potential of affecting society by developing and modeling lifelong learning and socially responsible citizens.

References

Barton, M. H. (2001). Coming full circle: Teaching for beyond the classroom. In F. J. Stephenson, Jr. (Ed.), *Extraordinary teachers: The essence of excellent teaching* (pp. 217–220). Kansas City, MI: Andrews McMeel Publishing.

Bielaczyc, K., & Collins, A. (1999). Learning communities in classrooms: A reconceptualization of educational practice. In C. M. Reigeluth (Ed.), *Instructional-design theories and models: A new paradigm of instructional theory* (Vol. 2, pp. 269–292). Mahwah, NJ: Lawrence Erlbaum.

Buskist, W., & Saville, B. K. (2001). Rapport building: Creating positive emotional contexts for enhancing teaching and learning. *American Psychological Society Observer, 14*(3). Retrieved from http://www.psychologicalscience.org/observer/0301/tips.html

Cohen, J. (1999). *Educating minds and hearts: Social emotional learning and the passage into adolescence.* New York: Teachers College Press.

Dewey, J. (1997). *Democracy and education.* New York: The Free Press.

Glynn, S. M. (2001). The psychology of teaching. In F. J. Stephenson, Jr. (Ed.), *Extraordinary teachers: The essence of excellent teaching* (pp. 95–100). Kansas City, MO: Andrews McMeel Publishing.

Hansen, D. T. (1998). The importance of the person in the role of the teacher. *Child and Adolescent Social Work Journal, 15*(5), 391–405.

Harwood, A. M., & Hahn, C. L. (1990). *Controversial issues in the classroom.* ERIC Digest. ED 327 453. Bloomington, IN: ERIC Clearinghouse for Social Studies/Social Science Education.

Jones, J. M. (1997). *Prejudice and racism* (2nd ed.). New York: McGraw-Hill.

Kovalik, S. J., & McGeehan, J. R. (1999). Integrated Thematic Instruction: From brain research to application. In C. M. Reigeluth (Ed.), *Instructional-design theories and models: A new paradigm of instructional theory* (Vol. 2, pp. 371–396). Mahwah, NJ: Lawrence Erlbaum.

Logue, C. M. (2001). Free speech in the classroom. In F. J. Stephenson, Jr. (Ed.), *Extraordinary teachers: The essence of excellent teaching* (pp. 175–183). Kansas City, MO: Andrews McMeel Publishing.

Mildred, J., & Zuniga, X. (2004). Working with resistance to diversity issues in the classroom: Lessons from teacher training and multicultural education. *Smith College Studies in Social Work, 74*(2), 359–375.

Murphy, M., & Valdez, C. (2005). Ravaging resistance: A model for building rapport in a collaborative learning classroom. *Radical Pedagogy, 7*(1). Retrieved from http://radicalpedagogy.icaap.org/content/issue7_1/murphy-valdez.html

Nelson Laird, T. F., Engberg, M. E., & Hurtado, S. (2005). Modeling accentuation effects: Enrolling in a diversity course and the importance of social action engagement. *Journal of Higher Education, 76*(4), 448–476.

Palmer, P. (1998). *The courage to teach: Exploring the inner landscape of a teacher's life.* San Francisco: Jossey-Bass.

Price, S. J. (2001). What I wish someone had told me: Advice to new teachers. In F. J. Stephenson, Jr. (Ed.), *Extraordinary teachers: The essence of excellent teaching* (pp. 203–210). Kansas City, MO: Andrews McMeel Publishing.

Rogers, C. R., & Freiberg, H. J. (1994). *Freedom to learn* (3rd ed.). New York: Macmillan College Publishing Company.

Torres, V., Howard-Hamilton, M. F., & Cooper, D. L. (2003). *Identity development of diverse populations: Implications for teaching and administration in higher education.* ERIC Digest. ED 479 151. Urbana, IL: ERIC Clearinghouse on Elementary and Early Childhood Education.

Umbach, P. D., & Kuh, G. D. (2006). Student experiences with diversity at liberal arts colleges: Another claim for distinctiveness. *Journal of Higher Education, 77*(1), 169–192.

U.S. Department of Health and Human Services. (n.d.). *Cultural competence resources for health care providers.* Retrieved June 20, 2007, from http://www. hrsa.gov/culturalcompetence/curriculumguide/appendixA.htm

Worchel, S., Coutant-Sassic, D., & Wong, F. (1998). Toward a more balanced view of conflict: There is a positive side. In S. Worchel & J. A. Simpson (Eds.), *Conflict between people and groups: Causes, processes, and resolutions* (pp. 76–89). Chicago: Nelson-Hall Publishers.

14

CREATING INCLUSIVE SCIENCE, TECHNOLOGY, ENGINEERING, AND MATHEMATICS (STEM) COURSES

Nilhan Gunasekera and Katherine Friedrich

This chapter focuses on research-based inclusive teaching practices that can address the "chilly climate" in STEM courses. It draws on the products of the Center for the Integration of Research, Teaching and Learning (CIRTL), which provide recommendations to improve the success of underrepresented groups. We define diversity in the broadest terms possible, to include ethnicity, gender, disability, learning style, socioeconomic status, sexual orientation, and other societal categories.

Sinking or Swimming? Student Experiences in STEM

Efforts have been under way for many decades to diversify the population of STEM students and practitioners. However, certain groups remain underrepresented in STEM. For example, as recently as 2004 (data for the most recent year available), only 4% of the STEM workforce was African American and 4% was Latino, even though these groups constitute 12% and 14% of the U.S. population, respectively (National Science Foundation [NSF], 2007). Women constitute only 27% of the STEM workforce (NSF, 2007).

A disparate process of attrition takes place during college and graduate school, filtering out nonmajority students (NSF, 2000, 2004, 2007; Thom, 2001). Women drop out of STEM majors at higher rates than men do (54%

vs. 33% at elite schools) (Seymour & Hewitt, 1997). This attrition continues in graduate school and even in postdoctoral work (Dowling, 1999; Hollenshead, Wenzel, Lazarus, & Nair, 1996). Much of the filtering during academic training has been attributed to pedagogy, from the messages conveyed (or not conveyed) by syllabi, to lack of peer interaction in the classroom, to teaching methods that align with certain learning styles (Rosser, 1993, 1997; Tobias, 1990).

Campus climate also influences student success. Undergraduates' academic experiences can be strongly affected by the general level of acceptance and social and financial support of students from underrepresented groups, as well as by mentoring (Alexander, Foertsch, Daffinrud, & Tapia, 1998; Cabrera & Nora, 1994; Maton, Hrabowski, & Schmitt, 2000).

STEM instructors can expand the pool of students who succeed in the field by improving students' educational experiences. The Center for the Integration of Research, Teaching and Learning (CIRTL), a National Science Foundation–funded network of six universities promoting the quality preparation of future STEM faculty, has developed resources to help faculty both support and benefit from classroom diversity. Some important areas to address include the following:

1. Learning Styles and Interests

Engineering courses tend to cater to certain learning styles and not to others; they are geared toward introverted students who do well in courses that are theory-based, deductively constructed, and not values-oriented (Felder, 1996). Such pedagogies often alienate those students who learn best in creative, cooperative settings that consider values and emphasize design and synthesis. Female students, in particular, feel alienated by traditional teaching methods in STEM fields (Rosser, 1993).

2. Academic Preparation

Students from certain socioeconomic or ethnic groups often do not have the opportunity to take advanced math courses in high school (Nettles, 2004). The lack of a collaborative community of learners can compound the academic struggle for these students (Treisman, 1992). Treisman (1992) initiated a program of intensive collaborative learning in mathematics to improve the performance of underrepresented minority students. Targeted training of at-risk students has since been used successfully at other institutions (Alexander, Burda, & Millar, 1997).

Although stereotypes exist about the preparation of some students, assuming that a given student is poorly prepared or well prepared because of his or her background or ethnicity may lead to interventions that are not appropriately targeted.

3. Technological Skills

STEM programs often assume previous experience with technology and good visualization skills. Spatial visualization is an important skill in STEM problem solving. Sorby (2001) has observed that female students are more likely than their male peers to lack experience with spatial visualization. Some universities now offer preparatory courses for students who are in need of visualization training.

Similarly, students' experience with mechanical work and with computers may influence their scientific career interests and skills (Gokhale & Stier, 2004; Tillberg & Cohoon, 2005). Relevant experiences include computer gaming, auto repair, and recreational activities involving computer hardware or electronics. These experiences are culturally defined in many countries as being appropriate for men but not for women. Class, ethnicity, learning style, physical disabilities, and regional background may also affect teenagers' access to computers, machines, and technology.

4. Social, Cultural, and Financial Support

Cultural isolation and lack of peer support for success, as well as unmet financial need, drive many students away from college, and especially from STEM. Maton, Hrabowski, and Schmitt (2000) found that integrating social and academic support was helpful in ensuring a culture of success for African Americans at the University of Maryland–Baltimore County.

In general, success in STEM requires considerable effort and dedication. This effort is especially challenging for students who have to work full time while attending school (Kane, Beals, Valeau, & Johnson, 2004).

5. Expectations and Stereotypes

Both female students and students of color experience exclusion and disrespect in college courses (Davis, 1993). Cabrera and Nora (1994) found that perceived racial prejudice and discrimination affected minority students' college experiences adversely. Often peers, not faculty, instigate these incidents. Instructors may not notice the problem or may not be sure what to do about it.

Women in STEM are sometimes harassed by their peers. Sixty percent of women scientists participating in one survey had experienced gender-based harassment (Ferreira, 2002).

Some lesbian, gay, bisexual, and transgender students may leave STEM fields and careers because they feel that they are not supported by their peers or by faculty (Worthington, McCrary, & Howard, 1998).

We often live up to the expectations others have of us. Thus, students from underrepresented groups who are aware of negative stereotypes face an uphill battle to "prove themselves" to their peers and to succeed in college and beyond (Moore, Madison-Colmore, & Smith, 2003; Perry, Steele, & Hilliard, 2003; Pinel, Warner, & Chua, 2005).

Diversity as an Asset: Changing the Classroom Climate

CIRTL has created a variety of resources to support STEM instructors in addressing diversity issues in their classrooms. The following recommendations are extracted from the literature review (Cabrera, Doyon, Friedrich, Roberts, Saleem, Hammargren, & Giovanetto, 2007) and *Reaching All Students*, a teaching manual (Sellers, Roberts, Giovanetto, Friedrich, & Hammargren, 2007).

1. Plan Your Course to Achieve Learning Outcomes, and Communicate These Expectations to Students

STEM students are often discouraged by lack of clear communication from their instructors (Tobias, 1990). Stating your expectations for students' performance clearly will make it much easier for them to excel in your classes. Such clarifications will also help students whose cultural background may differ from yours.

When planning a course or a discussion section, think carefully about the messages you want to communicate to your students. What skills do you want them to acquire or hone? How should they be able to apply their knowledge? You may wish to refer to Bloom's Taxonomy, reprinted in *Reaching All Students: A Resource for Teaching in Science, Technology, Engineering and Mathematics* (Sellers et al., 2007), for a rubric. Your choice of goals can guide you in designing appropriate activities.

A clear and straightforward syllabus can be a key communication tool. To set an inclusive tone in your classroom, you should include concise statements about accommodations for disabilities and for religious holidays. The Content Matters Syllabi Project (CIRTL Diversity Team, 2006), another CIRTL resource, provides many good sample syllabi.

In addition to formally discussing expectations, one should also address problems such as disruptive behavior or peer harassment immediately when they occur. *Reaching All Students* suggests building a trusting environment in the classroom through group work, and maintaining the role of facilitator even when correcting student assumptions.

2. Use a Variety of Teaching Methods Appropriate to Your Goals

Using a variety of teaching methods can help to engage many students who may otherwise consider changing their majors. Some engineering educators recommend including active learning, discussion of context, creative exercises, demonstrations, group work, and visual aids in STEM teaching (Felder, 1996). Additionally, several STEM-based pedagogies have been developed that focus on student-centered teaching, such as Bio Quest, Just-in-Time Teaching (JiTT), Process Oriented Guided Inquiry Learning (POGIL), Chemistry in Context, and Peer-Led Team Learning (PLTL) (Farrell, Moog, & Spencer, 1999; Gosser & Roth, 1998; Lewis & Lewis, 2005; Linneman & Plake, 2006; Novak, Patterson, Gavrin, & Christian, 1999; Peterson & Jungck, 1988; Schwartz & Bunce, 1994; Wamser, 2006).

3. Address Cultural, Ethical, and Social Issues in Your Field

The myth that STEM fields are devoid of cultural content or social relevance makes these fields less interesting to many people. In fact, scientific decisions have ethical and social consequences, just as business and policy decisions do.

Many students in STEM courses are likely to appreciate discussion of social problems in class. Rosser (1993) has written that such discussions are especially appropriate for engaging female students, who may be more interested in the societal consequences of science than their male peers.

The Content Matters Syllabi Project highlights a context-based chemistry course taught by Professor Catherine Middlecamp of University of Wisconsin–Madison that addresses uranium mining and use. The course integrates science, cultural awareness, and ethical questions (CIRTL Diversity Team, 2006). Another context-rich course, taught by Professor Donna Riley at Smith College, focused on the contributions of non-Western civilizations to engineering (Riley, 2003).

Another successful method involves using case studies to engage students in learning scientific concepts. Several good repositories of case studies exist for STEM disciplines (Herreid, 1994; State University of New York at Buffalo, 2005).

5. Seek Feedback from Students about Their Learning and Your Teaching

When introducing teaching innovations to the classroom, seeking feedback from students is essential. CIRTL's resource book contains extensive information on seeking and evaluating student feedback. The National Institute for Science Education (NISE) has developed the Field-Tested Learning Assessment Guide, or FLAG, a STEM-specific resource for assessing student learning (Ellis et al., 1999). The Student Assessment of Learning Gains, or SALG, is another useful online tool (Seymour, 2000).

It is important to analyze evaluation results carefully. Students who are accustomed to passively absorbing information may resent becoming active participants in the learning process. If you are a nonmajority instructor, your students may evaluate you less highly than they do your majority colleagues (Daufin, 1995). Despite these cautions, assessment is essential to improving one's teaching.

Conclusion

The history of science is rich in human and conceptual diversity. However, a number of groups continue to be underrepresented in STEM. The need to make STEM welcoming to these groups has become even more critical, since they are becoming an increasingly large fraction of the U.S. undergraduate population.

These pressures and demands challenge STEM instructors to implement changes in their teaching. CIRTL has created a variety of resources to help STEM instructors in this effort: a resource book that contains many inclusive teaching techniques, a collection of inclusive STEM syllabi, a set of case studies that can serve as conversation and reflection pieces, and summaries of educational research on diversity in STEM.

As educators adopt techniques that work for the increasingly diverse classrooms of the coming decades, they will become more effective at supporting the success of all students in STEM.

References

Alexander, B. B., Burda, A. C., & Millar, S. B. (1997). A community approach to learning calculus: Fostering success for underrepresented ethnic minorities in an emerging scholars program. *Journal of Women and Minorities in Science and Engineering, 3,* 145–159.

Alexander, B. B., Foertsch, J., Daffinrud, S., & Tapia, R. (1998). *The Spend a Summer with a Scientist (SaS) program at Rice University: A study of program outcomes and essential elements for success.* Madison: The LEAD Center, University of Wisconsin–Madison.

Cabrera, A., Doyon, K., Friedrich, K., Roberts, J., Saleem, T., Hammargren, C., & Giovanetto, L. (2007). Diversity resources literature review. Retrieved October 31, 2007, from http://www.cirtl.net/DiversityResources/resources/annotated-bibliography/

Cabrera, A. F., & Nora, A. (1994). College students' perceptions of prejudice and discrimination and their feelings of alienation: A construct validation approach. *Review of Education/Pedagogy/Cultural Studies, 16*(3–4), 387–409.

CIRTL Diversity Team. (2006). Content matters syllabi project. Retrieved October 31, 2007, from http://www.cirtl.net/DiversityResources/content_matters/

Daufin, E. K. (1995). Confessions of a womanist professor. *Black Issues in Higher Education, 12*(1), 34.

Davis, B. G. (1993). *Tools for teaching.* San Francisco: Jossey-Bass.

Dowling, J. (1999). The workplace: Opening remarks. *Annals of the New York Academy of Sciences. Women in Science and Engineering: Choices for Success, 869,* 94.

Ellis, E., Mathieu, B., Brissenden, G., Brower, A., Burgess, A., Daffinrud, S., et al. (1999). Field-tested learning assessment guide. Retrieved October 31, 2007, from http://www.flaguide.org/intro/intro.php

Farrell, J. J., Moog, R. S., & Spencer, J. N. (1999). A guided-inquiry general chemistry course. *Journal of Chemical Education, 76,* 570.

Felder, R. M. (1996). Teaching to all types: Examples from engineering education. *ASEE Prism, 6*(4), 18–23.

Ferreira, M. M. (2002). The research lab: A chilly place for graduate women. *Journal of Women and Minorities in Science and Engineering, 8*(1), 85–98.

Gokhale, A. A., & Stier, K. (2004). Closing the gender gap in technical disciplines: An investigative study. *Journal of Women and Minorities in Science and Engineering, 10*(2), 149–160.

Gosser, D. K., Jr., & Roth, V. (1998). The Workshop Chemistry Project: Peer-led team learning. *Journal of Chemical Education, 75*(2), 185–187.

Herreid, C. F. (1994). Case studies in science: A novel method of science education. Retrieved December 11, 2004, from http://ublib.buffalo.edu/libraries/projects/cases/teaching/novel.html

Hollenshead, C., Wenzel, S., Lazarus, B., & Nair, I. (1996). The graduate experience in the sciences and engineering: Rethinking a gendered institution. In *The equity equation.* San Francisco, Jossey-Bass.

Kane, M. A., Beals, C., Valeau, E. J., & Johnson, M. J. (2004). Fostering success among traditionally underrepresented student groups: Hartnell College's approach to implementation of the Math, Engineering, and Science Achievement (MESA) program. *Community College Journal of Research and Practice, 28*(1), 17–26.

Lewis, S. E., & Lewis, J. E. (2005). Departing from lectures: An evaluation of a peer-led guided inquiry alternative. *Journal of Chemical Education, 82,* 135.

Linneman, S., & Plake, T. (2006). Searching for the difference: A controlled test of just-in-time teaching for large-enrollment introductory geology courses. *Journal of Geoscience Education, 54*(1), 18–24.

Maton, K. I., Hrabowski III, F. A., & Schmitt, C. L. (2000). African American college students excelling in the sciences: College and postcollege outcomes in the Meyerhoff Scholars Program. *Journal of Research in Science Teaching, 37*(7), 629–654.

Moore, J. L., Madison-Colmore, O., & Smith, D. M. (2003). To Prove-Them-Wrong Syndrome: Voices from unheard African-American males in engineering disciplines. *Journal of Men's Studies, 12*(1), 61–74.

National Science Foundation. (2000). *Women, minorities, and persons with disabilities in science and engineering: 2000.* Retrieved June 13, 2007, from:http://www.nsf.gov/statistics/nsf00327/pdf/execsumm.pdf

National Science Foundation. (2004). *Women, minorities, and persons with disabilities in science and engineering: 2004.* Retrieved June 13, 2007, from: http://www.nsf.gov/statistics/wmpd/pdf/nsf04317.pdf

National Science Foundation. (2007). *Women, minorities, and persons with disabilities in science and engineering: 2007.* Retrieved June 13, 2007, from http://www.nsf.gov/statistics/wmpd/pdf/nsf07315.pdf

Nettles, M. T. (2004, August 18). *The pursuit of excellence in diversity: A focus upon preparation.* Presented at the CIRTL Diversity Institute Kickoff at the University of Wisconsin–Madison. Retrieved June 27, 2007, from http://www.cirtl.net/DiversityResources/news/kickoff/presentations/Nettles_DI_kickoff.pdf

Novak, G. M., Patterson, E. T., Gavrin, A. D., & Christian, W. (1999). *Just-in-time teaching: Blending active learning with web technology.* Upper Saddle River, NJ: Prentice-Hall.

Perry, T., Steele, C., & Hilliard, A. III. (2003). *Young, gifted and black: promoting high achievement among African-American students.* Boston: Beacon Press.

Peterson, N. S., & Jungck, J. R. (1988). BioQuest: Problem-posing, problem-solving, and persuasion in biology. *Academic Computing, 2*(6): 14–17, 48–50.

Pinel, E. C., Warner, L.R., & Chua, P. (2005). Getting there is only half the battle: Stigma consciousness and maintaining diversity in higher education. *Journal of Social Issues, 61*(3), 481–506.

Riley, D. (2003). *Pedagogies of liberation in an engineering thermodynamics class.* Paper presented at the American Society for Engineering Education Annual Conference and Exposition June 22–25, 2003 in Nashville, Tennessee.

Rosser, S. V. (1993). Female friendly science: Including women in curricular content and pedagogy in science. *Journal of General Education, 42*(3), 191–220.

Rosser, S. V. (1997). *Re-engineering female-friendly science.* New York: Teachers College Press.

Schwartz, A. T., & Bunce, D. M. (1994). Chemistry in context: Weaving the web. *Journal of Chemical Education, 71*(12), 1041.

Sellers, S. L., Roberts, J., Giovanetto, L., Friedrich, K., & Hammargren, C. (2007). *Reaching all students: A resource for teaching in science, technology, engineering and mathematics* (2nd ed.). Madison, WI: Center for the Integration of Research, Teaching and Learning.

Seymour, E. (2000). *Student assessment of learning gains.* Retrieved October 31, 2007, from http://ipconference.education.wisc.edu/, http://www.wcer.wisc.edu/salgains/instructor/

Seymour, E., & Hewitt, N. M. (1997). *Talking about leaving: Why undergraduates leave the sciences.* Boulder: Westview Press.

Sorby, S. A. (2001). A course in spatial visualization and its impact on the retention of female engineering students. *Journal of Women and Minorities in Science and Engineering, 7*(2), 153–172.

State University of New York at Buffalo. (2005). *The National Center for Case Study Teaching in Science case collection.* Retrieved April 26, 2005, from http://ublib.buffalo.edu/libraries/projects/cases/ubcase.htm

Thom, M. (2001) *Balancing the equation.* New York: National Council for Research on Women.

Tillberg, H. K., & Cohoon, J. M. (2005). Attracting women to the CS major. *Frontiers: A Journal of Women's Studies, 26*(1), 126–140.

Tobias, S. (1990). They're not dumb. They're different. A new "tier of talent" for science. *Change, 22*(4), 11–30.

Treisman, U. (1992). Studying students studying calculus: A look at the lives of minority mathematics students in college. *College Mathematics Journal, 23*(5), 362–372.

Wamser, C. C. (2006). Peer-led team learning in organic chemistry: Effects on student performance, success and persistence in the course. *Journal of Chemical Education, 83*(10), 1552–1556.

Worthington, R. L., McCrary, S. I., & Howard, K. A. (1998). Becoming a LGBT affirmative career adviser: Guidelines for faculty, staff and administrators. In R. Sanlo (Ed.), *Working with lesbian, gay, bisexual, and transgender college students* (pp. 135–143). Westport, CT: Greenwood Press.

15

TEACHING DIVERSITY THROUGH LITERATURE

Urging Voyages Toward Deeper Understanding

Nancy L. Chick

Does man love Art?
Man visits Art, but squirms.
Art hurts. Art urges voyages,
And it is easier to stay at home.

—Gwendolyn Brooks, "The Chicago Picasso"

This poetic excerpt reminds us that literature can lead to discomfort and resistance as well as new perspectives and deeper learning. Its presence in diversity studies, then, is crucial, but the map for such literary learning voyages may be unknown to those outside of English departments or even those who aren't well versed in the works and theories of noncanonical or specifically multicultural literatures.[1]

Literature's potential in learning suggests that it shouldn't be confined to the literature classroom. Literary narratives bring abstract theories, remote places, and statistics to life, deepening students' understanding of gender, race, culture, ethnicity, and class (Boyatzis, 1994). In other words, while social science lessons of diversity may *tell* students about the experiences of people of color, literature *shows* these experiences with greater impact. Indeed, researchers across the

---

[1] In literary studies and ethnic studies, the terms *multicultural, multiethnic,* and *of color* are used instead of *diversity.*

discipline have supported this value of literature in learning, especially when the goal is lasting, profound learning (Carter, 1993; Coles, 1989; Csikszentmihalyi & Larson, 1984; Howard, 1989; Polkinghorne, 1988; Vitz, 1990). Further, the inclusion of literature across the curriculum may facilitate students' cognitive development along Perry's (1970) positions from duality to relativism and toward Belenky, Clinchy, Goldberger, and Tarule's (1986) stage of constructed knowing as students realize the importance of context and perspective and recognize that knowledge and experience are constructed. The increasing awareness of context, perspective, and another's self also develops students' empathetic abilities, which are essential in understanding diversity.

In this chapter, I present four specific strategies for effectively using literature to facilitate deep learning about diversity. This discussion uses a theoretical perspective that can guide the development of additional strategies. Specifically, McLaren (1995) offers a typology of four forms of multiculturalism—"conservative," "liberal," "left-liberal," and "critical"—each representing a different way of thinking about difference and diversity. A conservative multiculturalist perspective sees "whiteness as an invisible norm" and thus encourages assimilation, viewing ethnic groups as "'add-ons' to the dominant culture" (p. 49). It explains the absence of equality in the United States by claiming some groups are culturally deprived and thus lack appropriate American values. In contrast, a liberal multiculturalist perspective assumes equality among groups, evident in the familiar "we're all the same" or "we're all just people" comments that deny differences between groups because, it asserts, acknowledging differences is itself a racist act. It explains any inequality by simply pointing to uneven opportunities that inhibit equal competition under capitalism. A left-liberal multiculturalist perspective emphasizes difference because focusing on equality erases significant, essential, exotic differences that are the result of "a primeval past of cultural authenticity" rather than history or culture, thus assuming that there is one, static, inherent, genetic definition of each culture (p. 51). Finally, a critical multiculturalist perspective critiques the previous perspectives and asserts that differences—including specific and varied differences "*between* and *among* groups"—are the "product[s] of history, culture, power, and ideology" (p. 53). In its challenges to the other perspectives' tendencies to exoticize or essentialize differences or erase them altogether and in its attention to multiple perspectives, specific examples and experiences, and contexts, critical multiculturalism offers guidelines for developing effective ways to teach and learn about diversity through literature.

Introducing Multicultural Literary Studies

A brief introduction to the field of multicultural literary studies grounds what may mistakenly be seen as isolated texts within larger disciplinary and institutional contexts. Such an introduction illuminates the history and study of multicultural literature, as well as its relationship to the university and issues of power. In the wake of the social and political changes in the 1960s, large numbers of students with racially and culturally diverse backgrounds enrolled in American universities, challenged many of their traditions, and insisted on content that represented their experiences, their ways of knowing, and their presence on these campuses (Gutierrez, 1995). As Ethnic Studies Programs emerged in response to these changes, so too did the formal disciplinary study of multiethnic literatures. After the 1968 watershed moment of Kiowa author N. Scott Momaday winning the Pulitzer Prize for fiction, publishing opportunities and attention to the variety of literatures produced by writers of nondominant cultures increased, and American literature courses gradually began including works by writers of more racially and culturally varied backgrounds.

Despite rich scholarly work on these literatures, the well-intended directives of regents, administrators, and others peripheral to the academic conversation have often oversimplified the subject of study to the "Big Four": African Americans, Native Americans, Latinos, and Asian Americans. Even within literary studies, the convenience of these groupings and their terms trumped their precision. Separate courses in multicultural literature or even more specialized courses in the literature of one of these groups emerged to facilitate in-depth study and have become more common than infusions of these literatures across the literary curriculum. The familiar list of four groups oversimplifies diversity in the United States by ironically making it seem less diverse—not to mention completely ignoring the diversity that blurs or extends our national borders, as international literatures and texts in translation are more often than not outside of diversity studies and requirements.[2] As a result, we risk giving the impression of homogeneous populations and literatures, conflating the experiences and texts of all the

---

[2] In fact, because multicultural literary studies focus on literature in the United States, I limit this brief chapter to this narrow field. International literature is treated separately in the discipline with different theories, scholars, and texts, many of which fall under the rubric of postcolonialism rather than multiculturalism. Only the latter meets most diversity requirements.

African diaspora, of well over 500 distinct Native American tribes, of all people with a heritage from anywhere south of the U.S. border or Spain, and of profoundly distinct Asian populations originating beyond our western borders. The familiar four implied by "diversity" also ignores the ethnic groups and literatures of some racially white ethnic groups, including those who experienced somewhat similar histories of oppression and conflict as the Big Four.

The 1989 publication of the first *Heath Anthology of American Literature* was a significant moment for teaching multicultural literature. Certainly, plenty of collections of noncanonical literatures had been published, but the *Heath* stood apart because of its breadth, depth, structure (chronological rather than culturally separate), heft, and integration (it's an anthology of American literature, not multicultural American literature). These traits reject the tendency to ghettoize multicultural literature into separate textbooks, courses, or even sections on a syllabus by considering them side by side with the canonical works of the time and with relevant contextual information. They thus reflect the critical multiculturalist's understanding of cultural differences and diversity and their richness. Contrasting the *Heath's* table of contents with anthologies organized by cultural group and then considering the implications of each (including what each suggests about diversity in the larger curriculum) can lead to thoughtful discussions about the tensions between separating the literature and infusing it across the curriculum—and the resulting place of "others" in developing knowledge and understanding.

Practicing Critical Multiculturalist Literary Analyses

Applying a critically multiculturalist perspective to the process of literary analysis is also effective in using literature to understand diversity. Literary analysis—or recognizing the literary elements such as genre or theme, rather than merely reading the texts as illustrations of a cultural perspective—reminds students that these are works of literature, deliberately constructed creative expressions within a variety of literary traditions, rather than the decontextualized thoughts of a solitary individual with no concern for how the ideas were expressed. Initially examining the similarities to traditional genres (novel, short story, autobiography, poetic form) or themes (love, family, coming of age) situates the text within the larger literary tradition and students' realm of the familiar. However, to avoid the liberal multiculturalist conclusion that these texts are "just like" canonical ones or simply about universal experiences, a subsequent activity should explore how the texts also revise these traditional forms and themes. Examining how they reflect specific cultural histories, cultures, ideologies, or ways of knowing leads to acknowledging the texts on their own terms and within their own contexts. Students shouldn't miss how these authors work both inside and outside of tradition and their complex relationships to power and voice. Such literary analyses support a critical multiculturalist stance that these writings must be read as products of specific people within specific groups at specific times in specific places, facilitating students' empathy and personal connections with the literature while also honoring the differences of another perspective.

Situating the Literature in Its Cultural Contexts

The historical and cultural contexts for multicultural literature are essential companions to the texts themselves in the critical multiculturalist's effort to acknowledge and accommodate differences and situate those differences within history and lived experience. Because these contexts are often unfamiliar to students, a necessary element of reading these literatures is developing a "fresh cultural intelligence" that integrates "the history, the myths and legends, the racial and ethnic experience behind those works" (Maitino & Peck, 1996, p. 12). Such an approach rejects the practice of interpreting the text in isolation from context because such a reading limits recognition of textual elements that emerge from its contexts—and thus limits an understanding of the text—and would easily lend itself to a liberal multiculturalist's focus on universals and sameness. Admittedly, such practices are often taught with the best of intentions, including the disciplinary attention to close reading and the pedagogical desire to have students "relate to" the texts, but they erase the richness, differences, and cultural identities of the literature, the authors, and the characters. As with the approach to literary analysis, connecting students to the text can be a starting point, but only a starting point.

At the other end of the theoretical spectrum is reading multicultural literatures as products of social science, rather than as works of literature, which ignores the literary work of the text and treats a single author and a single text as representative of an entire group (Olivares, 1996). This illustrates the left-liberal multiculturalist's tendency of treating culture and ethnicity (and identity) as static and monolithic by generalizing from a single text that's read as ethnography. It is essential to recognize ethnicity as dynamic, complex, and "constantly recreated" (Sollors, 1984, p. 95). Practicing the literary analyses already described and including the cultural history of the text, rather than relying on the literary text itself to define an entire culture, are ways of avoiding this common tendency. Such contextual understandings help students make sense of parts of the text they don't understand, instead of using those moments to dismiss their hope of understanding as futile or to exoticize unfamiliar cultures with extreme and sometimes harsh judgments.

Teaching the Conflicts About, Between, and Within the Literature

A practice for helping students appreciate the differences between and among groups invokes Graff's (1992) call to "teach the conflicts" (p. 12). He encourages educators to avoid glossing over the societal and disciplinary debates, tensions, and conversations: such juxtaposition of competing and often complex texts, concepts, and perspectives facilitates students' more sophisticated understanding of a complex world. These conflicts emblematize the complexities of cultures—that is, diversity. Graff's goal is to engage students in the controversies that engage scholars and teachers and even those outside of the academy. By including critical and popular debates and the conflicts between disciplinary figures and theories, classrooms become sites that challenge tendencies toward oversimplifying, romanticizing, and monolithically representing complex groups, relationships, and power dynamics.

Graff's own realization of the potential of literature occurred when he was a student reading Twain's *The Adventures in Huckleberry Finn*. His professor included scholars' contradictory interpretations about the treatment of race in the novel and encouraged the students to enter the debates about how race is represented, who does the representing, how we think about representations over time, and if racism is excused because it's part of one's cultural and historical context. Such debates continue even today inside and outside the university (e.g., Smiley's 1996 cover story about Twain's novel in *Harper's*; Morrison's brief, accessible examination of blackness in Poe, Melville, Cather, and Hemingway [1993]) and can provide an effective literary snapshot into how marginalized groups have been represented by those in power—even when it appears they haven't been represented at all.

Presenting the debates within a single group can help represent the complexity of identity and culture and the variety of experiences that challenge monolithic representations. For instance, the turn-of-the-twentieth-century public debate between Booker T. Washington and W. E. B. DuBois about how to respond to inequality between Blacks and Whites prefigures the tension between the philosophies of Martin Luther King, Jr., and Malcolm X, attesting to its lasting relevance, the validity of both sides, and its significance in discussions about difference and power. Other differing perspectives within groups abound and provide opportunities to consider some of the major issues affecting diversity studies. For example, while some major Harlem Renaissance writers like Jean Toomer and Zora Neale Hurston claimed racelessness at times, their own writings and those of Langston Hughes and Claude McKay describe highly racialized experiences, deliberately invoke and celebrate blackness, and even indict Whites for slavery, Jim Crow, lynching, and other continuing racial problems. Speaking from the middle of this tension, Countee Cullen's poem "Heritage" asks "What is Africa to me?" This set of African American texts from the same literary era illustrates complex yet not uncommon perspectives about race from within a single group.

In this context, it's easier to understand the challenges facing multicultural writers, especially when expected to represent an entire group. Because of the urge to correct stereotypes, multicultural writers are often pressured to prioritize selective accuracy and positive images over all else. For instance, criticisms are directed at Alice Walker's *The Color Purple* for its representation of abusive Black men (Whitaker, 1992), Maxine Hong Kingston for her adaptations of Chinese myths (Chin, 1999; Chu, 1997), and Sherman Alexie for including popular culture with Native American culture and for showing alcoholism on the reservation (Bird, 1995; Evans, 2001; Tellefsen, 2005). These conflicts have no easy answers. Such problematizing of identity—showing diversity and complexity even within groups—helps students understand more about difference and power.

By teaching literature through a critical multiculturalist perspective, instructors will help students recognize some of the historical and cultural sources for the complexity and richness of what we call diversity. Beginning with the broader landscape of multicultural literary studies opens up issues of power, canonicity, and the literary tradition that affect these authors and their texts. Integrating critical multiculturalist analyses of literary elements helps students value the literature as more than utilitarian textbooks, just as contextualizing the literature historically and culturally helps them approach the stories with greater empathy and "cultural intelligence" (Maitino & Peck, 1996, p. 12). Finally, facing the conflicts about, between, and within the literature prevents an oversimplification of culture, difference, and diversity itself. Students will be better equipped to intellectually and emotionally engage with the people they encounter and honor the stories they live. Ultimately, the potential for literature in learning about diversity calls for further study, but these four best practices, undergirded by an effective theoretical foundation, provide a more informed roadmap for the journey toward understanding.

References

Belenky, M. B., Clinchy, B. M., Goldberger, N. R., & Tarule, J. M. (1986). *Women's ways of knowing: The development of self, voice, and mind.* New York: Basic Books.

Bird, G. (1995, Fall). The exaggeration of despair in Sherman Alexie's *Reservation Blues. Wicazo Sa Review, 11*(2), 47–52.

Boyatzis, C. (1994). Studying lives through literature: Using narrative to teach social science and promote students' epistemological growth. *Journal on Excellence in College Teaching, 5*(1), 31–45.

Carter, K. (1993). The place of story in the study of teaching and teacher education. *Educational Researcher, 22,* 5–12, 18.

Chin, F. (1999). The most popular book in China. In C. S. Wong (Ed.), *Maxine Hong Kingston's* The Woman Warrior: *A casebook.* (pp. 23–28). New York: Oxford University Press.

Chu, P. P. (1997, Autumn). Tripmaster Monkey, Frank Chin, and the Chinese heroic tradition. *Arizona Quarterly: A Journal of American Literature, Culture, and Theory, 53*(3), 117–139.

Coles, R. (1989). *The call of stories: Teaching and the moral imagination.* Boston: Houghton Mifflin.

Csikszentmihalyi, M., & Larson, R. (1984). *Being adolescent: Conflict and growth in the teenage years.* New York: Basic Books.

Evans, S. F. (2001, December 1). "Open containers": Sherman Alexie's drunken Indians. *American Indian Quarterly, 25*(1), 46–72.

Graff, G. (1992). *Beyond the culture wars: How teaching the conflicts can revitalize American education.* New York: W. W. Norton.

Gutierrez, R. A. (1995). Ethnic studies: Its evolution in American colleges and universities. In D. T. Goldberg (Ed.), *Multiculturalism: A critical reader* (pp. 157–167). Malden, MA: Blackwell.

Howard, G. S. (1989). *A tale of two stories: Excursions into a narrative approach to psychology.* Notre Dame, IN: Academic Publications.

Maitino, J. R., & Peck, D. R. (Eds.). (1996). *Teaching American ethnic literatures.* Albuquerque: University of New Mexico Press.

McLaren, P. (1995). White terror and oppositional agency: Towards a critical multi-culturalism. In D. T. Goldberg (Ed.), *Multiculturalism: A critical reader* (pp. 45–74). Malden, MA: Blackwell.

Morrison, T. (1993). *Playing in the dark: Whiteness and the literary imagination.* New York: Vintage/Random House.

Olivares, J. (1996). Entering *The House on Mango Street* (Sandra Cisneros). In J. R. Maitino & D. R. Peck (Eds.), *Teaching American ethnic literatures* (pp. 209–235). Albuquerque: University of New Mexico Press.

Perry, W. G. (1970). *Forms of intellectual and ethical development in the college years.* New York: Holt, Rinehart and Winston.

Polkinghorne, D. P. (1988). *Narrative psychology.* Albany, NY: SUNY Press.

Smiley, J. (1996, January). Say it ain't so, Huck: Second thoughts on Mark Twain's "masterpiece." *Harper's, 292,* 61–68.

Sollors, W. (1984). Nine suggestions for historians of American ethnic literature. *MELUS, 1,* 95–96.

Tellefsen, B. (2005, Summer). America is a Diet Pepsi: Sherman Alexie's *Reservation Blues. Western American Literature, 40*(2), 125–147.

Vitz, P. (1990). The use of stories in moral development. *American Psychologist, 45,* 709–720.

Whitaker, C. (1992, May). *Color Purple* author confronts her critics and talks about her provocative new book. *Ebony, 47,* 86, 88–92.

16

INTERNATIONALIZING THE PSYCHOLOGY CURRICULUM

Examples of Course Transformation

LeeAnn Bartolini, Afshin Gharib, and William Phillips

Many academic departments have engaged in diversity transformation projects over the last decade. These endeavors have generally focused on increasing faculty and student awareness of underrepresented groups and multicultural issues within the United States (Goldstein, 1995, 2005). Textbook authors have broadened the scope of research in standard college texts to include diversity perspectives. Attempts at incorporating these findings into the standard curriculum have varied by institution, department, and faculty member (Brewer, 2006).

In 2002 our university participated in a diversity transformation process that led to the creation of diversity-focused student learning outcome (SLO) goals across the curriculum. The focus of the initial course SLOs was to increase cross-cultural understanding and awareness of diversity within the United States. Although this is a laudable and essential goal, we quickly realized that students continued to receive a very Amerocentric view of most disciplines. For example, in many psychology courses, the majority of research incorporated into textbooks and readings is carried out at American institutions. It seems reasonable that a truly diverse "international" curriculum should include how topics are studied and understood globally (Sexton & Hogan, 1992). We incorporated the campus-wide diversity initiative SLOs into our courses, but in 2005 the department took this transformation process one step further and extended it to include international SLOs for selected courses. Transforming courses to incorporate international research and theory is possible in most disciplines, and we present our process of internationalizing a psychology department as a model. To begin this process, we recommend the formation of a departmental task force to select an initial list of core courses for international transformation. Once courses are selected, faculty can decide on international SLOs and develop appropriate assignments and assessments.

Although courses on international psychology exist in the United States, we were interested in how to begin infusing internationalism throughout our curriculum (Stevens & Wedding, 2004). A division of the American Psychological Association (Division 52) formed a working group on "Internationalizing the Undergraduate Psychology Curriculum" in 2004, but their findings were not available when we set out to begin to internationalize the curriculum in our department (Lutsky, Torney-Purta, Velayo, Whittlesey, Woolf, & McCarthy, 2005).

One issue we had to resolve right away was how to distinguish *international* from *cross-cultural* (terms that seem to have been used interchangeably). We developed a somewhat arbitrary rule of thumb that *international psychology* included research conducted in countries other than the United States, focusing on non-American populations. Wedding (2004) writes in *The Handbook of International Psychology* that international psychology aims "to capacity build through transnational research and practice, and to facilitate the development of an international curriculum" (p. 2). We attempted to be consistent with his definition. The increase in "cross-cultural" research content, which would include comparing different cultural groups within the United States or comparing native cultures to one another, was seen as a subcategory of internationalization.

Our approach was threefold: to create an international SLO and a corresponding assessment tool for several courses in the major; to create a grid of psychology departments around the globe that offered study aboard and internship opportunities for American students; and to compile a list of international psychological associations. This chapter addresses the process of developing and assessing international SLOs and provides examples that can promote similar efforts in different disciplines.

One way of internationalizing a course is to include research from journals published in other countries. Such journals are readily available for most disciplines. For example, a quick search of journals in the arts and humanities shows the following possible sources: *Film Journal International, Dance International, Theatre Research International, Plays International,* and *International Journal for Philosophy of Religion.* In psychology we identified dozens of useful journals, such as the *Journal of British Psychology* or the *Asian Journal of Social Psychology,* as well as journals specializing in international research, such as the *International Journal of Psychology,* the *International Journal of Mental Health,* and the *Journal of Cross-Cultural Psychology.*

Not all methods of internationalizing a course simply involve research in other countries or comparison of cultures. Within any discipline one can identify possible topic areas that could benefit from an international perspective. In psychology, for example, a course could be transformed by examining licensing procedures for clinicians, exploring mental health issues faced in other countries, and reviewing legal issues surrounding mental health. Seven examples of SLOs and assignments that will hopefully stimulate faculty thinking at other institutions are included below.

1. Career Development in Psychology

All majors in our department are required to take a course in career development, which up to now has focused on career opportunities within the United States for people with psychology degrees. The new SLO aims to increase student awareness of career opportunities in other countries.

SLO. Students will gain an understanding of the range of career opportunities available in the discipline internationally.

Assessment. Students will compare and contrast the job possibilities (and required training) at the undergraduate and graduate levels in at least two different countries. Students will then work in groups to prepare a PowerPoint presentation and oral report summarizing their findings.

Example. Students may look up job descriptions from other countries available on the Web. Some Web-based resources they can use include the international job listings on psychologyinfo.com, links available on psychologystudents.org, and information on apa.org.

2. Health Psychology

Health psychology is an upper-level elective open to students from all majors. The focus of the course is on how biological, psychological, and social factors influence health. In order to internationalize the course, a new assignment was added to raise student awareness of how local culture and customs around the world can influence health.

SLO.   Students will learn to analyze the relationship among culture, psychology, and health in a global context.

Assessment.   Students will select a health issue specific to a particular part of the world and find research articles relevant to the problem. Students will present an oral report on the health problem and the unique local factors that contribute to the success or failure of the attempts to treat the problem.

Example.   While infectious diseases such as HIV and malaria are a worldwide health concern, some areas, such as Africa, face an especially severe crisis (Hayes & Weiss, 2006; Mugambi, 2006). Africa has the largest population of patients with HIV, and certain cultural and sexual practices (including having multiple concurrent sex partners) in sub-Saharan nations contribute both to the spread of the pandemic and to the difficulties in controlling it. As part of fulfilling the international SLO for this class, students may report on the various biological, psychological, and cultural factors that make controlling the spread of HIV infections in sub-Saharan Africa such a challenge.

3. Abnormal Psychology

All psychology majors in our department are required to take at least one upper-level elective focusing on the social science approaches to psychology. Abnormal Psychology is one course that meets this requirement. Traditional courses in abnormal psychology rarely review global approaches to mental health. To transform the course, a new SLO was added to increase students' understanding of how mental illness is responded to globally.

SLO.   Students will be able to demonstrate how one mental illness is diagnosed, assessed, or treated globally.

Assessment.   Students will find a journal article that focuses on the diagnosis, assessment, or treatment of a mental disorder in another country, write a one-page description of their findings, and orally present the paper to the class. All students will therefore become familiar with more than one country, and their global awareness for how mental illness is diagnosed, assessed, or treated will expand.

Example.   Research has indicated that some symptoms of social anxiety disorders are culturally bound (Heinrichs, Rapee, & Alden, 2006). Students whose final research paper involves "living" with this disorder for the semester would incorporate these various culturally linked symptoms into their paper.

4. Social Psychology

Social Psychology is offered as another upper-level elective in our department that meets the social science elective requirement. To internationalize the course, students will be required to take advantage of the cultural diversity of their surrounding community.

SLO.   Students will gain a better understanding of cross-cultural differences in nonverbal behavior.

Assessment.   Students will conduct an observational study or a norm violation exercise to study people from at least two different cultural backgrounds; they will then share their findings in an oral report or short written reflection paper.

Example.   Research has indicated international and cultural differences in people's sense of personal space and the appropriateness of interpersonal

touching (Beaulieu, 2004; Gunnoe, 2004). Students could do a norm violation exercise in which they see how physically close they can stand to people
of different cultures before the subjects move away; they then report their
findings.

5. Physiological Psychology

All psychology majors in our department are required to take at least one
elective in some area of experimental psychology, including physiological
psychology. The new SLO for this course focuses on increasing the
student's appreciation for the role of culture in determining brain
development.

SLO.   Students will learn how both biological and cultural factors contribute to the way our brains work and gain an appreciation of how neu-
ropsychological research is conducted around the world.

Assessment.   Students will find at least two research articles published by
researchers from two different countries on some aspect of brain function
that seems to be influenced by culture. The research will be summarized and
compared in a paper.

Example.   Students may review studies on the differences in brain lateralization in different countries (Fagard & Dahmen, 2004; Ida & Mandal,
2003; Mayes, 1982). There is evidence that culture and upbringing influence
brain lateralization and specialization of function in brain hemispheres. For
example, in cultures where left-handedness is strongly discouraged, there are
higher rates of strongly lateralized individuals.

6. Cognitive Psychology

Introduction to Cognitive Processes is offered as an upper-level elective
course meeting the experimental requirement for the major. Internationalization
of a cognitive psychology course can take two routes: reviewing research conducted in other countries or examining how culture affects various cognitive
processes. The following is one example of the latter.

SLO.   Students will demonstrate an understanding that cultural differences influence cognitive processes.

Assessment.   Tests will focus on elements from lectures that deal with international issues and article reviews and summaries that incorporate an international component.

Example.   Flaherty (2005) demonstrated differences in articulatory suppression in speakers of different languages. Findings from studies on memory span have revealed that the number of syllables in words influences the number of words that can be recalled from short-term memory (commonly referred to as the syllable effect). That is, people can recall more items from a list of one-syllable words than from a list of three-syllable words. This manner of recalling impacts the common digit-span task found on most tests of intelligence. Native speakers of languages where the digits are multisyllabic (e.g., Korean, Hebrew, and Spanish, to name a few) will on average recall fewer items on a digit-span task. This can easily be demonstrated in class (if there is enough diversity) or as a "research project" conducted by students outside the classroom.

7. Sensation and Perception

The Sensation and Perception course is an upper-level elective meeting the experimental requirement for the major. As with cognitive psychology, such a course can be internationalized by exploring how culture affects our perception or by reviewing research conducted in other countries (e.g., Segall, Dansen, Berry, & Poortinga, 2002). The following is a good example of reviewing research.

SLO.   Students will become familiar with perception research being done in other countries, and specifically how this research adds to our knowledge of perception.

Assessment.   Students are required to find a research article (given a perceptual topic) that has been performed in another country or that addresses the effects of culture on perception. In turn, they will then present this research to the class using Microsoft PowerPoint (or some other presentation software).

Example. Liu, Wan, and Ng (2006) reported that native listeners of Mandarin were more accurate at determining tonal differences among different speakers of Mandarin. Also, Suzuki (1982) reported that native speakers of Japanese are selectively more sensitive to particular tones than non-native speakers. (Because it is difficult for students to know about such research, hints in the form of "topics to choose from" are given in a handout. This will require some preparatory work at first, but additions can be made as some students find other topics independently.)

We have begun incorporating these international SLOs, and student feedback has been positive. One effect has been increased discussion of international issues in the classroom. One challenge our students have been facing is finding English translations in full text for some of the international resources. Incorporating these new SLOs has meant abbreviating other parts of our courses, which has been challenging, but at the same time we have found that we are also learning about new areas of research.

Since transforming courses in our department, we have conducted workshops for faculty from other disciplines. Some disciplines find internationalization more natural, such as political science, business, anthropology, and sociology. Others disciplines, such as mathematics, chemistry, occupational therapy, and nursing, find the process more of a challenge. Nevertheless, faculty from these other disciplines at our workshops have reported having a generally positive experience. As discipline communication becomes more international, we hope that other departments may benefit from engaging in a similar exercise.

References

Beaulieu, C. (2004). Intercultural study of personal space: A case study. *Journal of Applied Social Psychology, 34*(4), 794–805.

Brewer, C. (2006). Undergraduate education in psychology: United States. *International Journal of Psychology. Special Issue: International Practices in the Teaching of Psychology, 41*(1), 65–71.

Fagard, J., & Dahmen, R. (2004). Cultural influences on the development of lateral preferences: A comparison between French and Tunisian children. *Laterality, 9*, 67–78.

Flaherty, M. and Moran, A. (2005). Articulatory suppression in bilingual and second language speakers. *International Journal of Cognitive Technology, 10*(1), 38–46.

Goldsten, S. (1995). Cross-cultural psychology as a curriculum transformation resource. *Teaching of Psychology, 22*(4), 228–232.

Goldstein, S. (2005). Cross-cultural perspectives in the psychology curriculum: Moving beyond "add culture and stir." In B. Perlman, L. McCann, & W. Buskist (Eds.), *Voices of experience: Memorable talks from the National Institute on the Teaching of Psychology* (pp. 45–57). Washington, DC: American Psychological Society.

Gunnoe, J. (2004). Gender and culture differences in touching behavior. *Journal of Social Psychology, 144*(1), 49–62.

Hayes, R., & Weiss, H. (2006). Understanding the HIV epidemic trends in Africa. *Science, 311,* 620–621.

Heinrichs, N., Rapee, R., & Alden, L. (2006). Cultural differences in perceived social norms and social anxiety. *Behaviour Research and Therapy, 44*(8), 1187–1197.

Ida, Y., & Mandal, M. (2003). Cultural differences in side bias: Evidence from Japan and India. *Laterality, 8,* 121–133.

Liu, H., Wan, M., Ng, M. L., Wang, S., & Lu, C. (2006). Tonal perceptions in normal laryngeal, esophageal, and electrolaryngeal speech of Mandarin. *Folia Phoniatrica et Logopaedica, 58*(5), 340–352.

Lutsky, N., Torney-Purta, J., Velayo, R., Whittlesey, V., Woolf, L., & McCarthy, M. (2005). *American Psychological Association Working Group on Internationalizing the Undergraduate Psychology Curriculum: Report and recommended learning outcomes for internationalizing the undergraduate curriculum.* Retrieved May 1, 2007, from http://www.apa.org/ed/pcue/international.pdf

Mayes, J. T. (1982). Hemisphere function and spatial ability: An exploratory study of sex and cultural differences. *International Journal of Psychology, 17,* 65–80.

Mugambi, J. (2006). The impact of HIV/AIDS on Kenyan rural women and the role of counseling. *International Social Work, 49,* 87–96.

Segall, M., Dansen, P., Berry, J., & Poortinga, Y. (2002). *Cross-cultural psychology: Research and applications.* London: Cambridge University Press.

Sexton, V. S., & Hogan, J. D. (Eds.). (1992). *International psychology: Views from around the world.* Lincoln: University of Nebraska Press.

Stevens, M. J., & Wedding, D. (2004). International psychology: An overview. In M. J. Stevens & D. Wedding (Eds.), *Handbook of international psychology* (pp. 1–23). New York: Brunner-Routledge.

Suzuki, T. (1982). Genetic study on tonal sense (like a schema) peculiar to Japanese people. *Journal of Child Development, 18,* 1–15.

Wedding, D. (Ed.). (2004). *The handbook of international psychology.* Oxford: Routledge.

17

EXPERIENTIAL ACTIVITIES FOR TEACHING ABOUT DIVERSITY

Carlos M. Diaz-Lazaro,[1] Sandra Cordova, and
Rosslyn Franklyn

Over the past 20 years there has been considerable progress in the inclusion of cultural diversity themes in the curriculum (Bronstein & Quina, 2003; Mio, 2003). However, this progress has not happened without considerable debate, as there are still a significant number of faculty who fail to see the relevance of such inclusion. In particular, there is still considerable uncertainty as to which teaching strategies are especially effective for teaching about diversity. This paper highlights the usefulness of experiential activities in teaching about diversity. Although we include relevant literature in the area, our approach is primarily based on our experience as instructors and students, and our information is influenced by our shared perspectives concerning cultural competency and social justice. We focus on sharing what has worked for us in incorporating issues of diversity into the curriculum, with the aim of providing instructors with useful information as they develop their courses.

We start by defining experiential learning and briefly highlighting the benefits of this teaching approach. We then survey the literature on the use of experiential approaches to teaching about diversity and provide examples of activities that we have found useful. Finally, we present a list of

[1]Dr. Diaz-Lazaro would like to express his gratitude to Dr. B. Beth Cohen. Without her friendship, mentorship, support, and most of all her encouragement to think outside the box, this chapter would not have been possible.

resources that we believe could help in incorporating experiential activities in teaching.

Learning by Doing

Learning can be a complex task that depends on variables such as the age of the learner, the teaching style of the instructor, the learning environment, and socioeconomic status. Much research has been conducted in the educational and psychological fields regarding the types and styles of learning. One such style is experiential learning.

Numerous definitions of experiential learning presently exist. In its simplest form, experiential learning is learning by doing, or using one's experiences as a learning tool. The concept is based on the Experiential Learning Theory, which suggests that concrete experiences help students comprehend information when they can reflect or recall on those experiences and actively put to use those concepts they are learning (Scales, Roehlkepartain, Neal, Kielsmeier, & Benson, 2006). Rogers (2006) believes that experiential learning can take three separate forms. In the first form, learning is characterized by unplanned experiences (i.e., getting lost, meeting new people) and is generally either unconscious or semiconscious. The amount and depth of that learning are largely contingent on how much emotion is involved, how much attention is given at the time of the event, how much conscious reflection is given to the incident, and how much reuse and reinforcement are given to the incident (Rogers, 2006). The second type of experiential learning involves testing all new material we encounter against our cumulative past experience, regardless of how the new material or information is obtained. If this is not done, all new material is divorced from acquired learning rather than being added or adjusted to one's current knowledge and perceptual base (Rogers, 2006). Finally, the third form of experiential learning includes all those planned activities that facilitators and/or tutors use to shape our planned learning (Rogers, 2006). For example, artificial experiences facilitate student application of new material to real life scenarios from which they can draw lessons. This style has also been termed active learning.

Much as Rogers (2006) described the active component of experiential learning, Blood (2006) defined actionable knowledge as part of experiential learning. According to Blood, to be actionable, knowledge must go beyond being knowledge for its own sake and must lead to behavior change in the form of choice (guiding decisions) or implementation (guiding actions). Ives and Obenchain (2006) adopted yet another definition of experiential education, this one based on the Association for Experiential Education's formulation, which states that experiential education is a process through which a learner constructs knowledge, skill, and value from direct experience. These authors believe that experiential learning should include opportunities for student direction, curriculum connections to the real world, and critical reflection.

No matter what definition or term is used to describe experiential education, the literature provides a useful framework that educators, instructors, tutors, and the like can use and incorporate into their current teaching models. According to Scales et al. (2006), experiential learning, or service learning, may be a valuable technique for student engagement and achievement in urban, majority non-White, schools. Wherever and however experiential learning is used, research has shown its effectiveness. Becoming involved in the learning experience may be what some individuals need to better grasp and conceptualize new material.

Teaching About Diversity Through Experiential Learning

Teaching about diversity can take many forms. For example, Hill (2003) suggests that diversity may be taught by including knowledge-based topics in different courses as well as focusing on student growth and self-awareness. Topics typically represented in diversity courses include racial identity development, privilege, acculturation, racism, and worldviews (Mio, 2003). Experiential approaches are one way to address these topics in the classroom. The literature on multiculturalism highlights the use of experiential learning in multicultural teaching and training (Arthur & Achenbach, 2002; Kim & Lyons, 2003). For example, personal and professional experiences have been reported to be more influential in developing multicultural competence than are ethical codes or professional guidelines (Hansen et al., 2006).

Various methods are implemented in teaching diversity, such as didactic methods and experiential activities. However, these teaching methods vary in their effectiveness and specific student learning outcomes (Arthur & Achenbach, 2002). The most effective methods are considered to be those that positively impact students' level of awareness, knowledge, and skills (Kim & Lyons, 2003). Furthermore, students report benefiting specifically from experiential learning activities (Arthur & Achenbach, 2002; Kim &

Lyons, 2003), and those who experience a general multicultural activity report feeling more aware, knowledgeable, and skillful (Carlson, Brook, Laygo, Cohen, & Kirkscey, 1998).

Didactic methods as exemplified by traditional lectures usually do not require much active student participation. Experiential methods, on the other hand, directly involve the learner by requiring active participation in games, role plays, or guided imagery. Didactic methods are more effective when combined with experiential activities, such as role plays (Kim & Lyons, 2003). In addition, games are considered more effective than film viewing and similar activities (Kim & Lyons, 2003). Although film viewing is considered a helpful multicultural teaching and training method, games lead to more personal awareness of attitudes and beliefs. Specifically, they promote learning by facilitating changes in attitude and learning retention, possibly because they encourage direct participation, engaging the player in a more intriguing, interesting fashion than other activities (Kim & Lyons, 2003). By involving students in something that encourages them to act freely, this type of training facilitates multicultural learning.

When experiential methods are employed correctly, learners achieve significant outcomes. For example, experiential approaches can play an important role in challenging an individual's worldviews about the self and others, such as views on White privilege or racial identity. Experiential methods lead to empathy and awareness of oneself and others (Arthur & Achenbach, 2002). Games such as *BafaBafa* and *Step Forward, Step Back* can increase awareness of other cultures and can help trainees evaluate their own prejudice and privilege (Kim & Lyons, 2003). They provide a safe and structured environment where students can explore different cultural issues, and experiential training methods allow trainees to cognitively and effectively process these issues (Kim & Lyons, 2003). In short, experiential learning has been supported by the literature as a key approach to addressing issues of diversity.

Why Use Experiential Learning in Teaching About Diversity?

Cognitive Restructuring Through Self-Referencing.   Learning involves a relatively permanent change in our mental associations or behavior as a result of experience (Ormrod, 1990). A key component of learning is thus the incorporation of new information within our cognitive schemas, which can be conceptualized as "workable structures to organize and anticipate data" that are experienced (Fiske, 2004, p. 143). Self-referencing can be defined as "the tendency to process efficiently and remember well information related to oneself" (Myers, 2007, p. 35). Based on self-referencing, we are more likely to access the information we have learned when we can relate it to ourselves. When using the traditional lecture style, students are more likely to intellectualize course material without making a meaningful connection to themselves and their life contexts. On the other hand, when students participate in experiential activities, they connect with diversity concepts firsthand, either by relating the material to a past personal experience or by encoding a new experience. Our schemas have been influenced by previous experiences with issues of diversity. Because these schemas have been developed primarily through experience, it makes sense that they will be more effectively challenged experientially, not conceptually. Experiential activities on diversity bring course concepts to a more personal level increasing then the likelihood of effective cognitive processing and memory retrieval, an example of self-referencing. Furthermore, these activities can challenge inaccurate beliefs and attitudes by restructuring our cognitive schemas.

Emotionally Laden Topics Call for an Appropriate Outlet. Although particular multicultural concepts and ensuing discussions have different emotional contents, most instructors of diversity courses grant that many concepts related to cultural differences evoke affective reactions among both students and faculty. Pinderhughes's (1989) research on differences between European American persons and people of color in dealing with issues of race supports this idea. Pinderhughes noted that in addressing issues of race and ethnicity European Americans (a) are generally unaware of whiteness; (b) struggle with the exploration of early images of race and color; (c) feel discomfort, struggle, and pain; (d) are challenged to break through denial, projection, rationalization, and enduring anxiety and pain; and (e) experience apprehension. Ethnic minorities, on the other hand, who commonly experience issues of race, must be able to live with ambiguity and may inadvertently protect European Americans by blaming themselves, cope with the stress by denying their racial identity, and denigrate those within their racial group who have not been able to achieve parity with European Americans (Pinderhughes, 1989). European Americans and ethnic minorities come from different perspectives that often impose significant barriers to communicating about racial identity and meaning. As a result, (a) frustration is high; (b) efforts to share and be heard often generate more heat than light; and, (c) anger is a common response for everyone (Pinderghughes, 1989).

In short, we contend that the use of traditional lectures or even large-group discussions to deal with emotionally laden concepts is not the best alternative. We recommend the use of structured experiential activities. However, a key component of successful experiential learning in dealing with issues of diversity is having sufficient time for processing and debriefing after the activity. Without the debriefing, students have difficulty making sense of what they have just experienced because they do not have a sounding board with which to reflect on the experience and process uncomfortable emotions. They then are more likely to blame their negative emotions (sadness, guilt, anger, etc.) on the discussion itself or on individuals from diverse groups to protect themselves from understanding that their emotions have personal meaning. The debriefing assists students by making emotions more manageable and helping them integrate this new information into their current schemas.

Relaxed Learning Environment.   Developing a relaxed learning environment in which students feel open to sharing their thoughts on these sensitive issues is quite instrumental. Although a certain amount of guardedness in sharing about one's biases and experiences with diversity serves as a healthy self-protection strategy, open dialogue is a key factor in the development of multicultural awareness. One of the tools we have used to create a relaxed learning environment is humor, which facilitates student learning (Garner, 2006; Hurren, 2005/2006). If students experience activities as fun, they will be more likely to positively approach the multicultural concepts involved with or following the activity. Humor can be incorporated through a diversity activity that exposes the lighter side of an issue or simply through entertaining activities that might not be related to the topic per se. The Alternatives to Violence Project (AVP), for example, incorporates in its workshops brief, fun activities called "Light and Livelies" (AVP, 1986). These activities aim at connecting people to one another and diffusing negative emotions through the use of humor and physical movement.

Resources: Where Do We Find These Experiential Activities?

A number of journals provide very useful information on experiential activities for teaching diversity. Books that could be useful include *One Hundred Ten Experiences for Multicultural Learning* (Pedersen, 2004), *Activities Handbook for the Teaching of Psychology: Volume 4* (Benjamin, Nodine, Ernst, & Broeker, 1999), (c) *Teaching About Culture, Ethnicity, and Diversity* (Singelis, 1998), *Handbook for Developing Multicultural Awareness* (Pedersen, 2000), *Decisional Dialogues in a Cultural Context* (Pedersen & Hernandez, 1997), and *Exploring Culture: Exercises, Stories and Synthetic Cultures* (Hofstede, Pedersen, & Hofstede, 2002). We have found particularly useful the incorporation of activities from social justice and community workshops. However, using experiential activities that have been developed as part of a larger training experience may involve skillful modifications. For example, some activities may assume previous knowledge of particular concepts and may create confusion if these are not familiar.

You can also modify existing activities or create your own. Once you are familiar with facilitating a number of experiential activities, you are likely to come to a point in which you feel comfortable developing your own activities. You must be well aware of your objectives and your audience. Most importantly, nothing can replace good preparation. The more detailed you are in describing the activity you are conducting, the better grasp you will have on managing not only foreseeable challenges but the unforeseeable ones as well.

Finally, although these are not books on experiential activities, we have found that *Promoting Social Diversity and Social Justice* (Goodman, 2001) and *Understanding Race, Ethnicity, and Power* (Pinderhughes, 1989) are valuable resources in teaching courses on diversity. Teachers must create an optimal classroom atmosphere that will manage classroom dynamics. The aforementioned books do a great job of assisting teachers and trainers in understanding how race, gender, ethnicity, and other social identities play out in classroom interactions.

Conclusion

Teaching about diversity poses significant challenges, especially when an instructor actively questions students' core beliefs about diversity and takes them out of their comfort zone. Students can resist the topics addressed.

Instructors must stay out of their comfort zone and challenge students to explore topics in more depth. All in all, it is a challenging yet extremely rewarding journey. The integration of experiential activities can certainly be a key to classroom effectiveness and can guard against the burnout that usually accompanies teaching these sensitive topics.

A final word of advice for instructors is to look outside their own discipline for ideas on how to teach about diversity. Disciplines such as education, social work, sociology, psychology, and cultural anthropology, among others, offer unique perspectives into human diversity. We also need to go beyond traditional academia. A number of social justice and community organizations have much to offer in addressing issues of diversity. Equally important is to go beyond local frames of reference. Our analysis needs to broaden to include international perspectives. Modeling our own self-awareness and risk taking to students will certainly go a long way. Experiential activities provide an excellent strategy for effectively and creatively accomplishing our learning outcomes, appropriately challenging our students, and allowing learning about diversity to be a transforming influence in their lives.

References

Alternatives to Violence Project. (1986). *Basic course manual.* Houston, TX: Alternatives to Violence Project.

Arthur, N., & Achenbach, K. (2002). Counselor preparation: Developing multicultural counseling competencies through experiential learning. *Counselor Education and Supervision, 42,* 1–13.

Benjamin, L. T., Nodine, B. F., Ernst, R. M., & Broeker, C. B. (1999). *Activities handbook for the teaching of psychology, Vol. 4.* Washington, DC: American Psychological Association.

Blood, M. R. (2006). Only you can create actionable knowledge. *Academy of Management Learning and Education, 5,* 209–212.

Bronstein, P., & Quina, K. (Eds.). (2003). *Teaching gender and multicultural awareness: Resources for the psychology classroom.* Washington, DC: American Psychological Association. Carlson, M. H., Brook, C. J., Laygo, R., Cohen, R., & Kirkscey, M. (1998). An exploratory study of multicultural competence of counselors in training: Support for experiential skills building. *The Clinical Supervisor, 17*(2), 75–87.

Fiske, S. (2004). *Social beings: A core motives approach to social psychology.* Hoboken, NJ: Wiley.

Garner, R. L. (2006). Humor in pedagogy. *College Teaching, 54,* 177–180.

Goodman, D. L. (2001). *Promoting social diversity and social justice: Educating people from privilege groups.* Thousand Oaks, CA: Sage.

Hansen, N. D., Randazzo, K. V., Schwartz, A., Marshall, M., Kalis, D., Frazier, R., Burke, C., Kershner-Rice, K., & Norvig, G. (2006). Do we practice what we preach? An exploratory survey of multicultural psychotherapy competencies. *Professional Psychology: Research and Practice, 37*(1), 66–74.

Hill, N. R. (2003). Promoting and celebrating multicultural competence in counselor trainees. *Counselor Education and Supervision, 43,* 39–51.

Hofstede, G. J., Pedersen, P., & Hofstede, G. (2002). *Exploring culture: Exercises, stories and synthetic cultures.* Yarmouth, ME: Intercultural Press.

Hurren, B. (2005/2006). Humor in school is serious business. *International Journal of Learning, 12*(6), 79–83.

Ives, B., & Obenchain, K. (2006). Experiential education in the classroom and academic outcomes: For those who want it all. *Journal of Experiential Education, 29,* 61–77.

Kim, B. S., & Lyons, H. Z. (2003). Experiential activities and multicultural counseling competence training. *Journal of Counseling and Development, 81,* 400–408.

Mio, J. S. (2003). On teaching multiculturalism: History, models, and content. In G. Bernal, J. E. Trimble, A. K. Burlew, & F. T. L. Leong (Eds.), *Handbook of racial and ethnic minority psychology* (pp. 119–146). Thousand Oaks, CA: Sage.

Myers, D. (2007). *Exploring social psychology* (4th ed.). New York: McGraw-Hill.

Ormrod, J. (1990). *Human learning: Principles, theories, and educational applications.* Columbus, OH: Merrill Publishing Co.

Pedersen, P. (2000). *Handbook for developing multicultural awareness* (3rd ed.). Alexandria, VA: American Counseling Association.

Pedersen, P. B. (2004). *One hundred ten experiences for multicultural learning.* Washington, DC: American Psychological Association.

Pedersen, P., & Hernandez, D. (1997). *Decisional dialogues in a cultural context: Structured exercises.* Thousand Oaks, CA: Sage.

Pinderhughues, E. (1989). *Understanding race, ethnicity, and power: The key to efficacy in clinical practice.* New York: Free Press.

Rogers, A. (2006). Learning from experience. *Adults Learning, 18,* 30–31.

Ruben, B. D. (1999). Simulations, games and experience-based learning: The quest for a new paradigm for teaching and learning. *Simulation and Gaming, 30,* 498–505.

Scales, P. C., Roehlkepartain, E. C., Neal, M., Kielsmeier, J. C., & Benson, P. L. (2006). Reducing academic achievement gaps: The role of community service and service learning. *Journal of Experiential Education, 29,* 38–60.

Singelis, T. M. (Ed.). (1998). *Teaching about culture, ethnicity, and diversity: Exercises and planned activities.* Thousand Oaks, CA: Sage.

18

ENLISTING THE PARTICIPATION OF STUDENTS IN DIVERSIFYING THE CURRICULUM

Susan B. Goldstein

O ver the past two decades there has been considerable attention to issues of diversity in the college curriculum, and a fairly extensive collection of resources has been developed to support faculty seeking to design and teach more inclusive courses. These resources address implementation issues (e.g., Clayton-Pedersen, Parker, Smith, Moreno, & Teraguchi, 2007; Ouellett, 2005), course content and pedagogy (e.g., Branche, Mullennix, & Cohn, 2007; Enns & Sinacore, 2005), and assessment (e.g., Garcia, Hudgins, Musil, Nettles, Sedlacek, & Smith, 2002; Williams, Berger, & McClendon, 2005). One aspect of curriculum transformation that has been neglected, however, is the critical role that students play in this process. Although publications have discussed student activism prompting curriculum revision (e.g., Simien, 2003) and students' reactions to diversity initiatives (e.g., Ervin, 2001; Mio & Awakuni, 2000), little attention has been given to efforts to enlist students as active change agents. This chapter discusses the benefits and challenges of such efforts and provides specific recommendations for facilitating the inclusion of students in transforming the curriculum.

Student involvement in curriculum transformation can take a number of forms, ranging from informal comments in class discussions to assignments that involve identifying sources of diverse perspectives and determining how to integrate them into the curriculum. In some institutions, student-run courses or courses that are co-taught with faculty may be an additional opportunity for student involvement.

There are several benefits to including students as active participants in curriculum transformation efforts. Students tend to oppose diversity initiatives that they perceive as forced upon them by faculty or administrators (e.g., Whitt, Edison, Pascarella, Terenzini, & Nora, 2001). Curricular change initiated by peers may be both better received and more personally meaningful, and may thus have a greater impact on learning and retention. In addition, once students are familiar with curriculum transformation strategies, they may be able to impact courses across campus, regardless of whether the instructor has made efforts to address diversity. Finally, involving students in curriculum transformation helps to create an institutional norm in which students, faculty, and administrators expect diversity to be an integral part of the educational experience.

Despite the benefits of enlisting the participation of students in diversifying the curriculum, studies indicate that student response to diversity initiatives vary widely (Whitt et al., 2001). Some students already recognize forms of bias in the curriculum because they find their own social group (e.g., race/ethnicity, gender, social class) marginalized or excluded. Participating in curriculum transformation may validate their experiences and provide tools with which to respond to curricular omissions and distortions. Students exposed to Women's Studies or Ethnic Studies may also become enthusiastic participants in curriculum transformation (Schmitz & Taranath, 2005). Courses in these disciplines often directly address issues of inequality in the organization and presentation of information and welcome students to challenge the status quo. However, many students may have never fully considered issues of diversity. Some White students may view intercultural sensitivity as important for those in diverse environments but see little need for multicultural education in predominantly White college settings (Rosenberg, 1998). Several studies have found students of color to be ambivalent about diversity programs. According to Ervin (2001), students of color may fear they are being unfairly burdened with the role of educating others about their ethnic/racial group's history or experiences and may expect faculty and administrators to respond to concerns in a culturally insensitive manner.

In order to encourage students to participate in curriculum transformation and to enable them to have a positive experience doing so, it is important to (1) provide students with information that makes a strong case for a transformed curriculum, (2) provide them with the skills necessary to undertake curriculum transformation efforts, and (3) create an environment in which students feel safe and enthusiastic about participating. The remainder of this chapter discusses strategies for accomplishing these three goals.

Making the Case to Students for Diversifying the Curriculum

Many students may not be convinced of the need for and value of curriculum transformation. It is important for students to learn that academic disciplines are not immutable entities but that the content and methods of a single discipline may vary across time and place depending on how they have been shaped by social, cultural, political, historical, environmental, economic, and religious factors. Chun (2000), for example, suggests that anthropologists in Taiwan tend to conduct more applied research than those in the United States or the United Kingdom because of the closer ties between the university and the state. Across academic disciplines, there are countless examples of how content and methods have been influenced by conditions that privilege White men (see, for example, Clark, Ayton, Frechette, & Keller, 2005, and Silver, 2007, on the fields of world history and medicine, respectively).

Once acquainted with the impact of such forces on academic disciplines, students will better understand why texts and other course materials may include statements about universal theories and constructs that, upon further examination, are actually culture-specific or biased toward particular social groups. Even in math and natural sciences courses, illustrations of theories and constructs, as well as pedagogical assumptions, may be culture-bound (B. Goldstein, 1994). An example of a culture-bound phenomenon typically presented as universal in psychology texts is *social loafing*. Latane, Williams, and Harkins (1979) used this term to describe their finding that when people work in groups, they tend to exert less effort than when they work alone. In fact, social loafing seems to be far from universal. Studies of women throughout the world (Karau & Williams, 1993) and men in some collectivist cultures (Earley, 1989; Gabrenya, Wang, & Latane, 1985) more frequently find evidence of *social striving*, a term developed by Gabrenya and colleagues (1985) to describe a situation in which people work harder in a group context. It is useful to point out such instances to students, guide them in discovering other false universals, and help them to explore how and why such distortions came to be. The case of social loafing, for example, resulted from research initially conducted exclusively with men in individualist societies.

Awareness of the sociocultural forces that shape a discipline may be facilitated by exposing students to the ways in which a discipline's content, methods, and pedagogical approaches differ throughout the world. For example, reading about indigenous sociological approaches (e.g., Awiwowo, 1999) makes explicit the limited perspective of Western sociology.

Curriculum Transformation Skills

In order to be effective change agents, students need to be trained in the specific skills necessary to understand and have an impact on curriculum transformation efforts. Key skills include the ability to (1) speak the language of curriculum transformation, (2) assess the level of inclusion in the existing curriculum, (3) identify biases in course content and pedagogy, and (4) seek diverse perspectives excluded from the curriculum.

Skill 1: Speaking the Language of Curriculum Transformation

Curriculum transformation is a complex concept that can be more easily discussed if students possess relevant vocabulary. For example, it is helpful for students to be able to understand the difference between inadvertently *omitting* as opposed to deliberately *excluding* people or ideas from the curriculum (Minnich, 1986). They should also be able to distinguish between *additive* and *integrative* or *transformative* approaches to curricular change, each term indicating successively greater change to the structure and content of the curriculum. Finally, it is important that they understand the concept of *marginalization*, which refers to situations in which diverse perspectives are presented as exceptions to the norm. Information on diversity may even be literally marginalized in that it appears only in supplementary materials, in the "boxes" of primary texts, or in a separate diversity chapter. Instructors can play a valuable role in modeling the appropriate usage of terms such as these.

Skill 2: Assessing the Curriculum

To be active participants in the curriculum transformation process, students need to be able to assess the degree to which course materials integrate diverse perspectives. According to Chuppa-Cornell (2005), the primary assessment tool for this purpose has been phase models. Several such models exist, with McIntosh's (1983, 1990) one of the most widely used and perhaps one of the most straightforward for students to grasp. McIntosh outlined five phases of curriculum "re-vision" based on her analysis of history curricula. This model has been applied to such varied fields as literature (Roses & Randolph, 1997), biology (Rosser, 1986), math (Kaiser & Rogers, 1995), psychology (S. B. Goldstein, 2005; Torrey, 1987), management (Betters-Reed, 1994), and architectural history (Kingsley, 1988).

Bartlett and Feiner's (1992, p. 561) application of McIntosh's phases to the field of economics illustrates this model. According to these authors, in the first phase, economics is taught as if race and gender are irrelevant because economic models are assumed to be "objective and universal." In the second phase, famous economists who are female and/or people of color are mentioned as additions to the curriculum, but no substantive changes are made to course content. In McIntosh's third phase, diversity enters the curriculum in the form of isolated issues, such as income discrimination (Bartlett & Feiner, 1992), in which gender and race/ethnicity are viewed in the context of deviations from the norm. McIntosh's fourth phase involves the modification of economic theories and methods to address issues that arise in phase three. In phase four, faculty and students question the universality of thought within the discipline and produce a body of literature that is more inclusive and thus more accurate. There would be no need for separate courses, such as *Economics of Race, Class, and Gender*, since all courses across the economics curriculum would fully integrate diverse perspectives. Reaching the fifth phase would require the redefinition of economics as a discipline, including a restructuring of economics topics and methods of inquiry.

To help students develop the ability to assess the level of curriculum transformation, instructors might present examples of the different phases or ask that students do so as an assignment. More advanced students might identify information that could bring the material to a more sophisticated level of transformation and discuss how they might integrate these materials without marginalizing them. In some courses it may even be appropriate to have students rewrite text excerpts to make them more inclusive of diverse perspectives (see Textbook Rewrite assignment in S. B. Goldstein, 2008).

Skill 3: Identifying Bias

Once students become familiar with different forms of bias, they will be able to identify them in curricular materials and formulate appropriate solutions. One widespread form of bias involves generalizations based on the experiences or analysis of the dominant group, such as European Americans or men. In scholarship on the U.S. civil rights movement, for example, information about African American men is generalized to all African Americans, with African American women "conspicuously absent" (Simien, 2003, p. 747).

A second form of bias is the use of ethnocentric standards of comparison. Discussing cross-cultural differences in terms of *Western* versus *non-Western*, for example, reinforces the notion that what is Western is central and thus the standard of comparison, and that all other cultures are less significant and less distinctive. The terms *White* and *non-White* produce a similar bias. Minnich (1986, p. 7) explained, "We can tell quickly how far a group is from the unprefixed defining center by how many prefixes that group carries in scholarship: There are poets, and then there are Black Third World women poets."

A third form of bias stems from the failure to acknowledge within-group diversity. A collection of essays from Mexico, for example, should not be described as voicing Latin American perspectives. Similarly, essays collected from predominantly White, North American college populations do not allow us to draw conclusions about "Western values" or "American behavior."

Finally, students need to be aware of bias in how knowledge is organized within a discipline. Olson (2001; Olson & Schlegl, 2001) has written extensively about the gender and cultural biases inherent in library classification systems. These include representing groups as exceptions (e.g., a category for "gifted women" but not "gifted men"), isolating topics from the mainstream (e.g., information on "Aboriginal North Americans" that is classified separately from other information on North American history and culture), omitting topics (e.g., independent churches in Africa), using an inappropriate classification structure (e.g., language groupings based on inaccurate assumptions), and using biased terminology (such as "Gypsy" as opposed to the more preferred "Rom"). Similar forms of bias exist in the titles and publication sources of scholarly articles. For example, whereas a study of the health beliefs of Americans of Mexican ancestry would be clearly labeled as such and may be published in a culture-specific journal such as the *Hispanic Journal of Behavioral Sciences*, research on the health beliefs of Americans of European ancestry may be labeled as a study of "American health beliefs" and may appear in a discipline-specific journal, such as *Social Science and Medicine* (S. B. Goldstein, 2005).

Skill 4: Seeking Diverse Perspectives

Once students are able to target areas of the curriculum for revision, they will need to be able to locate information on the missing perspectives. One strategy is to take a functional equivalence approach. According to Pareek and Rao (1980, p. 131), "functional equivalence of a behaviour exists when the behaviour in question has developed in response to a problem shared by two or more social/cultural groups, even though the behaviour in one society may be superficially quite different from the behaviour in another society." For example, students in a variety of science and social science courses are exposed to the steps and assumptions involved in the scientific method. If one focuses on the *function* of this method as a model of inquiry into the natural world, other methods that serve this function may present themselves for inclusion in a more diversified curriculum. Garroutte (1999) discusses models of inquiry into the natural world indigenous to some American Indian cultures that differ from the scientific method in a variety of ways, including the nature of evidence and assumptions about cause and effect, language, ethics, and the meaning of contradictory explanations.

A second strategy for identifying diverse perspectives is to shift attention to the social context of a phenomenon. For example, rather than having education students concentrate on individual motivation as an explanation for why students *drop out* of school, one might reframe this issue in terms of the schools' *failure to retain* students. The focus would then be on characteristics of the school environment that might contribute to this problem, thus allowing for a discussion of sociocultural influences on individual behaviors. By learning to seek functional equivalents and attending to the social context, students will more easily identify diverse perspectives absent from the curriculum.

Helping Students to Feel Safe Participating in Curriculum Transformation Efforts

A welcoming and supportive classroom environment is key to enlisting the participation of students in curriculum transformation efforts. Instructors can set a positive tone by presenting discussions of diversity as rare and exciting opportunities to learn about viewpoints with which we are unfamiliar or disagree. Since people typically spend time with others who have opinions similar to their own, classroom discussions may be one of the few venues in which such exchanges occur. Students will look to instructors as models for respectful and honest discussion. This means acknowledging our own assumptions, areas of ignorance, and emotional reactions in an open and nondefensive manner.

Students will likely feel safer in the classroom if clear guidelines for discussion are established. These guidelines might emphasize communicating respectfully, safeguarding confidentiality, allowing for multiple perspectives on a single issue, and never placing anyone in the position of spokesperson for his or her ethnicity or social group. Students may more readily comply with discussion guidelines if they play a role developing them.

It can also be helpful to familiarize students with the cognitive processes involved in stereotype formation and maintenance (see, for example, Schneider, 2003). Once students view stereotyping as a result of errors in information processing (for example, the tendency to attend to vivid cases and to make stereotype-congruent attributions), they are better able to discuss stereotypic comments without making personal attacks and to identify the types of information that would be required to disconfirm these stereotypes.

Students' cultural background has a significant impact on classroom-related behavior and thus participation. For example, classroom environments in which one needs to be very assertive or interrupt the instructor or other students in order to participate may systematically disadvantage students whose cultures do not encourage such behavior. Other culturally patterned behaviors relevant to the classroom setting include ease with expressing personal feelings (Lynch, 1997) and comfort in group activities (Chan, 2003). Allowing students a range of participation options may result in a classroom that is more inclusive.

In working with those college students for whom the campus and classroom environments represent unfamiliar cultures, teachers can serve as cultural insiders. Rather than misattribute difficulties in this setting to personal deficiencies, teachers can help students gain specific cultural knowledge, such as how to read a syllabus, lead a discussion, or use library databases. This cultural knowledge allows all students to be full participants in classroom discussion and the curriculum transformation process.

Conclusions

For instructors struggling with multiple demands in an already compressed semester, training students as change agents may seem an expendable task. Yet the benefits of doing so are significant: students who are informed, engaged, and empowered; instructors who are simultaneously supported and challenged in revisioning their courses; and an ethos of inclusiveness essential to successful transformation across the curriculum.

References

Awiwowo, A. (1999). Indigenous sociologies. *International Sociology, 14,* 115–138.

Bartlett, R., & Feiner, S. (1992). Balancing the economic curriculum: Content, method and pedagogy. *American Economic Review, 82,* 559–564.

Betters-Reed, B. (1994). *Toward transformation of the management curriculum: Visions and voices for inclusion.* Working Paper No. 269. Wellesley, MA: Center for Research on Women.

Branche, J., Mullennix, J., & Cohn, E. R. (Eds.). (2007). *Diversity across the curriculum: A guide for faculty in higher education.* San Francisco: Jossey-Bass.

Chan, C. S. (2003). Psychological issues of Asian Americans. In P. Bronstein & K. Quina (Eds.), *Teaching a psychology of people: Resources for gender and sociocultural awareness* (pp. 179–193). Washington, DC: American Psychological Association.

Chun, A. (2000). From test to context: How anthropology makes its subject. *Cultural Anthropology, 15,* 570–595.

Chuppa-Cornell, K. (2005). "The conditions of difficulty and struggle": A discovered theme of curriculum transformation and women's studies discourse. *National Women's Studies Association Journal, 17,* 23–44.

Clark, R., Ayton, K., Frechette, N., & Keller, P. J. (2005). Women of the world, re-write! Women in American world history high school textbooks from the 1960s, 1980s, and 1990s. *Social Education, 69,* 41.

Clayton-Pedersen, A. R., Parker, S., Smith, D. G., Moreno, J. F., & Teraguchi, D. H. (2007). *Making a real difference with diversity: A guide to institutional change.* Washington, DC: Association of American Colleges and Universities.

Earley, P. C. (1989). Social loafing and collectivism. A comparison of the United States and the People's Republic of China. *Administrative Science Quarterly, 34,* 565–581.

Enns, C. Z., & Sinacore, A. L. (Eds.). (2005). *Teaching and social justice: Integrating multicultural and feminist theories in the classroom.* Washington, DC: American Psychological Association.

Ervin, K. S. (2001). Multiculturalism, diversity, and African American college students: Receptive, yet skeptical? *Journal of Black Studies, 31,* 764–776.

Gabrenya, W., Jr., Wang, Y. E., & Latane, B. (1985). Social loafing on an optimizing task: Cross-cultural differences among Chinese and Americans. *Journal of Cross-Cultural Psychology, 16,* 223–242.

Garcia, M., Hudgins, C., Musil, C. M., Nettles, M. T., Sedlacek, W. E., & Smith, D. G. (2002). *Assessing campus diversity initiatives: A guide for campus practitioners.* Washington, DC: American Association of Colleges and Universities.

Garroutte, E. M. (1999). American Indian science education: The second step. *American Indian Culture and Research Journal, 23,* 91–114.

Goldstein, B. (1994). Cultural diversity and curricular coherence: New teaching and learning strategies for an increasingly complex world. In D. F. Halpern (Ed.), *Changing college classrooms* (pp. 109–127). San Francisco: Jossey-Bass.

Goldstein, S. B. (2005). Cross-cultural perspectives across the psychology curriculum: Moving beyond "add culture and stir." In B. Perlman, L. I. McCann, & W. Buskist (Eds.), *Voices of experience: Memorable talks from the National Institute on the Teaching of Psychology* (pp. 45–57). Washington, DC: American Psychological Society.

Goldstein, S. B. (2008). *Cross-cultural explorations: Activities in culture and psychology* (2nd ed.). Boston: Allyn & Bacon.

Kaiser, G., & Rogers, P. (1995). Introduction: Equity in mathematics education. In P. Rogers & G. Kaiser (Eds.), *Equity in mathematics education: Influences of feminism and culture* (pp. 1–10). London: Falmer Press.

Karau, S. J., & Williams, K. D. (1993). Social loafing: A meta-analytic review and theoretical integration. *Journal of Personality and Social Psychology, 65,* 681–706.

Kingsley, K. (1988). Gender issues in teaching architectural history. *Journal of Architectural Education, 41,* 21–25.

Latane, B., Williams, K., & Harkins, S. (1979). Many hands make light the work: The causes and consequences of social loafing. *Journal of Personality and Social Psychology, 37,* 822–832.

Lynch, E. W. (1997). Instructional strategies. In A. I. Morey & M. K. Kitano (Eds.), *Multicultural course transformation in higher education: A broader truth* (pp. 56–70). Boston: Allyn & Bacon.

McIntosh, P. (1983). *Interactive phases of the curricular re-vision: A feminist perspective.* Working Paper No. 124. Wellesley, MA: Center for Research on Women.

McIntosh, P. (1990). *Interactive phases of the curricular and personal re-vision with regard to race.* Working Paper No. 219. Wellesley, MA: Center for Research on Women.

Minnich, E. (1986). *Conceptual errors across the curriculum: Towards a transformation of the tradition.* Memphis, TN: Memphis State University Center for Research on Women.

Mio, J. S., & Awakuni, G. I. (2000). *Resistance to multiculturalism: Issues and interventions.* Philadelphia: Brunner/Mazel.

Olson, H. A. (2001). The power to name: Representation in library catalogs. *Signs: Journal of Women in Culture and Society, 26,* 639–668.

Olson, H. A., & Schlegl, R. (2001). Standardization, objectivity, and user focus: A meta-analysis of subject access critiques. *Cataloging and Classification Quarterly, 32,* 61–80.

Ouellett, M. L. (2005). *Teaching inclusively: Resources for course, department and institutional change in higher education.* Stillwater, OK: New Forums.

Pareek, U., & Rao, T.V. (1980). Cross-cultural surveys and interviewing. In H. C. Triandis & J. W. Berry (Eds.), *Handbook of cross-cultural psychology: Vol. 2. Methodology* (pp. 127–179). Boston: Allyn & Bacon.

Rosenberg, P. M. (1998). The presence of an absence: Issues of race in teacher education at a predominantly White college campus. In M. E. Dilworth (Ed.), *Being responsive to cultural differences: How teachers learn* (pp. 3–20). Thousand Oaks, CA: Sage.

Roses, L. E., & Randolph, R. E. (Eds.). (1997). *Harlem's glory: Black women writing, 1900–1950.* Cambridge: Harvard University Press.

Rosser, S. V. (1986). *Teaching science and health from a feminist perspective: A practical guide.* New York: Pergamon Press.

Schmitz, B., & Taranath, A. (2005). Positionality and authority in curriculum transformation: Faculty/student collaboration in course design (pp. 104–114). In

M. L. Ouellett (Ed.), *Teaching inclusively: Resources for course, department, and institutional change in higher education.* Stillwater, OK: New Forums Press.

Schneider, D. J. (Ed.). (2003). *The psychology of stereotyping.* New York: Guilford.

Silver, A. (2007). Diversifying medical ethics. In J. Branche, J. Mullennix, & E. R. Cohn (Eds.), *Diversity across the curriculum: A guide for faculty in higher education* (pp. 130–135). San Francisco: Jossey-Bass.

Simien, E. M. (2003). Black leadership and civil rights: Transforming the curriculum, inspiring student activism. *PS: Political Science and Politics, 36,* 747–750.

Torrey, J. W. (1987). Phases of feminist re-vision in the psychology of personality. *Teaching of Psychology, 14,* 155–160.

Whitt, E. J., Edison, M. I., Pascarella, E. T., Terenzini, P. T., & Nora, A. (2001). Influences on students' openness to diversity and challenge in the second and third years of college. *Journal of Higher Education, 72,* 172–204.

Williams, D. A., Berger, J. B., & McClendon, S. A. (2005). *Toward a model of inclusive excellence and change in postsecondary institutions.* Washington, DC: Association of American Colleges and Universities.

19

A SEAT AT THE TABLE
FOR EVERYONE

Exercises in Valuing Diversity

Christy Price, Lynn Boettler, and Laura Davis

It's the all-too-familiar scene in any pop culture movie about high school. The "different" student trudges through the cafeteria line, pays for her meal, and then with trepidation scours the hoards of tables for a seat, but more than likely ends up at a table by herself. Although some may contend that this is just the reality of high school, this lunchroom scene is often repeated throughout life. Whether in the workplace, the political system, religious institutions, or U.S. majority culture, many people are undoubtedly living in a world where there is not yet a seat at the table for everyone.

Despite the reality, students tend to consider themselves diversity-minded and open, but often their valuing of diversity rests more at a cognitive level than an affective one. Likewise, as teachers we often find that helping students achieve diversity-related learning outcomes that fall within the cognitive realm is easier than helping them achieve outcomes within the affective domain. For example, teaching students about the different customs and practices of other cultures is a much simpler task than cultivating in students an emotional appreciation of diversity. Helping students achieve affective outcomes is possible but often requires alternative forms of instruction than a traditional lecture and typically involves experiential learning or discussions that seek to transform students' thinking and beliefs. The question then becomes: What kinds of experiences can be provided for students that will generate such transformations?

In this chapter, our intent is to share diversity activities and resources that can produce meaningful and memorable experiences and can be utilized in a variety of disciplines. We provide descriptions of what students have identified as the most engaging, enlightening, and transformative activities; we hope you will find these lessons useful. Add to or adapt them to meet your own pedagogical needs. We have attempted to trace each activity to its original source, but many training activities have been passed along, borrowed, edited, and often completely revamped by literally hundreds of practitioners (Seelye, 1996). Additionally, as there are entire books devoted to increasing students' appreciation of diversity, we provide a few titles at the end of this chapter for reference and further reading.

Icebreakers and Introductory Activities

These brief activities are ideal for introducing diversity concepts or using diversity content to assist group members in getting acquainted with one another.

Diversity Bingo

Summary.   Diversity Bingo is played much like traditional Bingo. Participants are given a Bingo card that has descriptors in each of the boxes. The descriptors are characteristics of people (e.g., European American, African American, Christian, Muslim). Participants attempt to win "Bingo" by circulating around the room and requesting signatures from individuals who identify with and fit the different descriptors.

Origin.   The Curriculum Collection on Prejudice and Intergroup Relations at www.spssi.org/teach_cc_activities1.html has a similar activity that focuses more on cultural competence and was contributed by Michele Grossman-Alexander of Ohio State University. The SPSSI site provides information for ordering a version of the game created by the staff at Skidmore College.

Purpose.   Typically this game is used as a get-acquainted activity; however, if debriefing follows the game, more in-depth learning can take place. The game is intended to create greater sensitivity to individual experiences and differences and to provide an opportunity to get to know fellow participants.

Resources/Materials.   Create Bingo cards with 25 squares for all participants. Know the climate of your group with regard to diversity issues, and tailor the level of intimacy of your descriptors to match the environment and
participants. Each participant must have a writing instrument for signing the
BINGO card squares of other players. If the descriptors are designed to match
the individual group members, this activity often takes less than 10 minutes.
Debriefing time depends on the level of intimacy that is being sought.

Facilitation.   Provide each participant with a BINGO card and a writing instrument. As participants circulate and meet other group members
whose demography matches those on their cards, they have those members
sign the appropriate square of their BINGO card. The first participant to
receive five different signatures in a row (down, across, or diagonal) wins.
When the game is over, the facilitator leads a debriefing discussion regarding
the diversity of the group.

Sample Items for BINGO Squares.   Items such as the following may be used
as descriptors: (1) is from a rural area; (2) knows someone who suffers from a
mental illness; (3) went to high school with someone openly gay or lesbian; (4)
has a multiracial family; or (5) speaks a first language other than English.

The *"People Like You"*

Summary.   This activity gives participants a chance to think about
how and why humans group themselves according to outward appearances
and stereotypes.

Purpose.   This activity should make participants more aware of labels
and stereotypes. In addition, participants discuss how and why groups form
based on these distinctions.

Resources and Materials.   This activity requires a package of blank, mul-
ticolored stickers or labels. Before meeting with the group, the facilitator
draws small, barely noticeable symbols on each label. For example, one group
of labels could have stars on them, another group smiley faces, and another
group an "x." The symbols should appear on a variety of different-colored

labels; in other words, make sure that there is a star on at least one label of every color, and so on.

Time.   This activity takes 15 to 30 minutes, depending on the length and depth of the following discussion.

Facilitation.   As the participants enter, the facilitator gives a label to each participant and instructs her to place it on a specific part of the body (e.g., leg, arm, lapel, hands). The facilitator should say as little as possible. Once everyone is ready, the facilitator should say, "I am going to ask you to move around and form groups. Please go and find the people like you." Almost always, participants group themselves according to the color of the sticker they are wearing. It is again important that the facilitator not say too much; he or she should simply say, "Now I want you to group yourselves again, but this time you have to find a new group. Please find the people like you." Usually, most participants will then group themselves according to the symbol on their label rather than the color. After they have found these new groups, the facilitator should say, "You need to find another group. Once again, please find the people like you." At this point, the participants will usually realize that they can group themselves by the location of the stickers on their bodies.

Debriefing.   After participants have found their final group, the facilitator should ask them to sit down where they are and to look around at all of the groups. The facilitator should ask questions about how they decided to group themselves during each round of the simulation. Some good warm-up discussion questions are: *How did you decide to group yourself? Why did you decide to group by color first? Why did you use the symbols second? As the game went on, was it harder to find new ways to group yourselves with "people like you"?* Typically, participants will discuss how the color of the sticker was the easiest thing to notice but that even as the simulation progressed, they could always find a new category to use to group themselves. As the discussion progresses, the facilitator should try to introduce the following topics:

1. The color of the stickers is supposed to stand for race. Ask,
   Do you think race is one of the first ways we group ourselves together?

Where are places you have noticed this happening?

Why is race such an easy way to group ourselves?

2. The symbols on the stickers are supposed to stand for other "symbols" people project that we may be unconsciously using as a way to judge them. Ask,

   What are symbols people wear that we use to stereotype them?

   (For example, some people wear religious symbols, expensive clothing, or their hair long or short to make a particular statement.) Ask,

   What assumptions do you make about people who have a lot of tattoos?

   A girl who has a crew cut and wears men's clothes?

   A boy who dresses in pink?

   A person with a shaved head?

   Are these stereotypes always right or accurate?

   These symbols are sometimes not as quickly noticeable as race, but we are usually picking up on them whether we realize it or not.

3. The body placement of the stickers is supposed to stand for how we judge others physically. Ask,

   What are some stereotypes we make when someone is very tall? Very short?

   Extremely thin? Overweight?

   In a wheelchair?

   When are times you have judged someone based on physical appearance?

   Were your judgments accurate or not?

4. Finally, it is important to ask the class a few final questions. Ask,

   Why did you use the stickers as a way of grouping yourselves?

   Remind them that the only thing you told them to do was to "find people like you." Ask,

   Why did you use the stickers at all?

   How might you have grouped yourselves differently?

   This should bring up the most important question. Ask,

   Why did you split into smaller groups in the first place? As the prompt was "find the people like you," and as you are participants in an activity together, aren't all of the people in here "people like you"? You could have been one big group rather than several groups based on the labels you were wearing.

These final questions can lead to a discussion of how humans always seem to find new ways to group themselves *with* some and *against* others. However, as the sticker simulation shows, we often have more in common with others than we think if we look past these artificial labels and distinctions.

Stereotyping Headbands

Summary.   This activity simulates what it feels like to be stereotyped. Participants wear headbands that provide an unknown label for them. They are asked to mingle and treat one another in a stereotypical fashion based on their unknown label. As the mingling progresses, participants are asked to guess their label based on the way other participants treat them.

Purpose.   The purpose of this activity is to identify stereotypes that lead to prejudice and discrimination. In addition, the activity motivates participants to rethink their behavior and attitude toward others.

Resources/Materials.   Using card stock and string or elastic, the facilitator creates one stereotyping headband per participant. Ideas for headbands should be based on common stereotypes in your region. Possible suggestions for stereotyping headbands include: *Teenager, Elderly Person, African American, Asian, Middle-Eastern, White, Homeless, Physically/Visually Challenged, Gay, Transgendered, Overweight, HIV Positive, Unwed Mother, Democrat, From a Rural Area, From an Urban Area, International Student, Fraternity/Sorority Member, Football Player, Cheerleader, Art Major, etc.*

Time.   In a group of 30 participants it will usually take about 10 minutes for everyone to identify his or her headband. Allow at least 15 minutes for discussion of how it felt to be stereotyped.

Facilitation.   Each participant randomly picks a headband without looking to see what headband he or she has chosen. Participants choose a partner and put a headband on the partner without allowing the partner to see the label. Participants are instructed to circulate around the room and mingle with group members. As they mingle, they are to treat one another based on their headband as they might stereotypically be treated in society. As the mingling progresses, participants must guess the label on their headband. After they do so, they may sit down. The game continues until all participants have guessed the label on their own headband. Afterwards, participants should discuss how they were treated and how it felt to be stereotyped.

In-Depth Exercises

These activities take more time than the introductory activities, explore diversity issues more intensely, and provoke deeper reflection.

A Class Divided: Video and Discussion Activity (50 minutes)

Summary. This video shows original footage from Jane Elliot's controversial 1973 lesson on discrimination as conducted at Riceville Elementary in Riceville, Iowa. Elliot separated her third graders based on their eye color, creating both prejudice and discrimination among them. Years later as adults, Elliot's class reflects on the impact of her lesson. Jane Elliot conducts her same lesson with adults in a prison and in a work setting.

Available for purchase at http://www.pbs.org/wgbh/pages/frontline/shows/divided/.

Prime Time Live Hidden Camera Videos: The Fairer Sex, True Colors, Age and Attitudes, and The Ugly Truth (20 minutes each)

Summary. These videos are excerpts from the television show *Prime Time Live* produced by ABC News. The segments focus on discrimination based on sex, race, age, and physical attractiveness. Hidden cameras reveal sexism, racism, and ageism.

Available for purchase through
CorVision
http://www.corvision.com
e-mail: corvision@aol.com
1359 Barclay Blvd.
Buffalo Grove, IL 60089

Contemporary Movies with Diversity Themes

Summary. Participants view a diversity-based movie either in class or on their own and discuss their reaction to the film. Depending on group size, one movie or more than one movie may be chosen, and participants may be divided into groups.

Movies with diversity themes include *Crash, Bend It Like Beckham, Mask, Hotel Rwanda, Transamerica, Smoke Signals, The Laramie Project, Saving Face, Remember the Titans, Boys Don't Cry, Brokeback Mountain, Soul Man, The Crying Game, Girl Interrupted,* and *My Family.*

Everyday Life Diversity Blog

Summary.   Students participate in a semester-long blog or journal related to diversity issues. The writing prompts ask students to examine the subtle effects of racism or other types of bias that exist around us in our daily lives.

Purpose.   This exercise aims to help students think about the covert and subtle influences of racism and other types of bias that are encountered in various activities and elements of public life, such as in the entertainment industry, advertising, politics, and the arts. The exercise increases students' awareness of racial and gender stereotyping in the world around them.

Resources and Materials.   This activity works best when using a blogging Web site so that students can read others' writing and have interactive discussions. There are a variety of free blogging sites available; Xanga.com is one popular option many teachers have used. However, if desired, this activity could be adapted to a more traditional written journal that could be shared in small groups during class.

Time.   This activity works best if used over the course of an entire semester.

Facilitation.   To help students think about how subtle racism and other forms of bias can be, the teacher can begin the discussion with media images so that students can get an immediate visual example. Two good photographs to use are the "looting" versus "finding" photos published during hurricane Katrina and the infamous *TIME Magazine* cover that features an artificially darkened mug shot of O. J. Simpson. Ask: *Do you think images like these subtly reinforce our stereotypes that some colors are "bad" and some are "good"? Why or why not?* Next, let the class know that they are going to be investigators for a semester and that their task will be to find instances where they see racial and/or gender (or any other diversity issue you would like to address) stereotyping occurring in daily life. Students are given a variety of activities over the course of the semester (found below). After each activity, they write a blog or journal exploring their observations and are required to comment on the entries of at least two other classmates to start discussions and hear others' opinions.

BLOG 1: ADVERTISING. Writing Prompt: Find a commercial or print advertisement that you think conveys a message about race or gender. Describe the ad and examine what it is trying to say. What positive images of race or gender does it convey? Negative ones? Do you think the images or stereotypes found in this ad are true or not? Why or why not? Do you think this ad is capable of changing and/or reinforcing people's opinions of a certain race or gender? Why or why not?

BLOG 2: MUSIC, MOVIES, and TV. Find a movie, show, or song that you think displays a negative stereotype or image of race or gender and one that you think is trying to portray a positive image of race or gender. What messages are being sent to the consumer, and why do you perceive these messages as positive or negative?

BLOG 3: POLITICS AND THE LEGAL SYSTEM. Research a law that you think is unfair or discriminatory on the basis of race, sex, or sexual orientation. Give the official title of the law and a brief description of it. Why do you think this law is discriminatory? If you were a lawmaker in this country, how would you revise this law and why?

BLOG 4: RELIGION. Find and summarize a newspaper or journal article that discusses religious intolerance or discrimination. What do you think the author of the article is trying to say? Have you ever experienced discrimination because of religion? What times in history can you think of when people were discriminated against based on their religion? What are some stereotypes you think of when you hear about different religions?

References

Seelye, H. N. (1996). *Experiential activities for intercultural learning.* Boston: Intercultural Press.

SECTION FOUR

DIVERSITY AND ONLINE
ENVIRONMENTS

20

DIVERSITY AND DISTANCE EDUCATION

Cultural Competence for Online Instructors

Savitri Dixon-Saxon

I n a recent lifespan development course, a learner repeatedly referred to a client she worked with as a "Black female adolescent." In almost every account of this client, she mentioned the client's race. I kept scrutinizing what she was saying to understand the relevance of the client's race. I finally started to conclude that the learner was presenting this client from a deficit model because of her race. I kept trying to get this learner to understand that she was doing a disservice to the client and all African American people. My sensitivity to this matter was lost on her, and I started to get incensed that this student refused to develop in a culturally competent way. As I am African American, I started to feel that this student was exacting her privilege as a member of the dominant group to not consider how detrimental it was to a marginalized group to insinuate that any pathology is somehow related to their group membership.

Finally, one day after presenting a final challenge to her to reconsider her habit of saying "this Black client" every time she referred to this client, without explaining the relevance of the term to the dynamics or the client issues, the student responded (paraphrased):

> I hope you will believe that I am saying this client's race and ethnicity are
> important. I find that a lot of White people want us to act race-neutral, or

pretend that race and ethnicity don't matter. I find that my race and ethnicity are very relevant to the way people respond to me, provide service to me, and support me. I hope you'll forgive me, but I really believe that what this client experiences is often a result of the way society treats African American women like her and me.

This scenario illustrates some of the greatest challenges of instruction in an online environment. I read her words and assumed that she was White, and she read my words and assumed that I was also. We were both operating under the presumption that most of the people in the environment would have majority group membership. The online environment forces us to be resourceful and use senses other than sight and investigative skills to determine who learners are and to understand how, when, and why diversity is relevant in each discourse. We must learn how to facilitate a culturally inclusive academic environment in the online classroom.

In addition to briefly describing the diversity of online learners, this chapter focuses on those areas in which online instructors need to develop cultural competence to facilitate a culturally inclusive academic environment and community. It also discusses the competencies and considerations necessary for course developers and administrators to demonstrate cultural competence and facilitate effective learning for a diverse population in the online education environment.

Characteristics of Online Education Learners

As online education evolves, there is increasing emphasis on providing an interactive environment for the adult learner searching for career advancement opportunities, knowledge that will enhance his or her professional role, an opportunity to demonstrate expertise gained from experiences, and an opportunity to add new knowledge to a field through research, all the while managing numerous personal responsibilities like family, work, community involvement, and leisure activities. This makes online education very attractive to learners with significant family responsibilities (Kinser, 2003) like caring for parents or young children, learners in remote areas, learners with limited financial resources, and learners who work at least 40 hours per week and sometimes more.

People from diverse backgrounds who have traditionally had limited access to the campus learning environment are also attracted to distance learning environments for the same reasons already mentioned (Smith & Ayers, 2003). There are also people in the distance learning environment with marginalized status. At Walden University, where I am employed, as of May 2005, 76% of the learners at the institution were women; 15% were African American; 4% were identified as Latino American; and 2% were identified as American Indian/Alaska Native. The average age of doctoral students was 42 years, and the average age of master's students was 36 years. Although these numbers don't reflect differences due to religion, ability, sexual orientation, language, and geography, they give us some indication that the online education classroom is a diverse environment.

Diversity Competence for Faculty

What are the standards of cultural competence in an online environment? This discourse can begin by identifying what these learners need from online instruction. This section focuses on six areas in which online instructors should develop cultural competence in the online classroom.

Identifying Contributing Diversity Factors

The opening example of a classroom interaction shows us that we need to obtain an accurate picture of those issues that impact the psychosocial identity and sociopolitical context of each individual in the course, including the instructor. Many would argue that because those factors are not obvious to everyone in the online environment, each student has equal access to the course discussion and an increased opportunity to be evaluated objectively. That's a reasonable assumption, but it is not reality.

Because online students have limited face-to-face interactions with their peers, I could argue that to an even greater extent than normal they view issues and learning through their own self-oriented lens. As they go through each course, students reveal more and more about who they are and what they value. However, as demonstrated in the opening example, simple phrases can be interpreted differently depending on the experience and group membership of the speaker.

Instructors should use all opportunities to find out who their learners are and what matters to them. For example, reading the postings in informal discussion areas and any other areas where students introduce themselves can help to provide the students with an understanding of who they are. Instructors should ask students to share information about their family structure, professional lives, geographic locations, and professional experiences.

Additionally, instructors should understand how their own group membership impacts the online classroom experience for each learner. Students are not the only ones who come to the distance learning environment with preconceived ideas about who will be in that learning medium. Instructors must understand that their own identity, life experiences, and group biases contribute greatly to the dynamics of the online classroom. Instructors should have the skills to use this knowledge to benefit the classroom experience. When instructors disclose who they are, they give students permission to disclose who they are. Of course, we encourage students in the online environment to proceed cautiously as they share personal information. However, students' ability to share culture, values, and experiences as they relate to newly acquired knowledge has the potential to enhance learning and make for a richer discourse.

Providing Support During Debate

Learners in the online classroom sometimes "carry the baggage" of past educational experiences. For some learners, the academic environment has been a stimulating place of freedom and validation, but for other learners, past experiences have not left the impression that the academic environment is supportive and validating for people like them. Such is the experience of privilege and marginalization, respectively. Students who have experienced privilege in academic settings are willing to share their ideas and opinions and are usually very practiced at articulating their ideas. Students who have felt marginalized traditionally are less eager to participate in a meaningful way, and many times are less practiced at doing so.

Providing support means fostering learner development in ways that allow for every student to get involved and participate in a meaningful way. Asking questions about the ideas shared, providing prompts that allow diverse students to demonstrate their expertise, creating assignments that reflect various worldviews, challenging students to think beyond their own worldview, and openly confronting biased language and ideas expressed in the classroom are all examples. Course assignments should give students the opportunity to apply newly acquired knowledge to community and societal issues while challenging them to consider culturally and contextually relevant solutions. One of the culminating assignments in the online program with which I am affiliated is the creation, implementation, and presentation of a mental health intervention in response to a community need. This action research project is designed to teach students how to engage cultural brokers and major community stakeholders in the design and implementation of a mental health intervention. The project reflects knowledge accumulated throughout the program about mental health counseling, and it gives students the opportunity to demonstrate their own understanding of the world while acknowledging that this is not the only consideration when designing effective programs.

Building Community in the Online Classroom

Most online educators believe that instruction goes far beyond demonstrating expertise in content and facilitating learning around course content. Supporting the developmental needs of students in a variety of areas is also critical (Kinser, 2003), and online instructors have to be the cultural brokers for their institutions. In that role, they are responsible for participating in community development, communicating institutional policies and resources, and providing support services to students. Establishing and maintaining a community in a classroom is one of the most important facets of being a culturally competent distance educator. Building a community in the online environment means accounting for individual community members' strengths and limitations in a way that benefits the collective. The quality of the intellectual debate and learning increases as a sense of community is developed.

Online instructors can provide opportunities for students to work together in group activities, allowing enough time for group cohesion and performance. Trying to manage group activities in a short time frame can be counterproductive to students gaining any real knowledge from each other, sharing their areas of expertise, and building community.

Instructors can also foster connections through discussions. As students explore issues relevant to their own experiences and communities, instructors should direct them to classmates with similar interests and ideas, as well as to those who possess divergent ideas.

Finally, instructors can also allow students to generate special topics for discussion that allow learners to demonstrate personal expertise in an area.

Establishing a Flexible Climate

Online educators often strive for quality, timely responses to their students. In an asynchronous environment, there have to be periodic points at which the instructor monitors and evaluates effectiveness, knowledge acquisition and retention, and skill development. However, many online learners have several competing responsibilities in their lives that compete with course deadlines. I once had a professor remark, "Why do all of our students have sick relatives that they have to care for and children with major illnesses?" I replied, "Because they are at points in their lives where they have to care for other people and have chosen an online education because this is the only way for them to fulfill their academic goals." Cultural competence means being flexible and distinguishing between equality and equity.

In many ways flexibility means being considerate. To maintain an inclusive environment, instructors should consider the needs of those students who are not native English speakers or are not speakers of the English spoken in the United States. Many English speakers in North America use colloquialisms that are not common to people in other parts of the world, and some are only common to those in a particular geographic region. I once remarked that a famous researcher was "my girl" in an effort to demonstrate that I could relax in the academic environment and that I was really fond of this researcher's work. One of the students remarked that I must be a really proud parent if this person was my daughter. This student understood only the literal meaning of my words, and I felt foolish that I had not considered this interpretation.

Understanding Diverse Learning Agendas and Learning Styles

This area above all others requires collaboration between instructors and course developers. In the online education environment, there are various motivating factors for higher education pursuits. Some students pursue online education because it will result in job promotions, informed community and client advocacy, salary increases, professional credentials, and job security. Each of these motivating factors has a great impact on how students present in the classroom community.

In the process of facilitating learning, instructors must be able to acknowledge these varied agendas and respond with appropriate instruction.

Some students' needs are met by exploring course content philosophically, whereas others need absolute and concrete information. Some students need to access pertinent and relevant information quickly or efficiently, whereas others want the opportunity to explore a variety of directions with each new idea presented in the classroom.

Some learners prefer an interactive environment where they have the opportunity to benefit from others' learning process. Others prefer to receive information in a structured way with little interaction with or influence from peers. The challenge of online education is to provide a comfortable learning environment for both these groups of people.

How we support diverse learning styles impacts students' success, satisfaction, retention, and referrals. Anakwe, Kessler, and Christensen (1999) found differences in attitudes about distance learning between those people with an individual orientation and those with a collectivist orientation. Online instruction should reflect an acknowledgment of the impact of culture and learning styles.

Maintaining Confidence and Personal Limits

One of the most rewarding aspects of online education is that instructors have the opportunity to learn so much from students. However, some instructors find it difficult to embrace this opportunity. Instructors have to be confident enough to allow students to demonstrate their areas of expertise, even if this knowledge and expertise are beyond the instructor's knowledge base.

Students' worldviews and personal and professional experiences shape their understanding and application of the information shared in the distance learning environment. Although this is also true of land-based learning settings, students in the online learning environment have fewer limitations with regard to how much information they can share in the course. Many learners want their past experiences validated by both their instructors and their peers.

Whereas in other environments students might easily accept the professor's role as an authority and expert in the classroom, many students in the online education environment expect an environment of mutual respect and authority. This presents a challenge for both instructors and students. Some students and faculty are not comfortable with this paradigm. Online instructors need to establish a climate in which students expect to share and receive information that enhances the classroom experience, but they also need to be skilled at managing this flow of information for precision and accuracy.

Cultural Competence of Course Developers and Administrators

Thus far, I have focused on the cultural competence of instructors, but a comprehensive discussion of this topic should also address the cultural competence of course developers and university administrators. These two groups of university agents have a great influence on students' perception of a culturally inclusive climate.

Course Developers

As institutions increase online education resources, more are employing the support of course developers, people trained in the best practices in online education pedagogy and course presentation. Course developers usually collaborate with instructors to deliver a product that meets the needs of the students and the academic program. Their challenge is to devise courses, textbooks, and other instructional materials that reflect the needs of diverse groups. Course assignments should provide opportunities for cooperative and individual learning and also provide students with the opportunity to tailor learning to their individual, community, and professional needs. Designers should also provide students with options for assignments that reflect their various learning styles, as well as instructional materials in varied formats.

Administrators

Establishing a culturally inclusive environment in online education starts with a commitment to this idea from the program and university administrators. Administrators can demonstrate this commitment in a variety of ways. One of the first steps is including diversity and inclusiveness outcomes in strategic plans, thereby challenging every agent of the organization to demonstrate how his or her work and skills support these goals. Administrators should hire faculty with diverse professional backgrounds and research interests and should provide support for research and other scholarship that benefit diverse groups. Finally, administrators should provide support and training to help faculty foster diversity in the online education environment.

The Enduring Challenge of Diversity in Online Education

I started this chapter with a description of an actual event demonstrating that the written word, devoted to a specific topic, often does not give clues about who a person is regarding her gender, race and ethnicity, ability, age, socioeconomic status, sexual orientation, or religion. However, all of those things can moderate the learning process for students. Online instructors must continually account for diversity without knowing what kind of diversity exists in a particular classroom community. As more online education opportunities are offered to higher education consumers, educators must learn to be more aware than they are now of students' language, socioeconomic status, culture, political climate, and religion. The creation of opportunities for a more diverse exchange in the intellectual debate also needs to become the norm.

References

Anakwe, U. P., Kessler, E. H., & Christensen, E. W. (1999). Distance learning and cultural diversity: Potential users' perspective. *International Journal of Organizational Analysis, 7*(3), 224–243.

Kinser, K. (2003). Diversity within the virtual classroom. *New Directions for Institutional Research, 118,* 69–77.

Smith, D. R., & Ayers, D. F. (2006). Culturally responsive pedagogy and online learning: Implications for the globalized community college. *Community College Journal of Research and Practice, 30,* 401–415.

21

USING EDUCATIONAL TECHNOLOGY TO TEACH DIVERSITY CONTENT

Mary Jo Blazek
Magdalena Linhardt

D iscussions of what constitutes diversity content are likely to yield a range of ideas in classrooms as well as among teaching faculties. We prefer Tomes's (2005) definition: "Diversity or multiculturalism is not a code word for ethnic minorities or people of color, but also includes age, disability, gender, sexual orientation and for the first time in a very long time at APA, religion." Using a broad definition expands student appreciation of diversity and serves the context in which we teach. If students equate diversity only with racial and ethnic differences, given the demographics of some areas, students may fail to connect course material to their life experiences.

A front-page article from the *Portland Press Herald* (July 23, 2006) with the headline "UMaine Teacher Program told to widen diversity" described the problem of "too few minority students and faculty" and pointed to a critical aspect of the diversity-related content for classes: the characteristics and experiences of the audience. Via distance education technologies, students attending our classes may be anywhere in the state (or beyond). Knowing your student population is essential to preparing class material on diversity.

The *Portland Press Herald* (August 5, 2006), in an article with the headline "Maine's black population doubles," compared census data from 2000 to 2005 that showed a 99% increase in the black population, which went from 6,760 to 13,456. Furthermore, 2005 census data showed that Maine has the oldest population in the United States, with a median age of 40.6 years

(Churchill, 2005). This is reflected in the University of Maine at Augusta, which serves primarily place-bound students. In an upper-level psychology class on aging, students begin the semester by sharing their age to demonstrate class concepts. In the fall semester 2005, the age range of the 73 students responding was 19 to 79, with a median age of 41.

Considering such diversity among students, one cannot assume that everyone defines diversity in the same way. Plank and Rohdieck (2007) suggest that students are diverse and arrive in the classroom with unique experiences and identities, most of which are invisible to educators. In efforts to expand the range of perspectives represented in class materials, instructors should be aware of the mission of an organization entitled Students for Academic Freedom (SAF), which promotes intellectual diversity on campus and defends the right of students to be treated with respect by faculty and administrators regardless of their political or religious beliefs. One part of the proposed SAF Academic Bill of Rights indicates that "curricula and reading lists in the humanities and social sciences should respect the uncertainty and unsettled character of all human knowledge in the areas by providing students with dissenting sources and viewpoints" (Students for Academic Freedom, 2007).

Is it possible for instructors to present all possible diverse perspectives? Is it possible to know who might disagree or be offended by a topic, theory, example, or thought that comes up in the context of a class or class materials? The likelihood that someone might be offended by anything, especially in classes dealing with controversial, disputed topics that are still under research, appears to be high.

Teaching via technology does not provide the instructor with traditional cues (facial expressions, body movement) that face-to-face settings offer. Students may "leave" a class (in a traditional classroom as well as those delivered through educational technologies) without seeking clarification on an issue or without the instructor's awareness of their personal interpretation of the material. Furthermore, students may feel discomfort with class materials, something said by a peer, or something said by the instructor in interaction with a peer. Such offense often only surfaces in student evaluations after the course is completed.

Because it is impossible to know the life experience and views of every student, statements should be included in syllabi such as "Due to the nature of this course, some content areas may offend some individuals. Controversy is an important aspect for course discussion matters and may be subject to differing opinions." Instructors need to be careful in giving opinions because the past histories and experiences of others are unknown, and offense or insult can take place without the instructor realizing it.

It is essential to consider the possibility of unintentional offense or insult during the use of electronic classroom discussion boards or e-mail. This also holds for classes that are entirely Web-based and for the increasing use of e-platforms to supplement classes. Educational technologies used to supplement traditional class formats need to include similar statements about what and how comments are posted and the impact such comments may have on others. Electronic communications, void of context and nonverbal cues, are fertile ground for miscommunication and misinterpretation. Because technological platforms also provide an environment of seeming anonymity, some users may give little thought to how comments will be interpreted by others. Such educational technologies, while providing a means to enrich course discussion, come with increasing responsibilities for faculty in monitoring and setting limits.

It may not be possible to include all aspects of diversity in class materials, and teaching about diverse groups may actually lead individuals to feel that their viewpoints or individual aspects of diversity have been left out. What appears necessary is not only to teach specific content related to common diverse characteristics (i.e., race, gender, culture, age, ability), but to also provide a framework for understanding the influence of any aspect of difference.

The teaching activities and assignments we share below are adaptable to a variety of class formats. We have used them in Web-based, asynchronous online classes as well as with large statewide interactive television classes (one-way video, two-way audio, in real time); they can also be used in traditional classrooms.

Examples of Technology Used in Courses

The course Psychosocial Rehabilitation provides a rich base for teaching diversity. Estimates indicate that 5.4% of the adult population in Maine have a severe mental illness, not including those who are institutionalized or homeless (U.S. Census Bureau, 2008). Additionally, approximately 160,000 children and adolescents were diagnosed with serious mental disturbances, and over

17% of these children were living in poverty. Yet, at the end of 2000 the total number of inpatient psychiatric beds in the state totaled 126, resulting in many children and adults with serious mental illness living in communities throughout the state (U.S. Census Bureau, 2008).

Viewing people with disabilities as a specific cultural group within a diverse society is a new development (APA Task Force on Diversity Issues at the Pre-college and Undergraduate Levels of Education in Psychology, 1998). As a result of the Americans with Disabilities Act of 1990, nondiscrimination and equal opportunity are to be provided for individuals with physical, sensory, or mental disabilities. Most university administrations and academic departments have begun to recognize that people with disabilities face difficulties similar to those of other minority populations.

Bringing diversity into the classroom involves educating our students and raising awareness about disabilities. Course e-platforms like BlackBoard© enable the instructor to connect students to Web links that contain state and federal documents pertaining to disability issues as well as current materials that are not covered in textbooks.

Aging, death, and dying are often marginal topics in college classes and textbooks. We offer a Web-based, asynchronous course on death and dying with content on diversity surrounding aging and terminal illness. One assignment used in this course, Five Wishes, a form of living will, requires students to complete self-reflection exercises on important relationships in their lives, as well as on goals and decisions for the rest of their lives. We also use this project to facilitate discussions about end-of-life issues in families. Considering the rural character of the state of Maine, discussions surrounding this project bring significant insight to students regarding diversity among families. Online, Web-based classes can also use discussion boards to incorporate current social issues, such as the assisted suicide controversy in the media surrounding the Schiavo family in Florida.

Other classes in our curriculum present the opportunity to raise awareness of people with a history of trauma, including that resulting from genocide, imprisonment, intrafamilial violence, substance abuse, sexual abuse and rape, child pornography, and even terrorism. These experiences influence mental health and personality development, creating a diverse group of people with different coping skills. Using movies and Web links to explain these different psychological conditions and their impact, as well as treatment options and self-help groups, can open students to a range of resources offering explanations of different psychological conditions and describing the immediate help available.

Assessment and planning classes also have an unsurpassed opportunity to bring the Diagnostic and Statistical Manual of Mental Disorders Fourth Edition Text Revision (DSM-IV-TR) into classrooms via the Internet. However, students may also be learning how to do assessment through problem solving and hands-on exercises. One technique is to use case histories that include diverse populations (e.g., 80-year-old Hispanic male with Alzheimer's; 18-year-old African American female with unwanted pregnancy attempting suicide). In online, Web-based classes or statewide interactive television classes using an e-platform such as BlackBoard© to supplement interaction, students can create the initial interview, assessment tools, medical and family history, and case formulation before they write the service plan. Through this educational technology they can create lives of patients with diverse background and intervention needs.

Storm and Todd (1997) offer a number of exercises that can easily be adapted to different class settings and that require students to consider how diversity affects thought, behavior, and experiences. One particular activity is the Rambo and Shilts Story Transforming Exercise. In this exercise, the instructor reads the story of Cinderella to the class. In Web-based classes a link is provided to the story online. Students are then divided into groups of four, and within the small groups each student is assigned a different character—stepmother, eldest stepsister, younger stepsister, prince—and asked to briefly rewrite the story from the perspective of that character. Students then share their revision of the story with their small group, and class discussion follows on the differences among stories. One student's comments during discussion of this activity were: "I learned through this exercise that we ultimately do view situations from our own perceptions. It was truly amazing to me, because there are so many times when I have thought that what I am thinking must be the same way that every one else is thinking, or my way of looking at it is the right way. . . . I can see how misunderstandings in communication can easily occur between people, especially when they come from different cultures and are of different genders" (G. M. Sylvia, personal communication, February 26, 2006). Finally, Internet searches can yield a range of useful resources for classes related to diversity, although care needs to be taken to evaluate Web sites and to monitor sites because they can move or no longer be available without notice. Web links are especially useful for online classes or those using a supplemental e-platform course management system.

References

APA Task Force on Diversity Issues at the Pre-college and Undergraduate Levels of Education in Psychology. (1998, February). Disability as diversity: A guide for classroom discussion. *APA Monitor on Psychology, 29*(2).

Churchill, C. (2005, March 11) Census: Maine now nation's oldest state. *Portland Press Herald,* p. B4.

Kim, A. S. & Huang, J. (2006, August 5). Maine's black population doubles. *Portland Press Herald,* p. A1.

Plank, K. M., & Rohdieck, S. V. (2007). The value of diversity: Diversity involves more than celebrating differences. *NEA Higher Education Advocate, 24*(6), 5–8.

Quimby, B. UMaine teacher program told to widen diversity. (2006, July 23). *Portland Press Herald,* p. A1.

Storm, C. L., & Todd, T. C. (1997). *The reasonably complete systemic supervisor resource guide.* Boston: Allyn & Bacon.

Students for Academic Freedom. (2007). *Mission and strategy.* Retrieved October 15, 2008, from http://www.studentsforacademicfreedom.org

Tomes, H. (2005, September). Diversity's unmet needs. *Monitor on Psychology, 36*(8), 37.

U.S. Census Bureau (2008). *USA QuickFacts.* Retrieved October 15, 2008, from http://quickfacts.census.gov/qfd/states/23000.html

22

DEVELOPING GLOBAL CONNECTIONS

Connecting Students in Cross-cultural Online Teaching Activities

Cindy J. Lahar

The first time I heard a student exclaim, "Wow, they are just like me!" I was teaching at Miyazaki International College (MIC) in Japan. I often heard comments like that in my classroom because comparative culture is a primary focus of the MIC curriculum. However, it was not just the Japanese students who said this, but also their new friends across the globe, a group of college students in Massachusetts whom my students had "met" and been working with via an online discussion board. That was in 1999. While teaching at MIC I connected five different classes with university classes in the United States, and since my return to the United States I've continued these collaborative efforts. It doesn't matter what side of the Pacific one is on; each connection has allowed college students to interact with students "just like themselves" but from a different culture. Students consistently report high enthusiasm for these online cross-cultural exchanges (Lahar & Shaw, 2001). Students also value learning not only the differences between cultures, but also the similarities (Lahar, 2004, 2006).

This chapter describes some online cross-cultural discussions that have increased students' global exposure and, in turn, global awareness and cultural competence. When we talk about diversity, we often speak of multiculturalism in the United States, but educators are also increasingly speaking of diversity beyond our borders and about developing a globally competent student (McMurtie, 2007; Nelson, 2007; Whalley, Langley, & Villarreal, 1997). Today the need to interact as global citizens is essential and has become increasingly important to curriculum designers in education (ACE, 2006; Bond & Scott, 1999; Czarra, 2002). Internationalizing the curriculum is essential in an interdependent global village (Loveland, 2007).

After first considering learning outcomes for online cross-cultural collaborative ventures, I provide some examples and practical suggestions for developing connections for your courses. I describe the format of online discussion boards that I have used, as well as some lessons I have learned, including the challenges as well as the successes.

Learning Objectives and Learning Outcomes

What do you want your students to learn when interacting online with students from afar? If we want our students to learn more about the perspectives of others (Simoni et al., 1999), then it is especially beneficial to expose them to different peoples, cultures, and perspectives. Establishing a computer connection between classes from around the globe could involve activities from increasing computer skills to developing world-mindedness. Outcomes from interacting with people from another culture can allow students to find new perspectives on core class concepts, learn about new traditions, build skills in cross-cultural communication, and build general intercultural skills—all useful for interacting in today's global society.

Despite the difficulty of measuring learning outcomes related to intercultural and international learning (Fallon, 2004; Longerbeam & Sedlacek, 2006; Mundhenk, 2006; Wright, 2005), there are a number of benefits beyond global learning that occur when students engage in online cross-cultural connections between classrooms (Dunn & Occhi, 2003a; Fisher, 2000; Koontz, Li, & Compora, 2006; Mason, 1998). Let's turn to a practical discussion of how to develop these connections.

Making the Connections: Technology and Planning

Cyberspace is constantly changing and growing, and with the advent of blogging and social networking, many college students are coming to the classroom with an array of skills for connecting with others online. Instructors are using blogs (Penrod, 2007; Reichard, 2005), discussion boards, and other online dimensions to supplement traditional courses (Richardson, 2006), and as distance education becomes more widespread, students and faculty are becoming more experienced with course management systems (such as Blackboard). Whatever the platform, an online experience provides opportunities for new types of learning (Collison, Elbaum, Haavind, & Tinker, 2000; Dunn & Occhi, 2003b; Koontz et al., 2006). A sampling of some of the many technologies that can be used to establish connections between individuals or classes is presented in Table 22.1. Some of these technologies need to be hosted on a server and typically maintained by an information technology (IT) department. These include course management programs such as Blackboard and commercial products such as WebBoard. Other technologies can be accessed and used directly because they do not need to be hosted locally. For example, anyone can sign up for free at Yahoo! Groups and create an online space where people can post and read messages, photos, and files.

An example of a free resource designed especially for educators is *Edublogs* (http://www.edublogs.org). Because blogs are a familiar enterprise for students today (social networking sites such as Myspace and Facebook employ blogging), students can adapt quickly to the format. Blogs give both the reader and the authors a forum for creativity and self-expression without

TABLE 22.1
Technology Options for Developing Online Collaborations*

Examples of commercial and open-source products that need to be hosted on a network:	
Course management programs	WebCT; Blackboard; Moodle
Discussion boards	WebBoard; AnyBoard; Vanilla; WWWBoard
Examples of software hosted on an external server:	
Free** message board hosting	Free Boards; Groupboard
Blogs	Edublogs, Blogster
Social networking sites	Ning; WebCrossing Neighbors; Facebook
Miscellaneous collaborative tools	Carnegie Foundation KEEP toolkit; Google Groups; Yahoo! Groups; Classroom 2.0; Wikispaces; Eduspaces

*Any of the specific tools listed above can be found with an Internet search. A more comprehensive list can be found at http://thinkofit.com/webconf/index.htm.

**Typically supported by advertising in the form of pop-up or banner ads.

censorship. But although blogs allow for the development of community, they also allow errors, biases, and even rude comments to be viewed. The question of whether you want your students' work or discussions to be freely available online should be asked early in the development of any connection. If a connection is developed within a course management program (such as Blackboard), then students need a password to access the discussion and the contents remain private. Although Table 22.1 offers a sampling of the many technological options for setting up collaborative connections, it is important to understand that the possibilities are changing every day.

If one wants to develop a cross-cultural connection, one must also find a partner class to work with from a culture of interest. The intercultural e-mail classroom (IECC) site (http://www.iecc.org) is a good place to start when looking for other classes around the globe. This free service began as a site to find e-mail pen pals, and according to its Web site has grown to include nearly 8,000 teachers in over 80 countries today. Requests for partners at this site range from "class seeking to build English skills" to "class looking to discuss finance and business." You can browse the messages or post a request. IECC has separate areas for requests in higher education and requests in the K-12 levels. Other groups are focused primarily on partnerships among K-12 educators, including United Nation's Cyber School Bus (http://www.un.org/cyberschoolbus/); Epals (http://www.epals.com); and the People to People International's School and Classroom Program (http://www.ptpi.org/programs/SchoolClass.aspx). Many of these groups also work with the Friendship Through Education initiative (http://www.friendshipthrougheducation.org), which links individuals and groups together from nations around the globe.

Direct networking with other teachers can also be a great way to initiate a partnership with another class. My first online link grew from a conversation with a colleague at a conference; we thought it would be "fun" to have our students collaborate online as we both were teaching the same course. Indeed, it was fun, and we also learned that it was a lot of work! Some connections can be student-driven (for example, you could create an open blog for students to write entries), but the more fruitful connections may take significant time on the part of the teachers involved. If you expect to post multiple assignments that need to be assessed or many discussion topics that need to be read, this will necessitate time beyond the traditional course demands. As with adding assignments to any course, this demand may impact not only teacher workload but also grading policies, student workload, and more.

Teachers also need motivation to develop these online connections, as well as the skills with the necessary computer hardware and software, the access to the computers, and time! There are probably an endless number of questions to consider before taking on a new online collaborative effort. By thinking carefully about the extent to which an online connection will take your time in and outside of class, you should prepare for how it might impact not only your workload but also the workload of your students. I was surprised to find that I needed to spend a lot of in-class time introducing the online environment and facilitating the online discussions. Although it is impossible to foresee all of the challenges in creating and facilitating an online cross-cultural partnership, there are many questions you can ask yourself in anticipation of such a venture (Lahar, 2006; Lahar & Shaw, 2001). Have you considered, for example, the number of students enrolled in your courses? Too many students may result in an overwhelming number of postings to a discussion board, and too few students will frustrate those who want to have more participation from others. Before looking at some of the sample online links, here is a list with some of the many questions to ask yourself if you want to add an online connection between classes.

- What are the learning goals and outcomes?
- What projects, assignments, and work will be required of the student?
- How much time do you expect students to put into the online work?
- How will you foster participation and interaction among students?
- How will students be assessed for their online participation?
- How much of the discussion will be student-driven and how much teacher-driven?
- What weight will this work have in the overall grading scheme of the class?
- How long will this collaboration be in place?
- Is the number of students involved in each class adequate, but not too large?
- What level of technological expertise do you have?
- Do you have technological support at your institution?
- Do you have Internet access in your classroom?
- Do students all have access to the Internet outside of class?
- Do you have contingency plans for technological failures?

Issues are also likely to appear as the collaboration unfolds (Collison et al., 2000; Lahar & Shaw, 2001; Powers & Guan, 2000). Dedication from both sides of the collaboration is needed for success. When working across cultures, language may be a barrier for students in one or both classes, and that problem may impact success as well. We can never anticipate all the potential problems, but considering issues of technology, teaching philosophy, and styles and objectives can help avoid problems with developing online cross-cultural connections (see also Hanna, Glowacki-Dudka & Conceição-Runlee, 2000; Koontz et al., 2006; Miller & Miller, 2000; Oliver & Herrington, 2000; Palloff & Pratt, 2001).

Sample Cross-cultural Connections

My first cross-cultural online connections were formed as content-based assignments added to my traditional Developmental Psychology class in Japan. Using a discussion board, my students were able to post messages to an online space shared by Ray Shaw's Developmental Psychology class at Merrimack College in the United States. Figure 22.1 shows the entry page of our discussion board at the end of a semester. Each title on the left, such as *Introductions* and *In the News,* represents a thread in the online environment. A thread is a series of messages between students; hence by viewing an entire thread one can see the evolution of the discussion. The number of messages is listed after each thread title; for example, there were 69 messages in the *Introductions* thread by the end of the term. Since our students were learning parallel content, we were able to present course-related topics for shared discussion, incorporate the same writing assignments, and introduce a collaborative research assignment fitting to both classes. We coordinated short writing assignments ("thought" assignments) so that students could share their writing. As a whole, this online experience served multiple learning goals, including practice of English skills for the Japanese students, exposure to the diversity of ideas both within and between cultures, collaborative research development and reporting, and even advancing basic computer skills (in 1999 and 2000 many college students had not mastered the fundamentals of typing or had little practice searching the Internet).

We were pioneers when we first set up these discussion boards. Over time we found that presenting prompts related to current events provided some good starting points for conversations. In the end we learned that each semester-long connection resulted in a mix of freely flowing conversations between students and conversations devoted to content-based,

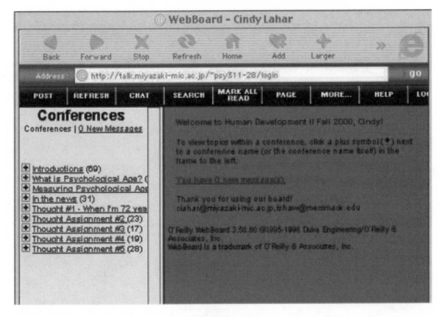

FIGURE 22.1

Screen shot from WebBoard connecting a class in Adult Development in Japan at Miyazaki International College with one in the United States at Merrimack College

teacher-directed topics and assignments. Although certain assignments were specifically aimed at helping students develop collaborative skills, at the same time students were able to learn from each other about daily life in another country.

In another example, my Introductory Psychology class in Japan connected with a psychology seminar course at Rochester Institute of Technology in New York. A screen shot of this discussion board is presented in Figure 22.2. We shared three short assignments during this connection. One used Goldstein's Cleanliness Beliefs Survey (Goldstein, 2000, pp. 17–22), a short series of questions that ask people to rate their level of agreement to statements such as *Shoes should be removed before entering the house* and *One should shower or bathe daily.* Students in both classes collected data, pooled the data, and submitted it to the discussion board, whereupon the teachers posted the comparisons. Figure 22.3 shows a screen shot of that data. We followed with discussions of the differences between the cultures. One Japanese student

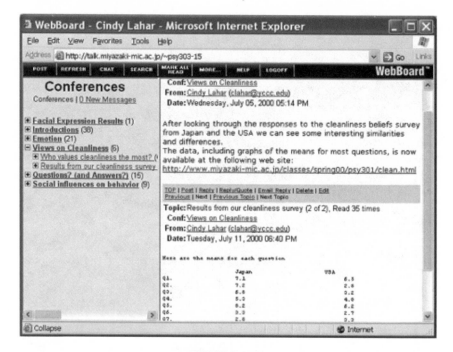

FIGURE 22.2

Screen shot of the online discussion board connection between a class at Miyazaki International College in Japan and a class at Rochester Institute of Technology in the United States

responded, "I have some image that Japanese people value cleanliness more than other countries. I think we don't see much trash in the street . . . but I think that it can be sometimes too cleanly [sic]. Many people take a bath and wash their hair twice a day." A student from New York wrote, "I think both countries value cleanliness, but in different ways and degrees," and another followed with "I would expect that Japanese would consider themselves as more clean because there is less diversity within the culture as compared to America." Some thought regarding the different cultures is evident from these interactions.

The types of activities that students may complete online can range from those directed by the instructors to those that are completely student led. The examples seen in Figures 22.1 and 22.2 employed a mix of student-led discussion areas and teacher-led discussions. In the first example (see Figure 22.1), each student was required to complete a series of short writing assignments

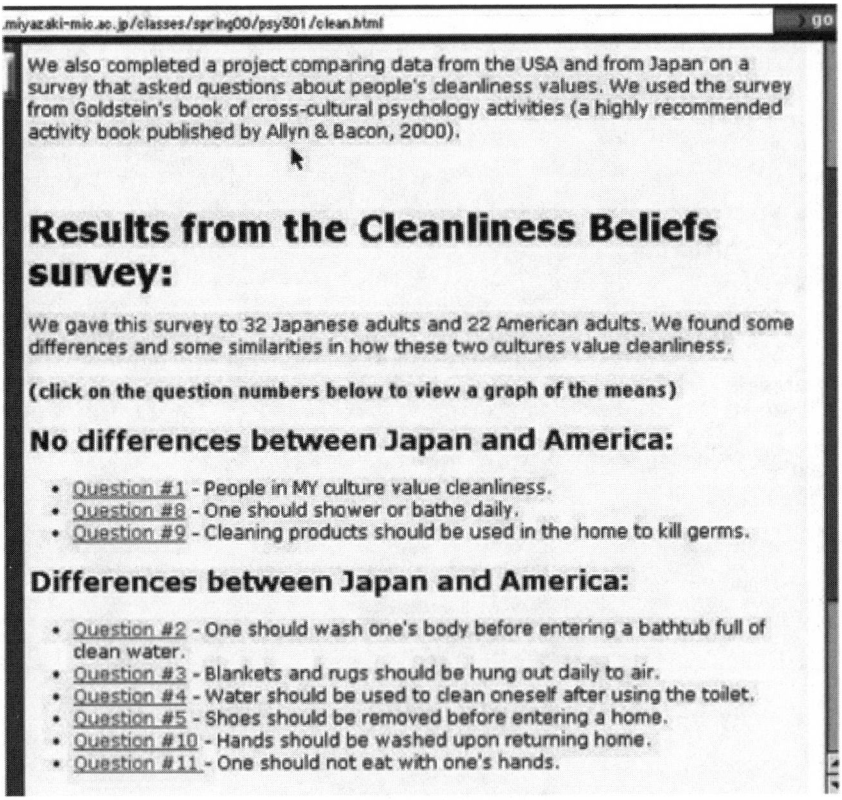

.miyazaki-mic.ac.jp/classes/spring00/psy301/clean.html

We also completed a project comparing data from the USA and from Japan on a survey that asked questions about people's cleanliness values. We used the survey from Goldstein's book of cross-cultural psychology activities (a highly recommended activity book published by Allyn & Bacon, 2000).

Results from the Cleanliness Beliefs survey:

We gave this survey to 32 Japanese adults and 22 American adults. We found some differences and some similarities in how these two cultures value cleanliness.

(click on the question numbers below to view a graph of the means)

No differences between Japan and America:

- Question #1 - People in MY culture value cleanliness.
- Question #8 - One should shower or bathe daily.
- Question #9 - Cleaning products should be used in the home to kill germs.

Differences between Japan and America:

- Question #2 - One should wash one's body before entering a bathtub full of clean water.
- Question #3 - Blankets and rugs should be hung out daily to air.
- Question #4 - Water should be used to clean oneself after using the toilet.
- Question #5 - Shoes should be removed before entering a home.
- Question #10 - Hands should be washed upon returning home.
- Question #11 - One should not eat with one's hands.

FIGURE 22.3

Web page developed to summarize an online collaborative project between a class in Japan and one in New York

about the topics of the course, and students learned much from each other by posting messages that included parts of these assignments. In addition, students wanted to converse about topics besides the class material. We opened a new thread about current news, which allowed students to choose their own topics for discussion. Likewise, in Figure 22.2 you can see a thread titled "Questions." We added this forum in response to students' desire to ask non-course-related questions of their counterparts overseas.

Online cross-cultural discussion topics can occur in the context of any discipline, and assignments can be of any form adaptable to the online environment. The variety of topics that developed in a recent collaboration between a sociology class of mine and a cross-cultural communication class

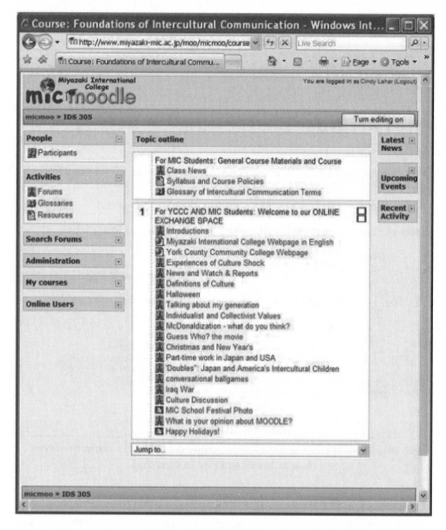

FIGURE 22.4

View of the topics in a discussion board at the end of term. This board was shared by an Intercultural Communication class in Japan and an Introduction to Sociology class in America using Moodle

in Japan can be seen in Figure 22.4. Using a course management technology called Moodle, we developed forums (essentially discussion threads) on various topics covered in one class or the other. There were no shared assignments in this link, simply open discussions between the students that created an authentic context for Japanese and American students to discuss class material as well as topics of personal interest. This example takes relatively little time to set up and can unfold naturally through time. On the other end of the continuum are assignments that are more directive and/or collaborative. Sample activities can range from presenting and working on a case study as a group to reviewing and discussing books, art, or music. Rowley (2006) introduced a collaborative project in which students developed concept maps for complex concepts. Whittlesey (2001) describes over 75 activities that could be used in courses to expand diversity understanding. Many of these are easy to employ in the online environment. The new edition (2008) of Goldstein's handbook has a host of teaching activities for diversity issues. Whether the students' online work is directed entirely by teacher assignments or takes the form of student-driven open discussions, when students have the opportunity to connect online with others overseas, we create a valuable component to a course that serves to enhance global competence.

Conclusions

Since 1999 I have developed 18 online cross-cultural connections by connecting classes in Japan with those in the United States. One of the greatest advantages of these electronic communicative activities is that they present opportunities for "real communication with real people, and not just an academic exercise" (Occhi & Fauss, 2005, p. 26). Rather than having a teacher present information about a new culture, the students are able to develop their knowledge firsthand, at their own pace, and often directed toward their own interests. There is added flexibility and autonomy for the student, as well as improved attitudes toward learning (Fisher, 2000). Furthermore, international collaborative learning can enhance not only student motivation and accountability but also critical thinking (Gokhale, 1995), creativity, and thoughtfulness (Fisher, 2000).

Online and cross-cultural experiences help spice up learning, and students enjoy the experience. Cross-cultural exchanges such as those described here can increase students' understanding of other cultures. Exposing students to the global community and to broader perspectives is something that any single lecturer can rarely provide and was a positive experience for these students. Students appreciated opportunities to share their opinions in an online environment and were often most surprised to find that there were both similarities and differences between the cultures. No longer is it only students who plan to work overseas that need to understand other cultures. It may be argued that today all of our students need to develop intercultural awareness and global perspectives. The international conversations students have had online with those from another culture have opened their eyes to seeing the world in new ways and, in turn, allowed for firsthand development of their personal global education.

Overall, students have enjoyed having the walls of the classroom expanded to include the world. Next we will be adding a new country to the mix by connecting U.S. social science classes with some at the Royal University of Phnom Penh in Cambodia. I suspect I'll be hearing the same old thing: "Wow. They are so different, and yet they are just like us!"

Acknowledgments: The collaborations described in this chapter have included many dedicated instructors, including Dr. Raymond Shaw of Merrimack College, Dr. Matthew Isaak of Rochester Institute of Technology (now at the University of Louisiana), and the following five professors at Miyazaki International College: Jeff Maggard, Dr. Hiro Toyota, Jeff Mok, Dr. Debra Occhi, and Roberta Golliher.

References

ACE (American Council on Education). (2006). American Council on Education's statement on International Learning. Retrieved December 27, 2007, from http://www.acenet.edu/AM/Template.cfm?Section=Home&CONTENTID=19461&TEMPLATE=/CM/ContentDisplay.cfm

Bond, S., & Scott, J. T. (1999). From reluctant acceptance to modest embrace: Internationalization of undergraduate education. Chapter 3 in S. Bond & J. Lemasson (Eds.), *A new world of knowledge, Canadian universities and globalization.* Retrieved January 2, 2008, from http://www.idrc.ca/openebooks/893-7/

Collison, G., Elbaum, B., Haavind, S., & Tinker, R. (2000). *Facilitating online learning: Effective strategies for moderators.* Madison, WI: Atwood Publishing.

Czarra, F. (2002). Global education checklist for teachers, schools, school systems and state education agencies. Occasional paper #173, The American Forum for Global Education, New York. Available at http://www.globaled.org

Dunn, C. D., & Occhi, D. J. (2003a). Contesting cultural representations: Using Internet-mediated communication for cross-cultural education. *Electronic Magazine of Multicultural Education, 5*(2). Retrieved June 10, 2007, from http://www.eastern.edu/publications/emme/2003fall/dunn_occhi.html

Dunn, C. D., & Occhi, D. J. (2003b). Iowa meets Miyazaki: Bringing coursework to life through a cross-cultural electronic exchange. *Education About Asia, 8*(2), 40–44.

Fallon, D. (2004). *Accepting, embracing and striving: Describing student responses to diversity issues.* Unpublished report for the Carnegie Academy for the Scholarship of Teaching and Learning. Retrieved June 10, 2007, from http:// www.cfkeep. org/html/snapshot.php?id=68805538647627

Fisher, M. M. (2000). Implementation considerations for instructional design of web-based learning environments. In B. Abbey (Ed.), *Instructional and cognitive impacts of web-based education* (pp. 78–101). Hershey, PA: Idea Group Publishing.

Gokhale, A. A. (1995). Collaborative learning enhances critical thinking. *Journal of Technology Education, 7*(1). Retrieved January 19, 2006, from http://scholar.lib. vt.edu/ejournals/JTE/jte-v7n1/gokhale.jte-v7n1.html

Goldstein, S. (2000). *Cross-cultural explorations: Activities in culture and psychology.* Boston: Allyn & Bacon.

Goldstein, S. (2008). *Cross-cultural explorations: Activities in culture and psychology* (2nd ed.). Boston: Allyn & Bacon.

Hanna, D. E., Glowacki-Dudka, M., & Conceição-Runlee, S. (2000). *147 practical tips for teaching online groups.* Madison, WI: Atwood Publishing.

Koontz, F. R., Li, H., & Compora, D. P. (2006). *Designing effective online instruction: A handbook for web-based courses.* Lanham, MD: Rowman & Littlefield Education.

Lahar, C. J. (2004). *How can students develop a sense of multiculturalism and global awareness?* Unpublished report for the Carnegie Academy for the Scholarship of Teaching and Learning. Retrieved June 10, 2007, from the Carnegie Foundation's Web site: http://www.cfkeep.org/html/snapshot.php?id= 9913664469415

Lahar, C. J. (2006, October). *Developing global connections: Connecting students in cross-cultural online teaching activities.* Presentation at Reaching Out: Best Practices in Teaching Diversity and International Perspectives Across the Psychology Curriculum, Atlanta, Georgia.

Lahar, C. J., & Shaw, R. J. (2001, June). *Cross-cultural connections for psychology classes.* Poster presented at the annual meeting of the American Psychological Society, Toronto, Canada.

Longerbeam, S. D., & Sedlacek, W. E. (2006). Attitudes toward diversity and living-learning outcomes among first- and second-year college students. *NASPA Journal, 43*(1). Retrieved May 30, 2007, from http://publications.naspa.org/ naspajournal/vol43/iss1/art3/

Loveland, E. (2007, November/December). Recreating disciplines with a global mindset. *International Educator, 16*(6), 4.

Mason, R. (1998). *Globalizing education: Trends and applications.* New York: Routledge.

McMurtie, B. (2007). The global campus: American colleges connect with the broader world. *Chronicle of Higher Education, 53*(26), A37.

Miller, S. M., & Miller, K. L. (2000). Theoretical and practical considerations in the design of web-based instruction. In B. Abbey (Ed.), *Instructional and cognitive impacts of web-based education* (pp. 178–191). Hershey, PA: Idea Group Publishing.

Mundhenk, R. (2006). Principles of good assessment. Pre-Meeting Workshop, American Council on Education Internationalization Collaborative. Retrieved January 3, 2008, from http://www.acenet.edu/AM/Template.cfm?Section= Search&Template=/CM/ContentDisplay.cfm&ContentID=15913

Nelson, P. D. (2007). The globalization of psychology: What does it mean? *The Educator, Newsletter of the APA Education Directorate,* Spring/Summer 2007, pp. 1–4.

Occhi, D. J., & Fauss, R. (2005). Integrating language and content goals through cross-cultural electronic exchange. In M. Apple & E. Shimo (Eds.), *Working together: Making a difference in language education* (pp. 20–27). Miyazaki, Japan: Miyazaki Chapter of the Japan Association for Language Teaching.

Oliver, R., & Herrington, J. (2000). Using situated learning as a design strategy for web-based learning. In B. Abbey (Ed.), *Instructional and cognitive impacts of web-based education* (pp. 178–191). Hershey, PA: Idea Group Publishing.

Palloff, R. M., & Pratt, K. (2001). *Lessons from the cyberspace classroom: The realities of online teaching.* San Francisco: Jossey-Bass.

Penrod, D. (2007*). Using blogs to enhance literacy: The next powerful step in 21st-century learning.* Lanham, MD: Rowman & Littlefield Education.

Powers, S. M., & Guan, S. (2000). Examining the range of student needs in the design and development of a web-based course. In B. Abbey (Ed.), *Instructional and cognitive impacts of web-based education* (pp. 178–191). Hershey, PA: Idea Group Publishing.

Reichard, D. A. (2005). *Incorporating blogging in a free speech course: Lessons learned.* Retrieved January 19, 2006, from http://www.academiccommons.org/ctfl/vignette/blogging-in-free-speech-course

Richardson, W. (2006). *Blogs, wikis, podcasts and other powerful web tools for classrooms.* Thousand Oaks, CA: Corwin Press/Sage.

Rowley, C. T. (2006). Teaching diversity online: Using concept maps to enhance learning outcomes. In A. J. Canas & J. D. Novak (Eds.), *Proceedings of the 2nd International Conference on Concept Mapping.* Retrieved May 30, 2007, from http://cmc.ihmc.us/cmc2006Papers/cmc2006-p85.pdf

Simoni, J. M., Sexton-Radek, K., Yescavage, K., Richard, H., & Lundquist, A. (1999). Teaching diversity: Experiences and recommendations of American

Psychological Association Division 2 members. *Teaching of Psychology, 26*(2), 89–95.

Whalley, T., Langley, L., & Villarreal, L. (1997). Best practice guidelines for internationalizing the curriculum. Victoria, British Columbia: Province of British Columbia, Ministry of Education, Skills and Training and the Centre for Curriculum, Transfer and Technology.

Whittlesey, V. (2001). *Diversity activities for psychology.* Boston: Allyn & Bacon.

Wright, B. D. (2005). *Thinking about good assessment—some questions.* Pre-Meeting Workshop, American Council on Education Internationalization Collaborative. Retrieved January 3, 2008, from http://www.acenet.edu/AM/Template.cfm?Section=Search&Template=/CM/ContentDisplay.cfm&ContentID=17342

SECTION FIVE

METHODS AND TECHNIQUES FOR FACULTY AND DIVERSITY TRAINERS

23

PLEASED TO MEET YOU

*Introducing Multicultural Competence and
Diversity Awareness to Your Students*

Karen Cone-Uemura

A number of factors influence how people think, feel, and behave, including the culture(s) in which they are raised. For this reason, incorporating multicultural awareness and diversity education into the curriculum is crucial to creating a solid foundation from which further teaching and learning can occur. This chapter begins by reminding the reader of the importance of teaching diversity awareness and multicultural education. It then reviews the meaning of multicultural competence, touches on some of the challenges in teaching this topic, and covers some evidence-based techniques for teaching. Finally, it provides an innovative way to introduce multiculturalism and diversity awareness in the classroom.

Race and ethnicity is one area that illustrates a shift in demographics and highlights one of the dimensions of diversity that needs to be addressed in the classroom. The United States is becoming increasingly more ethnically and racially diverse; by the year 2050, it is projected that European Americans will cease to be the numeric majority in the United States (U.S. Census Bureau, 2008).

Another area in which trends are shifting is age. By the year 2050, the U.S. Census Bureau (2008) projects that the number of people over the age of 65 will have almost doubled from the beginning of the century. Diversity in other areas, such as national origin, gender, socioeconomic status, education level, sexual orientation, religion, and ability level, continues to receive attention in psychology and other professions (Aronson, Venable, Sieveking, & Miller, 2005; Iijima Hall, 1997; Moore, Madison-Colmore, & Lott Collins, 2005; Weng, 2005).

Psychology has embarked on institutionalizing the importance of diversity awareness and multicultural competence through its development of the American Psychological Association's (APA) Guidelines on Multi-cultural Education, Training, Research Practice, and Organizational Change for Psychologists (2002) and through its establishment in 1979 of the Office of Ethnic Minority Affairs (Office of Ethnic Minority Affairs, 2004). In addition, multiculturalism is a criterion for accreditation in APA's applied training programs (Fowers & Richardson, 1996). The disciplines of medicine, law, and education also address the importance of developing multiculturally aware practitioners (Aronson et al., 2005; Moore et al., 2005; Weng, 2005).

Multicultural competence has been described as including three parts: awareness (including a recognition and ownership of one's own beliefs), knowledge, and skills (Aronson et al., 2005; Fowers & Davidov, 2006; Kim & Lyons, 2003; Pedersen, 1990; Sue, Bernier, Durran, Feinberg, Pedersen, Smith, & Vasquez-Nuttal, 1982). In some cases, a fourth dimension of "relationship" is included (Middleton et al., 2005; Sodowski, Taffe, Gutkin, & Wise, 1994). To be effective, professionals serving diverse clients should *ideally* possess multicultural awareness, knowledge, and skills. *Realistically*, people, including students enrolled in courses that address diversity, are at different points on the continuum of diversity awareness, multicultural competence, and their own ethnic identity development, including White racial identity (Brown, 2004; Middleton et al., 2005). Currently, most educators are middle class and of European descent (Hansen & Williams, 2003; Middleton et al., 2005). It is important to consider other areas where they might also enjoy a privileged position, including education level, age, ability, sexual orientation, language, and more.

One of the great challenges of teaching difficult topics such as diversity awareness is increasing students' awareness, knowledge, and skills without creating resistance by putting them in situations that cause them to feel threatened or afraid that their own values are being attacked (Brown, 2004). Placed in such a situation, most of us would feel defensive if the instructor failed to create a safe environment. Because "cross-cultural attitudes and beliefs are often intimately related to one's emotions" (Hansen & Williams, 2003, p. 204), an unsafe environment opens the door to student defensiveness and resistance. However, students can benefit from a certain amount of provocation and can explore the foundations of their beliefs to gain a better personal understanding (Mills, 1998). Once they have this self-awareness, they will be more receptive to learning about and understanding others (Weng, 2005).

To effectively teach multiculturalism, it is crucial that educators are aware of their own ethnic identity and able to acknowledge their own limitations. The more sophisticated a European American is in regards to White attitude development, the more he or she perceives himself or herself to be multiculturally competent (Middleton et al., 2005). Developing White racial identity awareness is an emotionally laden experience. Educating European Americans on diversity and multicultural competence is a delicate balancing game: students need to feel safe and not judged, yet learning about these issues requires them to take a critical look at their own beliefs and values. The trick is to personally engage and guide them on incorporating their awareness into the other aspects of cultural competence, namely, knowledge and skills. "Knowledge without personal meaning is passionless, while personal belief without knowledge is blind" (Mills, 1998).

Although there is a growing body of literature on the components of multicultural competence, not much research exists on the most effective methods for teaching them (Kim & Lyons, 2003). Techniques that involve the participants' thoughts and feelings have been touted as being successful in helping people learn better (Eckloff, 2006; Mills, 1998). Because emotions are involved, didactic strategies may not suffice in truly getting the messages across (Kim & Lyons, 2003). A multimodal instructional approach is effective in helping students learn (Brown, 2004). Experiential techniques that personally engage the participants combined with class discussion can be particularly effective in teaching "sensitive topics such as intercultural awareness and sensitivity" (Aronson et al., 2005, p. 17). Students' active engagement in the learning process through experiential activities is effective in helping them acquire multicultural skills (Brown, 2004; Kim & Lyons, 2003).

Multiculturism and Diversity Awareness Activity

I recently presented a workshop at a Best Practices for Teaching Psychology conference on an innovative method for introducing diversity and multicultural awareness in an educational setting. By modeling a concrete, guided activity, I taught workshop participants how to confidently introduce the topic of multiculturalism and diversity to their students. I presented tips on how to create a safe, nonjudgmental environment in which further exploration and discussion on diversity could occur and provided instructors with a template they could readily tailor to their classroom setting. Post-activity discussion generated ideas instructors could use to help their students safely examine their own biases and stereotypes as they embarked on the study of diverse cultures and people. The remainder of this chapter explains this activity so that the reader can implement it in his or her own classroom.

Basic Overview

This activity is designed to be an introduction to the topic of multiculturalism and diversity. Its main purpose is to decrease student resistance to the topic and open their minds to further exploration and learning. It presents a brief introduction to important multicultural competencies but is not designed to provide in-depth training. Further instruction on diversity awareness and multicultural competence should be covered in subsequent class sessions.

In this exercise the entire group, including the instructor, are active participants. In showing her willingness to be part of the activity, the instructor creates safety by decreasing the power differential in the classroom. Additionally, the instructor models her own investment in the importance of multicultural awareness and diversity by placing herself in the role of facilitator and colearner rather than in the role of one who imparts knowledge and evaluates performance. To further create safety, the instructor tells the students that there are no right or wrong answers, only answers that are the truth for each person. Emphasis is placed on the importance of not being judgmental and being willing to explore one's own thoughts, feelings, beliefs, and behaviors. Students are validated for their willingness to share their points of view and told how important their opinions are for their own growth as well as the development of others. The instructor shares with the class that she, too, is continuing to grow and learn and reinforces the value each student brings to the course.

Necessary Materials

- PowerPoint slides or overhead transparencies
- Projector
- Paper
- Pens/pencils

Specific Steps and Descriptions of Slides

The basic format of this lecture is slides and group discussion. Handouts of the various slides can be made and distributed to the participants. If this is the first time the instructor has met the group, he can briefly introduce himself, giving his name, position, and place of employment and purposely avoiding details of his life. Upon presenting the first slide, the instructor asks the students to take out a piece of paper and rate themselves from 1 to 10 (1 being the lowest degree) on a number of dimensions of cultural awareness that are presented as bullet points. The first slide contains items taken from Sodowsky et al.'s Multicultural Counseling Inventory (MCI) as reported in Aronson et al. (2005): *Cultural Understanding, Self/Other Understanding, Social Comfort, Communication, Recognizing Differences,* and *Freedom From Bias.* Although the MCI is created with psychologists in mind, it is useful in helping students begin to get an idea of their own degree of perceived competence in a few areas of diversity and multiculturalism.

The instructor explains the contents of the slide and answers questions to clarify any misunderstanding. *Cultural Understanding* refers to a student's comprehension of "variables such as racial identity, ethnicity, acculturation, worldviews, sociocultural influences, and value differences" (Sodowsky et al., 1994, p. 139). *Self/Other Understanding* refers to a person's examination of her own beliefs and attitudes as the starting point to understanding others'. *Social Comfort* is the ease that a person experiences in the presence of people from other cultures. The *Communication* factor relates to a person's ability to recognize the differences that exist in styles of conveying meaning to each other, as well as the principle that there is no one "right" way. *Recognizing Differences* means that a person is not color-blind and appreciates diversity rather than attempts to negate it. *Freedom From Bias* means personal awareness of one's own prejudices and the ability to acknowledge them. The definitions assigned may differ slightly from the MCI's originators' meanings, but the intent of this activity is to promote introspection that opens the door to diversity and multicultural awareness, knowledge, and skills. For further details on multicultural competencies, I suggest the reader refer to the American Psychological Association's *Guidelines on Multicultural Education, Training, Research Practice, and Organizational Change for Psychologists* (2002). The instructor can inform the students that he is using the instrument in a very unscientific manner, emphasizing that students should rate themselves not on where they think they should be but on what is honestly true for them right now. These ratings are for themselves and will not be shared with anyone else. After everyone is done, the instructor asks students to put these ratings aside and take out another piece of paper.

The number of slides needed for the next part of the activity depends on the number of students in attendance. According to the total number of students, the instructor requests they count off to form appropriately sized smaller groups. I find that groups of 5 to 10 people work well. The instructor does not explain that students will later be breaking into smaller groups. The participants write their number on their sheet of paper so they will remember it. Next the instructor presents a number of slides with descriptions of various people and tells them that the number they have corresponds with the vignette they are assigned. The instructor suggests they write down the descriptions given. Then the instructor presents the vignettes one at a time on a PowerPoint slide or overhead transparency, verbally reading each aloud.

Creation of the vignettes is where the instructor becomes intimately involved with the process. This involvement is unbeknownst to the students at this point. Prior to the class, the instructor picks and chooses aspects of herself, past and/or present, that she is willing to share with her students. She then mixes and matches these self-truths to create different vignettes. Each vignette, although composed of features unique to the instructor, should actually appear to be distinct individuals. For example, I have worked with incarcerated women at risk for transmitting or contracting HIV. Many of my clients worked as prostitutes to procure drugs. I developed close psychotherapeutic relationships with these women. One of my vignettes was: "Has been in & out of jail; has had intimate relationships with women who have worked in the sex industry; been known to hang out regularly with addicts." Another fact about me is that I was a top student in high school (thus illustrating the fact that instructors can use information about themselves that occurred many years ago!), initially studied engineering in college, and finally graduated from University of California at Berkeley with a degree in nutrition and clinical dietetics. The vignette created from this disparate information was: "Received various scholarships; graduated third in high school class; graduated from UC Berkeley w/honors; engineering major." The purpose of illustrating these vignettes is to provide ideas for instructors who want to use this activity. The vignettes must be composed of aspects of the instructor's own life, past and present information that is mixed and matched to present seemingly distinct individuals.

Once the vignettes are all presented, the instructor asks each participant to write about the person in his or her vignette. The instructor tells students to put aside political correctness and just describe how they think each person is in regards to age, sex/gender, race/ethnicity, education level, socioeconomic status, looks, and so forth. They are to make as detailed a description as possible. To facilitate the process, the instructor can ask the group such questions as: What type of transportation does the person use? Where does the person live? What kind of job does the person have? What kind of spirituality does the person practice? What are his or her hobbies? The instructor presents a slide with a number of facets of diversity—age, race/ethnicity, physical characteristics; SES, educational level, current occupation, religion, partner status, children, ability level, hidden disabilities, anything else—and explains that these are some of the areas of diversity on which students can base their descriptions. He leaves the slide up for student reference. He then asks them to draw a picture of what they think the person in their vignette might look like.

After the entire group has come up with their individual vignette descriptions, the instructor asks them to group with others who have the same vignette. After brief introductions in their small groups, the students share their individual descriptions with each other. Each group chooses a scribe and a reporter who will share the group's findings with the larger group. The instructor circulates and checks the progress of each group, facilitating the process as necessary. After approximately 20 minutes in this small-group activity, the students regroup as a whole. Each small group shares their group findings with the larger group.

After all groups have shared, the instructor asks how they would feel if the people represented by the vignettes could see the students' descriptions and portraits. The instructor reassures them that this is all part of the exercise and encourages them to make note of their thoughts and feelings at this moment, knowing that the people in the vignettes will be able to see their depictions. The instructor makes a mental note of the participants' responses and leaves the room. After a pause (during which I try to eavesdrop without being seen) the instructor reenters the room and discloses that she is actually the person in all the vignettes. She shares with the group how each of the characteristics describes a part of her identity. The instructor then processes the responses and asks students to share what they learned through doing the activity.

Some ideas for processing include the following:

1. How did it feel to be asked to describe the people in the vignettes? What was going through the minds of the students as they were describing the vignettes? It is important that the instructor explain how unsettling and anxiety-provoking the exercise may be and that this is part of the provocative nature of gaining multicultural competence.

2. What went on for the students on learning that the vignette people were real and would be privy to the students' written and illustrated depictions of them? Hopefully they felt somewhat uncomfortable, thus creating an increased awareness of their own biases and worldviews.

3. Encourage students to question and examine their own worldviews. Where did they learn them? What influences them? The instructor shares with the students that she also has her own set of cultural perspectives that are not superior to any of theirs. By modeling recognition that we all have areas in which to continue growing, including being made aware of our own blind spots, instructors create safety that can encourage further diversity awareness and multicultural competence. The instructor emphasizes that the purpose of the exercise is to merely heighten our awareness of our own biases, not to necessarily rid us of them. This exercise is just an opportunity to question and examine our own worldviews without the expectation of making any changes. After all, awareness is the first step toward multicultural competence!

The last slide of the presentation is titled "Multicultural Competence" (MC) and outlines the following bullet points:

- MC competence starts with active self-exploration, thus leading to increased self-awareness (recognition of our own values, biases, limitations).
- It includes knowledge about others' worldviews.

- It also encompasses skills and actions.
- And finally, it is aspirational; there's no limit to developing multicultural competence!

The instructor explains that the crux of this lesson is to help us recognize how our own experiences, beliefs, opinions, heritage, and views play a part in how we perceive ourselves and others. The students have now all embarked on the next phase of multicultural awareness and diversity exploration. The instructor encourages them to review the initial cultural awareness ratings they gave themselves and to rerate themselves now and at different points in the future as they continue to gain multicultural competence.

In summary, the purpose of this chapter is to give instructors an innovative method for introducing the topics of diversity awareness and multicultural competence to their students. By using an action-oriented, game-like activity in a safe environment, we can more personally involve our students, an important aspect when presenting emotion-laden topics such as diversity and multicultural awareness. The goals of this activity are to increase student awareness of the many ways in which we are diverse; introduce the idea of worldviews; increase awareness that we all have our own internalized biases based on our own cultures; cultivate appreciation for one's own cultural viewpoints while learning to appreciate the ideas of those who have different cultural beliefs; and remind students of the aspirational aspect of multicultural competence. We must constantly examine our own beliefs and own our biases to remain open to those who are from cultures different from our own.

References

American Psychological Association. (2002). *Guidelines on multicultural education, training, research practice, and organizational change for psychologists.* Washington, DC: American Psychological Association Press.

Aronson, K. R., Venable, R., Sieveking, N., & Miller, B. (2005). Teaching intercultural awareness to first-year medical students via experiential exercises. *Intercultural Education, 16*(1), 15–24.

Brown, E. L. (2004). What precipitates change in cultural diversity awareness during a multicultural course: The message or the method? *Journal of Teacher Education, 55*(4), 325–340.

Eckloff, M. (2006). Using sociodrama to improve communication and understanding. *ETC: A Review of General Semantics, 63*(3), 259–269.

Fowers, B. J. & Richardson, F. C. (1996). Why is multiculturalism good? *American Psychologist, 51*(6), 609–621.

Fowers, B. J., & Davidov, B. J. (2006). The virtue of multiculturalism. *American Psychologist, 61*(6), 581–594.

Hansen, C. E., & Williams, M. R. (2003). Comparison of cross-cultural course changes: From traditional lecture course to contemporary course with biblio-learning, video-learning, and experiential exercises. *Journal of Instructional Psychology, 30*(3), 197–206.

Iijima Hall, C. C. (1997). Cultural malpractice: The growing obsolescence of psychology with the changing U.S. population. *American Psychologist, 52*(6), 642–651.

Kim, B. S. K., & Lyons, H. Z. (2003). Experiential activities and multicultural counseling competence training. *Journal of Counseling and Development, 81,* 400–408.

Middleton, R. A., Stadler, H. A., Simpson, C., Guo, Y., Brown, M. J., Crow, G., Schuck, K., Alemu, Y., & Lazarte, A. A. (2005). Mental health practitioners: The relationship between white racial identity attitudes and self-reported multicultural counseling competencies. *Journal of Counseling and Development, 83,* 444–456.

Mills, J. (1998). Better teaching through provocation. *College Teaching, 46*(1). Retrieved July 14, 2007, from Academic Search Premier.

Moore, S. E., Madison-Colmore, O., & Lott Collins, W. (2005). Appreciating multiculturalism: Exercises for teaching diversity. *Journal of African American Studies, 8*(4), 63–75.

Office of Ethnic Minority Affairs. (2004). *Special section: In celebration of the 25th anniversary of the Office of Ethnic Minority Affairs.* Retrieved December 13, 2007, from http://www.apa.org/pi/oema/march2004specialsection_25thann.pdf

Pedersen, P. (1990). The constructs of complexity and balance in multicultural counseling theory and practice. *Journal of Counseling and Development, 68,* 550–554.

Sodowsky, G. R., Taffe, R. C., Gutkin, T. B., & Wise, S. L. (1994). Development of the multicultural counseling inventory: A self-report measure of multicultural competencies. *Journal of Counseling Psychology, 41*(2), 137–148.

Sue, D. W., Bernier, Y., Durran, A., Feinberg, L., Pedersen, P. B., Smith, E. J., & Vasquez-Nuttal, E. (1982). Position paper: Cross-cultural counseling competencies. *The Counseling Psychologist, 10,* 45–52.

U.S. Census Bureau. (2008). Press Release: An Older and More Diverse Nation by Midcentury. Released: Thursday, Aug. 14, 2008. Retrieved October 27, 2008, from http://www.census.gov/Press-Release/www/releases/archives/population/012496.html

Weng, C. (2005). Multicultural layering: Teaching psychology to develop cultural self-awareness. *Clinical Law Review, 11,* 369–403.

24

INTERCULTURAL SIMULATIONS AND GAMES

Having Fun While Discussing Serious Matters

Ly U. Phan

In 2003, the American Association of Colleges for Teacher Education hosted a special conference in Wisconsin to discuss the challenges of teaching an increasingly diverse student population (AACTE, 2003). This conference reflected a growing national movement to address diversity in the classroom. However, as educators continue to recognize the importance of integrating diversity-related topics into curriculums, they also face the challenge of implementing that mission.

Garcia and Soest (2000) note the intensified pressure on educators to assume the responsibility of caring for students' emotional and learning needs. Educators must find the right approach to accomplish the integration of diversity-related topics, particularly because discussing diversity requires that both educators and students discover and disclose their own personal prejudices and stereotypes. This chapter explores the use of simulations and games to address sensitive and serious diversity-related issues. It includes a discussion of the challenges and advantages of this pedagogical approach and lists additional resources for further exploration of the method.

The Need to Address Diversity in the Classroom

In 2000, the National Center for Education Statistics reported that, of the elementary and secondary teachers in public schools, 84% were Caucasian, 7%

were African American, 6% were Hispanic, and less than 3% were from other ethnic groups (U.S. Department of Education, 2003a; U.S. Department of Education, 2003b). In contrast, the students whom they were teaching differed dramatically; members of minority groups accounted for almost 40% of students (U.S. Department of Education, 2003a). In addition, 20% of school-age students came from homes in which English was not the primary language. The difference between teachers' and students' compositions presents a unique challenge to teachers: how to best educate a student population that is progressively more culturally and linguistically diverse.

Even though the discrepancy in demographic composition is not the main issue of this volume (though an important issue in its own right), it does illustrate the current dynamic between teachers and students that has led to the need for more cross-cultural awareness in the education system. When people who are on various points of the cross-cultural continuum come together, conflicts often arise from the articulation and interpretation of verbal and nonverbal language, cultural stereotypes, and the high level of anxiety toward people in "other groups" (Henderson, 1994). Students from different cultural backgrounds bring with them different sets of values and customs as well as various learning styles. Irvin (1990) found that this contrast was partly accountable for school failure among African American students. The Children's Defense Fund (1991) reported that children of color are more likely to drop out of school than their Caucasian classmates. Specifically, the dropout rate of African Americans, according to the National Center for Education Statistics (2003a), was 13%, and of Hispanics it was 35.5%. The consequence is an alarming crisis not only for the education system but also for the development and well-being of the nation as a whole. Although the presence of students of color is undeniably increasing in most classrooms nationwide, the need to do something pedagogically different is not as obvious to many educators. A survey by the National Center for Education Statistics (2001) indicated that only 32% of teachers felt prepared to address diversity and only 26% felt the need to participate in professional development to assist students with limited English proficiency. Studies investigating the relationship between teachers and students of color show fewer interactions and lower expectations (Garibaldi, 1992; Guerra, Attar, & Weissberg, 1997); others indicate that teacher involvement has a significant impact on the level of engagement of African American students (Pang & Sablan, 1998; Tucker, Zayco, Herman, Reinke, Trujillo, & Carraway, 2002).

Advantages and Challenges of Using Simulations and Games to Teach Diversity

Beginning in the 1990s, the movement toward active-learning pedagogy attracted teachers and instructors who were interested in an alternative to the traditional lecture-based teaching (Bonwell & Eison, 1991; Michael & Chen, 2006). Some of the most common active-learning pedagogies were small-group discussion (Cooper & Robinson, 2000; Smith, 2000), role play (McDaniel, 2000), debate (Garrett, Schoener, & Hood, 1996; Pernecky, 1997), and web-based demonstration (Browne & Funnell, 1998; Kocour, 2000; Marrs, Blake, & Gavrin, 2003). Educators and trainers, such as the Association for Business Simulation and Experiential Learning, who advocate this pedagogy, quote Confucius, "I hear and I forget. I see and I remember. I do and I understand" (Gentry, 1990).

"Active learning and teaching" here refers to the employment of a variety of techniques that require students to do more than listen; students must analyze, synthesize, and evaluate the information at hand (Chickering & Gamson, 1987). However, in spite of the advantages of using simulations and games, there are several challenges and barriers to this pedagogy (Bonwell & Eison, 1991).

Change in the Instructor's Role.   In introducing simulations and games, the instructor changes from provider of knowledge to facilitator of discoveries. Once started, a simulation or game can take on a life of itself. The outcome depends on the dynamic of the group as well as on the characteristics of individual members. Effectively using simulations and games requires that instructors recognize that there are two components of teaching, namely, the content and the process (Thiagarajan, 2001). "Content" refers to concepts, constructs, and theories, and "process" refers to the class discussions and activities used to demonstrate content. Advocating and using simulations and games in the classroom do not necessitate choosing process over content. With some thoughtful preparation, it is possible to achieve a well-balanced mix between content and goal-oriented process through simulations and games.

Time.   Preparation for simulations and games can be time-consuming in the beginning. One must first identify the intended goals of the lecture and then select the appropriate simulation or game so that the class agenda can be structured accordingly. This chapter presents a collection of relatively easy yet effective activities. Once you have become familiar with the practice of using games and find it fascinating, you can explore more complex exercises from the additional resources at the end of the chapter. Many resources are available through books and at various Web sites. Once comfortable with using these simulations and games in your classroom, you will find that it gets easier (and faster) to create lesson plans that lead to rich learning experiences.

Risk.   Using simulations and games involves a certain level of risk (i.e., of nonparticipation, losing control over the class, and using a non-traditional method). However, with adequate preparation such risks are minimized. Furthermore, the benefits of taking such risks outweigh the dangers. I believe that all educators hope to leave a lasting impression in their students through their teaching. This pedagogical approach offers a way to achieve this dream.

On the brighter side, the use of simulations and games has a number of advantages: ease of tension, creation of a welcoming environment where everyone opens up about emotions and attitudes, and best of all, fun. In a highly diverse class, there is a moderate amount of anxiety toward people whose backgrounds are different from one's own (Van Der Zee, Ali, & Haaksma, 2007). In national surveys and interviews of 9,100 college students at 28 private and public universities, students hesitated to discuss racial and multicultural issues but openly discussed their casual sex lives (Levine & Cureton, 1998). By inviting students to participate in a non-threatening exercise such as a simulation or game, instructors help reduce the discomfort that could occur when one is asked either to examine one's own biases or to address any deep resentment toward members of another ethnic group. The goal is to select and plan the sequence of activities so that students gradually recognize a range of emotions (e.g., fear, intimidation, resentment) or attitudes (e.g., prejudice, stigmatization).

Simulations and Games for Icebreakers

Barnga

This card game was developed by Thiagarajan (2006). It takes between 20 to 30 minutes to play the game and about the same amount for debriefing. The minimum number of participants is 8, but the best game involves 20 to

40 players. Students are divided into four-person groups to learn and play a new card game. Group members learn the rules of the game and then play a few practice rounds. Once familiar with the rules for winning, instruction sheets are removed and everyone must adhere to complete silence. No spoken words or drawings can be used to communicate; players may gesture to express themselves. The winner of each table rotates to a different table to play new rounds. What students do not know is that each table has a different set of rules for winning; therefore, the winner who arrives at a new table will play with different rules than those at that table. The purpose of this game is to help students discover the discomfort, misunderstanding, and conflict among people with different backgrounds. Each table is analogous to a culture with which we are intimately familiar; the interactions with members of "other groups" bring out the unspoken assumption that everyone operates with the same set of values and traditions. The book comes with detailed instruction on how to facilitate different variations of the game, preprinted rule sheets for copying, and suggestions for debriefing. All you need is this book and one deck of cards for each group.

Ball of Yarn

I have not been able to identify the original source of this icebreaker. I modified it for the purpose of introducing diversity topics. This activity begins with the facilitator listing three to five facts about himself or herself (e.g., name, birth order, favorite food or hobby). The facilitator then throws the ball of yarn to another person while holding on to the end of the string. The next person is instructed to catch the ball and say one thing that he or she has in common with the facilitator before introducing his or her own facts. Repeat these steps until everyone in the room has a chance to introduce his or her own set of facts. The result of the icebreaker is a tangled web of yarn that symbolizes the interconnectedness among people despite differences. This game is best carried out with group sizes ranging from 10 to 60 participants; the larger the group, the longer it takes. Too large a group might create difficulty in passing the ball of yarn.

What's in a Name?

Lambach (1996) described an interesting way to help develop a sense of community among strangers. The number of people taking part determines the amount of time it takes to play this game. The facilitator first writes his or her name on the board or overhead and then discloses some information related to his or her name. For example, I would write "Ly Uyen Phan" on the board and say "My name is Ly Uyen Phan; on my birth certificate it was written 'Phan Thuy Uyen Ly.' In the Vietnamese culture we list our family name first. Some people pronounce my name 'Lie' but the correct pronunciation is 'Lee.' When I was in high school, I combined my middle and first name to create 'Uyenly' so that people would not call me 'Lie.'" Then I add that I share the same initials *LP* with my father, my brother, my sister-in-law, and my two nieces. Lambach (1996) recommended that the extent to which the facilitator elaborates his or her disclosure provides a model for others to follow. Once the facilitator is finished, he or she passes the marker on the next person to explain his or her name. When the game is completed, participants will have learned more about each other and felt a sense of community. If someone does not say anything, the facilitator may prompt by asking whether he or she likes the name or, if given a choice, would have some favorite alternatives. Usually, people have a lot to say about their names, leading to a rich discussion about commonalities and differences.

Simulations and Games for Exploring Differences

Bafá Bafá

The Bafá Bafá game by Shirts (1974) was originally developed to help improve relationships between U.S. Navy sailors and the local people. Participants are divided into two groups that have two distinctive cultures, namely, Alpha and Beta. Participants are given materials to help them learn about their specific culture. The game requires a minimum of 12 participants, but it is best to have between 18 and 35. Once familiarized with the values, traditions, and customs of their assigned culture, a few visitors from each side are exchanged; the dynamics of the game unfold when visitors encounter the "strangeness" of the other culture; participants experience real-life discomfort when differences clash. Participants also have an opportunity to explore the biases and stereotypes used to judge people who are different. In the discussion that follows, participants examine their personal experiences with the simulated activities. This simulation is a great transition into learning about the unique characteristics of a particular culture or country, such as how people treat women and elders. If you are working with students in fifth through eighth grade, a simplified version called Rafá Rafá is more appropriate. Both Bafá Bafá and Rafá Rafá are available for purchase from Simulation Training Systems (www.stsintl.com).

Brief Encounter

If you have too restricted a budget to purchase either Bafá Bafá or Rafá Rafá for your class or you prefer a simpler activity, there is an alternative simulation called Brief Encounter (Peace Corps, 1996). This simulation serves a similar purpose but has no kit of preprinted cards, tokens, and cassette tapes. In Brief Encounter, participants are divided into two distinctive cultures, Pandya and Chispa; group members interact with each other according to the assigned culture. Interactions with members of the other culture bring out understanding of cultural differences, values contrasts, and an appreciation for the challenges of working with people from different cultures. Brief Encounter is part of a free downloadable 102-page collection of similar activities titled *Looking at Ourselves and Others* (Peace Corps, 1996).

Chatter

Chatter is another simulation from *Looking at Ourselves and Others* that will always catch participants off-guard. Each participant receives an etiquette strip of paper with instructions to follow when the conversations begin. Here are some examples from pages 28 and 29 of the booklet:

"It is impolite to shout, so talk softly. Whisper. Even if people cannot hear you, do not raise your voice."

"It is polite and reassuring to reach out and touch someone. Touch people on the arm or the shoulder when you speak to them."

"It is impolite to stare at people, so avoid eye contact. Look at the floor or the speaker's shoes. Do not look at the speaker's face."

"It is friendly to share your thoughts and feelings without any inhibition, so make several self-disclosure statements. Describe your intimate feelings about different subjects. Ask personal questions of the other members of the group."

"It is impolite to speak impulsively. Whenever somebody asks you a question, silently count to seven before you give an answer."

Interactions among participants accurately simulate the real-life experiences that occur when people from different cultural backgrounds come together at work, grocery stores, airports, and many other places. If participants follow the etiquette instruction well, you will always have a lively period of interactions with laughter. Some students look very anxious, while others enjoy themselves immensely. In the debriefing discussion, participants discover the key learning objectives of the exercise, namely, that we often judge other people according to what we think is "normal" and that prejudice is often the result of unfamiliarity with other people's customs and traditions. Debriefing usually serves as a good transition into a discussion of cultural differences, cultural biases, and issues related to acculturation.

Additional Resources

As you can see from the previous examples, using simulations and games can provide a fascinating new way to teach about diversity. The following are some sources that provide engaging ways to introduce your class to issues of diversity. Each can be modified for the objectives and time limitation of your classes.

Looking at Ourselves and Others (Peace Corps, 1996).   As already mentioned, this is a collection of activities designed by Peace Corps volunteers worldwide. These exercises target issues related to cross-cultural differences, acculturation, and intercultural communication. This 102-page booklet is available for download at http://www.peacecorps.gov/wws/publications/looking/index.cfm.

Thiagi Workshop, Inc.   This is a consulting firm that designs and trains performance-based workshops. Its Web site (http://www.thiagi.com) contains hundreds of free activities as well as advice on how to effectively facilitate an interactive session. Visitors may also subscribe to the group's monthly newsletter, which is filled with new advice, games, and simulations.

Experiential Activities for Intercultural Learning (Seelye, 1996).   This book contains a collection of 32 exercises that are highly appropriate for discussion of issues related to diversity.

Teaching About Culture, Ethnicity, and Diversity: Exercises and Planned Activities (Singelis, 1998).   This is another good resource that contains 28 simulations and games.

Diversity Activities for Psychology (Whittlesey, 2001).   This workbook contains a collection of 78 exercises covering a wide range of topics in psychology. It also organizes a matrix to suggest which exercises are best for a particular topic.

References

American Association of Colleges for Teacher Education. (2003, September). *Culture, language, and student achievement: Recruiting and preparing teachers for diverse students.* Proceedings and background materials of the Wingspread conference, Racine, WI. Washington, DC: Author. (ED 484 653)

Bonwell, C., & Eison, J. (1991). *Active learning: Creating excitement in the classroom. AEHE-ERIC Higher Education Report No.1.* Washington, DC: George Washington University, School of Education and Human Development.

Browne, T., & Funnell, D. (1998). Using CAL and the Web for first-year geography methods teaching. *Journal of Geography in Higher Education, 22*(3), 393–401.

Chickering, A. W., & Gamson, Z. F. (1987). Seven principles for good practice. *American Association of Higher Education Bulletin, 39,* 3–7.

Children's Defense Fund. (1991). *The state of America's children.* Washington, DC: Author.

Cooper, J. L., & Robinson, P. (2000). Getting started: Informal small-group strategies in large classes. *New Directions for Teaching and Learning, 81,* 17–24.

Garcia, B., & Soest, D. V. (2000). Facilitating learning on diversity: Challenges to the professor. *Journal of Ethnic and Cultural Diversity in Social Work, 9*(1–2), 21–39.

Garibaldi, A. M. (1992). Educating and motivating African American males to succeed. *Journal of Negro Education, 61,* 4–11.

Garrett, M., Schoener, L., & Hood, L. (1996). Debate: A teaching strategy to improve verbal communication and critical-thinking skills. *Nurse Educator, 21*(4), 37–40.

Gentry, J. W. (1990). *Guide to business gaming and experiential learning.* East Brunswick, London: Nichols/GP Publishing.

Guerra, N. G., Attar, B., & Weissberg, R. P. (1997). Prevention of aggression and violence among inner-city youths. In D. M. Stoff & J. Breiling (Eds.), *Handbook of antisocial behavior* (pp. 375–383). New York: John Wiley.

Henderson, G. (1994). *Cultural diversity in the workplace: Issues and strategies.* Westport, CT: Greenwood.

Irvin, J. J. (1990). *Black students and school failure.* New York: Praeger.

Kocour, B. G. (2000). Using Web-based tutorials to enhance library instruction. *College and Undergraduate Libraries, 7*(1), 45–54.

Lambach, R. (1996). What's in a name? In H. N. Seelye (Ed.), *Experiential activities for intercultural learning* (pp. 53–55). Boston: Intercultural Press.

Levine, A., & Cureton, J. S. (1998). *When hope and fear collide: A portrait of today's college student.* San Francisco: Jossey-Bass.

Marrs, K. A., Blake, R. E., & Gavrin, A. D. (2003). Web-based warm up exercises in just-in-time teaching. *Journal of College Science Teaching, 33*(1), 42–47.

McDaniel, K. N. (2000). Four elements of successful historical role-playing in the classroom. *History Teacher, 33*(3), 357–362.

Michael, D., & Chen, S. (2006). *Serious games: Games that educate, train, and inform.* Boston: Thomson Course Technology.

National Center for Education Statistics. (2001). *Teacher preparation and professional development.* (NCES 2001-088)

Pang, V. O., & Sablan, V. A. (1998). Teacher efficacy: How do teachers feel about their abilities to teach African American students? In M. E. Dilworth (Ed.), *Being responsive to cultural differences: How teachers learn* (pp. 45–65). Thousand Oaks, CA: Corwin Press.

Peace Corps. (1996). *Looking at ourselves and others.* Washington, DC: Author.

Pernecky, M. (1997). Debate for the economics class—and others. *College Teaching, 45*(4), 136–138.

Seelye, H. N. (Ed.). (1996). *Experiential activities for intercultural learning.* Boston: Intercultural Press.

Shirts, G. (1974). *BaFa BaFa.* Del Mar, CA: Simulation Training Systems.

Singelis, T. (1998). *Teaching about culture, ethnicity, and diversity.* Thousand Oaks, CA: Sage.

Smith, K. A. (2000). Going deeper: Formal small-group learning in large classes. *New Directions for Teaching and Learning, 81,* 25–46.

Thiagarajan, S. (2001, June). Can training games really teach? *Play for Performance, 3.*

Thiagarajan, S. (2006). *Barnga: A simulation game on cultural clashes.* Boston: Intercultural Press.

Tucker, C. M., Zayco, R. A., Herman, K. C., Reinke, W. R., Trujillo, M., & Carraway, K. (2002). Teacher and child variables as predictors of academic engagement among African American children. *Psychology in the Schools, 39,* 477–488.

U.S. Department of Education, National Center for Education Statistics. (2003a). *Digest of education statistics, 2002.* Washington, DC: Author. (NCES 2003-060)

U.S. Department of Education, National Center for Education Statistics. (2003b). *Early estimates of public elementary and secondary education statistics: School year 2001–2002.* Retrieved June 14, 2007, from http://nces.edu.gov/edstats/

Van Der Zee, K. I., Ali, A. J., & Haaksma, I. (2007). Determinants of effective coping with cultural transition among expatriate children and adolescents. *Anxiety, Stress, and Coping: An International Journal, 20*(1), 25–45.

Whittlesey, V. (2001). *Diversity activities for psychology.* Boston: Allyn & Bacon.

25

THE USE OF ACTION LEARNING TECHNIQUES IN A RACE RELATIONS COURSE

Peter L. Kranz, Sylvia Z. Ramirez, and Nick L. Lund

ction learning methods have been used successfully in teaching French
(Drew, 1990) and nursing (Thompson, 1990) within university classrooms. However, there is a paucity of literature describing the use of
these techniques in social science courses focusing on cultural diversity. Many
action techniques are derived from Jacob L. Moreno's psychodrama theory and
practice (Blatner, 2000; Gershoni, 2003; Starr, 1977). Crucial dimensions of the
method involve having individuals act out and/or disclose personal truths that
relate to their current unique experiences. A primary goal is gaining new insights
into personal problems and discovering helpful, constructive solutions.

Action techniques can enhance learning in cultural diversity courses. It is
time to move beyond discussions of the need for diversity awareness to courses
that provide active participation and substantive bases for changes in attitudes
(Hansen & Williams, 2003; Ocampo, Prieto, Whittlesey, Connor, Janco-
Gidley, Mannix & Sare, 2003). Traditional cultural diversity courses that are
limited to lectures, readings, question asking, and examinations can result in
students being passive observers and complacent consumers. Classroom learning needs to be an active and interactive process for all participants. This paper
describes action learning techniques that were effectively implemented in a
university race relations course (Kranz & Lund, 2004). The class was offered in
multiple sections to approximately 90 undergraduate students during a six-year
period at a state university in the southeastern United States during the early

1970s, a period of significant racial tension. Each section was composed of 10 to 12 students, with approximately even numbers of Black and White students because that was the ethnic composition of the university at that time. The course instructor (first author) is a licensed psychologist who has extensive training in psychodrama and race relations.

In the course, there was minimal emphasis on class lectures, note taking, and the use of examinations and papers as grade determinants. Experiential aspects of the class were emphasized. A primary objective was for students to openly examine their own and others' perceptions, feelings, attitudes, and behaviors related to race. A second important objective was for this experience to reduce prejudicial beliefs and enhance sensitivity and activism regarding diversity issues. The instructor subjectively evaluated students based on their personal growth, participation in course activities, discussion of assigned readings, and logs describing their reflections. Students kept personal journals in which they reflected on their beliefs and attitudes, as well as current and past experiences. The instructor read and commented on the students' logs on a weekly basis. The readings focused on racial issues, including books such as *Autobiography of Malcolm X* (Haley, 1966), *Black Rage* (Grier & Cobbs, 1968), *Confessions of a White Racist* (King, 1971), and *Roots* (Haley, 1976).

While Kranz and Lund (2004) described their teaching methods in general terms, this paper focuses on the learning techniques that were implemented in the course, most of which have their underpinnings in psychodrama. The following action techniques were used: (a) speaking in the first person; (b) taking responsibility for one's words; (c) telling one's personal story; (d) using a semi-structured format; (e) openly sharing beliefs and experiences; (f) altering seating arrangements to enhance student interactions and critical listening; and (g) using role reversal. Two role reversal techniques that were used outside the classroom were a seven-day live-in home stay with a family of the opposite race and a visit to a historically Black college or university (hereafter referred to as Black college/university). This paper is based on the instructor's observations, qualitative student feedback, and a 20-year follow-up study (Kranz & Lund, 2004).

Rules for the Class

At the outset, the instructor created basic guidelines for the class structure. First, students were allowed to express themselves as they wished as long as they were honest and took responsibility for their speech. This guideline permitted each student the freedom of not having to feel guarded based on political correctness. Second, verbal threats and physical confrontations in any form were not permitted. By holding to these guidelines, students had to consider and develop new ways of self-expression and control so that the other racial group might accurately hear and listen to their concerns. When needed, the instructor encouraged and assisted students in communicating strong feelings more effectively. The students were instructed to communicate in their own vernacular, while using a voice tone that was consistent with the words expressed. Most students recognized that this active voice was a more effective means of communication. Other important class rules were that all students were to be respected even if their particular views or perspectives differed from those of others, and that what was expressed was to be kept within the class and not discussed with others outside the class. At first, these guidelines were problematic, as the majority of students had strong, deep-seeded views about the other group. However, in time and with active participation in building trust, many of these negative views were tempered by class activities, resulting in more positive personal relationships among the students.

Action Techniques Used in the Classroom

Speaking in the First Person and Taking Responsibility for One's Words

Students were strongly encouraged to speak in the first person when addressing each other. An insistence on ownership of personal statements and feelings helped eliminate comments hidden behind third-person usage. Although this process was initially difficult for most students, it became easier with practice and was an extremely beneficial technique in moving students to a deeper and more personal and honest level of racial awareness and understanding. Students had the freedom to use their own vocabulary and level of affect without fear of censorship.

Telling One's Own Story

As with psychodrama, it was important for participants to tell their own stories and experiences. Their personal stories evolved throughout the course. Inner voices of intense emotions and feelings, such as anger, fear, and anxiety, emerged with greater profundity. As the semester progressed, they became more comfortable recognizing and sharing different parts of themselves related to racial relationships. The instructor encouraged the students and ascertained how far they could be pushed in their self-exploration, thereby reducing the chances that they would "shut down" and not openly share their stories. Students were surprised when other classmates accepted their struggle and reinforced their honesty and openness.

The dialogue for many in the mixed racial groups was cathartic because it was the first time the students had unleashed strong feelings of pain and anguish that were based on years of prejudice and discrimination. Most participants reported that, for the first time, the other racial group truly listened to their feelings and stories, and they themselves actually confronted their prejudices. The experience involved not only relating personal stories but also critically and constructively analyzing other participants' assumptions and experiences. Students could not state unfounded statements or generalizations about either their or the other racial group without being challenged. Although this process created discomfort, it helped students clarify their thoughts.

Using a Semistructured Format

Many class activities were based on a semistructured, uncensored format in which spontaneity was encouraged. This kept students focused in the present and prevented them from using rehearsed inner voices of self-protection. The process led to unexpected and worthwhile discoveries about themselves and the impact of prejudice on their lives. Students often became supportive of each other as they listened and participated in each other's personal struggles with prejudice. Active participation in seeking constructive solutions to their intense struggles frequently led to closer class bonding. An example was the required live-in home visit. Each student's experience depended on the interaction between the student and the particular family's circumstances, dynamics, and activities.

Openly Sharing Beliefs and Experiences

Students were encouraged to relate their particular truths and beliefs without restrictions of political correctness or worry about how the other racial group would perceive them. The instructor emphasized that all views were to be heard, respected, and explored as to possible origins and criteria of belief. Class sessions were based on stripping away well-defended emotional layers that had protected the core of the students' realness. Since this was a gradual, carefully guided process, students were quite willing to be forthcoming. The instructor's and fellow students' support and questions were critical aspects of this process. The more students revealed about themselves, the more others were encouraged to do the same. In this process of building trust, students were more able to critically examine underlying well-guarded and deep-seeded issues of racial prejudice.

Altering Seating Arrangements to Enhance Student Interactions

Another action technique used to examine issues between the two racial groups was altering the class seating arrangement. Initially, the groups voluntarily sat apart from each other. However, classroom chairs were easily movable, which allowed for a variety of seating arrangements. Most students reported that the use of dyads in the beginning of the semester enhanced more open exchanges between Blacks and Whites. Also, this particular one-to-one configuration reduced fearfulness in verbal exchanges; thus, students were less guarded in both listening to others and responding openly to issues of prejudice. As the semester progressed, the number of students in the groups was gradually increased from dyads to groups of up to six. Students reported that the small group size enhanced their comfort level in sharing and resulted in stronger, personal connections with other students. Prejudices were explored at deep levels, entanglements of distrust were undone, and racial misunderstandings were greatly reduced.

An alternate seating arrangement that had an obvious effect on group dialogue was the circle, which can easily be utilized in many classroom situations. When chairs were placed in a circle, students had face-to-face contact with each other. Another effective seating variation was the creation of two circles, with a small interior circle surrounded by a larger one. Various configurations were placed within the smaller circle, such as Black males and White females. The inner group of students was then instructed to dialogue about their racially related views, feelings, and issues. The outer group (which was the "audience") was required to listen but could not initially respond to the inner circle's dialogue. At the conclusion of the dialogue, the audience then had the opportunity to react to the inner circle's dialogue. This particular arrangement of inner and outer circles was extremely valuable in that many students stated that, for the first time, they listened critically to others. Not allowing the outer circle to comment focused their attention on what was being said, especially regarding the impact of race on themselves and others. This type of insight might have been missed if students in the outer circle had thought about how to respond rather than only listen. These seating arrangements can be transferred to other situations in which issues of difference need to be explored, such as those involving ethnicity, economic status, geographic location, religion, and gender. For example, within a class dealing with gender issues, the circle seating arrangement could be set up with males in the inner circle and females in the outer circle.

Using Role Reversal

Another successful action learning technique was to have students sit on the floor, close their eyes, and warm themselves up to a role reversal exercise. With their eyes closed, they were to imagine that their skin color was of the other racial group. In this process, everything in their lives was to remain the same except for their skin color. It was important not to rush the warmup. After they opened their eyes, they discussed the impact of this change on their lives. Students needed to think about what their lives would be like in the new circumstance and also to consider how this dramatic change would make them feel in the deepest personal sense. This exercise was clearly unsettling for many students because they realized that their lives would be very different. Some relationships with families and friends that had been positive were now strained or threatened because of this experience. During this role reversal, some students expressed feelings of anxiety, fear, and sadness about the altering of current relationships. Students also indicated that they had not realized the profound impact that skin color and prejudice had on their lives.

Action Teaching Techniques Outside the Classroom

Live-in Home Visit

Another role reversal was a class requirement of a seven-day home visit by each student with a family of the other race during the last third of the course. This exercise, during which White students spent a week living in a

Black family's home, and vice versa, proved to be a powerful growth experience for both groups. To facilitate the visit, the instructor contacted families in the region who were willing to participate, but class members then had to make all their own arrangements with the families. Students reported that the home visit was a profound experience that resulted in real breakthroughs. It enabled them to reduce fears about the other racial group, rethink long-held prejudices, and achieve better racial understanding.

Visit to a Black College/University

A key class requirement was either a one-day or weekend visit to a Black college/university. The instructor obtained approval from the institution's administration for the visit. The class interacted with the host university's students, faculty, and staff in a variety of settings. The initial impact of this role reversal experience was different for each racial group. Many White students, who had never been in an educational or similar setting in which they were a distinct racial minority, felt intimidated, uneasy, and fearful when they realized that most of the faces and voices around them were Black. Most White students expressed that they felt that they would be ignored, rejected, and/or physically confronted. By the end of the visit, the White students' fears and concerns tended to abate because of positive interactions with Black students on the campus. For many of the visiting Black students, this was the first time they were in a higher educational setting in which they were in the majority. Their newfound comfort level significantly helped lower their defenses, and they reported that they felt like they were "coming home."

Summary and Discussion

Action learning techniques were used effectively to facilitate students' personal exploration in a university race relations course. The class format was semistructured, and spontaneity of expression was stressed. Students were strongly encouraged to speak in the first person, take full responsibility for their words, tell their stories and experiences through their own eyes, speak without constraints of political correctness, and respect the beliefs and experiences of other students. Class meetings focused on gradually stripping away layers of emotional defenses so that students would carefully examine personal, well-guarded, and deep-seeded issues of racial prejudice. Other effective action techniques included role reversal during in-class and outside class exercises, and changing seating arrangements to enhance critical listening and personal connections. The action learning techniques utilized in this course could easily be used in a variety of disciplines and do not need to be used in their entirety. Rather, the selection should be based on the instructor's comfort level, expertise, and relevance to the course. For example, the visit to a Black college/university is not appropriate for all diversity courses.

Since the course content and experience can be highly emotional and personally sensitive, it is recommended that the instructor be clinically trained and have significant experience in cultural diversity and group process. A detailed, written description of course expectations about the depth of required student participation should be provided and discussed in the first class meeting. There should be a clear understanding that students can withdraw "without prejudice" if they are not willing to participate fully in the course.

Improving racial relations is critical in advancing cultural understanding in an increasingly diverse world. In a 20-year follow-up study, class members were interviewed about the impact of this course on their lives. Participants reported that the action learning techniques employed in the course were very effective in bringing about lifelong, positive changes in their attitudes, beliefs, and actions regarding members of other races (Kranz & Lund, 2004). In conclusion, students suggested that similar courses using techniques described in this paper would be useful in fostering better racial understanding and interactions, especially if offered early in one's educational experience.

References

Blatner, A. (2000). *Foundations of psychodrama: History, theory, and practice* (4th ed.). New York: Springer.

Drew, N. (1990). Psychodrama in nursing education. *Journal of Group Psychotherapy, Psychodrama and Sociometry, 43*(2), 54–61.

Gershoni, J. (Ed.). (2003). *Psychodrama in the 21st century: Clinical and educational applications.* New York: Springer.

Grier, W. H., & Cobbs, P. M. (1968). *Black rage.* New York: Basic Books.

Haley, A. (1966). *The autobiography of Malcolm X.* New York: Grove Press.

Haley, A. (1976). *Roots.* New York: Garden City.

Hansen, C. E., & Williams, M. R. (2003). Comparison of cross-cultural course changes: From traditional lecture course to contemporary course with biblio-learning, video-learning, and experiential exercises. *Journal of Instructional Psychology, 30*(3), 197–206.

King, Larry L. (1971). *Confessions of a white racist.* New York: Viking Press.

Kranz, P. L., & Lund, N. L. (2004). Successful teaching techniques in a race relations class. *Journal of Psychology, 138*(4), 371–383.

Ocampo, C., Prieto, L. R., Whittlesey, V., Connor, J., Janco-Gidley, J., Mannix, S., & Sare, K. (2003). Diversity research in teaching of psychology: Summary and recommendations. *Teaching of Psychology, 3,* 5–18.

Starr, A. (1977). *Rehearsal for living: Psychodrama.* Chicago: Nelson-Hall.

Thompson, M. C. (1990). An action-oriented lesson for second-year college French students. *Journal of Group Psychotherapy, Psychodrama and Sociometry, 43*(2), 82–84.

26

KEEPING IT REAL

Authenticity in the Diversity Learning Environment

Kelley D. Haynes

As the field of diversity education emerges, it is vital to establish best practices. One such practice, the utilization of authenticity in teaching, can be a very useful strategy in the successful dissemination of information about diverse groups. Additionally, an authentic instructor or trainer promotes an environment of personal awareness and reflection for trainees (Cranton & Carusetta, 2004).

Authenticity can be defined several ways; my definition comes from pioneering research conducted by Patricia Cranton and Ellen Carusetta (2004). In their paper, authenticity is described as having knowledge about ourselves as distinct and separate from other human beings. They identified five domains for authenticity in teaching: self, other, relationship, context, and critical reflection. Faculty members who participated in the study understood *themselves* as teachers and also as persons. They were aware of *others* as human beings in the teaching and learning environment, especially students, but sometimes as colleagues and individuals outside the classroom. These instructors were aware of and carefully defined their *relationships* with students. They held an understanding of how the *context* of teaching influenced self, other, and relationship. Finally, the faculty members engaged in *critical reflection* within the aforementioned categories (Cranton & Carusetta, 2004).

This chapter addresses how one can integrate unique diversity learning environments with authentic expression in each of the aforementioned domains. I utilize personal reflections and stories to provide the reader with applied scenarios in each domain.

The Domain of Self

In this domain, two factors are most important: instructors' own biases (Sue & Sue, 2003) and their identity development (Moore, Madison-Colmore, & Lott Collins, 2005). To work toward authenticity and positive ways of thinking about others, instructors must explore their personal biases. Instructors that do so come to understand their own identity and that of their students (Moore et al., 2005).

Derald Wing Sue and David Sue (2003) address the importance of becoming aware of one's personal bias in their model describing culturally competent mental health professionals. In this model of cultural competency, one of three essential competencies is having an awareness of personal values, biases, and assumptions. Mental health professionals are encouraged to examine how their own personal judgments and values influence competent work within their professional environments. To become culturally competent and authentic in the learning environment, instructors and trainers need to do the same.

Instructors and trainers must also become aware of others' cultural identity development, which can be described as a transformational process (Sue & Sue, 2003). Over time, individuals transition across several stages in relating to themselves and others as cultural beings. Several theorists engage this concept, resulting in an array of identity development models for racial, sexual orientation, feminist, and other cultural groups (Cross, 1991, 1995; Helms, 1995; Kim, 1981; McCarn & Fassinger, 1996; McNamara & Rickard, 1989; Parham & Helms, 1985; Ruiz, 1990; Sue & Sue, 2003).

Teacher dignity is also important. As described by R. Bruce McPherson (2001), it has three core components: the capacity to go beyond teaching and produce student learning; the ability to appear confident to one's students; and the ability to be authentic and influence others to become authentic. In transmitting authenticity to students, teachers give clear indications as to who they are, what they have to offer to students, and what they expect from students. Students' respect for such teachers promotes the dignity of teachers.

I find journaling and dialoguing with others useful strategies in identifying personal values relating to topics of diversity. During a recent trip to Europe, I spent many hours journaling about my own attitudes toward race, culture, social class, and gender in other countries. It was rewarding to identify, through journaling activities, my own values regarding these issues. I also spent time contemplating my experiences of and statuses within various cultural identity development processes.

I have also found that having discussions with other faculty members or diversity trainers can help me gain a better sense of my personal values in relation to diversity. I am part of a teaching community that takes opportunities to discuss experiences with students, and in these discussions I have had further opportunity to process personal experiences with diversity.

The Domain of Other

Using a variety of teaching techniques ensures that the needs of each learner are more likely to be met. Moore et al. (2005) identify several activities that are useful in multicultural education, including field trips, self-reflective activities, retreats, class presentations, and field observation.

In my own teaching, I incorporate experiential, intellectual, and applied learning activities to meet the needs of multiple learning styles and preferences. A few of these are described below.

Self-Reflective Activity

Learners choose two films, preselected by me, to view during the learning cycle. After viewing a film, a learner composes a term paper examining her personal reactions to diversity issues in the film. The purpose of the assignment is for the learner to acknowledge any personal stereotypes and the potential impact of those judgments in interacting with diverse populations.

Case Study

Periodically throughout the learning cycle, learners are required to engage in group analyses of case studies. Some case studies are borrowed from an external source (Sue & Sue, 1999), and others I have personally created. The case studies are designed to increase student awareness of critical incidents that might take place in cross-cultural interactions. In groups, students are required to identify diversity issues and discuss goals for each case. The purpose of these activities is to help students apply multicultural theories to tangible situations.

Diversity Interview

Students are required to interview a classmate about topics of diversity. The goal is to learn as much as possible about an individual across several domains of diversity. When interviewed, students are given the option of role-playing or playing themselves. Interviewers are provided with a list of questions to begin the interview and are encouraged to ask additional questions as the interview progresses. The purpose of this activity is to acclimate students to exploring topics of diversity with others.

The Domain of Relationship

For many instructors and trainers, engaging in heated discussions about emotionally charged issues is a formidable yet crucial component to their teaching. In these cases, setting expectations of student-teacher and student-student interactions can become an important issue.

Rasheed outlines an approach designed to help students communicate in diversity learning environments. In this model, through dialogue and discussion, students develop a critical awareness of diverse experiences. Rasheed (2002) asserts that dialogue creates not only a conversation about differences but also a space for addressing the lived experiences of another. It is an approach that addresses the dimensions of difference and diversity while acknowledging our common humanity.

Parker J. Palmer addresses the idea of creating an educational community in the learning environment. In such an environment students and teachers are engaged in a communal learning process that is ultimately centered on the subject. Students and their instructors or trainers are in "a classroom in which the best features of teacher- and student-centered education are merged and transcended by putting not teacher, not student, but subject at the center of our attention" (Palmer, 1998).

Years ago as a new instructor, I found myself involved with teacher-centered and student-centered debates in the diversity learning environment. In one case, students became angry at comments made by a classmate about a specific racial group. I handled the situation by allowing and, at times, encouraging the class to direct its energies toward this student. The outcome was more anger and a lack of shared understanding about the subject matter. Since that time, I have come to utilize the communal learning model. At the outset of each learning cycle, I educate students about the differences between dialogue and discussion versus debate. Throughout the learning cycle, I encourage dialogue by redirecting debate toward class discussions.

The Domain of Context

For many, the diversity learning environment is a social microcosm into which instructors and trainers, along with their students and trainees, carry a unique experience of their social systems. Racial and political dynamics, current political issues, and other social issues surrounding diverse populations are significant. They may also impact an instructor's ability to successfully teach about these potentially emotionally charged issues. For instance, an instructor or trainer addressing discrimination in social class systems faces potential challenges when teaching and training students who are unexposed or resistant to such issues.

Because the sociopolitical climate is influential in the diversity learning environment, it can be useful for instructors to acknowledge that living in the current social context impacts dialogue in and out of the classroom. A useful strategy in discussing these issues is described by Moore et al. (2005). Instructors select a current sociopolitical issue (hot topic) from the social context of the learning environment to discuss within the learning context.

Moore et al. (2005) describe an additional assignment, the community assessment, that can also be useful. For this assignment, learners are required to gather descriptive data about a community. They then do exploratory research that describes the current economic conditions, current issues, and/or other important issues facing that particular community.

I am presented with many opportunities to discuss hot topics in diversity learning environments. On one occasion, students discussed a graduate professor's comments about feeling "voted down to a second-class citizen."

The comments were made the morning after a gay marriage rights bill was not supported in a public election. Learners were given the opportunity to discuss different viewpoints and to consider the lived experiences of individuals on both sides of this political issue.

The Domain of Critical Reflection

Instructors moving toward authenticity engage in an open and mindful consideration of themselves and their teaching. Instructors must determine the appropriate mechanisms by which they can critically reflect on their teaching (Cranton & Carusetta, 2004).

Teaching portfolios are useful resources for critical reflection (Lyons, 2006; Tigelaar, Dolmans, De Grave, Wolfhagen, & Van der Vleuten, 2006). In the Lyons (2006) model for creating teaching portfolios, reflection is a critical and essential component. Lyons asserts that "through reflection a teacher revisits and inquires into his/her own teaching, assessing what succeeded or failed and why" (p. 156). Elements of the Lyons teaching portfolio include an introduction, a teaching philosophy, materials such as a course syllabus, activities students are asked to perform and do, and student work, examinations, and projects.

In my own experience, relationships with colleagues offer an environment for critical reflection about my teaching. In these relationships, I engage in reciprocal discussion about teaching methods in diversity classes. My colleagues are also available to discuss my difficult moments with students in diversity learning environments and successful and unsuccessful techniques for discussing topics with students. The expertise of my colleagues, and the warmth created by the openness in these relationships, are indispensable to my own critical reflection on teaching in the diversity learning environment.

References

Cranton, P., & Carusetta, E. (2004). Perspectives on authenticity in teaching. *Adult Education Quarterly, 55*(1), 5–22.

Cross, W. E. (1991). *Shades of black: Diversity in African American identity.* Philadelphia: Temple University Press.

Cross, W. E. (1995). The psychology of Nigrescence: Revising the Cross model. In J. G. Ponterotto, J. M. Casas, L. A. Suzuki, & C. M. Alexander (Eds.), *Handbook of multicultural counseling* (pp. 99–122). Thousand Oaks, CA: Sage.

Helms, J. E. (1995). An update of Helms's White and people of color racial identity models. In J. G. Ponterotto, J. M. Casas, L. A. Suzuki, & C. M. Alexander (Eds.), *Handbook of multicultural counseling* (pp. 181–191). Thousand Oaks, CA: Sage.

Kim, J. (1981). The process of Asian American identity development: A study of Japanese-American women's perceptions of their struggle to achieve personal identities as Americans of Asian ancestry. In D. W. Sue & D. Sue (Eds.), *Counseling the culturally diverse* (p. 133). New York: Wiley.

Lyons, N. (2006). Reflective engagement as professional development in the lives of university teachers. *Teachers and teaching: Theory and practice, 12*(2), 151–168.

McCarn, S. R., & Fassinger, R. E. (1996). Revisioning sexual minority identity formation: A new model of lesbian identity and its implications. *Counseling Psychologist, 24*(3), 508–534.

McNamara, K., & Rickard, K. M. (1989). Feminist identity development: Implications for feminist therapy with women. *Journal of Counseling and Development, 68,* 184–193.

McPherson, R. B. (2001). Teacher dignity: An antidote to burnout? *Education, 104*(2), 199–203.

Moore, S. E., Madison-Colmore, O., & Lott Collins, W. (2005). Appreciating multiculturalism: Exercises for teaching diversity. *Journal of African American Studies, 8*(4), 63–75.

Palmer, P. J. (1998). *The courage to teach: Exploring the inner landscape of a teacher's life.* San Francisco: Jossey-Bass.

Parham, T. A., & Helms, J. E. (1985). Relation of racial identity attitudes to self-actualization and affective status of Black students. *Journal of Counseling Psychology, 32,* 431–440.

Rasheed, M. (2002, November). *A dialogical perspective for teaching diversity.* Paper presented at the annual meeting of the North American Association of Christians in Social Work, Rochester, NY.

Ruiz, A. S. (1990). Assessing, diagnosing and treating culturally diverse individuals: A Hispanic perspective. *Psychiatric Quarterly, 66,* 329–341.

Sue, D. W., & Sue, D. (1999). *Counseling the culturally different: Theory and practice* (3rd ed.). New York: Wiley.

Sue, D. W., & Sue, D. (2003). *Counseling the culturally diverse: Theory and practice* (4th ed.). New York: Wiley.

Tigelaar, D., Dolmans, D., De Grave, W., Wolfhagen, I., & Van der Vleuten, C. (2006). Portfolio as a tool to stimulate teachers' reflections. *Medical Teacher, 28*(3), 277–282.

27

COPING STRATEGIES FOR DIVERSITY SCHOLARS

Kelley D. Haynes

U niversity instructors experience various forms of occupational stress, including emotional exhaustion, job dissatisfaction, lack of productivity, stress-related health problems, and consideration of job change. Professionals engaged in jobs (such as teaching) that involve responsibility for the well-being of others are particularly vulnerable to stress. University instructors can also become emotionally exhausted from interacting with large numbers of students and other university officials (Blix, Cruise, Mitchell, & Blix, 1994).

University instructors who address topics of diversity (diversity scholars) face additional challenges. Mangaliso describes teaching diversity as "a challenging, daunting, and rewarding task for both teacher and student" (2004, p. 2). Among its challenges is managing learner resistance to topics of diversity and the instructors who teach the topics, which often exhibits itself through "anger, silence, avoidance, and passivity toward participating in the process" (Jackson, 1999, p. 27). Diversity scholars often become strained and stressed because of ongoing interactions with learner resistance in their classrooms.

This chapter briefly defines stress and then discusses the occupational stress, including student resistance, that is experienced by instructors who address topics of diversity. It also discusses a variety of coping strategies for

---

*General concepts of the chapter evolved from 'Avoiding Burnout' presented at Best Practices in Teaching Diversity & International Perspectives across the Psychology Curriculum by Dr. Kelley Haynes and Dr. Christina Camp in October, 2006.

managing stress, giving special consideration to minority group instructors, who face unique stressors. It concludes by offering strategies that I have found to be successful in managing the stress I have experienced as a diversity scholar.

Defining Stress

Stress can be defined in many different ways (see Gurung, 2006, for a review). The simplest way to define stress and one that allows for subjective differences and physiological and psychological components is that stress is the upsetting of homeostasis (Cannon, 1929), or the state of balance within one's body.

Richard Lazarus (1966) devised the first psychological model of stress. Lazarus saw stress as the imbalance between demands placed on the individual and the individual's resources to cope. He argued that the experience of stress differed significantly among individuals, depending on (1) how they interpret the event and (2) the outcome of specific thinking patterns called appraisals.

All of us are faced with demands. According to Lazarus, these demands are just *events* until *we deem them* to be stressful. For some, teaching about diversity is stressful, and for others it is not perceived as such. The main cognitive process at work is that of making *appraisals*. Lazarus suggested that we make two major types of appraisals when facing any potentially stressful event. During primary appraisals, we ascertain whether the event is positive, negative, or neutral. If negative, we determine whether it is harmful, threatening, or challenging. A harm (or harm-loss) appraisal is made when we expect to lose or actually lose something of great personal significance. For example, when we break up a close relationship, we lose a confidant; we may lose support from an ex-partner or the love of a parent who is dying. Other losses include harm to one's self-esteem with the loss of a job, or physical harm and loss from a diagnosis of a terminal illness. Threat appraisals are made when we believe the event will be extremely demanding and will put ourselves at risk for damage. If you think a bad performance on an upcoming project can severely ruin your reputation, you are seeing the project as a threat. If you appraise the situation as a challenge, you believe you can grow from dealing with the event and may even look at the positive ways you can benefit from it.

A diversity scholar appraising a student's negative comments and challenges as harmful to the professor's influence in the class is experiencing a threat appraisal. An instructor might appraise negative course evaluations as a harm appraisal, believing his or her employment is at risk. Still other diversity scholars may interpret these situations as meaningful to student learning, appraising the events as challenge appraisals.

Stress can be positive or negative, and healthy stress reduction involves identifying environmental and situational stressors. Sources of stress cannot be entirely avoided, but individuals can use a variety of techniques to prevent or reduce stress. Experts advise seeking advice from a medical professional when stress symptoms become severe (Harvard Medical School, 2006).

Learner Resistance

When learners are exposed to topics of diversity, they either accept those ideas or reject them. According to Lather, those who reject ideas early on are unable to embrace and find value in diversity. Learners who accept the ideas may find the new information exciting and liberating, drawing strength from the experience. Others experience a variety of negative emotions, including guilt, fear, and hopelessness. Reacting to negative emotions, these learners may reject the information, blame the instructor, or become passive in the classroom. Still others may become angry and display hostile behavior (Lather, 1991).

Roberts and Smith (2002) propose that learners cannot "learn to think critically without experiencing some discomfort and taking some individual responsibility" (p. 296). Learners who experience discomfort, however, can become resistant and respond to instructors negatively. Schmitz, Stakeman, and Sisneros (2001) report that learners in their study expressed resistance through negative journal entries and closed body language and facial expressions. Learner resistance was strong and quick, and learners expressed anger via evaluations but provided no specific feedback (Schmitz et al., 2001).

Learners display resistance to diversity education in several ways. Whitehead and Wittig (2004) discuss learner reactions to a prejudice-reduction program. Students who participated in the study expressed different negative evaluations of the program. Some students simply denied prejudice, refuting that they held negative beliefs and attitudes about diversity groups. Students in this category experienced the program as an accusation of prejudice. The most common form of resistance was portraying lessons as uninteresting. A third category of students resisted the program by seeing diversity as protecting them against prejudice. These students employed unqualified interpretations of diversity issues, suggesting that "anti-prejudice lessons are not necessary for them, as they have already learned to be tolerant." This stance inoculated them "against potential challenges" to their beliefs (p. 276). Finally, other students normalized self-segregation, prejudice, and intergroup tension, implying that self-segregation was positive and denying any evidence of prejudice or intergroup tension in their contexts (Whitehead & Wittig, 2004).

Mildred and Zuniga (2004) support the notion that resistance may be different for each learner. They suggest that diversity scholars face similar challenges to those of other instructors who deal with resistance to the instructor's classroom management, learner expectations, and overall group process. Other learners may display resistance because they are not ready for the challenging aspects of diversity education: the unresolved emotional and psychological issues and the cognitive dissonance created by acknowledging personal bias, prejudice, and stereotypes (Mildred & Zuniga, 2004).

The current sociopolitical climate may also influence resistance. Mildred and Zuniga (2004) state that "some students might prefer to remain on an intellectual level, while for others, passive resistance may represent a reasonable defense against overwhelming and intolerable feelings of hopelessness" (p. 367). Instructors are cautioned not to overwhelm students but rather to use resistance as a positive asset to facilitate student learning and success (Mildred & Zuniga, 2004).

Finally, Jackson (1999) addresses transference resistance as an additional type of learner resistance to diversity education. Jackson paraphrases work by Comas-Diaz and Jacobsen in the following quote:

> Some students may experience professors as hostile or ambivalent, depending on the student's history of dealing directly with these issues. Students of color may project their own negative stereotypes about class and color onto the faculty member and experience him or her through these projections. Euro-American students are also likely to project negative stereotypes onto the faculty member if they feel unsafe in class. These projections can result in a complex combination of experiences for the professor to negotiate as a result of inter- and intraracial transference resistance. (p. 32)

With transference resistance, diversity scholars may experience verbal attacks, acting-out behavior such as not turning in assignments, and poor evaluations (Jackson, 1999).

Diversity Scholar Stress

For most diversity scholars, the goal is helping navigate learners through difficult emotions in a process of understanding the lived experiences of diverse individuals and groups as well as understanding societal oppression and other historical social issues. Schmitz et al. (2001) state that because learners "come with a range of values, cultural histories, and prejudices," diversity education "can be like walking through a minefield" (p. 613). Organista, Chun, and Marin (2000) agree, stating that diversity scholars will invariably experience negative reactions from learners, despite their willingness to address learner sensitivities.

Diversity scholars may experience learner resistance as "disorienting" and "misplaced". They may also be "caught off guard" by the strong negative reactions of learners. Although diversity scholars must be prepared to utilize coping strategies to deal with the stress created by this resistance, teaching these courses can be emotionally draining (Jackson, 1999, p. 30). High levels of emotional exhaustion in university instructors has been positively correlated with higher work stress scores, health problems as a result of stress, and consideration of job change. Emotional exhaustion has negatively correlated with satisfaction with teaching, work productivity, and perceived ability to cope with job stress (Blix et al., 1994).

Minority Scholars

Although all diversity scholars are vulnerable in their classrooms and their institutions, those who belong to minority groups are particularly vulnerable. These scholars may be seen as having a personal agenda and pushing that agenda onto learners and other faculty members (Mildred & Zuniga, 2004). This perception can add a unique source of occupational stress. In addition, professors who belong to minority groups are often seen by students as less competent and less qualified than professors from majority groups. These assumptions are based on unfounded prejudice, bias, and stereotypes. Lee and Janda report that students may lack appreciation for the opportunity to be educated by scholars from backgrounds differing from their own. These students also rate minority scholars lower on end-of-course evaluations (Lee & Janda, 2006).

Minority stress is described as stress created by the concurrence of minority status and dominant culture values and the resulting conflict with the social environment (Meyer, 1995). It can be experienced as "alienation" and "the internalization of negative societal evaluations" (Smith & Ingram, 2004). It "arises not only from negative events, but from the totality of the minority person's experience in dominant society" (Meyer, 1995, p. 39). Minority scholars as diversity instructors encounter learner resistance as well as minority stress. This combination may result in significant emotional strain.

For ethnic minority persons, perceived racism contributes to race-related life stress. Racism can become a form of emotional abuse for ethnic minority persons. It involves "negative, rejecting, and/or demeaning societal messages". These messages undermine self-esteem, contributing to life stress (Franklin, Boyd-Franklin, & Kelly, 2006, p. 16). Schmitz et al. (2001) indicate that information shared by an ethnic minority scholar may be misinterpreted by a learner from a different ethnic background. In this case, learners can be especially critical of faculty of color.

Lesbian, gay, and bisexual (LGB) scholars also face challenges. Waldo (1999) states that these challenges may come from "strong antigay attitudes and behaviors in American society" (p. 218). Heterosexism, Waldo argues, is a source of minority stress and a contributor to work-related stress for LGB individuals. Heterosexism can produce prejudice, social stigma, and discrimination (Waldo, 1999). Smith and Ingram (2004) report that minority stress leads to psychological stress in LGB individuals. These findings are especially true for LGB individuals whose occupation involves working in a majority (heterosexual) context (Waldo, 1999).

Feuhrer and Schilling (1985) reported that women in academia were underrepresented, seen as atypical, and seen as violating normative standards. Because of these factors, female faculty members were at risk of "being stigmatized, isolated, and even ostracized" (p. 33). Discrimination toward women is not limited to academia. Kaiser and Miller (2004) reported that women experience prejudiced attitudes across a number of situations and contexts. Sexist incidents have included "gender role stereotyping and prejudice, demeaning comments and behaviors, and sexual objectification" (p. 174). Struggles with gender discrimination within their institutions and academic fields of study, combined with the stress of managing student resistance, creates a formidable amount of stress to be managed by diversity scholars in this category.

Coping Strategies

A study by Knoop (2001) indicates that occupational stress can be reduced if employees engage in work roles that are intrinsically valuable. In this study, extrinsic work values were inversely related to job stress but intrinsic work values were slightly more related. Knoop states that work values are "conducive to one's welfare" and that they depend on "individual interpretation," are "accessible only to personal experience," and are "acquired over time" (p. 832). When workers are enriched (when their jobs are intrinsically and extrinsically valuable), occupational stress is greatly reduced or eliminated. Work values investigated in the study include "esteem from others, achievement through meaningful work and the use of one's abilities and knowledge" (p. 835). Based on the findings, Knoop states that "meaningful work alleviates such stress symptoms as feeling worthless, trapped, troubled, hopeless, and disillusioned; . . . esteem from others makes people feel more optimistic, happy, and energetic; . . . a sense of achievement reduces feelings of tiredness, exhaustion, and weariness" (p. 835).

Iwasaki, Mactavish, and Mackay (2005) investigated how involvement in leisure activities counteracts, manages, and reduces stress. In their study, participants acknowledged the benefits of leisure as a strategy for preventing and reducing stress. Their results indicate three categories of leisure that can reduce stress. The first is "leisure space" (p. 91). Creation of leisure space included participating in activities that were personally rewarding and did not involve taking care of the needs of others. Specific activities were participation in social and cultural events and travel. Second, participants utilized leisure as a palliative coping strategy. In this category, leisure was used as a means to "divert thoughts about stress" (p. 93). Specific activities in this category were reading, going on power walks, listening to music, and traveling. Finally, in a third category, leisure activity was used as a means to provide balance and counteract stress. Specific activities here included volunteer work and culturally meaningful activities.

A range of techniques, including relaxation training (breathing exercises, progressive muscle relaxation, guided imagery), healthy nutrition, regular exercise, social support, journaling, spiritual and religious practices, and cognitive restructuring, have been identified as useful stress prevention and reduction strategies (Gurung, 2006). The emerging field of positive psychology can also provide useful strategies to build optimism and reduce stress. A personalized stress-relief plan can be used to "manage stressful situations better and even prevent stress from building in the first place". Personalized plans should be practiced 10 to 20 minutes each day for one to two weeks before making adjustments or changes (Harvard Medical School, 2006, p. 42).

Conclusion

I agree with Mangaliso (2004) that teaching diversity is a "challenging, daunting, and rewarding" (p. 2) task. I conclude by offering a list of strategies that have helped me manage the stress I experience as a diversity scholar. I have also incorporated strategies that other diversity scholars have shared with me. These strategies are as follows:

1. *Teach a variety of courses.* Teaching a variety of courses allows diversity scholars to experience students in other, less resistant environments, and vice versa.
2. *Take "time off" from teaching diversity courses or teach diversity courses only once a year.* Taking time off allows diversity scholars to recharge emotionally and psychologically.
3. *Develop support circles with other instructors in your institution, especially other diversity scholars.* Participate in weekly or monthly process meetings addressing difficulties with learner resistance and other stressors.
4. *Connect with diversity scholars at other institutions.* Participate in local, state, national, and international conferences or access diversity scholars through other resources such as the Diversity-Teach listserv at http://www.bsu.edu/archives/diversity-teach-l.html.
5. *Establish camaraderie with other professors in your department.* Gaining allies in the academic department is personally and professionally beneficial for diversity scholars.

This list is not exhaustive. Diversity scholars are encouraged to investigate additional strategies that would be most advantageous to them in their unique contexts.

References

Blix, A. G., Cruise, R. J., Mitchell, B. M., & Blix, G. G. (1994). Occupational stress among university teachers. *Educational Research, 36*(2), 157–169.

Cannon, W. B. (1929). *Bodily changes in pain, hunger, fear and rage.* Oxford, England: Appleton.

Feuhrer, A., & Schilling, K. M. (1985). The values of academe: Sexism as a natural consequence. *Journal of Social Issues, 41*(4), 29–42.

Franklin, A. J., Boyd-Franklin, N., & Kelly, S. (2006). Racism and invisibility: Race-related stress, emotional abuse and psychological trauma for people of color. *Journal of Emotional Abuse, 6*(2–3), 9–30.

Gurung, R. A. R. (2006). *Health psychology: A cultural approach.* San Francisco: Wadsworth.

Harvard Medical School. (2006). *Stress management techniques for preventing and easing stress.* Boston: Harvard Health Publications.

Iwasaki, Y., Mactavish, J., & Mackay, K. (2005). Building on strengths and resilience: Leisure as a stress survival strategy. *British Journal of Guidance and Counselling, 33*(1), 81–100.

Jackson, L. (1999). Ethnocultural resistance to multicultural training: Students and faculty. *Cultural Diversity and Ethnic Minority Psychology, 5*(1), 27–36.

Kaiser, C. R., & Miller, C. T. (2004). A stress and coping perspective on confronting sexism. *Psychology of Women Quarterly, 28,* 168–178.

Knoop, R. (2001). Relieving stress through value-rich work. *Journal of Social Psychology, 134*(6), 829–836.

Lather, P. (1991). Staying dumb? Student resistance to liberatory curriculum. In C. Lazarus, R. S. (1966). *Psychological stress and the coping process.* New York: McGraw-Hill.

Lee, G., & Janda, L. (2006). Successful multicultural campus: Free from prejudice toward minority professors. *Multicultural Education, 14*(1), 27–30.

Mangaliso, Z. (2004). *Teaching multiculturalism in a predominantly White class.* Paper presented at the annual meeting of the American Sociological Association, San Francisco, CA.

Meyer, I. H. (1995). Minority stress and mental health in gay men. *Journal of Health and Social Behavior, 36,* 38–56.

Mildred, J., & Zuniga, X. (2004). Working with resistance to diversity issues in the classroom: Lessons from teacher training and multicultural education. *Smith College Studies in Social Work, 74*(2), 359–375.

Organista, P. B., Chun, K. M., & Marin, G. (2000). Teaching an undergraduate course on ethnic diversity. *Teaching of Psychology, 27*(1), 12–17.

Roberts, A., & Iyall Smith, K. (2002). Managing emotions in the college classroom: The cultural diversity course as an example. *Teaching Sociology, 30,* 291–301.

Schmitz, C., Stakeman, C., & Sisneros, J. (2001). Educating professionals for practice in a multicultural society: Understanding oppression and valuing diversity. *Families in Society: The Journal of Contemporary Human Services, 82*(6), 612–622.

Smith, N. G., & Ingram, K. M. (2004). Workplace heterosexism and adjustment among lesbian, gay, and bisexual individuals: The role of unsupportive social interactions. *Journal of Counseling Psychology, 51*(1), 57–67.

Waldo, C. R. (1999). Working in a majority context: A structural model of heterosexism as minority stress in the workplace. *Journal of Counseling Psychology, 46*(2), 218–232.

Whitehead, K., & Wittig, M. (2004). Discursive management of resistance to a multicultural education programme. *Qualitative Research in Psychology, 1,* 267–284.

SECTION SIX

DIVERSITY ACROSS
EDUCATIONAL SETTINGS

28

TEACHING DIVERSITY IN THE HIGH SCHOOL CLASSROOM

Amy C. Fineburg

High school classrooms are microcosms of diversity. Students of varying backgrounds and abilities take classes together and learn to work together. The challenges teachers face as they facilitate this environment make for a rich opportunity to address diversity issues. While this chapter focuses on high school teaching, college and university faculty deal with many of the same issues as the population of students entering college becomes more diverse.

The ways in which students are diverse in high school classrooms are as numerous as the ways in which people are diverse. In a typical day, a teacher sees variations in color, gender, socioeconomic status, ability level (physical and cognitive), parenting status, sexual orientation, and religious beliefs, often with several variations within the same individual. Sometimes teachers assume that their students believe or will react in similar ways to lessons or examples used in class, and this assumption can lead to uncomfortable or difficult situations during class. People tend to use their own filters when interacting with others, and teachers are not immune to this tendency. Rosenthal and Jacobson (1966) exposed this tendency in teachers with his classic study of how teachers' expectations influence students' IQ scores. Rosenthal provided teachers with profiles of students' IQ scores, casting some students with low IQ and others with high IQ. The students' IQ scores at the end of the study reflected the expectations the teachers had of them: those cast with lower IQ scores had lower scores and those cast with higher IQ scores had higher scores. The powerful effect of teacher expectations highlights how important it is for teachers to pay attention to their own stereotypes about diverse students so that unintended, negative outcomes do not occur.

Preservice teachers receive some undergraduate training in diversity issues, but the training is mainly focused on issues related to students with disabilities. Further training while teaching depends on school or district requirements or the teachers' personal desire to learn ways to address diversity. To say that teachers are underprepared to deal with diversity issues is an understatement. It is imperative to make more concerted efforts to equip teachers with the skills needed to handle diversity in their classrooms.

Areas of Diversity in High Schools

Students with Disabilities

Schools primarily focus on diversity issues related to learning, such as learning or physical disabilities. Students must be placed in a learning environment that provides the most learning opportunities with the least restrictions. Students with disabilities are accommodated in the traditional classroom in a variety of ways. Those who are mainstreamed into the regular classroom often have an Individualized Education Plan (IEP) that is devised by a team of educators and the students' parents; the plan sets goals and outlines strategies that must be used with the student to help foster success. Some students require very little intervention, perhaps only preferential seating or a quiet environment in which to take tests. Others need more substantial accommodations, which may include learning a modified curriculum or having tests read to them. Students with more challenging issues (e.g., autism, profound cognitive disabilities) may have a co-teacher trained in special education who works alongside the regular classroom teacher assigned to them. These co-teachers provide extra or specialized instruction that the regular classroom teacher may not have time to provide.

A typical high school teacher may have as many as 10 students in any given class with an IEP. IEPs can be devised for students with any number of cognitive, behavioral, and physical issues, and teachers must keep track of what each student's accommodations are. Keeping up with the legal and educational implications of IEPs can be daunting for schools with few resources and stretched personnel. Not all schools can afford to hire co-teachers for every student who needs one, so many co-teachers work with several students at a time.

Teachers who work with students without a co-teacher may find it difficult to manage the IEP requirements for all their special education students.

Students from Minority Backgrounds

Teaching students from various racial, ethnic, and language backgrounds is more complex than it seems. A student who identifies with a particular racial, ethnic, or language group does not always behave in ways that are radically different from peers. Teachers must also consider their own stereotypes about students' backgrounds and how those stereotypes would affect learning. Additionally, teachers should not expect their minority students to represent their group for the majority students. Simply looking like one who is from a particular group does not mean that one identifies with that group or knows about the image that group has in the majority culture. To ask one student to speak for an entire group might instill further stereotyping with majority students instead of enhancing dialogue. Teachers should make every effort to show students how the similarities and differences in students enrich perspectives.

Teachers have moral and legal obligations to ensure that students are treated equally and fairly. They should be on the lookout for signs of bigotry and bullying to keep these activities from continuing. Additionally, teachers should monitor their own behavior to keep prejudices at bay.

Students and Sexual Orientation

The issue of sexual orientation has become an important one. Students are increasingly aware of the difficulty associated with being homosexual in public school. Teachers can play a pivotal role in the lives of students concerning sexual orientation issues. Just as teachers need to be aware of community and personal notions of racial, ethnic, or language groups, so must they also be aware of notions about sexual orientation. If a community is particularly prone to heterosexism or homophobia, teachers should be sensitive to students who may be potential victims of abuse or prejudice. Additionally, teachers should be mindful of their own stereotypes about homosexuals. Even if a teacher is homophobic or heterosexist, he or she cannot sacrifice the primary responsibility of protecting the welfare of students in his or her charge. Teachers must guard against treating students negatively because of differences, even if those differences may not be in sync with personal values.

Emphasizing Diversity Through Instructional Choices

Differentiated Instruction

One way to emphasize diversity in a classroom is to teach in a differentiated way. Differentiated instruction, pioneered by Carol Ann Tomlinson, promotes the idea that teachers should craft lessons that meet the individual needs and interests of students rather than lessons that require students to fit into a particular mold. Tomlinson (2001) suggests that teachers often teach in ways that tap into their own interests and strengths, often ignoring the ways that engage students in learning. Teachers also neglect to acknowledge that learning can be assessed in multiple ways. Traditional pen-and-paper assessments have their place, but not to the exclusion of other alternative assessments. Teachers can use differentiated methods such as portfolio assessments or performances that tap into student needs and interests. Some students may not test well because of language difficulties, cognitive limitations, or emotional issues, so alternative assessments and activities can help those students demonstrate their learning more effectively. Teachers who use differentiated instructional techniques focus on aligning activities with learning goals and helping students be active and responsive. These techniques focus on clarifying concepts repeatedly and using assessment as a teaching rather than an evaluation tool. Differentiated instruction provides teachers with a way to teach that is more flexible and responsive to the diversity of students found in today's classrooms.

Course Organization

By evaluating the needs of students with disabilities, the backgrounds of students, and the social atmosphere of each class, teachers can craft a course that addresses the particular diversity needs of their students. For example, high school psychology allows for teachers to make curricular choices that maximize student interest and instructor expertise. Psychology teachers do not have to teach the course from a chronological perspective. They can pick and choose areas to emphasize and can alter the order of topics to teach. Teachers may want to restructure their courses to emphasize diversity without teaching diversity as a separate topic. One quick way to emphasize diversity through course sequence is to teach social psychology topics at the beginning of the course. Social psychology topics, such as prejudice and stereotyping, individualism and collectivism, and obedience and conformity, lend themselves to discussions about social issues. Teachers can then move to topics about the nature of scientific knowledge (methodology), how biology and environment interact (biological bases of behavior), and how thinking and problem solving occur (cognition). Each of these topics can enlighten students about how people are both similar and different, stimulating powerful conversations about diversity in specific ways.

Teachers in other subjects can also make organizational choices that address diversity issues. History teachers can teach thematically instead of chronologically, addressing themes such as human rights, war and revolution, and immigrant issues, all of which highlight diversity issues. In this way, history teachers can teach the important knowledge of history while focusing on issues students need to deal with in a diverse classroom. English and language arts teachers can organize their courses in similar ways, choosing readings that emphasize diversity issues and encouraging students to read works that further expound on issues such as women's roles in society, prejudice and discrimination, and religious tolerance. Even science teachers can teach about diversity issues when discussing evolution and biological processes. Helping students see how people are similar when looking through a wide lens can be a key step in dispelling prejudice.

Infusing Diversity Instruction

Teachers may be hindered by local policies from organizing their courses in unique ways. An option for teachers in this situation is to infuse diversity instruction throughout the course. Teachers can make diversity issues a priority when discussing topics that are part of the standard curriculum. For example, in a high school psychology or science course, teachers should emphasize cross-cultural research studies that explore different cultural populations, testing whether psychological concepts apply to non-White, non-collegiate populations. Several interesting studies have shown that concepts that apply to traditional research populations (White, male, undergraduate psychology students) do not also hold true for non-traditional populations. This type of emphasis in methodology also highlights the importance of teaching the dangers of overgeneralizing. Simply because a study shows an effect on the participants does not mean that the results can be applied to all others everywhere. The results of the study are only applicable to those who resemble the participants of the study. Typically, researchers try to address this issue using random sampling from the population, but knowing the population from which the sample was taken is important to knowing whether the study is generalizable to others. As teachers present concepts to students, they must be mindful of the population the study was conducted with and whether the results would apply to their particular populations of students.

Another example is in teaching biopsychology. Teachers can highlight diversity issues in several ways, such as by discussing the interplay of biological and environmental influences. As people bring their own biological predispositions to the world at birth, their environment interacts to influence behavior. This interplay helps explain why people are so similar and yet so different. Even identical twins, who are genetically the same, become separate individuals because no environment is exactly the same for any two people. Students can begin to appreciate that whereas human genetic predispositions lead us to behave similarly, environmental influences create variations in the exact reactions people might have. If students can see similarities in the people around them and understand how and why people are different, they can embrace diversity rather than fear it.

This type of diversity infusion is not limited to psychology courses. History and English courses can also infuse diversity by emphasizing alternative interpretations of historical events and literary works. For instance, a history teacher might discuss the abolitionist perspective when discussing the Civil War or an English teacher might propose a feminist critique of a novel the class is reading. These types of diversity instruction show students that not everyone views history or literature in the same way. Science teachers could also point out diversity issues when teaching about evolution. The ways in which species have adapted to environmental changes shows that differences among people and nonhuman animals represent strengths rather than weaknesses. This perspective can help students look at the diversity around them in a positive rather than a negative light.

Progress Begins in a Classroom

It may seem a bit naïve to suggest that teachers can change the world by pointing out or by specifically teaching about diversity issues in their courses. But perhaps it is not so much naïve as it is necessary. Many teachers often spend more time with their students than do the students' parents, and they are therefore one of the most important influences on a students' life. Teachers have the burden of helping students get ready for the "real world," and that burden includes helping students appreciate the diversity in that world. If teachers do not expose students to the diversity they will encounter, students will be unprepared for the challenges living in a diverse world presents. Teachers have a responsibility to teach specifically about diversity either through a course organization that emphasizes diversity or through classroom discussions and activities that highlight diversity. If they do not, the mission will be a failure.

Additionally, teachers need to be aware of the diversity in their own classrooms and their own stereotypes that may affect learning. The atmosphere teachers facilitate each day can determine whether diversity is accepted or rejected. Teachers who openly recognize their own prejudices and the prejudices of their students can cultivate an environment that tackles diversity issues instead of shunning them. Teachers can also be on the lookout for instances where students do not embrace diversity. However, they must avoid making students uncomfortable by pointing out how they are diverse. If teachers can navigate the teaching of diversity well, students can gain a positive appreciation of the world around them, paving the way for the next generation of students and teachers to embrace diversity even more effortlessly.

Cooperative Learning Activity: *Positions of Privilege and Institutional Racism*

To address diversity from the very beginning of class, I use activities that address group dynamics and socioeconomic diversity. A very successful activity, originally developed by Sandra Lawrence (1998), is called *Positions of Privilege and Institutional Racism*. The following descriptions are taken from the *Thinking About Psychology: Teacher's Resource Manual* by Charlie Blair-Broeker and Randal M. Ernst (2004):

Concept

This provides a powerful experiential exercise that challenges White, middle-class students to see their privileged position and to question their assumptions about the less privileged.

Materials

The activity requires packets of materials that small groups of four or five students will use to create a mobile. Some packets contain minimal materials, say, a 12-inch wooden dowel, a single coat hanger, two pieces of construction paper, and a spool of thread. Other packets contain additional materials, with the most lavish consisting of, say, three dowels, two coat hangers, string, fishing line, precut wire, 10 pieces of colored paper, felt-tip markers, crayons, pipe cleaners, streamers, scissors, ribbon, pom-poms, glue, and tape.

Description

Begin by dividing your class into small groups and giving them 15 minutes to compose a working definition of a concept related to social psychology, for example, social justice, equity, tolerance, or peacemaking. As each group works on reaching consensus, place a packet of materials in close proximity to the group. After 15 minutes, instruct each group to use the next 30 minutes to use the materials provided in their packet to create a mobile representation of their definition. If you want to enhance the feeling of privilege and discrimination during this session, walk around the room praising groups that have a surplus of materials (Look at how good this mobile looks! They always do such a good job!) and criticize groups that do not have adequate materials (Why can't you do as well as this other group?). At the end of the mobile construction period, ask the students to demonstrate their finished products to the class. Conclude with one open-ended question: "What was it like for you to participate in this exercise?" An additional follow-up assignment can ask students to reflect in writing about their experience.

Discussion

Students will likely have several different reactions to this activity. They will quickly notice which groups have more and which have less. Additionally, the privileged group will either act compassionately toward the underprivileged or purposely create a horrible mobile knowing that whatever they produce will be praised. Underprivileged groups will give up and become belligerent toward the teacher, or they will try to overachieve to prove they are as good as the other groups.

Lawrence suggests that White undergraduates tend to view racism as synonymous with personal prejudice and thus rarely consider racism as deeply rooted in systems of advantage. Institutional racism typically leads to inequalities in resources that the more privileged have trouble seeing. At the same time, they blame the less privileged as responsible for their own unfortunate circumstances. Lawrence reports that groups with minimal resources not only feel frustrated but, noticing the lavish materials of the more privileged groups, also complain to each other about the unfairness of the exercise. Feeling robbed and cheated, they are often reluctant to display their creation, knowing they could have done better had they been given better resources. Later, these students note that by having momentarily stood in someone else's shoes, they gained a new perspective on the real privilege they enjoy in society. In contrast, those in the privileged groups are unlikely to notice the inequality of resources. They recognize the difference only in follow-up discussion when the less privileged share their feelings. In fact, initially the wealthy wonder about the motivation, creativity, and organizational skills of the poorer groups. In later reflections, they explain how the demonstration "surprised," "rattled," or "jolted" them into a better understanding of the advantages they receive because of their positions in society.

References

Blair-Broeker, C. & Ernst, R. M. (2004). *Thinking about psychology: Teacher's resource manual.* New York: Worth.

Lawrence, S. M. (1998). Unveiling positions of privilege: A hands-on approach to understanding racism. *Teaching of Psychology, 25,* 198–200.

Rosenthal, R. & Jacobson, L. (1966). Teachers' expectancies: Determinates of pupil's IQ gains. *Psychological Reports, 19,* 115–118.

Tomlinson, C. A. (2001). *How to differentiate instruction in mixed-ability classrooms* (2nd ed.) Alexandria, VA: Association for Supervision and Curriculum Development.

29

DIVERSITY ISSUES IN COMMUNITY COLLEGES

Robin Hailstorks

Community colleges were originally established in the early twentieth century to create a highly skilled workforce at the local level that would ensure America's competitiveness globally. Although it has been more than 100 years since the first community college was established, the mission of community colleges remains the same: to provide high-quality instruction to local residents that is accessible, affordable, and responsive to the workforce development needs of local businesses (American Association of Community Colleges [AACC], 2006).

Today, administrators, faculty, and staff at community colleges find themselves at a crossroad. While the mission of the community college remains the same, the public and political demand for accountability in higher education requires community colleges to demonstrate their institutional effectiveness by maintaining high standards of excellence and, at the same time, holding firm to their position on open admissions.

Community Colleges in Context

Although community colleges have a similar mission, there is no *one-size-fits-all model* for community colleges. Community colleges are diverse in terms of their size, type, and student population. Currently, there are 1,195 community colleges in the United States and 31 tribal colleges that are also considered community colleges. In fact, all tribal colleges were established first as community colleges. Moreover, there are community colleges that are considered historically Black colleges and universities (HBCUs) as well as Hispanic serving institutions (HSIs) (AACC, 2006).

With more than 6.5 million students enrolled annually for credit and another 5 million students enrolled for noncredit, community colleges have become the single largest sector of higher education. Yet American community colleges are the nation's overlooked asset. This finding is particularly troubling because community colleges are the most diverse institutions of higher education in terms of their student populations. According to the College Board's National Commission on Community Colleges, community colleges are the Ellis Island of American higher education, the crossroads at which K-12 education meets colleges and universities, and the institutions that give many students the tools to navigate the modern world (National Commission on Community Colleges [NCCC], 2008). One cannot possibly discuss diversity issues in higher education without considering the challenges and opportunities that American's community colleges present.

The National Commission on Community Colleges released a report in January 2008 titled *Winning the Skills Race and Strengthening America's Middle Class: An Action Agenda for Community Colleges* (NCCC, 2008). The authors of this report argue for a new Community College Competitive Act that makes universal public education through the associate degree the minimum expectation in society. Because most of the jobs created in the twenty-first century will require postsecondary training, community colleges may become the institution of first choice for those who are seeking an opportunity to become members of the middle class. In short, the American community college may become the passport for upward mobility.

Community colleges will continue to play a prominent role in higher education. Recent economic trends in higher education, coupled with the public perception that a college education will afford you a better-paying job, have almost guaranteed that more Americans will be attending community colleges in the years to come. As the cross-section of Americans attending community colleges changes, the promises of America's community colleges will be realized.

Diversity Issues in Higher Education

Diversity issues in higher education are generally discussed in the terms of how to increase the number of racial and/or ethnic minorities on campus. For the most part, these conversations don't get beyond the demographic profiles of students, faculty members, or administrative staff on campus. They usually end when institutions are able to demonstrate how they have met their benchmarks for student recruitment and faculty hiring. Yet we know that diversity has to do with strategies or policies designed to achieve particular goals, whereas affirmative action has to do with policies or initiatives designed to address past discrimination. In higher education, what is often perceived as a conversation about diversity is really a conversation about recruiting underrepresented groups.

But what exactly do we mean by the term *diversity*? *Diversity* refers to the strategies or policies that are implemented to achieve certain goals or objectives in order to increase awareness of and responsiveness to cultural differences. These goals or objectives can become part of a larger diversity plan of action or can be subsumed in the college's strategic plan. *Cultural diversity* is an inclusive term that encompasses many forms of diversity and that takes into consideration the rich diversity that currently exists within our society.

Higher education needs to define not only diversity issues but also strategies and policies to address these issues. Generally speaking, a great deal of emphasis has been placed on how to achieve diversity, but far too little emphasis has been placed on why achieving diversity is important (American Association of University Professors and the American Council on Education, 2000). Moreover, new models need to be presented so that colleges and universities can make their case for diversity by presenting evidence that diversity does work.

Diversity in Community Colleges

Infusing cultural diversity into the curriculum at community colleges is challenging. While faculty members encounter more racially and culturally diverse student populations in their classrooms, the curriculum at community colleges does not necessarily reflect this vast multiculturalism. There is often resistance to making changes to the curriculum to reflect the changing demographics of the U.S. population. The greatest tension exists between addressing U.S. multiculturalism and addressing globalization. The struggle is often defined as "either or" rather than "both and" so that students can gain from both perspectives.

In reality, the curriculum at community colleges does address both continuums of the debate regarding multiculturalism and globalization.

However, the integration of this content tends to be slow and not evenly distributed throughout the curriculum. Part of the difficulty has to do with faculty not understanding the difference among the concepts multiculturalism, globalization, and cross-cultural studies. Often these concepts are used interchangeably, which makes matters worse when one is trying to have an intellectual discussion on how to infuse diversity in the curriculum.

What is often involved in this debate is the number of credit hours already imposed on many programs of study. Many of the educational programs at community colleges have demanding curriculums that cannot possibly accommodate any additional courses. Cultural diversity courses are often perceived as electives and therefore do not get the same support as general education courses or courses in the major. When faculty members approve courses that meet their college's cultural diversity requirement, these courses are often substituted for other courses that are more closely aligned with the existing curriculum. In some cases, diversity requirements are simply dropped from the curriculum so that students can complete degree requirements or can transfer to four-year institutions without losing credit hours.

Recently, there has been a backlash against advocating for diversity courses and training in higher education. Part of the backlash has to do with the larger issue of affirmative action, and part is related to how these courses are taught. It is also hard to advocate for cultural diversity in higher education when diversity courses are poorly constructed or when training programs are not well developed.

Although infusing cultural diversity into the curriculum at community colleges is challenging, community colleges are in a unique position to share their programs and models for working with diverse populations because they are by design diverse educational institutions. Administrators, faculty, and staff at community colleges work closely with leaders in their local communities to solve problems and to create action plans for addressing these problems. For faculty at community colleges, the issue isn't so much how to achieve cultural diversity in the curriculum but how to use the rich diversity that exists within community colleges to demonstrate to the other sectors of higher education that achieving diversity is beneficial. In addition, community colleges are mostly concerned about closing the achievement gap between the prepared and underprepared college student. For this reason, diversity issues in community colleges are focused on student success and achievement.

Diversity Challenges

On a micro level, the greatest diversity challenge for community colleges is how to allocate resources for prepared and underprepared college students. Administrators at community colleges must determine how to allocate resources so that every student is treated fairly and given a reasonable opportunity to achieve success. What this means is that administrators at community colleges must provide reasonable resources so that any student who attends a community college has the same opportunity to be successful as any other student enrolled in the same institution. Students are encouraged to use the services available to them to increase the probability of their academic success. There are counseling, academic support, and social support services available to students attending community colleges.

The challenge of meeting the needs of a diverse student population is even greater when you factor in the range of ability levels of students attending community colleges. Underprepared students present an interesting challenge for community colleges because their number has increased steadily over the past decade, and community colleges use considerable resources to meet their needs. At the same time, however, community colleges have begun honors programs to attract talented students to their campus to improve their public image and to meet the needs of honor students who want to attend college locally. Community colleges now offer a broader range of courses and educational opportunities to address the needs of these students. Honors students are seeking an academic challenge in a smaller setting so that they can get individualized attention. Honors programs are highly selective and require faculty committed to teaching these courses. These programs help community colleges improve their public image, while developmental education programs reinforce the stereotypical image of community colleges.

Another major diversity issue at community colleges is the number of full-time and part-time faculty members teaching courses at these institutions (National Center on Education Statistics [NCES], 2004). While the ratio of full-time to part-time faculty members in higher education in general has decreased considerably during the past decade, it has grown disproportionately at community colleges. Part of the reason for this rapid growth in adjunct faculty is purely economic: It's simply cheaper to hire adjunct faculty to replace full-time faculty when they retire. The other part of the justification for hiring record numbers of adjunct faculty members has to do with the growth of community colleges in general. There is a record number of first-generation college students attending community colleges. There is also a record number of ethnic minority students attending college for the first time who have chosen community colleges as their institution of first choice.

Adjunct faculty members who teach at community colleges are diverse because many do so to meet their financial obligations. Moreover, some adjunct faculty members work full-time or are retired but want to teach to stay active. These types of professionals are very attractive to administrators at community colleges because they bring a wealth of experience and expertise to the college campus. They also tend to be loyal college employees who provide great service to the institution.

Hiring practices and patterns in higher education are a huge issue that is beyond the scope of this chapter, but it needs to be addressed briefly here so that the implications of these practices can be understood in a broader context. If higher education continues to hire adjunct faculty to replace retiring faculty members, women and ethnic minorities will have a harder time finding full-time faculty positions in higher education. The ripple effect of this practice will be fewer women and ethnic minorities in faculty roles and fewer women and ethnic minorities in administrative roles in the near future. This is a diversity challenge for all institutions of higher education, not just community colleges.

On a macro level, community colleges face the challenge of what types of institutions they will become: degree-granting institutions or technical colleges. There is a great deal of tension around this issue as institutions study this question. Limited resources and pressure from state legislatures will drive some community colleges to rethink their goals and strategic plans. Now more than ever before, community colleges must work collaboratively with many partners to develop a strategic plan that takes into consideration workforce development needs and, at the same time, the educational needs of local citizens.

Perhaps no diversity issue in higher education has received more national attention than the educational disparity between women and men in the larger society (Lewin, 2006). More women are attending college at record numbers, and the gap between college-aged African American females and males is even wider (NCES, 2005a). No one seems to have an answer to this dilemma, but community colleges are especially hard pressed to address this issue because a disproportionate number of African American males begin their college education at community colleges. However, more African American females complete the degree requirements for an associate of arts degree at community colleges. With the exception of the science, technology, engineering, and mathematics (STEM) areas, women outnumber men in college by a ratio of two to one (NCES, 2005b). However, African American females earn a disproportionate number of bachelor's degrees in the STEM areas. The question being raised by the larger society is how do we achieve parity for men?

Community colleges have begun social support groups to address the needs of male students who are ethnic minority members and to provide mentors for male students seeking educational support. Community colleges have also provided leadership training opportunities that target male students and have worked collaboratively with businesses and organizations at the state level to address this issue. Recommendations have been set forth, and policymakers are providing resources to address this problem.

Promising Practices in Diversity

There are a number of promising practices for diversity in community colleges. One is the Achieving the Dream: Community Colleges Count (2005), a multiyear national initiative designed to help more community college students succeed. This initiative is particularly concerned with helping students who have traditionally been unsuccessful in college: low-income students and ethnic minority students. Funded by a number of foundations and supported by national partner organizations, this initiative will impact institutions by bringing about lasting change in institutional culture; data-driven policy about how to define and achieve student success; public engagement about shaping policy that addresses student success; and new knowledge based on research that will drive the institutional forces to make the necessary changes to increase student success.

Another promising practice is the joint program of South Carolina's Community Colleges and Clemson University, Call ME Mister, an initiative designed to address the critical shortage of African American teachers. This program targets undergraduate students enrolled in teacher education programs who are from diverse backgrounds and who have an interest in teaching in low-performing schools. Students are afforded tuition assistance in exchange for working with students attending schools in low-income areas. This program was created by South Carolina's visionary education leaders.

Excelencia in Education is a national organization designed to apply knowledge to public policy and institutional practice to accelerate Latino student success in higher education. *Excelencia* has been examining Hispanic serving institutions (HSIs) and documenting their progress in achieving success among Latino students. It is projected that 25% of the college-aged students in the nation will be Latino students. Almost half of all Latino undergraduates in 2003–2004 enrolled in 6% of the institutions in higher education known as HSIs. *Excelencia* in Education is studying these trends to help policymakers and institutional leaders promote practices that support higher educational achievement for Latino students and all students.

The American Indian Higher Education Consortium (AIHEC), founded in 1972, represents 34 colleges in the United States and one Canadian institution. AIHEC's mission is to support the work of these colleges and the national movement for tribal self-determination. AIHEC publishes a journal that promotes four main objectives: to maintain commonly held standards of quality in American Indian education; to support the development of tribally controlled colleges; to promote and assist with the development of legislation for American Indians in higher education; and to encourage the participation of American Indians in the development of higher education policy.

There are many promising diversity-related practices in community colleges in the twenty-first century, far too many to cover in this brief chapter overview. The reader is encouraged to visit the American Association of Community College's Web site (http://www.aacc.nche.edu/) to learn more about these practices and to receive regular updates on programs that target community college faculty, students, and administrators. What is certain is that the future of America's community colleges is bright and full of promise. As we move ahead, the role of community colleges in promoting cultural diversity will become more transparent in higher education.

References

Achieving the dream: Community colleges count. (2005). Retrieved from http://www
.achievingthedream.org/default.tp

American Association of Community Colleges. (2006). *About community colleges.* Retrieved March 24, 2008, from http://www.aacc.nche.edu/

American Association of University Professors and American Council on Education. (2000). *Does diversity make a difference?* Retrieved from http://aaup.org/ AAUP/issues/diversity/div-aa-resources.htm

Lewin, T. (2006). *At colleges, women are leaving men in the dust.* Retrieved from http://wwwnytimes.com/2006/07/09/educat/09college.htm/

National Center on Educational Statistics. (2004). *National study of postsecondary faculty.* Retrieved from http://nces.ed.gov/pubsearch/pubsinfo.asp?pubid= 2006179

National Center on Educational Statistics. (2005a). *Gender differences in participation in and completion of undergraduate education and how they have changed over time.* Retrieved from http://nces.ed.gov/das/epubs/2005169

National Center on Educational Statistics. (2005b). *Trends in educational equity of girls and women: 2004.* Retrieved from http://nces.ed.gov/pubs2005/equity/

National Commission on Community Colleges. (2008, January). *Winning the skills race and strengthening America's middle class: An action agenda for community colleges.* Retrieved March 24, 2008, from http://collegeboard.com/ communitycollege/prof/nccc.html

30

ASSIGNMENTS AND COURSE CONTENT IN TEACHING DIVERSITY

Champika K. Soysa, Lori J. Dawson, Bonnie G. Kanner,
Marc J. Wagoner, and Emily G. Soltano

This chapter highlights strategies to achieve diversity awareness at a liberal arts institution. Many students at our institution are the first in their families to attend college. Few have traveled even 50 miles to the closest big city, let alone out of the state or the country. Like many other institutions, our college is located in a city that has some ethnic and racial diversity, but the college community is predominantly Caucasian. Our students, therefore, have had limited exposure to the spectrum of diversity issues. The college's five-year strategic plan includes increasing diversity and global perspectives in various domains across campus. The Psychology Department offers specific courses on diversity (e.g., race, women, culture) and incorporates this content in other courses across the curriculum as well. This chapter describes two course assignments used to teach diversity issues and two approaches to teaching about diversity in courses dedicated to examining racism and culture. The content presented here can be easily adapted for a range of courses and cultural contexts.

Portfolio Assignments for a Course on Prejudice

The objectives of this second-year course included understanding theories of prejudice and discrimination and challenging assumptions about socially defined "majority" and "minority" groups. Portfolio assignments were designed to help students explore their own social identity; gain a greater appreciation for people in social groups other than their own; examine privilege, prejudice, and stigma; and reduce prejudice.

One component of the portfolio assignments was attendance at extracurricular lectures that allowed students to learn from the experiences of people with social identities that differed from their own and/or that of their instructor. Students attended lectures and wrote brief reaction papers to them. The course was taught in the spring semester to allow students to take advantage of college programming for Black History Month (February) and Women's History Month (March). Examples of these programs include "Stuck on the 'N' Word: Hip-Hop and Race" a talk sponsored by the Diversity Office, "Biphobia" a talk sponsored by the Gay-Straight Alliance, and a showing of the movie *North Country* followed by a panel discussion on sexual harassment sponsored by the Women's Forum.

Students also completed a series of exercises that varied by topic, difficulty, format (in or out of class; individual vs. group projects), and level of self-reflection. Early assignments examined commonly held stereotypes to allow students to begin talking about difficult issues such as prejudice and privilege without "owning" anything yet. As the semester progressed and trust developed within the classroom, the exercises became more complex and often more personally challenging, especially for those students who identified as coming from positions of privilege.

A few representative examples of portfolio assignments used in class follow:

1. In an in-class group activity on stereotyping, students were divided into groups of five to six people. Each group was given a socially defined category (e.g., based on race, gender, sexual orientation, social class, age, ability status) to discuss and was asked to report the following back to the class: descriptive and prescriptive stereotypes they learned about the group, the source of stereotyped information, and how much contact they had had with members of that group.

2. Short, outside-class assignments used the Internet or other media to find relevant stories in the news, required online attitudinal surveys, critiqued media portrayals of stigmatized groups, and calculated the wage gap.

3. In another exercise, students were given five sheets of paper and asked to write the name of someone close to them on each sheet. They were asked to imagine that they woke up that morning with a sexual orientation that differed from the one they had the day before. A wastebasket was placed in the center

of the room, and students were instructed to discard the name of anyone who would no longer accept them with their new orientation. The exercise continued with people being "thrown away" to different degrees based on how much that individual would accept them with their new sexual orientation.

4. One of the assignments that students found most challenging was based on readings and class discussion of theories of minority identity development (Cass, 1984; Cross, 1971; Downing & Roush, 1985) and White racial identity (Hardiman & Jackson, 1992; Helms, 1990). Students chose which model best related to their own life experiences and then wrote their "autobiography" as it related to their identity development, either as a majority group member developing a sense of racial awareness or as a person who identified most strongly as having a minority status (e.g., based on race, gender, sexual orientation, disability status).

In keeping with the aforementioned course goals, assignments were based on prejudice reduction research. Several assignments utilized cooperative learning groups that allowed students to get to know each other better (Aronson & Bridgeman, 1979; Desforges, Lord, Ramsey, Mason, Van Leeuwen, & West, 1991; Dovidio & Gaertner, 1999; Pettigrew, 1997); some challenged existing belief systems (Monteith, 1993; Rokeach, 1973); and others focused on empathy and perspective-taking (Galinsky & Moskowitz, 2000). Although no formal assessments were conducted on how well these assignments promoted course goals, student response to the portfolios was consistently positive.

Interview Exercise on Discrimination

Experiential activities are useful in teaching diversity-related content (Simoni, Sexton-Radek, Yescavage, Richard, & Lundquist, 1999). Examining the effectiveness of such strategies, Yoder and Hochevar (2005) found that student performance improved more with active learning techniques than with other formats. Based on the empirically supported value of active or experiential learning, an interview exercise was developed to teach fourth-year students about discrimination.

The interview exercise can be used in any course in any discipline, but supervision is crucial. The goal of the exercise was for students to learn about an area of discrimination that they had not experienced themselves by interviewing someone who had experienced racism, sexism, heterosexism, ableism, or classism. Women, for example, could not study sexism. Class discussion addressed how multiple group identities intersect in any one individual (e.g., race, gender, and sexual orientation), with varying degrees of power associated with each aspect of identity. An Asian American man may have male privilege in some contexts, for example, while experiencing racial discrimination in others. When the exercise was described, students reported having limited interaction with people who experience discrimination and expressed discomfort about addressing the topic. They were reassured, therefore, that the classroom was a safe learning environment where the basis of interaction was mutual respect.

In preparation for the assignment, basic interviewing skills were reviewed (Trull, 2005). Students read discipline-specific content on multicultural issues, in this case, mental health (Corey & Corey, 2007). Following class discussion on how to frame questions and organize interview content, students formulated questions addressing the domain of discrimination selected for study while considering the individuality of their interviewees. The instructor provided extensive feedback on the initial questions, and students reworked them as necessary. Informed consent was obtained from interviewees, emphasizing that the interview was a course assignment that included a class presentation, that participation was voluntary, and that confidentiality would be maintained. The interviews were conducted in privacy and were about 20 minutes long.

Students gave 15-minute presentations on their interviews. The instructor used the presentation content to highlight emerging themes of discrimination both within domains (e.g., gay interviewees spoke of heterosexual fear regarding HIV contamination) and across domains (e.g., interviewees were hesitant to label their experiences as discriminatory). Consequently, students participated in co-constructing their understanding of diversity issues in the classroom, based on experiential learning.

The *Interview Exercise Evaluation* was developed to examine the effectiveness of the exercise as a teaching tool ($N = 16$). The evaluation contained 15 questions. One question asked about the area of discrimination investigated in the interview; 12 quantitative questions with responses ranging from 1 (*low agreement*) to 5 (*high agreement*) constituted two subscales, the *Student Status Subscale* and the *Benefits of Exercise Subscale;* and two qualitative questions addressed the challenges and benefits of the assignment. The *Student*

Status Subscale gathered retrospective data about students' pre-interview status regarding issues of discrimination ($M = 3.06$, $SD = 0.82$, *Cronbach's alpha* = .71), which yielded a midrange score. Subscale items included the following: current experience with these issues; comfort in articulating these issues; and discussion of these issues outside class. The *Benefits of Exercise Subscale* addressed student reports about the interview exercise ($M = 4.44$, $SD = 0.41$, *Cronbach's alpha* = .64), which elicited a high score. Examples of items on this subscale were the following: feedback on interview questions; usefulness of their own and other students' interviews; recognition of shared/unique features of discrimination within/across domains; and recognition of the need to know more. The difference between these subscale scores indicated that students did not randomly respond to questions, $t(15) = 6.09$, $p < .001$. In the qualitative responses, students stated the following challenges: fears of offending the interviewee and/or appearing ignorant; difficulty developing questions; and general nervousness. Regarding the benefits of the exercise, students said they learned about discrimination and resilience; enjoyed hearing peer presentations; learned more than from reading the textbook; liked constructing their own questions; and learned about the interview process. In sum, the interview exercise was an effective teaching strategy for addressing how discrimination is experienced by people in their daily lives.

Pop Culture as a Source of Racism and Sexism

Expressions of racism and sexism are far less overt than they have been (Devine, 1995; Wilson, 2006). Teaching this fact to Caucasian students about race, or men regarding gender, when they have been led to believe that race and gender play no role in their social worlds, can be a jarring experience. What follows was the groundwork for a first-year seminar called "Social Representations of Race and Gender," which could be incorporated into most social science curricula. The purpose was to talk about the influence of popular culture on race and gender, how stereotypes are infused into popular culture and promoted by cultural value systems, and Social Cognitive Theory (Bandura, 1989) as an explanation of stereotype construction.

The discussion began at a place that is familiar to students: popular culture, which is both a mirror for our social environment and a resource that establishes socially normative behavior. It must be initially established that popular culture is built on the flawed reasoning (e.g., stereotypes) of members of that culture. As such, it is an inaccurate source of normative information.

Students' experiences as members of particular races, genders, and classes help determine the meaning of their experience of popular culture. The demographics of the audience should determine how we talk about what popular culture presents to each student and how this relates to their classmates.

The first substantive discussion stemmed from the first writing assignment, in which students wrote about what makes each race and gender distinct. They found that identifying true distinctions was harder than expected. The aim of the exercise was for students to note the limited number of "true" differences between races and genders as opposed to perceived differences that exist as a function of social construction. They additionally noted that their actual "resources" for such information (e.g., music, television) were not what they had imagined. That is, while their *values* regarding race and gender developed from spirituality, friends, and family, their *information* about race and gender came from that source they took for granted, popular culture.

Students were introduced to definitions of stereotyping, prejudice, and discrimination (Allport, 1954). The initial discussion was about race, both theoretically and in terms of media portrayal (Glassner, 2000). They were shown how the terms *stereotyping* and *prejudice* are distinct both from one another and from the way popular culture defines them. Specifically, *stereotypes* refer to beliefs that all members of a particular social group fit a certain set of behavioral or trait-related descriptions, while *prejudice* refers to our evaluation of those traits. In popular culture, one often finds an oversimplification, and either term is used to refer to any discussion that may or may not include objectionable content about a stigmatized group. Students were additionally introduced to definitions and ideas on feminism (Faludi, 1991, 2000; hooks, 1984). Texts by Faludi and hooks addressed feminist issues, including gender representation in the media. The feminist argument of bell hooks is that sexism and racism are inseparable because both are examples of systematic social oppression. Students engaged with this material through both critical reading and writing. They were given this grounding so that they could grasp the more advanced material that was introduced later.

Social Cognitive Theory (Bandura, 1989) was a valuable tool for students on the interplay between the self and the media as a source of behavioral and attitudinal information. The central elements of the theory were the most important for students to understand: (1) humans learn by observing others and by doing; and (2) individuals model the behavior of others with whom they identify. This information was applied to what students learn from popular culture about race and gender.

The idea was to help students begin to see the process whereby information in popular culture influences their race- and gender-oriented perspectives. The end goal of the course was to introduce students to the view that much of their misunderstandings regarding race and gender comes from sources of information that are deeply embedded in our cultures.

Teaching the Cultural Framing of Development

The primary goal for this fourth-year seminar on cultural development was for students to develop a comprehensive understanding of what it means to argue that one develops in culture. When this is achieved, students understand that they, along with all individuals, have developed in and are functioning within a culture, and that who they have become could be fundamentally different had they developed in another culture. To attain this goal, course content and activities enabled students to appreciate fundamental diversity across cultures and therefore in development, without encouraging them to rank cultures and developmental outcomes using their own cultural norms as the standard.

One method in the course involved rich ethnographic readings that conveyed aspects of cultures that varied greatly from those the students knew. The reading discussed (Seymour, 1999) describes a life in which women's roles are defined in terms of caring for in-laws, their husband, and children; parents choose their children's spouses; children co-sleep with parents; and mothers decide for their children when their basic needs are met.

Along with the reading, students answered questions designed to elicit their reactions, which typically included the following:

"Don't these women know their rights?"
"Those women are just slaves to the family!"

"I'm glad I live where I can choose my own husband!"
"It is child abuse to force-feed a child!"

Students then answered questions that prompted them to reflect on their reactions. What beliefs and values did they have that were being violated or contested by what they were reading? Students' responses included assertions that in our culture or country we believe the following: men and women are equal; women have rights; children have rights; people choose who they marry; children know best what they want and need.

Students answered these questions as a class and were prompted to connect cultural practices and settings to cultural values, norms, and beliefs. For example, students came to connect the practice of individuals choosing their own spouses with beliefs that all individuals lead their own lives and are responsible for their own decisions.

As students became more aware that they were judging others in relation to their own unique cultural system of values, norms, beliefs, practices, and settings, the focus shifted to how others from differing cultures might view their values, norms, beliefs, practices, and settings. Students learned that members of the rural Indian culture often saw students' parents as neglectful and/or unloving because they forced their children to sleep alone, allowed them to undereat or overeat, and made them pay the consequences for poor marriage decisions with high divorce rates.

Students' growing ability to reflect on and articulate how their reactions to other cultures were framed by their particular cultural viewpoint opened the door to their appreciation that people in other cultures act differently because they have different values and beliefs. Students began to rethink their earlier strong reactions to the reading. For example, the interpretation that arranged marriages meant that parents are intrusive and overcontrolling could now also be understood as parents acting on the belief that, because of their greater experience and their attentive care of their children, they know better than children, even adult children, what children's needs are.

The interactive processes of helping students articulate the values, norms, expectations, practices, and settings of their own culture in relation to those of another culture were crucial to attaining the central goal of the course. By coming to appreciate that everyone functions within a culture and that cultures can vary fundamentally, students learned that no one culture is the norm against which all others can be interpreted. Only then could the fundamental tenets of cultural psychology, that development cannot possibly occur somehow "outside" of its cultural context, begin to have any concrete meaning. The readings that provided rich descriptions of different cultures greatly facilitated this process.

Conclusion

As described in the assignments and course approaches discussed here, it is important to consider (a) the composition of the student audience, i.e., the degrees or limits of the diversity they represent, (b) the sources of the instructor's social identity, (c) students' level of exposure to diverse populations, and (d) students' extent of knowledge about diversity issues and their impact on all people. Overall, the teaching strategies addressed here emphasize the importance of examining ourselves (students and faculty), the reciprocal relationship between ourselves and others, and the cultural contexts in which we learn our conceptualizations of self and other. Our hope is that these techniques foster greater understanding of diversity in all its forms as a means of decreasing prejudice and discrimination in our students and others that they, in turn, might teach.

References

Allport, G. W. (1954). *The nature of prejudice.* Reading, MA: Addison-Wesley.

Aronson, E., & Bridgeman, D. (1979). Jigsaw groups and the desegregated classroom: In pursuit of common goals. *Personality and Social Psychology Bulletin, 5,* 438–445.

Bandura, A. (1989). Human agency in Social Cognitive Theory. *American Psychologist, 44,* 1175–1184.

Cass, V. (1984). Homosexual identity formation: Testing a theoretical model. *Journal of Sex Research, 20,* 143–167.

Corey, M. S., & Corey, G. (2007). Understanding diversity. In *Becoming a helper* (5th ed., pp. 182–217). Pacific Grove, CA: Thomson-Brooks/Cole.

Cross, W. (1971). The Negro-to-Black conversion experience: Toward a psychology of black liberation. *Black World, 20,* 13–27.

Desforges, D., Lord, C., Ramsey, S., Mason, J., Van Leeuwen, M., West, S., et al. (1991). Effects of structured cooperative contact on changing negative attitudes towards stigmatized groups. *Journal of Personality and Social Psychology, 60,* 531–544.

Devine, P. G. (1995). Prejudice and out-group perception. In A. Tesser (Ed.), *Advanced social psychology* (pp. 467–524). New York: McGraw-Hill.

Dovidio, J., & Gaertner, S. (1999). Reducing prejudice: Combating intergroup biases. *Current Directions in Psychological Science, 8,* 101–105.

Downing, N., & Roush, K. (1985). From passive acceptance to active commitment: A model of feminist identity development for women. *The Counseling Psychologist, 13,* 695–709.

Faludi, S. (1991). *Backlash: The undeclared war against American women.* New York: Three Rivers Press.

Faludi, S. (2000). *Stiffed: The betrayal of the American man.* New York: Three Rivers Press.

Galinsky, A., & Moskowitz, G. (2000). Perspective taking: Decreasing stereotype expression, stereotype accessibility and in-group favoritism. *Journal of Personality and Social Psychology, 78,* 708–724.

Glassner, B. (2000). *The culture of fear: Why Americans are afraid of the wrong things.* New York: Basic Books.

Hardiman, R., & Jackson, B. (1992). Racial identity development: Understanding racial dynamics in the college classroom and on campus. In M. Adams (Ed.), *New directions for teaching and learning: Vol. 52. Promoting diversity in college classrooms: Innovative responses for the curriculum, faculty, and institutions* (pp. 21–37). San Francisco: Jossey-Bass.

Helms, J. (1990). *Black and white identity: Theory, research, and practice.* Westport, CT: Greenwood Press.

hooks, b. (1984). *Feminist theory: From margin to center.* Boston: South End Press.

Monteith, M. (1993). Self-regulation of prejudiced responses: Implications for progress in prejudice-reduction efforts. *Journal of Personality and Social Psychology, 65,* 469–485.

Pettigrew, T. (1997). Generalized intergroup contact effects on prejudice. *Personality and Social Psychology Bulletin, 23,* 173–185.

Rokeach, M. (1973). *The nature of human values.* New York: Free Press.

Seymour, S. C. (1999). The patrifocal family: Growing up female in the old town. *Women, family, and child care in India: A world in transition* (pp. 52–101). Cambridge: Cambridge University Press.

Simoni, J. M., Sexton-Radek, K., Yescavage, K., Richard, H., & Lundquist, A. (1999). Teaching diversity: Experiences and recommendations of American Psychological Association Division 2 members. *Teaching of Psychology, 26,* 89–95.

Trull, T. J. (2005). The assessment interview. In *Clinical psychology* (7th ed., pp. 141–172). Belmont, CA: Thomson-Wadsworth.

Wilson, T. C. (2006). Whites' opposition to affirmative action: Rejection of group-based preferences as well as rejection of blacks. *Social Forces, 85*(1), 111–120.

Yoder, J. D., & Hochevar, C. M. (2005). Encouraging active learning can improve students' performance on examinations. *Teaching of Psychology, 32,* 91–95.

31

BEYOND THE CLASSROOM

An Experiential Model for Developing Multicultural Competence

Angélica M. Díaz-Martínez and Letizia A. Duncan

D iversity within the United States has grown significantly (Schmitt, 2001; U.S. Census Bureau, 2001). Increasing levels of immigration are permanently changing the makeup of the population. This growing diversity is reflected in many areas of American life, including the workforce, education, and the mental health system. One topic that has been receiving a great deal of attention is the need to develop diverse and culturally competent professionals and educational literature in fields such as healthcare, education, and business. For example, according to the Final Report of the Commission on Ethnic Minority Recruitment, Retention, and Training in Psychology (American Psychological Association, 1997), there is a need for training programs in psychology that make students, faculty, and professionals "aware, knowledgeable, and skilled in the area of multicultural psychology" and for "professional and scientific psychology training programs [that] incorporate multicultural issues in all aspects of curriculum and field training." In the field of medicine, research indicates that surgeons as a population are not consistent with U.S. demographics (Andriole, Jeffe, & Schechtman, 2007). Additionally, the *U.S. Pharmacist* (Diggs & Berger, 2004) featured an article that discussed inequalities, the impact of racism, stereotyping, and the need for culturally competent pharmacy care. In business, the notion of diversity is also picking up speed. Companies like IBM have found that recognizing cultural differences and amalgamating these differences into the corporate culture increases sales (Thomas, 2004). Concurrently, the need to develop more effective research programs that evaluate the efficacy of these initiatives is important. It is evident that multicultural issues are relevant to all disciplines.

This chapter discusses one approach to developing cultural competency in what at first glance appears to be a geographically small area of the United States, that is, Monmouth County, New Jersey. At second glance, however, the reader will see that New Jersey is a cultural microcosm and is representative of the many institutions where faculty are striving to better incorporate diversity into and across the curriculum. The chapter provides a detailed look at how one hospital-based internship program increased cultural competency.

As teachers, professors, and supervisors, we have a responsibility for educating the next generation of professionals. The program described in this chapter follows many of the tenets of the model developed by the National Center for Cultural Competence (2007) that was modified from Cross, Bazron, Dennis, and Isaac's work in 1989. In particular, the program described in this chapter specifically addresses the importance of assessing cultural competence to provide an opportunity for students to be exposed to information related to different cultures and an overall appreciation for diversity.

The cultural competence project took place at Jersey Shore University Medical Center's (JSUMC) Department of Behavioral Health. JSUMC is a full-service teaching medical center with over 500 acute care beds. The Behavioral Health Services (JSBHS) combine a number of programs that treat over 7,000 patients each year. These programs serve a broad and diverse range of ethnic minority, socioeconomic, and age groups, as well as a wide range of diagnostic groups across multiple levels of care.

Diversity in New Jersey

According to the U.S. Census Bureau (2007), New Jersey's diverse population numbers 8.7 million and surpasses the national averages with regard to African American, Hispanic, and Asian populations. Monmouth County, which JSBHS serves, reflects a diverse group of people as well. Its population is 78.9% White (non-Hispanic), 8.1% African American, 4.9% Asian, and 7.6% Hispanic, with about 1.5% who are of mixed-race Hawaiian/Pacific

Islander or American Indian/Alaska Native. The two towns closest to JSBHS, Neptune Township and Asbury Park, both contain a large minority population. Neptune Township's demographics (U.S. Census Bureau, 2000a; U.S. Census Bureau, 2000b; U.S. Census Bureau, 2006) are as follows: 39.9% African American, 5.6% Hispanic, 1.5% Asian, and 2.9% other. Asbury Park's African American population is 66.4% of its total, while Whites, Hispanics, Asians, and others make up the remaining 33.6%. As these statistics reflect, the population is diverse in the communities surrounding the medical center; thus local issues in New Jersey are very similar to the problems that are occurring nationwide.

The Project: Goals and Rationale

There is growing evidence that being more open to diversity and working toward understanding others allows businesses (including healthcare) to compete in the marketplace more effectively (Brach & Fraser, 2002). Despite the apparent need for cultural competence training across all disciplines, there are often factors that make the development and introduction of these programs challenging. One of these is the resistance to change: that is, the concept "If it ain't broke don't fix it." As a result, presenting a training program focused on cultural issues may challenge the company culture (Brown, 2001). Further, some individuals (Brown, 2001) may feel that the notion of diversity will hurt them in the long run (i.e., their current and future potential for employment). According to Brown (2004), "Diversity training may also be perceived as a source of reverse discrimination" (p. 1). With these issues in mind, the new director of training and the JSBHS manager of performance improvement at JSUMC proposed to establish a core of multicultural competence within JSBHS. Once trained, this core group could then act as models and teachers for the rest of the staff.

Funding for this project was obtained through an American Psychological Association CEMRRAT grant that would allow JSBHS to train its predoctoral psychology interns, their supervisors (i.e., licensed psychologists), and JSBHS outpatient managers and supervisors (both are psychologists) in multiculturally competent treatment modalities, research, practice, and supervision. Further, the program would be open to all JSBHS staff in order to train nonpsychologists in multicultural competencies, since they too serve the diverse surrounding community. It is the responsibility of all educators to ensure that an improved awareness of cultural sensitivity exists on all levels of the staffing spectrum.

The *Multicultural Competence Program* was developed as required training for JSBHS's APA-accredited predoctoral psychology interns and was incorporated into the psychology staff's training curriculum. There were three predoctoral psychology interns and four supervisors. The training program ran for one year and contained three major elements: seminars, clinical case presentations, and data collections. The seminar or didactic portion was presented first, followed by the clinical presentation of a case from a multicultural perspective by each student participant. Data collection occurred at various points throughout the program.

Training Program and Data Collection

The seminar portion of the program incorporated working with different racial and ethnic groups, using culturally sensitive psychotherapy treatment models as well as highlighting the experiences of linguistic minorities, immigrants, and different races living within the United States. Seven speakers were obtained to present on these topics. The first speaker's presentation was entitled "Diversity Training." The purpose of this seminar was to introduce the topic of diversity and have students and faculty engage in exercises that aimed to broaden the minds of the students and staff to others' experiences. For example, one exercise involved lemons. The speaker separated the group into teams of two and asked each team to take a lemon from a grocery bag full of them. She then asked each team to name the lemon and create a life story for the lemon. Then all teams were asked to place the lemons back in the grocery bag. After reading the story to the group, teams were then asked to find their lemon in the bag. All teams were able to identify their particular lemon. The purpose of this exercise was to highlight that although people may fall into a particular group and may appear to look alike, as do the lemons, each person has his or her own story and is unique, just like each lemon.

The next four topics were related to working with particular populations. The presentation titles were as follows: *Diversity Issues While Working With the Chronically Mentally Ill, Working With the South Asian Population, Working With Children and Families of Color,* and *Working With African-Americans.*

The last two presentations were aimed at helping psychologists in training to expand their treatment repertoires, that is, develop culturally appropriate interventions and adapt an evidence-based psychotherapy treatment orientation to be more inclusive of culture. The titles of those presentations were as follows: *Developing Culturally Appropriate Interventions* and *Culturally Sensitive Techniques in Cognitive-Behavioral Techniques.*

All of the psychology interns were required to attend the Cultural Competence Trainings. The psychology supervisors were strongly encouraged to attend the trainings. Four supervisors interacted with the interns on their major rotations. These four supervisors attended most of the training sessions.

The clinical case presentation portion of the training program required each predoctoral psychology intern to present cases relevant to multicultural competence. The purpose was to give the students an opportunity to receive "supervision" that is culturally relevant while they explore the multicultural components of the cases, their own biases, and the application of the didactic material presented by the speakers. The case presentations also allowed for the opportunity to determine whether the education received would be transferred into practice. At least two of the supervisors were in attendance to evaluate the clinical cases that were presented by the interns; one of them, the director of training, has had extensive cultural competence training.

To determine the interns' and supervisors' satisfaction with the curriculum as well as its ability to convey the program's concepts, data were collected from several different perspectives:

1. Self-Rated Ability and Attitudes Toward Multicultural Competence. A demographics questionnaire and a "pre-test" and "post-test" (i.e., the same instrument) were developed to collect data about the each participant's attitudes toward cultural competence prior to and after training (see Table 31.1). The pre-test and post-test were developed after reviewing the following: *Multicultural Counseling Knowledge and Awareness Scale* (MCKAS) (Ponterotto, 2004; Ponterotto & Potere, 2003), the *Multicultural Awareness-Knowledge Skills Survey-Teachers Form* (MAKSS-Form T) (D'Andrea, Daniels, & Noonan, 2003), *The Handbook of Multicultural Competencies in Counseling and Psychology* (Pope-Davis, Coleman, Liu, & Toporek, 2003), and the learning objectives of each presentation scheduled for the seminar series. The self-assessment instrument developed for this pilot program contained a total of

TABLE 31.1
Means of Self-Assessments and Evaluations

Measure	Mean		
	Pre	Post	Overall
Ability and attitudes toward multicultural competency	3.65	4.09	
Seminar evaluations			4.60
Case presentations			
Intern 1			5.14
Intern 2			5.18
Intern 3			5.45

Note. Blanks indicate that data are not applicable.

25 items. Twenty-one items were assessed with a 5-point scale ranging from 1 (*strongly disagree*) to 5 (*strongly agree*). Four of the items were assessed with a 5-point scale ranging from 1 (*poor*) to 5 (*excellent*). These four items were converted to the previous scale for all calculations. An example of the items used is "In general, how would you rate your skill level in terms of being able to provide appropriate services to culturally different patients and their families?" The pre-test was given prior to the implementation of the program. The post-test was completed after the final seminar presentation.

2. Seminar Evaluations. Participants evaluated all seminars on a number of different factors, including how well the material was presented, the level of helpfulness, and the informative nature of the presentation. Ratings ranged from 1 (*not at all*) to 5 (*extremely*). Evaluations for all of the trainings were averaged to determine one overall average evaluation of the series of trainings.

3. Case Presentations. Each intern was rated on her ability to present a case from a multicultural perspective using the Cross-Cultural Counseling Inventory-Revised (CCCC-R)(Hernández & LaFromboise, 2004). The CCCI-R is a 20-item inventory. Two additional open-ended questions were added by the grant investigators that asked the raters to assess the intern's consideration of cultural, socioeconomic, gender, and other related areas in their case presentations as well as the intern's case conceptualization. Each of the 20 items was assessed using a 6-point scale ranging from 1 (*strongly disagree*) to 6 (*strongly agree*). The higher the score, the more it was perceived by the evaluator that the presenter demonstrated an understanding of the cultural issues affecting

the client. Upon completion of their case presentations, each intern was rated by at least two supervisors. These ratings were then averaged to obtain one score per intern.

Outcomes

There were a total of seven participants in this program. Three were predoctoral psychology students and four were internship program supervisors (doctoral-level psychologists). All of the participants were Caucasian females ranging in age from 27 to 62. Five participants reported that they were of European heritage, one was of Cuban American heritage, and one was of Polish Russian heritage. In addition, five participants were Roman Catholic, one was Jewish, and one was Unitarian. Participants were asked to rate their doctoral programs' multicultural training on a scale from 1 (*poor*) to 5 (*excellent*). The average rating was 3.85, indicating that on average participants rated their graduate training program between "good" and "very good" on multicultural competence.

Overall, the results of the pre- and post-assessment, the participant rating of the seminars, and the supervisory team's rating of each intern's ability indicate that this project was well received and had positive outcomes for all involved (see Table 31.1). In terms of participants' self-rated ability and attitudes toward multicultural competency, the results indicate that by the end of the training seminars the participants were more likely to agree with comments exemplifying multicultural attitudes and rate themselves as having "very good" skills. Based on the participants' evaluations of the seminars, the material was considered to be useful and helpful. In addition, participants gave numerous comments exemplifying the positive learning experiences of the training seminars. Finally, the results of the case presentations indicated that the participants had a good understanding of the cultural issues affecting the client presented.

Applicability to Other Disciplines

Striving toward the goal of diversity and cultural competency must start, in any profession or business, with a commitment. The commitment must be formally defined, obvious to the observer, and made directly by administration. Brown (2001) suggested that diversity training should "start . . . with a clear statement of values that includes explicit mention of participants' rights to express how they see things and how they feel about comments that are being made, within the boundaries of good group dynamic principles" (p. 4). Moreover, to be effective, the commitment to diversity needs to be more comprehensive than a one-time program that is offered in an orientation or an employee handbook. This project is an example of how starting small with an extensive program focusing on information/education and real-world application can improve individuals' multicultural competence and also begin to filter this positive experience out to the broader team. Including cross-cultural cases in business and law programs, teaching physicians or other healthcare workers concrete cultural differences, and training teachers and administrators in social skills that are culturally open and respectful of others are ways to effectively apply the knowledge provided in this chapter.

By structuring the educational program as described in this chapter, we learned that providing seminars to a group of individuals and having them present clinical cases from a cultural perspective increased the awareness and skills of our students and supervisors. The crucial piece of the program was the interns' case presentations, which required them to think about, incorporate, and apply the knowledge obtained through the seminars and the suggested readings, thus taking a step further toward becoming culturally competent.

There were at least two additional outcomes of this program. The cultural competence program gave us an opportunity to develop an in-house seminar series, Grand Rounds for Behavioral Health, that was relevant to the overall staff's training. At least one-third of the Grand Rounds presentations in the coming year will relate to cultural competence and/or diversity. Further, because the involved supervisors' knowledge and perception of cultural issues were enhanced through the training, they are likely to pass this knowledge along to the interns and other clinicians they supervise, thus continuing to contribute information and awareness to future generations of therapists.

How can a small psychology internship be applicable to other disciplines? Whether you are in academia, business, social sciences, or medicine or conduct research in a lab, it is important that students, employees, and administrators have a basic understanding and appreciation for religions, cultures, and life circumstances that may be different from their own. In today's world, cultural competence is not only a moral and ethical issue but an economic one as well. According to reports on the buying power of minorities (Humphreys, 2004), by 2009 "the combined buying power of African

Americans, Asians, and Native Americans will be more than triple its 1990 level of $242 billion, and will exceed $1.5 trillion, a gain of $1.1 trillion or 242 percent" (p. 2). The buying power of Hispanics will also grow immensely and will be greater than the increase of buying power across all races and ethnic groups. It is estimated that by 2009 it will be "$992 billion," which is an increase of "347.1 percent" (Humphreys, 2004, p. 6) when compared to 1990. In light of these statistics, it is important that all businesses, which include schools, universities, other learning centers, companies that sell goods and services, and healthcare institutions, continue to examine ways to help their employees enhance their level of competency in working with diverse populations. The program described provides one example of how focusing on basic aspects of competency and incorporating real-life examples can accomplish this goal.

References

American Psychological Association. (1997). *Visions and transformations: The final report of the Commission on Ethnic Minority Recruitment, Retention, and Training in Psychology.* Retrieved January 31, 2005, from http://www.apa.org

Andriole, D. A., Jeffe, D. B., & Schechtman, K. B. (2007). Is surgical workforce diversity increasing? *Journal of the American College of Surgeons, 204,* 469–477.

Brach, C., & Fraser, I. (2002). Reducing disparities through culturally competent health care: An analysis of the business case. *Quality Management in Health Care, 10,* 15–28.

Brown, B. L. (2001). *Diversity training: Myths and realities.* No. 13 (ERIC Database#ED454403). Retrieved June 6, 2007, from http://www.ericacve.org/fulltext.asp

D'Andrea, M., Daniels, J., & Noonan, M. J. (2003). New developments in the assessment of multicultural competence. In D. B. Pope-Davis, H. L. K. Coleman, W. M. Liu, & R. L. Toporek (Eds.), *Handbook of multicultural competencies in counseling and psychology* (pp. 154–167). Thousand Oaks, CA: Sage.

Diggs, A., & Berger, B. A. (2004). Cultural competence. *U.S. Pharmacist, 29.* Retrieved December 27, 2007 from http://www.uspharmacist.com/index.asp?show=article&page=8_1238.htm

Hernandez, A., & LaFromboise, T. D. (2004). Appendix C: Cross-Cultural Counseling Inventory-Revised. In C. A. Falender & E. P. Shafranske (Eds.), *Clinical supervision: A competency based approach* (pp. 243–244). Washington, DC: American Psychological Association.

Humphreys, Jeffrey M. (2004). *The multicultural economy 2004. America's minority buying power.* Georgia Business and Economic Conditions (pp. 1–26). Retrieved June 27, 2007, from http://www.selig.uga.edu/forecast/GBEC/GBEC043Q.pdf

National Center for Cultural Competence. *Conceptual frameworks/models, guiding values and principles.* Retrieved June 12, 2007, from www.http://www11.georgetown.edu/research/gucchd/nccc/foundations/frameworks.html#ccdefinition

Ponterotto, J. G. (2004). Appendix D: Multicultural Counseling Knowledge and awareness Scale. In C. A. Falender and E. P. Shafranske (Eds.), *Clinical supervision: A competency based approach* (pp. 243–244). Washington, DC: American Psychological Association.

Ponterotto, J. G., & Potere, J. C. (2003). The Multicultural Counseling Knowledge and Awareness Scale (MCKAS): Validity, reliability, and user guidelines. In D. B. Pope-Davis, H. L. K. Coleman, W. M. Liu, & R. L. Toporek (Eds.), *Handbook of multicultural competencies in counseling and psychology* (pp. 137–153). Thousand Oaks, CA: Sage.

Pope-Davis, D. B., Coleman, H. L. K., Liu, W. M., & Toporek, R. L. (Eds.). (2003). *Handbook of multicultural competencies in counseling and psychology.* Thousand Oaks, CA: Sage.

Schmitt, E. (2001, April 1). U.S. now more diverse, ethnically and racially. *New York Times.* Retrieved December 27, 2007, from http://query.nytimes.com/gst/fullpage.html? res=9505E2D6133FF932A35757C0A9679C8 B63

Thomas, D. A. (2004). IBM finds profit in diversity. *Harvard Business School Working Knowledge for Business Leaders.* Retrieved December 27, 2007 from http://hbswk.hbs.edu/cgi-bin/print

U.S. Census Bureau. (2000a). *Table DP-1. Profile of general demographic characteristics: 2000. Geographic area: Asbury Park City, New Jersey.* Retrieved June 28, 2007 from http://www.census.gov

U.S. Census Bureau. (2000b). *Table DP-1. Profile of general demographic characteristics: 2000. Geographic area: Neptune Township, Monmouth County, New Jersey.* Retrieved February 8, 2005, from http://www. census.gov

U.S. Census Bureau. (2001). *Population by race and Hispanic or Latino origin for the United States: 1990 and 2000 (PHC-T-1).* Retrieved December 27, 2007, from http://www.census.gov/population/www/cen2000/phc-t1.html

U.S. Census Bureau. (2006). *State and county quick facts (Monmouth County).* Retrieved February 8, 2005, from http://quickfacts.census.gov/qfd/states/34000.html

U.S. Census Bureau. (2007). *State and county quick facts (New Jersey).* Retrieved June 28, 2007, from http://quickfacts.census.gov/qfd/states/34/34025.html

ABOUT THE CONTRIBUTORS AND EDITORS

Craig E. Abrahamson, Ph.D., is a professor of psychology at James Madison University. He has also been a clinician for over 30 years, and he volunteers at a medical center providing therapy for trauma victims. Dr. Abrahamson has published articles, book chapters, and conference presentations in the areas of teaching pedagogy, psycho-physiological manifestations of trauma and dissociation from multicultural perspectives, human diversity, student motivation, and heart rate variability biofeedback in reducing anxiety among undergraduates.

LeeAnn Bartolini, Ph.D., is a professor of psychology at Dominican University of California. She teaches both undergraduate and graduate clinical psychology courses, as well as courses in the humanities and in the Women and Gender Studies minor. Her research interests include the internationalizing of psychology and student learning via honors trips to other countries. She maintains a local private clinical practice and is involved in a wide variety of community work.

Mary Jo Blazek, LCSW, is a professor of human services at the University of Maine at Augusta's Mental Health and Human Service program. She has extensive experience teaching courses offered state-wide through an interactive television network and in an asynchronous online format. A licensed clinical social worker; she was previously the director of licensing and evaluation for the Maine Department of Mental Health.

Lynn Boettler, M.A., is a full-time instructor in the First-Year Experience program at Kennesaw State University. She obtained her bachelor's and master's degrees from Truman State University and has completed extensive doctoral work in education from the University of Tennessee. With over 20 years of experience in higher education, her background in this field is varied and includes expertise in curriculum and program development, counseling, teaching, staff and faculty development, and student academic success.

Nancy L. Chick, Ph.D., is an associate professor of English at the University of Wisconsin-Barron County. She has authored articles on multicultural women writers, feminist pedagogy, diversity learning, and misconceptions and signature pedagogies in literary studies. She is the co-editor of *Exploring Signature Pedagogies: Approaches* *to Teaching Disciplinary Habits of Mind* (2009). She is a member of the board of directors for the International Society for the Scholarship of Teaching and Learning (ISSOTL).

Karen R. Cone-Uemura, Ph.D., recently graduated from the University of Utah. She has extensive training and experience in psychodrama and has authored an encyclopedia article on drama in the classroom. Dr. Cone-Uemura is a leadership fellow of the Asian American Psychological Association, Diversity Committee chair of the Utah Psychological Association, and will be working as a bilingual staff psychologist at the University of Utah's Counseling Center, emphasizing the areas of substance abuse and multicultural awareness.

Sandra Cordova, B.S., is a clinical psychology doctoral student at Argosy University in Dallas, Texas.

Karlyn Crowley is director of women's and gender studies and assistant professor of English at St. Norbert College. A recent article from her current project, *When Spirits Take Over: Gender and American New Age Culture*, is "New Age Feminism? Reading the Woman's 'New Age' Non-fiction Bestseller in the United States" and appears in *Religion and the Culture of Print in Modern America* (2008).

Laura Davis is an assistant professor of English at Kennesaw State University and teaches courses in composition, literature, and gender and women's studies. Her research interests include online learning and teaching with technology, faculty development, southern literature, gender studies, and diversity studies. She has published articles in *Pedagogy* and in the *Tennessee English Journal* and has given recent presentations at the Conference on College Composition and Communication and at the Flannery O'Connor Conference. In addition, she has co-led workshops on freshman student motivation at multiple colleges and universities.

Lori J. Dawson, Ph.D., is interim associate vice president for academic affairs and professor of psychology at Worcester State College in Massachusetts. Her research interests include the study of sexuality, physical abuse, sexual abuse, emotional abuse, sexual harassment, prejudice, and the juxtaposition of minority/majority statuses. Before entering academia, Dr. Dawson worked in various social service agencies including a shelter for homeless and battered families and residential facilities for abused children.

Neloufer de Mel, Ph.D., is professor of English and director of studies for the Faculty of Arts at the University of Colombo in Sri Lanka. She is the author of

Militarizing Sri Lanka: Popular Culture, Memory and Narrative in the Armed Conflict (2007), *Women and the Nation's Narrative: Gender and Nationalism in 20th Century Sri Lanka* (2001), and several essays on gender and cultural studies. She is also the recipient of several distinguished research awards.

Angélica M. Díaz-Martínez, Psy.D., is the chief psychologist and director of training at Jersey Shore University Medical Center and a volunteer/adjunct clinical assistant professor at Robert Wood Johnson Medical School. Her areas of interest are in training, cultural competence, and behavioral medicine, and she has several published articles and presentations in these areas. Dr. Díaz-Martínez is a graduate of the Graduate School of Applied and Professional Psychology at Rutgers, The State University of New Jersey.

Carlos M. Diaz-Lazaro, Ph.D., is an adjunct professor at Argosy University. He has several presentations and publications in the areas of multicultural competencies and Latino/a psychology. He is a licensed psychologist in the state of Texas where he serves as editor for the Latino/a Psychological Association of Texas Newsletter.

Savitri Dixon-Saxon, Ph.D., is an associate dean of the School of Counseling and Social Service, program director for the M.S. in Mental Health Counseling at Walden University, a licensed professional counselor in the state of North Carolina, and a national certified counselor. Dr. Dixon-Saxon has been a professional in higher education for the last 17 years, and she has been training students and professionals about diversity issues for just as long.

Letizia A. Duncan, Ph.D., is a graduate of Seton Hall University in the Counseling Psychology Doctoral program. She has worked with the persistently and seriously mentally ill population for over 10 years. Currently, she is the manager of performance improvement for Meridian Behavioral Health. In this role, she is responsible for coordinating the development, collection, aggregation, and reporting of quality initiatives throughout a wide variety of inpatient and outpatient behavioral health programs at two major hospitals.

Dana S. Dunn, Ph.D., is a professor of psychology and director of the Learning in Common curriculum at Moravian College in Bethlehem, Pennsylvania. The author or editor of eight books, his most recent book is *Research Methods for Social Psychology* (2009). A fellow of the American Psychological Association, Dunn will serve as president of the Society for the Teaching of Psychology in 2010.

Amy C. Fineburg, M.A., is the chair of the Department of Social Studies and teaches AP Psychology and psychology at Spain Park High School in Hoover, Alabama. She has authored teaching resources, book chapters, and articles on teaching high school psychology and positive psychology. Amy is an award-winning teacher and is an affiliate member of the American Psychological Association through Teachers of Psychology in Secondary Schools (TOPSS) and the Society for the Teaching of Psychology.

Rosslyn Franklin, M.S., is a clinical psychology doctoral student at Argosy University in Dallas, Texas.

Katherine A. Friedrich, M.S., is an associate editor for the School of Education at the University of Wisconsin–Madison. Her background is in journalism, environmental studies, and engineering. She has coauthored resources for inclusive teaching in science, technology, engineering and mathematics. These resources are available online at http://cirtl.net/diversityresources/.

Afshin Gharib, Ph.D., is an associate professor of psychology at Dominican University of California. His research interests include the cognitive and neural mechanisms of learning, focusing on the role of attention, timing, and response learning in operant conditioning and age-related changes in learning and memory. He is particularly interested in the effectiveness of antioxidants in reversing age-associated declines in cognition. He teaches or has taught Introduction to Psychology, Physiological Psychology, Statistics, and Research Methods.

Nilhan Gunasekera, Ph.D., is an assistant professor of chemistry at University of Wisconsin–Rock County. He received his Ph.D. in chemistry at the University of Minnesota in 2003. Prior to that in 1998, he earned a B.S. in comprehensive chemistry from the University of Wisconsin–Eau Claire with a minor in cross-cultural studies. After earning his Ph.D. his scholarly interests have expanded to include diversity in STEM education and chemical education. He has been part of a national five-year NSF grant as a faculty associate for the Center for the Integration of Research, Teaching, and Learning at the University of Wisconsin–Madison. In that capacity, and in addition to publications that train graduate students and STEM faculty in inclusive teaching, he has extensively traveled within the United States offering training workshops for graduate students in STEM teaching with diverse groups of people in mind.

Susan B. Goldstein, Ph.D., is a professor of psychology at the University of Redlands in southern California. She received her Ph.D. from the University of Hawaii while a grantee of the East West Center. She is the author of *Cross-Cultural Explorations: Activities in Culture and Psychology* as well as several articles on intergroup and intercultural relations.

Amy Hackney, Ph.D., is an assistant professor of psychology at Georgia Southern University. She received her Ph.D. from Saint Louis University. Her research interests are social cognition and social justice, with a focus on the role of stereotypes, prejudice, and discrimination in criminal justice decision making. She loves teaching social psychology, psychology of gender, psychology and law, and research methods.

Robin J. Hailstorks, Ph.D., earned her doctoral degree in developmental psychology at The Ohio State University. Dr. Hailstorks is the associate executive director of the Education Directorate for the American Psychological Association (APA) and director of the Office of Precollege and Undergraduate Education for the APA. She is the former chair of the Department of Psychology at Prince George's Community College in Largo, Maryland. She is an active member of the APA and the Eastern Psychological Association.

Kelley Haynes, Psy.D., is an associate professor of clinical psychology at Argosy University in Dallas, Texas. She has given presentations at numerous professional conferences and associations on the topics of multiculturalism and diversity issues related to clinical psychology. Haynes is also involved in clinical practice with the Center for Survivors of Torture in Dallas, Texas. She is a licensed clinical psychologist and member of the Society for Teaching Psychology Diversity Committee.

Bonnie G. Kanner, Ph.D., is professor of psychology at Worcester State College. Her research interests include the role of peers in social and cognitive development with children and adolescents, cultural understandings of marriage and relationships, the interaction of culture and biology in various aspects of social and cognitive development, and issues of pedagogy. Dr. Kanner has presented her most recent work at local and international conferences within the United States and abroad.

Peter L. Kranz, Ph.D., is an associate professor in the Department of Educational Psychology at University of Texas-Pan American in Edinburg, Texas. He has authored several articles on race relations based on a groundbreaking university class taught in the 1970s. He has also been a presenter at numerous regional and national conferences. His work has been recognized in the media by *The Lehrer News Hour*, National Public Radio, and the *Wall Street Journal*.

Janet E. Kuebli, Ph.D., is an associate professor at Saint Louis University where she is director of undergraduate studies in psychology. She is a developmental psychologist whose research and teaching interests include parenting and socialization processes in child development as well as the role of developmental processes during transitions from high school through college.

Accalia R. Kusto holds bachelor degrees in psychology and philosophy from Saint Mary's College and a master's degree in developmental psychology from Saint Louis University with a minor in research methods, as well as a graduate certificate in women's studies. Her research interests include the socialization of emotion regulation in children with a focus on how family practices and cognitive developments are related to understanding emotions.

Cindy J. Lahar, Ph.D., chairs the Biological and Social Sciences Department at York County Community College. Since receiving her Ph.D. in psychology from Brandeis University she has taught at universities in the United States, Canada, Japan, and Cambodia. She was named a Carnegie Scholar in 2003 and has received two Fulbright awards to Cambodia. She is also an adjunct professor of psychology at the Royal University of Phnom Penh.

Magdalena Linhardt, Ph.D., is an assistant professor of psychology and mental health at the University of Maine at Augusta (UMA). She finished her postdoctoral program at Boston University, Center for Psychiatric Rehabilitation in 1997, as well as a postdoctoral fellowship at the Boston Institute for Psychotherapy. Dr. Linhardt mostly teaches distance education courses via the interactive television system (ITV) or the internet for the Mental Health and Human Services program at UMA.

Nick L. Lund, Ph.D., is a professor emeritus at Northern Arizona University (NAU). Past positions include executive director at NAU in Yuma, associate vice president for academic affairs at Richard Stockton College of New Jersey, senior business manager at TRW, Inc. Space & Technology Group, and professor and chairman of the Psychology Department at University of North Florida.

David Matsumoto, Ph.D., is an internationally acclaimed author and psychologist. He received his Ph.D. in psychology from the University of California at Berkeley in 1986. He is currently a professor of psychology and director of the Culture and Emotion Research Laboratory at San Francisco State University, where he has been since 1989. He has studied culture, emotion, social interaction, and communication for 20 years, and has approximately 400 works in these areas.

Sandra L. Neumann, Ph.D., is an assistant professor of psychology at the Marshfield/Wood County campus of the University of Wisconsin. She is a social psychologist whose interests include teaching students with dominant social identities about discrimination, privilege, and social justice and researching factors that influence acceptance of or resistance to global warming.

Christy Price, Ph.D., has been teaching at the collegiate level for 17 years. She is currently a professor of psychology at Dalton State College. Dr. Price was honored with the newly created Excellence in Teaching Award at Dalton State in 2007 and the University System of Georgia Teaching Excellence Award for 2008/2009. As a recipient of an Institutional Foundation Grant Award, Dr. Price has conducted research on teaching techniques that influence student motivation.

Ly U. Phan, M.A., is an instructor of psychology at the University of St. Thomas in Houston, Texas. She incorporates her research interest in cultural intelligence into her teaching practices. The simulations and games presented in her chapter have been used in courses such as Industrial/Organizational Psychology, Inferential Statistics, and Psychometrics.

William Phillips, Ph.D., is an associate professor of psychology at Dominican University of California. He teaches courses about cognition, perception, learning, statistics, research methods, and psychology. His research interests include the cognitive processing of visual and touch information as well as student learning in the classroom.

Sylvia Z. Ramirez, Ph.D., is an associate dean at the University of Texas-Pan American in Edinburg, Texas. She received her Ph.D. in educational psychology from the University of Wisconsin–Madison. Her work focuses on multicultural issues in psychotherapy and consultation, and fears and anxiety in individuals with intellectual disabilities.

Thomas N. Robinson, III, Ph.D., is an assistant professor of psychology at Kutztown University. He is a coauthor of the introductory psychology textbook, *Understanding Psychology* (2007). His areas of expertise include the psychological predictors of racism, ethnic and racial identity development, and cultural influences on human development. Dr. Robinson teaches various psychology courses, including Psychology of the Black Experience, and consults in the area of multicultural competence and self-development.

Kumudini Samuel, M.A., is the director of Women and Media Collective Sri Lanka and has worked on women's rights issues since 1980. She was appointed to the Subcommittee on Gender Issues advising the plenary of the Sri Lankan Peace negotiations in 2002. Her writings address gender, conflict, and peace building. She is currently on the executive committee of DAWN (Development Alternatives with Women for a New Era) and the board of WUSC (World University Service, Canada).

Kathie E. Shiba, Ph.D., is a professor of psychology at Maryville College in Tennessee. She received her Ph.D. from University of California, Riverside. Her research and teaching interests include adolescent development, cross-cultural psychology, development of peaceful communities, and positive psychology. A founding member of Just Connections, she promotes participatory research involving an equal partnership between campus and community. She coordinates Project Lead, a leadership program for middle school youth, and leads diversity workshops through her work with the National Coalition Building Institute.

Paul C. Smith, Ph.D., is an associate professor of psychology, chair of the Institutional Review Board at Alverno College, and president-elect of the Alliance Française de Milwaukee. He has recently authored chapters such as "Assessing Students' Research Ideas" and "Teaching Critical Thinking about Difficult Topics" (with Kris Vasquez).

Emily G. Soltano, Ph.D., is an associate professor of psychology and interim chair of psychology at Worcester State College in Massachusetts. She researches language processing, teaching effectiveness, and most recently language development of internationally adopted children. She has presented at national and regional meetings. Dr. Soltano serves on the steering committee for the New England Psychological Association. She is a reader for the College Board AP Psychology Exam.

Champika K. Soysa, Ph.D., is an associate professor of psychology and director of women's studies at Worcester State College in Massachusetts. She studies pedagogical issues pertaining to differentials of social power. Her collaborations with students examine college student anxieties and their buffers. Her international research addresses culture and psychological distress, trauma and resilience, and sociostructural influences on ethnic identity and prejudice. She has presented and published her work in the United States and abroad.

Kris Vasquez, Ph.D., is an associate professor of psychology at Alverno College in Milwaukee, Wisconsin. She is chair of the Global Perspectives Ability Department, and serves as director of the Behavioral Sciences Research Center.

Marc J. Wagoner, Ph.D., is an assistant professor of psychology and chair of the Human Subjects Review Board at Worcester State College in Massachusetts. His targets of study include stereotyping, prejudice, and racism. He also studies the self and self-esteem, and the relationship between psychology and religion.

Karen Wilson, Ph.D., is a lecturer at the College of Staten Island and Saint Francis College in New York City. She received her Ph.D. in social psychology with a minor in research methodology from Saint Louis University. Her research interests include attitudes toward infidelity as well as HIV/STD risk perceptions in romantic relationships.

INDEX

NOTE: Page numbers followed by an "n" or a "t" indicate that the reference on the designated page is to a note or a table respectively.

PLEASE RETURN TO:

BENNETT D. KATZ LIBRARY
46 UNIVERSITY DRIVE
AUGUSTA, ME 04330

Items returned after stamped due date
are subject to a fine of 50 cents per day.
Renewals may be requested as follows:
online: http://ursus.maine.edu/patroninfo/
by email: uma.library@maine.edu
by phone: 621-3349.
Fines & overdue books will block access
to UMA library services and will be added
to student bill

DEMCO

JUL   7 2009